OTTOMANS AND ARMENIANS

Also by Edward J. Erickson

Mustafa Kemal Atatürk

Strategic Water; Iraq, Water and Security in the Euphrates-Tigris Basin, coauthored with F. M. Lorenz

Gallipoli, The Ottoman Campaign, published in Turkish as *Gelibolu, Osmanlı Cephesi*

A Military History of the Ottomans, from Osman to Ataturk, coauthored with Mesut Uyar

By the Light of a Candle, The Diaries of a Reserve Officer in the Ottoman Army: The WW1 Diaries of Ragip Nurettin Ege, translated by Gunes Ege-Akter, annotated by Edward Erickson

Gallipoli and the Middle East 1914–1918, From the Dardanelles to Mesopotamia, Published in Swedish as *Första Världskriget Del 5: Gallipoli och Mellanöstern*, published in Turkish as *Birinci Dünya Savaşı'nda Osmanlı: Dünya Savaş Tarihi*

Ottoman Army Effectiveness in W.W.I: A Comparative Study, published in Turkish as *Dünya Savaş'nda Osmanlı Ordusu (Çanakkale, Kutü'l-Amare ve Filistin Cephesi)*

Defeat in Detail, The Ottoman Army in the Balkans, 1912–1913, published in Turkish as *Balkan Harplerinde Osmanlı Ordusu*

Ordered To Die, A History of the Ottoman Army in the First World War, published in Turkish as *Size Ölmeyi Emrediyorum! Bininci Dünya Savaş'nda Osmanlı Ordusu*

The Euphrates Triangle, Security Implications of the Southeast Anatolia Project, coauthored with F. M. Lorenz

OTTOMANS AND ARMENIANS

A Study in Counterinsurgency

Edward J. Erickson

palgrave
macmillan

OTTOMANS AND ARMENIANS
Copyright © Edward J. Erickson, 2013.

First published in 2013 by
PALGRAVE MACMILLAN®
in the United States—a division of St. Martin's Press LLC,
175 Fifth Avenue, New York, NY 10010.

Where this book is distributed in the UK, Europe and the rest of the world,
this is by Palgrave Macmillan, a division of Macmillan Publishers Limited,
registered in England, company number 785998, of Houndmills,
Basingstoke, Hampshire RG21 6XS.

Palgrave Macmillan is the global academic imprint of the above companies
and has companies and representatives throughout the world.

Palgrave® and Macmillan® are registered trademarks in the United States,
the United Kingdom, Europe and other countries.

ISBN: 978–1–137–36220–9

Library of Congress Cataloging-in-Publication Data is available from the
Library of Congress.

A catalogue record of the book is available from the British Library.

Design by Newgen Knowledge Works (P) Ltd., Chennai, India.

First edition: November 2013

10 9 8 7 6 5 4 3 2 1

*This book is dedicated to the memory of
the late Professor Stanford J. Shaw
(emeritus UCLA and Bilkent University)
and to
Professor Dennis Showalter, Colorado College,
both of whom gave me incredible encouragement
and support as a novice author and historian*

Contents

CONTENTS

Maps, Figures, and Table

Maps

Figures

Table

ACKNOWLEDGMENTS

I would like to take this opportunity to acknowledge the many friends and colleagues who have helped me in the writing of this book. Without their generous and willing support, as well as critical commentary, I could not have written *Ottomans and Armenians*. Let me first identify Professor Hakan Yavuz, who teaches at the University of Utah in Salt Lake City, without whose unstinting and creative quest to help me find a publisher this book would still be an unpublished manuscript on my desk. Hakan connected me with my editor, Dr. Farideh Koohi-Kamali, at Palgrave Macmillan Publishing, who had the intellectual courage to support this work, in spite of its political incorrectness and contravention of our received historical wisdom. I would also like to thank Sara Doskow, also at Palgrave Macmillan, for her advice and guidance in steering me through the publication process. My appreciation goes to Newgen Knowledge Works for their unfailing support, patience, and careful work.

A number of my colleagues have been instrumental in leading me toward information and research opportunities that have been critical in framing my understanding of this subject. First among equals is my close friend and coauthor Professor Mesut Uyar (retired colonel, Turkish Army) at the University of New South Wales. Mesut's tireless efforts in guiding me with midcourse corrections and offering new information have had a monumental impact on this book. My friend and independent scholar Dr. Garabet Moundijian, obviously of Armenian heritage but wonderfully open-minded to the Ottoman experience, provided me with extremely valuable counterpoints and supporting information about the Armenian revolutionary committees. My very good friend and colleague Dr. Yücel Güçlü, a Turkish diplomat in the Ministry of Foreign Affairs, provided me with much information on the Ottoman narrative and sources. Finally, Professor Guenter Lewy, professor emeritus from the University of Massachusetts, was particularly helpful in sending me in search of German archival materials. These four scholars were kind enough to read portions of my manuscript and I acknowledge their monumental contributions in lending whatever balance I have achieved in this book.

Over the past years, I have enjoyed a number of personal conversations with scholars about the events detailed in this book. These include: Ara Sarafian from the Gomidas Institute; Suleyman Gokçe and Ela Görkem from the Republic of Turkey's Ministry of Foreign Affairs; and Professor Michael Reynolds of Princeton University, whose comments have been very valuable to me. Likewise, a number of scholars have read and commented on the manuscript. These include: Professor Jeremy Salt of Bilkent University, independent scholar Dr. Hilmar Kaiser, Professor Reşit Engener of Bosporus University, and David Saltzman of Saltzman and Evinch Law Partners. I also acknowledge the following individuals who have supported my efforts with encouragement and friendship: Professor Nur Bilge Criss at Bilkent University, Professor Michael Gunter at Tennessee Tech, Professor Dave Cuthell at Columbia University, Dr. Sinan Ciddi at the Institute of Turkish Studies, Professor Sean McMeekin at Kac University, Professor Doug Streusand and Professor Pauletta Otis at the Marine Corps University, Dean of Academics Dr. Doug McKenna at the Marine Corps Command & Staff College, Dr. Turhan Bykan in the United States, and Mr. Haluk Oral in Istanbul, Turkey.

Much of my research was conducted in Turkey and a number of friends, old and new, were of immense help in hosting and supporting my trips to Ankara. These are: PhD candidate Marlene Elwell from Bilkent University, independent scholar Mr. Bulent Yilmazer, independent scholar Ms. Sevin Elekdağ, the current director of the Turkish military archives (ATASE) Colonel Suat Akgül, and former director Dr. Ahmet Tetik (retired colonel, Turkish Army), translator at the military archives Mr. Yusuf Serdar Demirtaş, and Ambassador (retired) Ömer Engin Lütem of the Turkish Ministry of Foreign Affairs.

I would also like to gratefully acknowledge the University of Utah Press for allowing me to use material I have published in *War and Diplomacy, The Russo-Turkish War of 1877–1878 and the Treaty of Berlin* (M. Hakan Yavuz and Peter Sluglett (eds.); Salt Lake City: University of Utah Press, 2011) and the Chief of the Australian Army for material I have published in *1911, Preliminary Moves* (Peter Dennis and Jeffrey Grey (eds); Canberra: Big Sky Publishing, 2011). I would also like to thank Professor (Emeritus) John Hall of Saint Lawrence University and Lieutenant General Paul Van Riper (USMC, retired) for allowing me to quote their wisdom.

The superb maps included in this book are the work of my former command and staff college student and good friend Mr. Nick Sims of Woodbridge, Virginia and Professor Justin McCarthy at the University of Louisville.

Finally, I gratefully acknowledge the encouragement, support, and love given to me by my fiancée, Jennifer Collins, without whose willingness to leave me alone in isolation, I could not have finished this book.

Introduction

The conduct of such rebel elements rendered it necessary to remove them from the areas of military operations and to evacuate the villages serving as bases of operations and shelters for the rebels. To achieve this, a different course of action has begun to be implemented.

—*Decree from the Sublime Porte, Constantinople, May 31, 1915*[1]

INTRODUCTION

This is a military history of the Ottoman army and selected counterinsurgency campaigns, which it waged in the last days of the empire it served. It is a military history of insurrection and counterinsurgency in the Ottoman Empire from 1878 to 1915. The author recognizes that the use of the contemporary term "counterinsurgency" in this book is ahistorical in the sense that this term was not commonly used in the early twentieth century.[2] He would also like to note that this study leaves out a number of important Ottoman counterinsurgency campaigns in order to meet the limitations of the publisher's word count, examples of which are the Kurdish, Arab, Greco-Macedonian, and Sanussi rebellions.

It can be argued that the Ottomans were among the most active practitioners of counterinsurgency campaigning in the late nineteenth and early twentieth centuries. However, in the vast literature on counterinsurgency available in the early twenty-first century, there is very little scholarly analysis about how the Ottomans reacted to insurgency and then went about counterinsurgency. The book presents the thesis that the Ottoman government developed an evolving 35-year, empire-wide array of counterinsurgency practices that varied in scope and execution depending on the strategic importance of the affected provinces.

The book is organized chronologically to acquaint the reader with the origins and history of the largest insurgencies in the Ottoman

Empire of the time and with an understanding of how the Ottomans dealt with insurgency in the core and peripheral areas of the empire. After 1878, secret cell-like revolutionary committees arose in the more educated and urbanized Balkan and Anatolian provinces. Within these core areas of the Ottoman Empire, heavily armed Armenian and Macedonian revolutionary committees rose repeatedly in insurrection with the goal of autonomy or independence. The Ottoman counter-insurgency campaigns in response to these insurrections were kinetic and involved both large-scale combat operations of up to one hundred thousand men and, sometimes, smaller-scale expeditionary operations. Other minorities, such as the Yemenis and Albanians, in the empire's outer periphery, rose in rebellion as well with varied Ottoman military reactions. In these different places and circumstances, the Ottomans employed a wide variety of military forces, and counterinsurgency tactics, to suppress insurrection.

Elsewhere in the world, by the early 1900s, the Western powers established counterinsurgency and counterguerrilla strategies that centered on the relocation of people to concentration camps. The most well-known of these campaigns were Spain in Cuba, America in the Philippines, and Britain in the Boer republics. Population removal and relocation became established counterinsurgency practices, which, while often characterized by highly publicized human rights abuses, were generally acceptable to the governments of the world. These campaigns are described briefly because the contextual background and operational rationale regarding these tactics is important in developing a full understanding of the new counterinsurgency course of action taken by the Ottomans in 1915.

By 1908, insurrection in the core areas had been largely suppressed but rebellion continued in the periphery, which ended through negotiation by 1912 in favor of the insurgents. Although damaged, the powerful Armenian revolutionary committees remained in being and were an active presence in Ottoman affairs. The Ottomans themselves then created their own ad hoc Ottoman irregular military capability in the form of guerrilla advisors in response to Italy's 1911 invasion of Libya. After the Balkan wars of 1912–13, the Ottomans activated a formal institutional irregular warfare capability by creating the Special Organization, which was designed to instigate guerrilla warfare in the Balkans and in Russian Caucasia.

In the years prior to World War I, young Ottoman firebrands themselves had formed revolutionary committees, the most aggressively nationalist of which eventually seized control of the government. As world war approached, both the Armenian committees and the

Ottoman Special Organization developed significant irregular warfare capabilities in anticipation of conflict. In 1914, the outbreak of World War I created conditions that again brought the Ottoman state into direct conflict with the Armenian revolutionary committees. This was largely a result of the actions of the allied powers, which encouraged and supported the eastern Anatolian Armenian revolutionary committees to commit acts of terrorism and minor insurrections in early 1915. These small and localized, but widespread, acts of violence appeared to metathesize during a serious Armenian insurrection at Van in April 1915, which made the Ottoman government believe that an imminent Armenian insurrection was an existential threat to Ottoman national security. With almost the entire Ottoman army deployed on the active fronts, the Ottomans did not have the force structure necessary to deal with the Armenian insurrection as they had done previously. In the late spring of 1915, the Ottomans turned to a Western-style strategy of regional population relocation designed to separate the insurgents from their base of popular support. This strategy enabled the feeble Ottoman forces available in eastern Anatolia to defeat easily the surviving insurgent bands, thus ending the insurrection.

The book places the Armenian revolutionary movement within a chronological narrative of Ottoman counterinsurgency campaigns that establish a context for understanding the empire's geostrategic and military problems in dealing with its restive multiethnic population. It is the author's contention that the Ottoman government's 1915 shift to a counterinsurgency campaign, based on population relocation of some of the Armenians, came about because of two principal elements centered on an existential danger to national security in wartime. The first of these elements was the Ottoman government's belief that the Armenian revolutionary committees directly threatened the empire's military lines of communications. The second element was a critically weak military posture in the empire's core areas caused by the concentration of the Ottoman army in 1914 on the frontiers. As a result of these twined elements, the Ottoman government chose to pursue a counterinsurgency campaign against the Armenian revolutionary committees in 1915 from a weak position of constrained resources centered on population relocation explicitly designed to separate revolutionary insurgents from a base of popular support. This was a new course of action, previously unseen in either the core or the periphery, as articulated by the Sultan's decree of May 31, 1915, quoted at the beginning of this introduction.

The book establishes a comprehensive framework for understanding why the Ottoman state decided to relocate en masse the Armenian population living in six eastern provinces out of twenty in the empire in 1915. Although it is true that individuals, and large groups of Armenians, were relocated from all parts of the empire; provincial-scale relocations en masse were regionalized in just six militarily critical provinces in the empire's core, while elsewhere the relocations were limited to selected groups of Armenians. In fact, at the war's end in 1918, 350,000–400,000 Armenians from a prewar population of around 1.5 million remained in their homes in the Ottoman Empire. The question of why the Ottoman state thought a partial relocation was necessary has never been fully researched or brought to a definitive resolution by other scholars or authors and, to date, there is no satisfactory explanation as to why the eastern Armenians were relocated and those in the Constantinople area and western provinces were not. The book's treatment of the Armenian insurrection of 1915 and the Ottoman counterinsurgency response as a military event rather than as a political, social, or ideological event is a significant departure from all previous work in this area.

This is the military history of insurgency and the associated counterinsurgency campaigns, rather than a social and political history of the grievances of oppressed peoples, although the author recognizes that these themes are interconnected. This book advances the idea that Ottoman counterinsurgency policy and campaigning varied significantly between the empire's core and the periphery. It outlines the evolution of the heavily armed and militarized revolutionary committees and their subsequent insurrections, and details the corresponding evolution of reactive counterinsurgency policies, practices, and campaigns that the Ottomans used against them over a 25-year period. It explains that the Ottoman counterinsurgency campaign involving the relocation of the Armenian population from six Anatolian provinces in 1915 was the outcome of an evolving counterinsurgency policy nested within the context of a global war.[3] It illuminates why the Ottomans believed that the Armenian revolutionary committees were a genuine threat to national security in 1915 and why the Ottoman state chose a vigorous counterinsurgency policy based on relocation. The theme and objective of the book is to inform and understand more completely Ottoman counterinsurgency practices as these affected the empire's Armenian citizens.

All too often the research into what happened between the Ottomans and the Armenians has lost sight of the broad context and the interaction of insurgency-counterinsurgency that occurred from 1890 to 1915. Indeed, much of the contemporary literature about these events can only be characterized as inflammatory and tends toward the selective engagement of narrowly defined, and in some cases predetermined, political narratives. The contemporary Western narrative asserts that the Armenian insurrection of 1915 was never an "actual" threat to the security of the Ottoman state and that the Committee of Union and Progress (which was also known as the Young Turk party) manipulated the notion of an internal Armenian threat as a pretext for ethnic cleansing and genocide.[4]

The mechanics of the relocation and destruction of the Armenian population of eastern Anatolia in 1915 have been studied intensively over the past half century and have been the source of much controversy. Moreover, many Western historians have concluded that the Ottoman state and the Young Turks, in particular, conducted a genocidal policy of ethnic cleansing against helpless Armenians.[5] On the other hand, the modern official Turkish position maintains that military necessity and state security, endangered by a gathering Armenian insurgency, provoked the relocations and some of the massacres.[6] There is some kernel of truth in both of these positions, but neither fully explains what happened. In fact, as the Sultan's decree declared, the relocation of Armenians was the result of specific actions and was itself a different course action from what had gone before.

The book begins in 1878 and ends with the completion of the military counterinsurgency campaign in the fall of 1915. Readers should note that the tragic events involving the movement of the Armenians, which occurred during, and after, the conduct of the military campaign, are outside the framework of this narrative. The tragic story of the Armenian convoys and settling the displaced Armenians into camps in the Euphrates River valley is extensively documented elsewhere. For example, the massive slaughter of tens of thousands of Armenians while staging for movement or while in convoy, conditions that themselves were a consequence of relocation, are unrelated to this particular narrative. Likewise, the loss of life of captive Armenians in camps, the brief resurrection of the state of Armenia and its destruction, and the subsequent Armenian Diaspora are not germane to an explanation of why the Ottoman government decided to relocate them in the first place.

In a similar vein, the fact that tens of thousands of Ottoman Muslims were also slaughtered by their Christian neighbors—a fact sometimes advanced as reason enough to reciprocate—did not threaten national security either and has been left out of the story as well. In actuality, from the perspective of the 1915 Ottoman military, the causes and consequences of the Armenian rebellions were of little interest. The author has attempted to isolate the military factors affecting operations, which directly led to the relocation decisions of May 1915 and to the evolution of a counterinsurgency campaign based on the isolation of guerrillas and insurgents from the general population. This book simply helps in understanding why the Ottoman government conducted an evolving, and varied, array of counterinsurgency practices and, in particular, its campaigns against the Armenian revolutionary committees.

Arguably, the 1915 Ottoman campaign against the Armenian revolutionary committees was the last major counterinsurgency campaign waged by the Ottoman Empire prior to its collapse. Ottoman army operations against the Arab Revolt of 1916–18 are more accurately characterized as counterguerrilla or counterirregular, because these were oriented against armed military groups, rather than against the Arab tribes themselves. Finally, the Ottoman counterinsurgency campaign against the Armenian revolutionary committees presaged the greater, and more lethal, counterinsurgency campaigns of the twentieth century, and it served to inform the world that only a small proportion of a population, if actively encouraged and armed by outside nations and forces, is necessary for the conduct of an insurgency.

CHAPTER 1

Insurgency by Committee

The repeated failures to carry out the reforms...coupled with the methods of slow or wholesale "elimination" of which the Armenians have been the victims during the last thirty-five years have driven many of them to join or form revolutionary societies.

—Mr. Fitzmaurice, British Embassy,
Constantinople, August 10, 1913[1]

INTRODUCTION

The rise of late-nineteenth-century armed revolutionary committees (or societies) in the Ottoman Empire occupies a significant place in the literature of the relationships between the Ottoman state and its subject peoples. However, revolutionary committees were not unique to the Ottoman Empire, or even to the repressive multinational empires of the age, and appeared in the democracies as well. In fact, the character of insurgency in Europe, including the ways in which it was organized, planned, and executed, changed dramatically in the middle of the nineteenth century, when the inspiration for insurgency shifted from something that centered on a response to oppression to something that was centered on, and driven by, ideology and national identity. This change sprang not from deliberate and intensive doctrinal theorization and debate, but was rather more of an outcome of the age of Napoleon and the changing conditions brought about by the implementation of what came to be called the Concert of Europe.

In addition to containing France after the fall of Napoleon, the victorious European coalition partners sought to contain the French idea of nationalism, which threatened to infect the subject peoples of the continental empires. At the Congress of Vienna in 1815, Austrian prince August von Metternich forged an agreement between the monarchs of Europe to safeguard the old regimes against popular revolts. Known as the Concert of Europe, the monarchs pledged military cooperation between themselves in order to maintain their thrones against internal revolution. In turn, the willingness of monarchs to support one another by armed interventions with their armies made it increasingly difficult, if not impossible, for insurgent peoples or revolutionary groups to operate openly and successfully. The large-scale and poorly organized failed revolutions of 1830 and 1848 were proof of this and drove nails into the coffin of open rebellion. As a consequence, European revolutionaries and insurgents went underground and adopted new organizational architectures and tactics, which allowed them to survive and continue operations. Of note was the nearly simultaneous emergence of the Nihilist movement in Russia and the anarchist movement in Italy.[2] This was then followed by the evolution of a system of revolutionary committees, operating in secret, motivated by ideology and nationalism, and determined to use violence to advance their agendas.

In the wake of failed uprisings, Nihilism emerged in Russia after the Crimean War when intellectuals rejected the idea of legal gradualism as a means of societal change. Secret societies, such as the Circle of Tchaikovsky and the People's Will, that embraced the idea of violence to achieve political change were formed. Embedded in the Nihilist movement was the concept of "propaganda by deed" or the dramatic violent act, such as assassination or bombing, designed to strike fear into the mechanisms of authority (the assassination of Czar Alexander II in 1882, for example).[3] Radicalized workers and intellectuals also formed secret societies in Italy in 1869, which became known as the Anarchist Movement. The Anarchists, like the Nihilists, embraced violence and the idea of propaganda by deed. Anarchism soon spread to many countries, including France, Germany, and the United States, where because of its secretive nature, the authorities found it difficult to suppress.

In the Ottoman Empire, the philosophies, organization, and tactics of the Nihilists and Anarchists were adopted by ethnic Christian minorities as a vehicle by which they might achieve independence or autonomy. Two such groups of subject peoples, in particular, became associated with these ideas as the empire entered the twentieth century—the Armenians and the Macedonians. This chapter traces the origins and evolution of the Armenian and Macedonian revolutionary movements, which to the Ottomans were known simply as the "committees."

THE RISE OF THE COMMITTEE SYSTEM

Historically, revolts had been ongoing in the Ottoman Empire almost since its inception, but new waves of insurrections swept the empire in the nineteenth century, particularly in the Balkans between 1821 and 1878. The Balkan revolts were built around recently constructed nationalist identities and were quite successful in dismembering the empire's European provinces. In the classic sense, these movements were driven more by misrule and oppression than by ideology. Unfortunately for the Ottomans, the Congress of Vienna excluded the Ottoman state from the Concert of Europe and the Ottomans were left isolated from the military assistance available to the monarchs of Europe. Moreover, in some cases, European nations actively assisted the Christian subjects of the Ottoman sultan in overthrowing Ottoman rule. Notable examples included British support for the Greeks and Russian support for the Serbs, Romanians, and Bulgarians.

After 1878, a second wave of revolts swept through the Ottoman Empire, and the most notable were the Albanians who rose up in 1880, the Armenians in 1894, 1904–1905, and 1909, the Cretans in 1896, the Macedonians in 1896, the Kurds in 1908, and the Arabs in Yemen and the Hijaz as well as the Libyan Sanussi in the early twentieth century. The second wave of insurrections was driven, in part, by perceptions of Ottoman weakness as well as by a worldwide surge of political agendas based on nationalist identity. Most of the insurrections in the second wave were unsuccessful in achieving independence, but often led to great power interventions and interference in Ottoman domestic affairs.[4] This chapter will focus on the evolution of the Macedonian and Armenian revolutionary nationalist groups into well-organized and effective hierarchical systems of revolutionary committees.

The Congress of Berlin in 1878 left significant numbers of Christian ethnic minorities within the Ottoman Empire, who quickly and stridently demanded independence or union with their respective motherlands. Moreover, certain clauses of the treaty itself were designed to reform the empire's treatment of its Christian minorities. In particular, Article 23 obligated the sultan to reform the administration of the Balkan provinces, which when incompletely and sluggishly implemented by the Ottoman government directly led to discontent and unrest. After 1878, in Ottoman Macedonia,[5] and in the densely populated Armenian eastern provinces of Ottoman Anatolia, a number of groups emerged who fought the Ottomans (and among themselves) in attempts to gain control of the provinces. This situation coincided with the rise of what might be termed the "modern guerrilla organization," which was a result of the introduction of Russian Nihilism and Italian anarchism into radicalized revolutionary groups. These organizations were known to the Ottomans as committees, because of their tightly constructed organizational architecture, and their members were likewise known as *Komitacıs* (literally a member of a secret political organization and the word most commonly used by the Ottomans to describe the groups themselves).[6] The groups were organized hierarchically in a military-like chain of command that extended from the top echelons down to local village levels. They were generally formed initially outside of the empire by exiles or revolutionaries, who supported terrorist activity inside the Ottoman provinces.

Megerdich Portukalian formed the first internal committee (the Armenakans or the Armenagans) in Van in 1885. External committees were formed by the Armenians in Geneva in 1887 (the Hunchakian or Social Democratic Party) and in Tiblisi in 1890 (the Dashnaktsutiun or the Armenian Revolutionary Federation, ARF), which adopted extremely aggressive terrorist policies.[7] These two groups consolidated a preexisting network of decentralized revolutionary cells that were well armed and ideologically motivated. After 1892, the Armenian revolutionary organizations held world congresses, issued manifestos and proclamations, and secretly organized and trained military formations inside the Ottoman Empire.[8] At the same time, the external committees organized internal, and ostensibly peaceful, counterpart political committees inside the Ottoman Empire itself. These committees were legal, operated openly and were often composed of prominent locals such as teachers, priests, businessmen, and mayors.[9] The internal committees encouraged nationalism and promoted military activity, which was presented as self-defense against repression. Thus, the Armenian committees evolved a dual organizational architecture consisting of both legal political organizations and secret armed military cells.[10] The Armenian revolutionary structure then became the template used by other rebellious ethnic groups in the empire, and particularly for the Macedonians in the Balkans, to form their own revolutionary organizations.

The Rise of the Armenian Committees

The roots of the formally organized Armenian committees reach back to the early 1880s when a group of young Armenians led by Khachadour Geregtsian and Garabed Neshikian formed a clandestine organization in Erzurum.[11] This marked the beginning of the change from brigandage to revolutionary activity. The group called itself "Defender of the Homeland" and was dedicated to the purchase of weapons and military training. Several hundred Armenians were members and were organized into a decentralized structure of ten-man cells.[12] They established contact with fellow Armenians in Tiblisi and received assistance and weapons. Meetings were frequent and revolutionary groups gathered strength in Erzurum, Tiblisi, Yerevan, and Baku. By 1888, the movement coalesced in Tiblisi by establishing an organization called "Young Armenia," which was organized into "Droshak" or military cells.[13] Shortly thereafter, the Armenakan Party (Armenagan) established itself as a political party whose purpose was to "win for the Armenians the right to rule over themselves through revolution."[14] The activities of the Armenian committees were concentrated in the core provinces of the Ottoman Empire as shown in map 1.1.

The Armenakans began spreading revolutionary propaganda, smuggling arms, organizing military units, and, occasionally, engaging in armed action. The party was organized in groups of cells, under the direction of the Central Body, which all had both active and auxiliary members.[15] The group came to the attention of the authorities in May 1889, when a firefight broke out near Van in which two prominent Armenakan leaders were killed. Papers disclosing revolutionary objectives and letters to local supporters were found on the dead bodies.[16] According to Louise Nalbandian, "The Armenakans did not stop at mere defensive action, but also incited trouble and committed terroristic acts."[17] Hunted and persecuted by the Ottoman authorities, the party disintegrated and went underground. Although later reconstituted, by 1896, it was replaced by successor activist organizations.

The Social Democrat Hunchakian Party formed in Geneva in August 1887 was the first of the Armenian socialist political parties. Its founders were heavily influenced by the revolutionary articles in the journal *Armenia*, published in Marseilles by Mekertitch Portugalian. The new party's name was taken from the party newspaper *Hunchak*, meaning "bell" or "clarion" and its seven founders were young Russian students who followed a Marxist ideology. The new party's program was written by three of its founding members, Mariam Vardanian, Avetis Nazarbekian, and Gevorg Gharadjian.[18] The Hunchakians, or Hunchaks, were committed to autonomy, which would be followed by the creation of an independent and socialist Armenian state carved out of Ottoman Anatolia. Taking a cue from the Nihilists and Anarchists, the Hunchaks were committed to the use of violence and terror.[19] Hunchak methods and tactics included "Propaganda, Agitation, Terror, Organization, and Peasant and Worker Activities."[20] Not only were Ottoman officials and notables targeted for assassination, but Armenians, who worked with the Ottomans and who were regarded as "spies and informers" by the Hunchaks, were to be killed as well.[21]

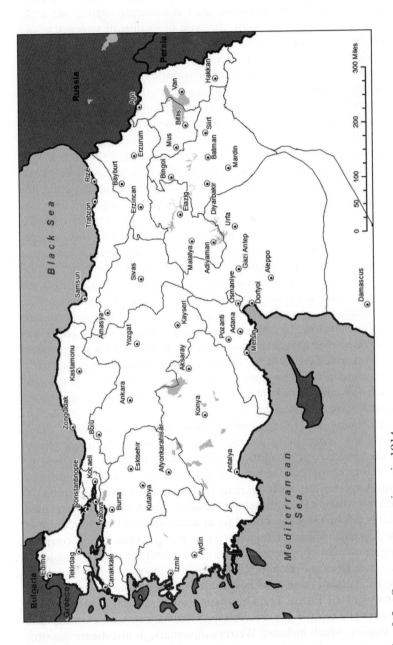

Map 1.1   Ottoman core provinces in 1914.

These tactics were designed to create secondary effects by inciting both Armenians and Ottomans into committing further atrocities and violence.[22] At some point, the cycle of small-scale violence would explode into a larger general insurrection. Like the Armenakans, the Hunchaks were organized into cells, composed of peasants and workers, which would become fighting units during the anticipated revolution. Operationally, the program hinged on the idea that "the most opportune time to institute a general rebellion for carrying out the immediate objective was when Turkey was engaged in a war."[23]

By 1890, there were hundreds of members inside and outside the Ottoman Empire and the party adopted a new name—the Hunchakian Revolutionary Party. In addition to the *Hunchak*, the party translated and published the works of Karl Marx into Armenian, including *The Communist Manifesto*. The party became very visible on July 15, 1890, when it staged the Demonstration of Kum Kapı, which was a public demonstration in the form of a procession to the Yildiz Palace. The demonstration's objectives were to rally support for Armenian issues and to present a petition to the sultan asking for reforms. When police blocked the procession violence broke out during which both police and demonstrators were killed or injured. The leader of the demonstration, Haruthiun Tjankulian, was arrested and sentenced to life imprisonment. In response to the harsh sentence, the Hunchaks accelerated their propaganda machine to highlight Ottoman oppression and atrocities.[24] The government kept a watchful eye on the party leaders and in 1893, brought trial and hanged a number of prominent Armenians including "the famous Hunchak hero and revolutionary pioneer, Zhirayr Poyadjian" in Yozgat.[25]

In August 1894, an actual rebellion broke out in Sason, which was characterized by Louise Nalbandian as one of the major efforts of the Hunchakian Revolutionary Party against the Ottoman government and Kurds. Nalbandian noted that Kurdish solidarity combined with Armenian agitation to create circumstances leading to conflict.[26] Led by Murat (Hambardsum Poyadjian), brother of the executed Zhirayr, Armenians responded to an attack on and the plundering of the Armenian village of Talori by refusing to pay taxes and by committing minor acts of aggression. The government regarded the violence as a rebellion and responded by sending troops. Murat mobilized the local armed bands and held out for a month against government forces and the Kurds. The Ottomans crushed the rebels and captured Murat. The Great Powers forced the Ottomans to send a commission of inquiry, which included Western diplomats, to investigate the situation; the results of this inquiry favored the Armenians.[27] Although the rebellion failed, it served to highlight the plight of the Armenians and generated sympathy for them in the West.[28]

A second major rebellion broke out on October 12, 1895, in nearby Zeytun, a town that had experienced rebellion previously in 1862 and 1877.[29] The local Hunchak leaders, identified as Aghassi, Apah, Heratchia, Neshan, Meleh, and Karapet, "hoped that the uprising of Armenians there would be quickly followed by Armenians throughout Cilicia."[30] Fighting spread to the nearby Armenian villages and lasted for four months, ending on February 1, 1896. According to an Armenian historian, the Ottoman army sent in a division of 8,000 soldiers reinforced by 30,000 irregulars.[31] Over the course of the four-month campaign, the Ottoman commander Remzi Pasha was replaced by Edhem Pasha for failing to subdue the insurgents, who numbered some 1,500 men.[32] The European Great Powers intervened diplomatically and forced the Ottoman government and the Hunchaks to accept a general armistice. The Armenians had to surrender all weapons and expel five foreign Hunchak revolutionary committee members but, in return, received tax amnesty and the promise of reforms.[33] Louise Nalbandian noted that the Armenians lost fewer men than the Ottomans and regarded the rebellion as a victory.

Determined to force their concerns into the public eye, Hunchak party leaders in Constantinople decided to act by presenting a "Protest-Demand" to the sultan.[34] The party leadership in the capital organized itself into the Board of Directors, which gave "instructions for nearly all of the revolutionary activity" and the Executive Committee, which organized and executed the instructions.[35] The Executive Committee's organizers were led by Karo Shakian (Heverhili Karon), who planned to conduct a peaceful demonstration.[36] After several months of secret meetings, Karo led thousands of demonstrators on September 18, 1895, to the Bab Ali gate, where he was arrested by the police without presenting his petition to the government. Rioting and violence immediately broke out during which scores of people were killed, while hundreds more were injured or imprisoned. Once again the bloodshed, this time in the capitol itself, deeply disturbed the Great Powers, which forced the sultan to introduce the Armenian reform program on October 17.[37]

The Hunchaks then fell out among themselves over the issue of political policy. A dissenting faction emerged, which took issue with the socialist positions of the party as expressed by the editor Avetis Nazarbekian in the *Hunchak*. They felt that socialism alienated the European governments and was counterproductive to the interests of the Armenian people. The subsequent ideological rift then split the party causing irreparable damage to its organization. The dissidents formed a splinter party called the Reformed Hunchakian Party in London in 1896. Nazarbekian continued to publish the *Hunchak* and maintained socialism in the Hunchakian Revolutionary Party's ideology. Although the Hunchak parties survived, the split weakened them to such an extent that they were incapable of serious revolutionary activity against the Ottomans after 1896.

To summarize the role of the Hunchaks in the development of revolutionary activity in the Ottoman Empire, it may be argued that they were the first group to combine all of the elements of a modern revolutionary movement. The organization was neither tribal nor did it engage large numbers of Armenians and, in fact, many Armenians opposed the movement. Rather the architecture of Hunchak leadership and organization might be more accurately described as a cadre and cellular structure that did not need widespread popular support. The organization was actively engaged in the construction of a nationalist identity and an associated ideology. The Hunchaks developed an active political policy of achieving independence supported by an accompanying military policy built around the creation of secret armed groups. They envisioned and employed tactics that maximized their small numbers and secretive cells, which included violence and terrorism designed to encourage and bring on widespread popular uprisings (ideally when the Ottoman Empire was engaged in a war). Although the Hunchak movement disintegrated as a revolutionary force in the mid-1890s, it was replaced immediately by a more sophisticated and more active Armenian revolutionary movement.

THE DASHNAKTSUTIUN

As the Hunchaks had emerged from expatriate groups in Western Europe, the Dashnaks grew out of a merger of Armenian groups in Russia.[38] Christopher Mikaelian, Stepan Zorian (also known as Rosdom or Kotot), and Simon Zavarian formed the Dashnaktsuthiun (or federation in Armenian) in Tiblisi in the summer of 1890.[39] Heavily influenced by Russian ideologies, the Dashnaks embraced socialism and opened discussions with the Hunchaks. At first, it appeared that the Hunchak organization would merge itself with the Dashnaks into a larger federation, but it maintained its separate identity. The newly formed Russian group then decided to call itself the Federation of Armenian Revolutionaries (*Hai Heghapokhakanneri Dashnaktsuthiun*), which was soon abbreviated to the commonly used Dashnaks.[40] The new party established its Central Committee in Tiblisi and began to publish *Droshhak* as a "rebellion promoting organ" of the party.[41]

The Dashnaks soon produced the *Manifesto*, which announced that the party had "declared a people's war against the Turkish government" and demanded the freedom of Ottoman Armenia.[42] They also encouraged Sarkis Googoonian to launch an expedition composed of about 125 Armenian revolutionaries from Russia into the Ottoman Empire. Googoonian's self-described "Divine Mission" departed on September 23, 1890, amid much fanfare and bedecked with patriotic Armenian flags, but collapsed with a week.[43] In fact, the expedition never even left Russian territory before Googoonian and 30 followers were captured by Cossacks and sent to prison.[44] Although a failure, Louise Nalbandian argued that Googoonian's aborted invasion led to an idealized Armenian vision of heroic and bloody self-sacrifice for the revolutionary cause.[45] The Dashnak committees fell into disarray for the next several years but revived themselves by convening a conclave.

The First General Congress of the Federation of Armenian Revolutionaries convened in Tiblisi in early autumn 1892, in order to sort out the following three points of dissention: revolutionary objectives, party organization, and methods and tactics to be used by the party. As the congress deliberated it reached general agreement and the introduction to the Dashnak's new program stated that the party's purpose was "to bring about the political and economic freedom of Turkish Armenia by means of rebellion."[46] Part one of the document continued with a compendium of demands centered on socialist ideology. This was followed by an explicitly violent and revolutionary set of methods and tactics that are listed here in their entirety.[47]

"The methods to be used by revolutionary bands organized by the party were the following:

1. To propagandize for the principles of the Dashnaktsuthiun and its objectives, based on an understanding of, and sympathy with, the revolutionary work.
2. To organize fighting bands, to work with them in regard to the above mentioned problems, and to prepare them for activity.
3. To use every means, by word and deed, to elevate the revolutionary activity and spirit of the people.
4. To use every means to arm the people.
5. To organize revolutionary committees and establish strong ties among them.
6. To investigate the country and the people and supply constant information to the central organ of the Dashnaktsuthiun.

7. To organize financial districts.
8. To stimulate fighting and to terrorize governments, informers, traitors, usurers, and every kind of exploiter. Because this idea is a key element in the committee's tactical methods, another translation of this point is offered: 'Fighting and using the weapon of terror on corrupt government officers, spies, traitors, grafters and all sorts of oppressors.'[48]
9. To protect the peaceful people and the inhabitants against attacks by brigands.
10. To establish communications for the transportation of men and arms.
11. To expose government establishments to looting and destruction."[49]

The final part of the new program dealt with the organization of the party. It was centered on decentralization and redundancy and established two Central Committees.[50] These committees would work in conjunction with each other and provide coordination and support to the movement. Like the Hunchaks, the vocabulary of the program was drenched in socialist and Marxist terminology, which alienated the shrinking Armenakan Party. And, while not particularly different from the Hunchak's program, the Dashnak's 1892 program highlighted the increasing radicalization of a violent element in the political development of the Armenian revolutionary parties.

Regional committees were immediately established in a number of cities on both sides of the Russo-Ottoman border and in Constantinople. Committees were also established in neighboring Persia and Tabriz became a hotbed of Armenian activity, where Tigran Stepanian built a small arms factory.[51] In short order, arms smuggling from Persia into the Ottoman Empire began in earnest via the Armenian monastery of Derik, which was just inside the Persian frontier.[52] Smuggling of arms and ammunition became so pervasive and frequent that the Ottoman authorities sent police and Kurds trying to suppress it. A major Ottoman cross-border raid against Derik on July 21, 1894, temporarily interrupted the operation but failed to stop it entirely. The period between 1892 and 1896 was one of preparation and organization for the Dashnaks during which they recruited men, began coordination with the Internal Macedonian Revolutionary Organization, spread propaganda, and armed and trained men. Several important regional congresses were also held in this period at which Rosdom advanced his General Theory Program in 1894, which provided further political guidance for the movement.[53] Rosdom's program also reaffirmed the objective "to attain political and economic freedom in Turkish Armenia by means of insurrection."[54] Map 1.2 shows the arms smuggling routes into Ottoman Anatolia.

In 1895, Rosdom became the "prime mover of the work of infiltration, arms transport and organization."[55] Dashnak *Gomidehs* (committees) and cells were established in a number of eastern Anatolian cities, including Trabzon, Erzurum, Erzincan, Van, Muş, Bitlis, Sason, and Hinis. Small-scale revolts soon broke out across the width of the Ottoman eastern Anatolian provinces. In September, revolts broke out in Zeytun and Sivas.[56] In October, the Armenian committees rose in Trabzon, Egin (known then as Mamutartu'l aziz), Develi (Kayseri), Akhisar (Izmit), Erzincan, Bitlis, Bayburt, Maraş, Urfa, and Erzurum. And in November, the Armenians of Diyarbakir, Malatya, Elâzığ (known then as Harput), Arapkir, Sivas, Maraş, and Muş rose in rebellion. On December 3, 1895, revolts broke out in Kayseri. The sheer number and timing of these incidents is hard to ignore or dismiss as reactive and spontaneous, rather than deliberately planned and orchestrated. The momentum of the movement accelerated at the end of 1895, when Serop Vartanian led a party of 27 *fedayees* (irregulars or militia fighters) to the villages of Sokhort and Akhlat to organize self-defense units.[57] Dasnabedian asserted that these efforts significantly

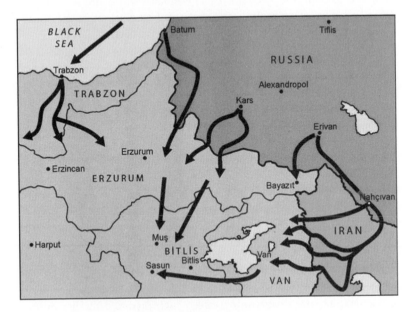

Map 1.2 Armenian arms smuggling routes.

contributed to saving Armenian lives in the oncoming revolt by providing the means for self-defense.

Over the winter of 1895–96, Dashnak activity in the province of Van became increasingly violent and centered on preparation for revolt.[58] The revolutionaries began killing fellow Armenians, who were not supportive of the ARF positions, including Bishop Boghos of Van and a number of lesser community leaders as well.[59] British consulate messages reported the killings and also noted that young Armenians were receiving military training in the Russian consulate.[60] The British also reported that Armenian groups in the city were openly planning rebellion and that this was common knowledge.[61] British vice consul W. H. Williams estimated that there were approximately 400 members of the Dashnak party in his area, and another 100 Hunchak members in Van, as he entered the critical summer of 1896.[62] Making things more volatile, Ottoman efforts at reform were slow and ineffective and, even more importantly, the government's efforts at halting Kurdish depredations against the Armenian population were a failure.[63] A Kurdish attack on four Armenian villages on March 30, 1896, killed 26 and wounded even more—with the Ottoman military force sent to assist the villagers arriving too late.[64]

The Armenian revolt began on a large scale on June 3, 1896, after months of provocation on both sides. Ottoman army reports recorded 23 revolutionary incidents prior to the outbreak and subsequent reports outlined premeditated and carefully planned preparations.[65] The three Armenian committees established a "Joint Directorate of Defense, which on the basis of prepared lists, deployed five hundred young men at 33 strategic positions."[66] In a situation much like Paris in 1871, the committeemen barricaded the streets to create fortified blocks held by highly motivated, trained, and well-armed men. The fighting in Van raged for three days, during which hundreds of combatants as well as civilians, both Muslim and Armenian, were killed in bitter house-to-house fighting. Attempts were made to negotiate a truce but these quickly collapsed when the Ottomans demanded that the ringleaders surrender themselves to the authorities. The revolt collapsed on June 10 and many of the surviving Dashnaks escaped and fled into the hills. Ottoman army reports listed 418 Muslims dead and 1,715 Armenians killed, as well as 363 Muslims and 71 Armenians wounded.[67] It is unclear today whether the lopsided ratios of Armenian killed to wounded, which should have been directly proportional, in reverse, to the number of dead, reflect the killing of wounded prisoners or the escape of wounded Armenians. In any case, the fleeing survivors were followed and attacked near the village of

Erciş, where many more were killed before the remaining made it across the border into Persia.

The most famous operation conducted by the early Dashnaks followed the Van uprising and is known today as the Ottoman Bank Demonstration, which occurred on August 24, 1896, in Constantinople.[68] The demonstration was actually not a demonstration at all, but an armed seizure of the bank by 26 Dashnak revolutionaries led by 17-year-old Babken Suni. The heavily armed men, carrying explosives, took over the entrances and threatened to blow themselves and the bank's occupants up unless their demands were met.[69] The demands include the appointment of a European high commissioner for Armenia, judicial and tax reforms, property return, refugee return, and a general amnesty for those condemned on political charges.[70] The Russian Embassy attempted to assist the Dashnaks with negotiations but the impatient Ottomans stormed the bank. Four of the Armenians died, including Suni, and eventually most the perpetrators were escorted out of the country. Riots broke out in the city immediately following the demonstration and the Dashnaks claimed that the Ottoman authorities slaughtered 6,000 Armenians. While this number is certainly exaggerated, there was enough death and destruction for the ambassadors of the Great Powers to send a Collective Note and a Verbal Note, on August 27 and September 2, respectively, to the Sublime Porte demanding an end to the killing.[71]

Although cross-border raids by Armenians and punitive Ottoman counter-raids into Persia and Russia continued into 1897, the bloody revolutionary episodes of 1895 and 1896 came to an end. As mentioned earlier, the Hunchak committees came close to dissolving as a result of internal strife and division. The Dashnaks, on the other hand, went into a period of retrenchment and rearmament. Meeting in Tiblisi from December 1896 through January 1897, the Dashnaks held their Second Regional Congress. Representatives from both Russia and the Ottoman Empire "examined various proposals regarding the tactical aspects of revolutionary activities."[72] The result of these deliberations was agreement on a revised strategy that was largely regenerative and aimed at the reconstitution of strength and position. The congress decided to build up a concentration of strength in Sason and to undertake the arming of its Armenian population. It directed revolutionary leaders such as Serop, Kourkan, Antranig (who was rapidly becoming a prominent figure in the movement and from whom more will be heard later in this book), and other military elements to move into the area. At the same time, they reached a decision that Cilicia and Dersim were "areas appropriate for revolutionary action" and to extend the "work of revolutionary organizing" to those locations.[73] The third major decision reached at the congress was more immediate and involved the launching of a punitive expedition, known as the Khanasor Expedition, from Persia into the neighboring Ottoman province of Van.

The idea behind the expedition was contentious with some prominent Dashnak leaders preferring concentration and rearmament to direct action.[74] Those in opposition included Ishkhan Arghoutian and Vartan. Other notables in the movement, such as Kristapor Ohanian and Nigol-Douman, insisted on pressing ahead with the offensive. This tension delayed the operation and polarized the *fedayee*, who had volunteered for the expedition.[75] The assembling of arms and equipment proved difficult but, nevertheless, planning continued and about 300 combatants gathered in Adrbadagan. Typical of volunteer units of the age, the men elected two leaders, Vartan as commander and Hovsep Arghoutian as second-in-command. The Central Committee approved these choices and appointed two *fedayees*, Pokhig and Akhber, as captains. Although he was an important advocate of the expedition, Nigol-Douman received a lowly lieutenancy. An advance force of 30 men carrying 40 rifles, led by Vazken, set out across the border on July 14. Later, after taking "solemn oaths," the main body of the expedition, some 253-men strong, departed on the night of July 24, 1897, and crossed the Persian-Ottoman border in the Araoul Mountains.[76] The next day, Vartan attacked and annihilated the camp of Kurdish tribal leader Sharaf Beg, losing 20 of his own men. Having met his objective of punishing his enemies and achieving a victory notable for propaganda purposes, the expedition withdrew and then disbanded.[77] It was the last such expedition launched from Persia as subsequent pressure from the Ottoman government persuaded Persian authorities to crush these activities and arrest the leaders.

To what extent was the Dashnak movement different from the Hunchak movement? As a revolutionary group, the Dashnaks certainly grew into a more highly evolved and heavily organized structure than the Hunchaks. The Dashnak political agenda and military policies were designed to be more deeply embedded in the population and it may be argued that the Dashnaks cast a wider net and deliberately appealed to a larger number of potential participants over a larger area (including the hierarchy of the Armenian Orthodox Church). In operational terms, the Hunchaks intended to incite and inflame both Armenians and Ottomans with acts of terrorism and violence; however, their actions were more spontaneous and driven by random events. The Dashnak program was more controlled, deliberate, and well-thought out. The evidence for this is the tailoring of the smuggling operations to heavily arm certain key locations for action, after which more carefully organized and larger-scale operations were undertaken. In essence, the Dashnaks attempted to design and execute operations on a much larger order of magnitude than the Hunchaks.

ARMENIAN COMMITTEE REORGANIZATION

The defeats and casualties inflicted on the Armenians committees in the rebellions of 1895 and 1896 produced a collapse of morale, especially among those members in the Caucasian committees that had borne the brunt of the fighting.[78] The hoped-for support from the international community to pressure the sultan failed to materialize and, from a practical point of view, the strategy of instigating open revolt proved disastrous. The ARF held its Second World Congress in Tiblisi from April through June 1898. From the congress emerged outcomes that were primarily operational and organizational. The most important military outcome was the articulation of "tactics for future action," which became the movement's military policy for the following years.[79] At the heart of the policy was a decision to concentrate military forces and armaments in a few key areas of the empire "in preparation for large-scale insurrections or demonstrations."[80] The congress then selected Constantinople, Cilicia, Sason, and Van, all of which contained numerically large Armenian populations, as areas for concentration. Whether this was a deliberate and functional response to the ineffectiveness of the widely scattered rebellions of the preceding years, which the Ottomans were able to crush individually, is unclear today. The congress established and selected a Responsible Central Committee with the power to oversee and direct military activities. Thus, in two simultaneous decisions, the committees concentrated military power geographically and centralized the means by which to employ it

The congress also reached agreement for a formal organizational structure and affirmed the arrangement established by the Second Regional Congress during the previous year. Two committees, the Western Bureau in Geneva and the Eastern Bureau in Tiblisi, were established with clearly defined jurisdictions (a line bisecting Anatolia running north to south from Giresun through Harput to Diyarbekir), each responsible for the subordinate provincial and city Central Committees in their areas. The two bureaus reported to the newly established "Body Representing the Will of the Dashnaktsutiun" (itself another organizational product of the congress) and were responsible for the organization of their areas and for the administration of party funds.[81] Within the Central Committees, local Responsible Committees were established to coordinate and conduct military activities while administrative support and political activities were left in the hands of local Central Committees, maintaining the cellular revolutionary organizational architecture. Thus, as the Armenian movement entered the twentieth century, a defined organizational structure emerged. Figure 1.1 shows the coherent and well-defined organization of the ARF committee in 1898.

The congress set a date to convene a Third World Congress at the end of 1900 but financial difficulties prevented this from happening. Instead, with the agreement of the bureaus and central committees, the Body Representing the Will of the Dashnaktsutiun met in April 1901 in Philippi, Macedonia. As finances were an immediate problem the body decided that "as an unavoidable measure for alleviating the financial crisis of the party, the Body adopted a plan of collecting funds through coercion."[82] According to Dasnabedian, "The plan was to secure, with threats and if necessary assassination, significant amounts of money from apathetic wealthy Armenians, in order to finance revolutionary and propaganda activities."[83] The collection was placed in the hands of the Central Committee for Constantinople for implementation and given the code name *Potorig* (storm). The body briefly considered the establishment of an Armenian Revolutionary Red Cross, as well as the cessation of negotiations with the Hunchaks, who were in the midst of organizational difficulties. Importantly, the body decided to begin the reactivation of armed groups, and to establish cooperation with the Macedonian committees, and also with the Committee of Union and Progress (also known as the Young Turks). In fact, an actual alliance was established in short order with the Macedonian revolutionary committees in the summer of 1901.[84]

The smuggling of arms from Russia and Persia continued, but after 1900, the practice of transportation of large shipments changed to one of "absorption." Smaller quantities of arms and ammunition were brought in by mule using this idea, which slowed delivery but insured that deliveries were not intercepted. The central committees also coordinated these movements into a number of main transportation routes, the principal lines of which ran as follows: (1) Salmasd to Van to Sason, (2) Nakhichevan to Van (direct via the Monastery of Saint Thaddeus), (3) Yerevan to Van (direct via Ararat), (4) Kars to Akhlat, (5) Kars to Sason with a branch toward Erzurum, (6) Batum to Sason.[85] The revitalized local committees also began a revival of violence directed against both Ottomans and fellow Armenians. The area around Sason, in particular, became a hotbed of activity and in

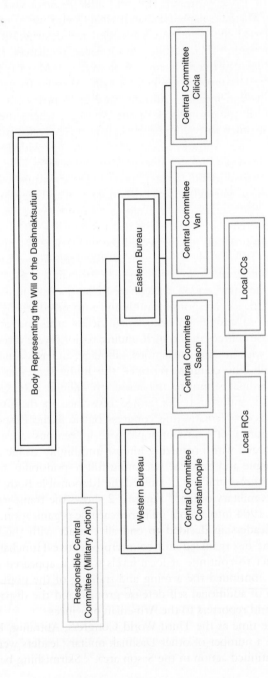

Figure 1.1 The Armenian ARF committee structure, 1898.

the autumn of 1901, Antranig, Kevork, and Magar assassinated a Kurdish tribal chieftain named Bshareh Khalil, who was responsible for the murder of the Armenian Serop and the destruction of the village of Sbaghank.[86] This resulted in Ottoman retaliatory raids on Armenian villages causing the Central Committee of Muş to organize "more resolute demonstrative military action" in order to attract the attention of the Europeans.[87] Antranig and 20 *fedayee*s entrenched themselves inside the Monastery of the Apostles, where they were attacked by Ottoman forces in a battle lasting three weeks. Although defeated in the end, Antranig's stalwart resistance provided a much needed propaganda and morale boost for the movement.

The years 1902 and 1903 formed a period of relative quiet when the party made a determined effort to concentrate men and arms in Sason, while spreading propaganda and recruiting in Muş. Externally in 1903, the ARF supported the Macedonian Illerdin uprising. By 1904, the coercive *Potorig* program had remedied the financial problems of the Dashnaks and the ARF was able to conduct the Third World Congress in Sofia in February and March. Because of Ottoman successes against the *fedayee* in the Sason region, the congress placed arms and money at the disposal of the local responsible body and authorized armed action. Plans were laid to smuggle in larger quantities of arms and ammunition and the committees in the surrounding regions were directed to support them with hit-and-run actions, sabotage, and assassinations.[88] Organizationally, the congress renamed the Body Representing the Will of the Dashnaktsutiun to the more streamlined ARF Council. Aware that the opportunity for armed resistance in the Ottoman capitol city was problematic, the congress replaced the Responsible Central Committee of Constantinople with a Demonstrative Body, which was charged with organizing intense and highly visible actions in Constantinople and Smyrna. Accepting full responsibility for self-defense the congress similarly organized the Responsible Body for the Caucasus as its military organ.[89] Figure 1.2 shows the transformation of the ARF in 1904 into a more militarily capable organization.

The ARF leadership decided to end all contact with the higher echelons of the disorganized and counterproductive Hunchaks, but allowed contact to continue at local levels when it appeared useful. The congress continued the arming and training of the population, the formation of additional self-defense groups, and the dispatching of operatives and reporters to the Armenian provinces.

At the same time as the Third World Congress, Antranig, Kevork Chvoush, and a number of other Dashnak military leaders were preparing for continued action in the Sason area.[90] Skirmishing began in

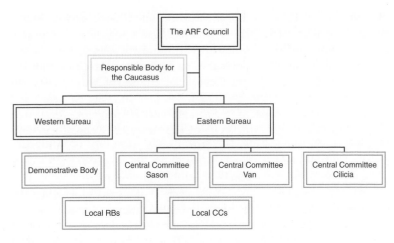

Figure 1.2　The Armenian ARF committee structure, 1904.

January and within a month heavy fighting broke out in the villages of Khiank and Dalvorig. The Ottomans massed their army against the Armenians and, by April, the fighting had become heavy.[91] Large battles took place in early April at Shenig and, later that month, another larger battle took place at Gelieguzan. However, by this time, the Dashnak's supplies of ammunition and food were dangerously low. The central committees attempted to send reinforcements and ammunition, but none of the relief efforts were successful. Beginning in May, the rebels disengaged and, with an escort of 115 *fedayee*s, evacuated the Armenian civilian population to the plains of Muş. The Armenian cadres and population suffered serious casualties during these operations.

The newly established Demonstrative Body in Constantinople began its military operations with a daring plan to assassinate Sultan Abdülhamid II using bombs. However, while the planners were training for the operation outside Sofia, some of the bombs detonated prematurely killing Kristophor, the principal organizer of the local ARF, as well as others.[92] The surviving plotters continued on and attempted to kill the sultan, who was riding in his carriage, on Friday, July 21, 1905, but the bomb exploded before the sultan arrived at the point of detonation.[93] Within weeks, the authorities discovered the location of the conspirators and apprehended them along with incriminating evidence implicating the ARF.[94] After another attempt to blow up the Ottoman Bank, the Demonstrative Body ceased operations in the capitol entirely.

Discouraged by the defeat at Sason and by the clumsy failures in Constantinople, the ARF Council met in Geneva in February and again in April of 1905. Neither of these costly operations had aroused sympathy in Europe and were judged to be counterproductive. Consequently, the council decided to "a) avoid localized clashes and instead prepare fully for large-scale movements in Van and Cilicia (in the case of the latter, preferably when Turkey was embroiled in a war); b) to carry out the Smyrna aspect of the Demonstrative Body's operations after the assassination of the Sultan; and c) to organize the province of Sivas in preparation for operations there in the future."[95] Moreover, the council decided "to move on from the phase of self-defense to revolutionary activity" and to publish a Plan of Action for the Caucasus.[96] It is clear from the ARF Council's meetings, and from its Plan of Action, that the Dashnaks intended to widen and broaden the war by increasing the scope of activity, and by expanding the battle space.

In the following years, the ARF coordinated an expansion of its Russian wing in order to confront Azeris and Tatars. As this absorbed ARF resources, it decreased Dashnak activity inside the Ottoman Empire, which, in fact, dropped off in 1906 and 1907. In turn, less costly demonstrative activities picked up in the eastern provinces. However, during this period, the party pushed so many men and resources to the Van Central Committee region that it was divided into two new Central Committee regions, called Sham, which included Van and its hinterlands, and Lernabar, which included the mountainous areas south of Lake Van (known to the Armenians as Shadakh). Despite the injunctions of the ARF Council, small battles still broke out when Armenian propaganda and organizing efforts brought down the wrath of the authorities.

Dasnabedian characterized the Fourth World Congress, held in Vienna from February 22 through May 4, 1907, as one of the "most important assemblies in the history of the Dashnaktsutiun."[97] The events in Russia had polarized the party between those who wanted to refocus operations against the Ottomans, and those who wanted to retain the momentum against the Azeris and Tatars. The party verged on the edge of breaking in half, but Rosdom and others acted as conciliators and reforged a common platform. In the end, the congress agreed to adopt several important policies. They rejected separation and agreed to pursue operations in both empires. Furthermore, they ratified and endorsed the ARF Council's Plan of Action for the Caucasus (also known as the Caucasian Plan). Much to the discomfort of the western Armenians members, the congress reenergized the party's socialist roots by embracing a social and economic agenda centered on workers and class struggle. More importantly for this work, the party reestablished its "essentially revolutionary tactics: rebellion, armed resistance against government forces, political assassination, demonstrative activity, armed popular self-defense, and political and economic strikes."[98] It is important to note here that the Dashnaks obviously understood that there were differences between offensive operations such as rebellion, political assassinations, and demonstrative activity and defensive operations such as armed popular self-defense.

Thus, by 1907, the ARF transformed itself again in its design for the waging of insurrection against the Ottoman Empire. The most important change came from the Second World Congress when the party decided on specific areas for the operational concentration of forces, those being Sason, Cilicia, and Van. This was supported by a sophisticated arms smuggling operation that was designed to equip the forces gathering in those locations for action. The party established what amounted to a general staff (the Responsible Central Committee) to coordinate military activities and provide operational direction to the effort. The ARF formalized coercion as a way to collect money and devised the means to gather and move financial resources in order to support military and political activities. The organizational architecture was solidified into a systematic chain of command that responded to central direction. Reconciliation between the Russian and Ottoman factions of the party was achieved and, finally, a revised coherent strategic plan evolved that focused on freeing the Caucasus from Ottoman rule. Taken altogether, the Dashnaks were proving to be a capable and formidable organization.

THE MACEDONIAN COMMITTEES

The Balkan committees formed in the early 1890s, when intellectuals from Ottoman Macedonia, who were ethnic Bulgarians, formed literary societies in Bulgaria, which were, in fact, thinly disguised nationalist movements.[99] On October 23, 1893, men of Bulgarian ethnicity and sympathies formed the clandestine Internal Macedonian Revolutionary Organization (hereafter called the IMRO) to counterbalance the increasing influence of Serbia in the Ottoman province.[100] Most of the founders were educated and had worked as teachers in Macedonia. They began by establishing a central committee and, in 1894, they established local committees in Istib, Prilip, and Manastir. Meanwhile, in Sofia, the local expatriate literary society transformed itself into the Young Macedonian Company, which shortly matured into the Fraternal Union. A competing Macedonian Committee also based in Sofia soon sprang up as well and, by 1895, it was apparent to the various groups that coordination was in order. Shortly thereafter the external groups in Bulgaria merged and became known as the Macedonian Revolutionary Organization (MRO).

The First Macedonian Congress convened in Sofia on March 7, 1895, and members of the IMRO attended thus establishing formal contact with the external MRO group. Two months later, the Bulgarian minister President Konstantin Stoilov met with the leaders and encouraged uprisings in Ottoman Macedonia with promises of Bulgarian support. The committees then began to organize themselves tactically into bands of armed irregulars in Bulgaria called *cheta* or *chete* for operations inside the Ottoman Empire.[101] Armed by the Bulgarian army and organized into four major *cheta* and several smaller ones, the bands crossed into eastern Macedonia in the summer of 1895, where they proceeded to raid and terrorize the Muslim population. Ottoman reprisals were swift and merciless against villagers believed to have assisted the intruders. Encouraged by their successes, the externals convened the Second Macedonian Congress in December in Sofia, and all the internal groups were invited as well. Out of this congress came a refined organizational architecture with a Supreme Macedonian Committee composed of eternals at the top and in charge of the movement. This attempt to control the movement by the externals led to a fracturing of relations between the MRO and the IMRO's central committee, which refused to recognize the Supremists (as the externals called themselves).[102]

Between 1896 and 1897, IMRO put in place a comprehensive committee system throughout Macedonia, which secretly organized *cheta* and trained them to use military weapons and tactics. Discipline was strict and the various local groups were compartmentalized so that the exposure or destruction of one would not endanger the rest. In November 1897, IRMO began a campaign of terror in Macedonia using assassinations and bombings. These internal tactics complemented the raids into Ottoman territory conducted by the Sofia-based externals. And, in 1899, at the Sixth Congress the two organizations agreed to work together.[103] Similar Serbian and Greek revolutionary groups emerged in the 1890s, although they do not seem to have been as violent as the Bulgarian movements. After 1900, the IMRO accelerated its preparations for insurrection by smuggling weapons into Macedonia, conducting military training, and inculcating nationalist propaganda into its network of revolutionary cells. Unfortunately, for the Bulgarian nationalists, the rift between the internal and external groups soon resurfaced, which, in turn, led to a badly coordinated insurrection.

The insurrection began in October 1902 in Djoumaia Bala (Cuma-i Bala), instigated by armed gangs of committeemen crossing the border. The Ottomans quickly contained the revolt and limited it to the northeastern corner of the Salonika province. This tactical reverse energized the IMRO to begin a comprehensive campaign of terror over the winter of 1902–1903, in preparation for a major pre-planned insurrection.[104] This was coordinated to coincide with the Armenian's Second Sason rebellion. The IMRO campaign targeted the Ottoman infrastructure: railroads (including the fabled Orient Express), bridges, tunnels, gas works, banks, and Ottoman police and army stations using bombs and raids by armed gangs. In May, the central committees began to orchestrate the actual uprising by organizing the *chetas* into tactical groups, evacuating supplies and villagers into the mountains, and prepositioning medical supplies.[105]

IMRO was at its strongest in the Manastir province and began the insurrection there on August 1, 1903, by immediately cutting Ottoman lines of communications and attacking isolated military and police outposts. This was followed closely by the seizure of narrow passes and bridges to isolate the area.[106] Inside the main area of operations the insurgents began to slaughter Muslim villagers. However, the well-prepared Ottomans ruthlessly suppressed the insurgency, finally crushing resistance in September. The fighting was so intense that it shocked the Great Powers, which intervened to stabilize the region but it was a blow from which the IMRO never recovered.[107] While the Ottomans defeated the Balkan *Komitacıs* in the first decade of the twentieth century, it was a bitter victory that resulted in a wide swath of destruction in the European provinces and created adverse publicity for the government. As will be shown, sporadic IMRO activities and localized revolts continued up until the Balkan Wars forcing the Ottoman army to maintain a continuous military presence, focused largely on internal security, in the region.

The Committee of Union and Progress

The third committee that is relevant to this period in late Ottoman history was neither Christian nor Armenian, but was composed largely of Westernized Muslim opponents to the anarchic rule of Sultan Abdülhamid II. Organized as the Committee of Union and Progress (*İttihad ve Terakkı Cemiyeti*), this party was often called "The Young Turk" party or the CUP.[108] The party grew out of a secret society of military cadets in Constantinople at the end of the 1880s, but a group of Imperial Medical School cadets calling itself the Ottoman Union Committee (*Osmanlı İttihad Cemiyrti*) formalized itself into a political committee in 1889. The committee, which advocated westernization and modernization, grew and received impetus from the efforts of Ottoman prince Sabahaddin, who had moved to Paris in 1899, and who had become an ardent advocate of reform. The prince formed the Society of Ottoman Liberals and then, in 1906, the League of Private Initiative and Decentralization.

Recognizing the success the Macedonian nationalists were having with exterior and interior committees, Dr. Behaettin Şakir, a rising young member of the committee, reorganized the committee along similar lines.[109] Şakir reorganized the CUP into functioning parallel elements, with the external group in Paris, and the internal one in Salonika. Mirroring the Macedonian model, the Paris committee managed external operations with subcommittees in Austria-Hungary, Bulgaria, and Romania, while the Salonika committee managed subordinate groups within the Ottoman Empire itself.

By 1904, disaffected army officers had also formed a number of secret committees, all of which carried the same phrase—*Vatan* (or motherland)—within their names. These committees flourished within the tolerant and westernized atmosphere of the Ottoman army's command headquarters in the Balkans. Unsurprisingly, the epicenter of the committees was located in Salonika at the Third Army headquarters. The CUP emerged in 1907 as the strongest and best organized of the military committees and absorbed the rest. The goals of the CUP were not insurrection aimed at independence, but rather the use of violence and terror to overthrow the sultan, in order to install a constitutional government. There was great divergence in the manner in which this might be accomplished with some officers favoring a coup d' état, while others advocating insurrection and guerrilla warfare.

In the fall of 1907, Arguni (Khachadur Malumian) and Şakir organized the Second Congress of Ottoman Opposition Parties in Paris. The co-organizers invited both the ARF and the CUP and Prince Sabaheddin somewhat grudgingly attended. Meeting from December 27 to 29, the ARF and CUP representatives brought differing proposals to the floor.[110] The ARF notably advanced both insurrection and terrorism as recommended strategies.[111] In the end, the congress issued a declaration agreeing that the parties would force the sultan to abdicate and reestablish a constitutional government. They also provided a tactical framework for accomplishing this, and it encompassed armed resistance, nonpayment of taxes, propaganda within the army so that it would not move against the committees and general rebellion. However, neither the congress participants nor the committees provided a means or plan to coordinate these activities and, in the end, it was the army that overthrew the government.

Events came to a head in April 1908, when a CUP attempt to assassinate the chief of the Salonika military police failed, causing the sultan to dispatch an investigative team with broad powers to deal with the committees. This occurred at about the same time as the negotiation of the Revel Agreement, which potentially threatened to dismember the empire's Balkan provinces. Enraged by these developments, a number of CUP members began localized violence that included assassinations, guerrilla warfare, and mutiny. This led to a generalized rebellion by the younger officers of the Third Army stationed in what was then called Ottoman Macedonia. Now actively confronted by his own military, Sultan Abdülhamid II agreed, on July 23, 1908, to restore the 1876 Constitution.

The CUP differed from the Armenian and Macedonian committees because it consisted not only of members of the imperial family, but also of serving professional army officers, both of whom wanted to reform a decaying system. It was not committed to the dissolution of the Ottoman Empire but rather sought to preserve it. The CUP did not seek, at least at this moment in history, to create a nationalist identity and instead advocated westernization and modernization as the means to oppose the increasing interventions and influence of the European powers. The sultan stood in the way of this agenda and this brought the CUP into temporary alignment with the ARF. The IMRO was not invited to the 1908 Paris congress because the Ottoman army was engaged in an ongoing and intensive counterinsurgency against it in Ottoman Macedonia.

It is important to note here that, prior to 1908, the secret committees of the CUP, although arguably never as violent as the ARF or IMRO, involved many Ottoman army officers who later rose to high positions in the Ottoman government and military.[112] In effect, this collective experience provided the Ottoman government and high command in World War I with men who understood the dynamics of secret revolutionary committees from the perspective of practitioners.

THE CONSTITUTIONAL PERIOD

The period from July 1908 through January 23, 1913, represents a time in which the Armenian committees enjoyed a relatively cooperative relationship with the Ottoman government. The reasons for this, from the Armenian perspective, were that the committees felt, under a parliamentary framework, that the oppressive practices of the government were likely to change.[113] With the restoration of the constitution, the formerly illegal and secret committees became openly legal political parties. The ARF even went so far as to embrace a public position endorsing participation in government, reconciliation, and the abandonment of the idea of an independent Armenia.[114] Rosdom and Anton (Simon Zavarian) enthusiastically orchestrated political campaigns as vigorously as they had planned military ones. ARF field workers were dispatched to the provinces containing significant Armenian populations; for example, Dro went to Diyarbakir as a political organizer.

In the first elections, ten Armenian representatives were elected to the Ottoman parliament.[115] At the same time, the CUP was unable to handle the stress of compromise required by the democratic process and began to fragment. In truth, the Ottoman Armenians made a better transition from secret revolutionary committee to legal political party than the Ottoman Turks. This was a product of the Armenian committee's comparatively well-organized leadership, tight discipline, and institutional strength. Moreover the strength of a preexisting organizational architecture in the major western cities, and in the eastern Anatolian provinces, was a huge political asset as well. Whether the CUP ever intended to partner in a meaningful way with the Armenians is problematic and it may be, as stated by Justin McCarthy, that "simply put, the Dashnaks were a necessary element in the electoral and parliamentary coalition that kept the CUP in power."[116] The ARF certainly was aware that it had its feet planted on shaky ground and maintained its organizational self-defense architecture intact and continued to smuggle arms and ammunition into the empire.[117]

Unfortunately for the advocates of representative parliamentary government, mutinous demonstrations by disenfranchised regimental officers broke out in Constantinople on April 13, 1909, which led to the collapse of the government. Characterized as a counterrevolution, chaos reigned briefly and several people were killed in the confusion. Finally, the military intervened and the ad hoc Action Army, led by Ottoman Third Army officers, who were members of, or sympathetic to, the CUP, arrived in the capital from Salonika to restore order on April 24, 1909. The political result was that the CUP took a much more active and forceful role when the government was reconstituted in June.

At the same time, a major outbreak of violence, known today as the Adana Massacres, shook ARF-CUP relations to the core, almost destroying the hitherto cooperative alliance. All sources agree that the violence apparently began in a vineyard near Adana on April 12, 1909, involving armed Muslim Turks and Armenians.[118] However, the narrative breaks down from that point on with pro-Turkish authors blaming the Armenians and pro-Armenian authors blaming the Ottomans.[119] The Armenian narrative presented these events as a deliberately conducted large-scale massacre, while the Ottomans presented it as a deliberate instigated episode of violence, rapidly escalating out of control into an insurgency, which had to be quelled by the army.[120] Direct testimony by neutral international observers is similarly conflicted, but it seems that enough atrocities were committed by each side so that any number of conclusions could be drawn from the violence, which lasted about a week. The new Ottoman governor, Cemal Pasha, appointed in August, estimated that 17,000 Armenians and 1,850 Muslims died in the violence.[121]

The truth of what actually happened is almost impossible to recover and reconcile today. The author believes that young Armenian men, who were armed by the revolutionary committees, unwisely became involved in gunplay over a minor problem with their Muslim neighbors. The Ottoman authorities overreacted, provoking a more dangerous response from the Armenians. The conflagration quickly spread into the city proper where it had the appearance of a revolt. In turn the Ottoman authorities brought in military forces and ruthlessly stamped out both real opponents, while at the same time massacring thousands of innocent people. It stands as one of the blackest marks against the Ottoman government during the Hamidian and constitutional period.

Surprisingly, and despite the disturbing events in Adana, the ARF leadership remained committed to cooperation with the CUP, which promised to punish the perpetrators and compensate the victims.[122] The ARF convened its Fifth World Congress in Varna, Bulgaria, from August through September 1909 and, in light of the reestablished constitutional government, decided to discontinue its underground activities and place its military forces "in the service of protecting the constitution and the freedoms it brought."[123] However, the Adana Massacres alarmed so many of the participants that the congress reaffirmed the right to self-defense and, in a positive act, decided to retain military capability stating that "in the case of danger that the Dashnaktsutiun will enter the stage with all of its forces."[124] With its last vestiges of goodwill and cooperation, the ARF formed a Joint Body with the CUP in January 1910, to investigate the Armenian complaints and the government promised to send inspectors out to the eastern provinces to document them. Unfortunately, the left wing of the CUP (including Talat, Şakir, Nazım, and Cavid), which was supportive of collaborative efforts with the ARF, was out of power.

The year 1910 brought renewed problems in the eastern provinces between Armenians and Kurds, which were characterized by what amounted to land grabs perpetrated against Armenian peasants. Unfortunately, when these cases went to court, Muslim judges frequently upheld the claims of the Kurds and Ottoman Muslims, which further inflamed tensions.[125] Sporadic violence directed against Armenians, which that included murder and thievery, continued but overall the incidents of violence against Armenians declined.[126] Nevertheless, as promised reforms failed to materialize, relations between the CUP and ARF continued to deteriorate in 1911. A particular problem for the CUP was that it did not exercise a high degree of local political power or control over many of its adherents in many of the eastern provinces and cities. Compounding this situation, some Kurdish tribes were beginning to feel the stirrings of nationalism at the instigation of the Russians. In August and September 1911, the ARF held its Sixth World Congress in Constantinople itself. Concerned with the broken promises of the Ottoman government, the congress penned a declaration outlining the conditions under which the ARF would continue to work with the government. The congress examined the organizational structure of the party, but made no changes, with one exception. The congress was convinced that deteriorating political conditions in the empire made "probable the necessity of resorting to self-defense"[127] and the congress elected a Self-Defense Body, which was fully empowered to direct all military affairs.

The Ottoman parliament dissolved on January 15, 1912, and political campaigns began almost immediately. The CUP launched a manipulative campaign designed to take advantage of opposition weakness that also included intimidation and violence. The CUP swept the elections of 1912, with CUP candidates and supporters taking 170 of 284 available seats.[128] The tactics of the CUP troubled many Armenians, who already felt let down by the broken promises of the Young Turks. This led to a break between the ARF and the CUP. On May 5, 1912, the ARF presented a notice to the CUP officially severing relations to the Young Turks. The break became public the following month when the Western Bureau printed an official announcement directed to "Ottoman Citizens" and the June issue of *Droshak* ran an editorial about it.[129]

Throughout the constitutional period, the Armenian committees generally refrained from violent activity and abided by their promises to work within the constitutional processes. Nevertheless, uncertain as to a successful resolution of their grievances and status, they continued to smuggle arms and ammunition into the Ottoman Empire and they continued to train men to use them. The highly disciplined ARF military command and control architecture remained intact and received a boost when the Fifth World Congress revitalized the command structure by activating a Self-Defense Body. While peaceful during the period of constitutional government, the Armenian committees retained and even improved their full military capability.

EFFECT ON THE OTTOMANS

In the author's view, there were two serious outcomes that affected the Ottomans as a result of these nationalist insurrections by committee. First, over a period of some 20 years, the operations of the *Komitacıs* in the Balkans and in eastern Anatolia came to dominate the collective Ottoman military mind; much like the Sepoy Mutiny of 1857 affected the British army.[130] Insurgency by committee became, and remained, a persistent concern of the Ottoman government and army until the final days of the empire. The intellectual focus and interest of an entire generation of the Ottoman officer corps shifted from conventional warfare to counterinsurgency campaigns. In the operational sense, the experiences and backgrounds of the army's professionals likewise shifted away from large-scale conventional operations toward proficiency in small unit operations focused on the suppression of internal insurrection. Second, and perhaps more importantly, there was a change in Ottoman understandings of the nature of insurgency as evidenced by Ottoman military responses. In fact, the rise of the revolutionary committee architecture itself represented a fundamental shift in how insurrections were conducted within the Anatolian and Balkan provinces of the Ottoman Empire.

Although insurrection had been nearly a constant throughout its history, rebellion in the Ottoman Empire, before the committees, tended to be leader-centric or tribal.[131] It was often driven by heavy taxation or conscription rather than by nationalist aspirations and the insurrections were led by clearly identifiable local or regional leaders.[132] In a sense, until the late nineteenth century, insurrections in the Ottoman Empire were characterized by an apolitical leader-centric and tribal organizational architecture. As a result, traditional Ottoman counterinsurgency strategies and tactics focused on the hunt for the leader and on punishment for his followers by Ottoman army expeditionary columns.

The reality of the rise of the *Komitacıs* forced a paradigm shift in the Ottoman intellectual approach to the question of insurrection because the committees distributed the leadership down through and into the population itself. The club-like political front structure of the legal wings and the cell-like structure of the violent armed secret wings created a web of networked local leaders, who were embedded in the very fabric of the societies of particular nationalist minorities. The preponderance of *Komitacıs* leaders were teachers, intellectuals, merchants, and priests. In many locations, the *Komitacıs* leaders were mayors and public officials. In effect, the rise of the committees transferred responsibility for rebellion from individual tribal leaders into collective responsibility for insurgency onto entire segments of the population. This paradigm shift in the nature of insurrection itself made it nearly impossible to localize and isolate those responsible for the problem forcing the Ottomans, in turn, to evolve new counterinsurgency methods.

This page intentionally left blank

CHAPTER 2

Counterinsurgency in the Empire's Core

The immediate aim of the revolutionists has been to incite disorder, bring about inhuman reprisals, and so provoke the intervention of the Powers in the name of humanity.

—*Sir Phillip Currie, British Embassy, Constantinople, March 28, 1894*[1]

INTRODUCTION

The demographic and economic core areas of the late Ottoman Empire were its Turkey-in-Europe provinces in the Balkans and the provinces of the Anatolian heartland, both of which were strategically essential for the continued preservation of the Ottoman state. Unfortunately, after the Russo-Ottoman War of 1877–78, in the core areas the Ottoman military faced renewed conventional threats from external enemies as well as new unconventional threats from the internal Macedonian and Armenians revolutionary committees. In response to these threats, the retention of core areas became a strategic imperative that drove the reorganization and redeployment of the Ottoman Army into a military posture with which it could handle the situation. As a result, in the period from 1878 through the First Balkan War of 1912, the Ottoman army evolved a variety of effective counterinsurgency practices in order to deal with the new operational and tactical problems created by the emergence of the revolutionary committees. However, this institutional focus on counterinsurgency came at a price and led to the creation of a generation of Ottoman officers who were highly specialized in low-intensity conflict at the expense of professional skills in conventional war.

"The Berlin Peace Treaty recast the Ottoman Balkan possessions in such a way that it was not militarily feasible to defend them against either foreign aggression or internal insurrection."[2] Nevertheless, Bismarck's Congress of Berlin Treaty, signed on July 13, 1878, had a profound effect on the military posture of the Ottoman Empire as it entered the twentieth century, particularly with regard to its military deployment and operations. After 1878, the recast situation in southeastern Europe forced the Ottoman Empire to dedicate more and more of its scarce military resources toward the defense of the Balkans. This outcome was largely due to the vulnerable geographic position of the Ottoman's remaining Balkan provinces imposed by the Congress of Berlin and by the increasingly strident and dangerous insurgent activities that the agreement seemed to encourage. This chapter explores the relationship between the Congress of Berlin and the evolution of Ottoman counterinsurgency practices in the empire during the period 1878–1913.

In political terms, while reducing the "Greater Bulgaria" created by the Treaty of San Stefano, the Congress of Berlin served to create the modern country of Bulgaria, which, by 1885, included the province of Eastern Rumelia as well. The strategic consequence for the Ottomans was monumentally disastrous in that the new Bulgaria cut deeply into Ottoman territory in Europe thereby partially isolating the five western Balkan provinces of Kosovo, Iskodra, Janina, Manastir (Macedonia), and Salonika. Moreover, the creation of Bulgaria nearly severed overland communications with the region, and the single-track railroad from Constantinople through Salonika to Skopje remained the only significant route available to the Ottomans.[3] This made communications with the Ottoman western provinces very vulnerable to interdiction while simultaneously making the resupply of military forces stationed there problematic. Unfortunately for the empire, in strategic terms the Berlin agreement created a theater of operations, the maintenance of which was critical to the national security needs of the Ottoman Empire, but which had no strategic depth against its new Bulgarian neighbor. Unwilling to abandon the isolated provinces because of their large populations and productive economies, the Ottomans felt forced to defend them. Unfortunately, the nearly bankrupt Ottomans did not have the financial resources to defend the entirety of the overextended empire. As a result, the Ottomans made a series of military policy decisions that prioritized the defense of their European provinces. In turn, this prioritization of effort shortchanged other theaters of operation and led to the evolution of a variety of differing counterinsurgency practices. By the time of World War I, these practices evolved into practices that significantly affected Ottoman policy decisions regarding the Armenian insurrection in 1915.

CHANGES IN OTTOMAN STRATEGIC POLICY AND PRIORITIES AFTER 1878

The principal military legacy of the Congress of Berlin was the creation of a new and unfavorable strategic geography which pushed back the frontiers resulting in the creation of a Bulgarian state that projected like a salient into the Ottoman European provinces. This was aggravated, in turn, by the permanent loss of the fortress zones along the Danube frontier in Europe and in the border areas around Kars and Batum in Caucasia. Combined with massive losses of men and equipment, the treaty immediately put the Ottoman Empire in a strategically defensive posture. The Ottoman strategic response was predictable and resulted in a major reorganization of armies, the construction of a new series of modern fortresses to replace the ones that were lost as a result of the Congress of Berlin, and a movement toward military modernization. Unfortunately, as the new Christian kingdom of Bulgaria grew larger and more dangerous, the Ottomans, now hamstrung by inadequate finances, were forced to constrict and prioritize their military spending and outlays in line with strategic threats. This was the result of the creation of the Ottoman Public Debt Administration in 1881 by the Great Powers, which forcibly reduced government expenditures in order to pay European creditors.[4] Thus, between 1880 and 1911, Ottomans built and gathered a disproportionate share of the empire's military strength in the Balkans at the expense of other regions.

Prior to the Russo-Turkish War of 1877–78, there were three Ottoman field armies with headquarters and operational areas in Europe—the First in Constantinople, the Second in Şumnu (essentially in what is now Bulgaria), and the Third in Manastir (in what is now Macedonia).[5] The European front absorbed about 55 percent of the field forces with the remainder spread evenly between Caucasia, Mesopotamia, and Arabia.[6] The organization of these armies was not standardized and varied greatly with local combinations of divisions and independent regiments. During the war, the Second Army was largely destroyed or captured by the Russian armies making the postwar restructuring of the Ottoman army an immediate priority. It took the Ottomans several years after the Treaty of Berlin to reorganize into seven numbered field armies, implementing the new structure in March 1881, and, at the same time, also standardizing their divisions along European lines.[7] In Thrace, the Ottomans reconstituted the Second Army with its new headquarters in the city of Edirne.[8]

In terms of force structure, the field armies were each identically organized with two infantry divisions, an artillery division, and a cavalry division. The infantry divisions contained four infantry regiments each and, for the purposes of this chapter, the infantry regiment will be used as the basis for analyzing force structure and deployments. Under the 1881 reorganization, the three Ottoman field armies in Europe deployed a total of 24 infantry regiments with the army's remaining 32 regiments assigned to the other four field armies (this meant that the Ottomans deployed 42 percent of the force in Europe). This well-balanced deployment was made possible by the creation of a weakened Bulgarian state in 1878 and by the removal of a direct Russian threat to southeastern Europe. However, the situation changed in 1885 when the Bulgarian annexation of East Rumelia placed an increasingly powerful Bulgarian adversary on the doorstep of Edirne (Adrianople) and Constantinople.

The creation of a new strategic threat in European Thrace forced the Ottomans to again reconsider the army's strength and deployment. In 1888, a modernized reserve system was created, which added 16 reserve infantry regiments to each field army in the event of war (thereby adding 48 infantry regiments to the wartime defense of the European provinces).[9] However, this alone was insufficient to guarantee the defensive integrity of the European front and, to strengthen the European front, the peacetime manning levels of the infantry battalions assigned to the Second and Third Armies were raised to wartime authorizations of 800 men per battalion, while the First Army authorizations were raised to 500 men.[10] In the empire's other armies, infantry battalion peacetime manning levels were maintained at 400 men (only 50 percent of wartime authorizations). This increase in manning strengthened the Ottoman European forces, but the vastly increased numbers of men brought commensurate increased costs in provisioning, equipping, and billeting.[11]

As a young and vigorous Bulgaria grew in conventional military power, it also encouraged revolutionary movements in Ottoman territory that forced the Ottomans to send even more troops to the European provinces. In 1894, the Ottoman army added four active infantry divisions to its force structure, of which two went to the Third Army in Macedonia. Moreover, by 1907, the Second Army in Edirne had grown to 16 regiments while the Third Army grew to 24 regiments (making it the largest Ottoman field army). This gave the three Ottoman armies in Europe 57 percent of the army's combat power but, under the army's higher manning levels on its European fronts, over 70 percent of the army's infantry rifle strength.[12]

Further reorganization and modernization occurred between 1908 and 1911 creating army corps that brought the Ottoman army in line with contemporary European practices.[13] As a part of this, the Third Army headquarters moved to Caucasia, while the Second Army headquarters was shifted to Salonika absorbing the former Third Army area and assuming operational responsibility for the Ottoman provinces in Europe. The First Army headquarters remained in Constantinople but assumed command of the Edirne fortress. On the eve of the Balkan Wars in 1912, Ottoman forces assigned to defend Europe had grown to 63 percent of the force structure (89 infantry regiments of a total of 141 in the army) manned at near war establishments.[14]

Similarly, the national security and police force (originally named the *Zabtiye* or law enforcement), which was founded in 1840, transformed in the 1870s into a national gendarmerie (*Jandarma*), which reflected the shifting strategic priorities of the empire. In 1888, European advisors reorganized the gendarmerie along military lines by including military training and ranks into the organization.[15] As it militarized and grew in size and capability, the *jandarma* assumed internal responsibility for field operations against terrorists and guerrillas. At the beginning of the twentieth century, the Ottoman *jandarma* was a well-led, well-trained, and competent force that was an integral component of the Ottoman internal security structure. The deployment of the *jandarma*, a force of over 26,000 men by the 1890s and modeled on the French system, reflected the national security priorities of the military in which over 40 percent of its strength was stationed in the European provinces.[16]

This robust growth of Ottoman military and paramilitary force structure was matched by the construction of new modern fortresses to make up for the loss in 1878 of the Danube fortress quadrilateral (Silistre, Zistovi, Vidin, and Plevne) and the Caucasian fortresses (Kars, Ardahan, and Batum). Starting in the early 1880s, the Ottomans chose a number of important cities as defensive complexes and began to fortify them similarly to efforts then ongoing in Belgium, France, and Germany. This was a substantial effort that was very expensive. In Macedonia, Ottoman engineers, closely advised by German officers, turned Janina and Scutari into major fortresses and established secondary fortress complexes in Salonika, Manastir, and Kosovo (as well as 16 other fortified towns).[17]

Complementing these defenses, the Ottomans heavily fortified the city of Edirne and the fortress line at Çatalca, which lay astride the key avenue of approach from Bulgaria to Constantinople. These major fortresses became the operational hubs around which the defense of Ottoman Europe was established.[18] The major fortresses consisted of concentric rings of self-sufficient forts about three kilometers outside the city that contained heavy artillery emplaced inside bombproof brick and earth fortifications. These forts were connected by entrenchments and later connected by telephone wires as well. By the twentieth century, the ring of forts was moved out to about ten kilometers from the city centers.[19] In Caucasia, the Ottomans heavily fortified the city of Erzurum as well as smaller efforts at Trabzon, Van, and Samsun. Thus, in the 30-year period after 1878, Ottoman military policy shifted toward the static defense of the empire's European and Caucasian frontiers, prioritizing the construction of fortresses in the Balkan provinces.

The nearly total defeat at the hands of the Russians in 1878 also led the Ottoman sultan Abdülhamid to undertake dramatic reform efforts in rebuilding his shattered armies.[20] The most well-known and farreaching of his reforms lay in the selection of Germany to approach for assistance in the retraining and reforming of the Ottoman army. Initially, the sultan approached France, a traditional ally and friend; however, the French ignored the request and, in May 1880, Abdülhamid's request was accepted by the Germans instead. Led by Colonel Kaehler the first three German officers reached Constantinople on April 29, 1882.[21]

From these small beginnings, the German military mission began the retraining of the Ottoman officer corps. Under Kaehler's successor, Colmar von der Goltz, the mission had a great effect on the curriculum of the Ottoman War Academy by creating a mirror image of the German War Academy. This ensured that German theories of war, operational principles, and planning and training methods took intellectual root in the Ottoman army.[22] Moreover, almost immediately, Ottoman army weapons procurement began to shift toward German manufacturing firms, such as Krupp and Mauser, in efforts to reequip Ottoman forces.[23] By 1888, for example, the army's artillery forces had acquired over a thousand quick-firing German field guns.[24] The army also procured hundreds of thousands of rifles, pistols, and other military equipment from Germany. Beyond this, the German military mission had little apparent immediate impact; indeed, because of the financial costs the sultan rejected most of the German recommendations regarding the creation of a modern reserve system and modern army organization. In fact, the real impact of the German presence was strategic in that it began the long process, which ultimately blossomed into a friendly military relationship and alliance between the two nations.[25]

In sum, these policies (force structure increases, fortification, and military reform) militated some of the negative strategic effects imposed by the Congress of Berlin. The army gradually deployed the bulk of its strength in Europe and it created a new heavily armed fortress system that blocked key avenues into the empire's Balkan provinces. Over time, the army was reequipped predominately with up-to-date German weapons and, over a generation, its senior officers were trained to plan and execute campaigns like their German mentors. Unfortunately for the empire, in the end, none of these measures would compensate for the geographic penalty imposed by the creation of an aggressively expansionist Bulgaria, which acted as salient cutting deeply into the transverse communications between Constantinople and the western provinces.

The Evolution of Ottoman Counterinsurgency Practices in Europe

During the period 1878–1912, the primary strategic threat to the Ottoman Empire was not external attack by a neighboring country, but rather insurrection by nationalist groups seeking political autonomy or independence, the most active of which were the Bulgarian and Armenian *Komitacis* in Macedonia and Caucasia, respectively. As shown previously, the costly strategic reinforcement of the Ottoman armies in the Balkans closely paralleled the growth of both the Bulgarian state and the growth of the internal and external revolutionary *Komitacis*. The strategic "bill payers" (to use a modern expression) for the increasing costs of security in Europe were the Ottoman field armies in the remaining theaters of operations (Caucasia, Mesopotamia, and the Arabian and North African provinces), which over time were denuded of men and equipment.[26] This asymmetric concentration of conventional forces in the Balkans, in turn, forced the Ottomans to consider alternative operational solutions to the insurgency threats elsewhere. An outcome of this situation was the parallel development of resource-driven counterinsurgency practices by the Ottoman military.[27] In Europe, the powerful Ottoman Second and Third Armies increasingly focused on counterinsurgency operations as the terrorist threats mounted. These operations, conducted in the relatively small Balkan geographic theater of operations by strong regular forces, closely mirrored the contemporary western counterinsurgency practices of the age and were successfully executed.

As the *Komitacis* matured in strength and capability during the early 1890s, the Ottoman army had no formal doctrines about counterinsurgency warfare. Indeed, the military philosophy of the age was based on conventional Napoleonic warfare interpreted by Clausewitz and Jomini, which concentrated almost exclusively on wars between the regular forces of nation states. The major defining small guerrilla wars of the era had yet to be fought and the lessons learned about effective counterinsurgency practices had yet to be written down.[28] This absence of formal and comprehensive doctrines left the door of practical application wide open for interpretation by individual officers. This intersected with Ottoman foreign policy, which, after 1878, was focused on keeping the Great Powers from intervening in domestic crises within the empire involving Christian minorities. This imperative drove the army to find quick and effective solutions when revolts broke out. Thus the question of how to suppress revolts as rapidly as possible in the Ottoman Empire was left entirely to field army commanders.[29]

Ottoman commanders and their staffs were not formally trained in counterinsurgency tactics, however, the Ottoman army and its officers intensively, but informally, studied contemporary counterinsurgency campaigns and small wars. The most notable example was Pertev Pasha, who was an Ottoman general staff officer and a protégé of General Colmar von der Goltz. Pertev and von der Goltz maintained an active correspondence concerning the lessons learned from the Boer War.[30] Von der Goltz also mentored Ahmet İzzet Pasha throughout this period and the two maintained an active professional friendship. Ahmet İzzet later commanded the tactically and operationally successful Ottoman counterinsurgency campaign in Yemen in 1911–12, an effort that involved 29 infantry battalions.

It is known that counterinsurgency operations were actively discussed at the Ottoman War Academy in the period 1905–14, although the subject itself was not a part of the regular course curriculum.[31] The reason for this was because the wily and paranoid Abdülhamid, fearful of being overthrown by his own officer corps, forbid the inclusion of the subject of counterinsurgency as a taught course (as he also did for any courses involving political theory and thought). Callwell's *Small Wars*, for example, was never translated into Ottoman, although it was translated into French (as Petites Guerre in 1899) and both the English and French editions were privately available in the empire. In spite of these prohibitions, the academy and war college trained officers, who were all fluent in at least one European language, read widely and maintained active understandings of contemporary military affairs.[32] It may be easily argued that the Ottoman officer corps was well grounded in its collective knowledge of what the Western world was doing in the way of small wars and counterinsurgency at the dawn of the twentieth century.

For small-scale rebellious outbreaks in the Balkans, the Third Army turned to the formation of provisional detachments (*müfreze*) or small self-sufficient expeditionary forces that were tailored toward specific missions. Typically such detachments were commanded by a colonel and consisted of several thousand soldiers with artillery (a typical detachment in the suppression of the Bosnian revolt consisted of four battalions and an artillery battery).[33] In practice, the detachments were positioned around the affected area of insurrection and then drove inward on a convergent point. Any rebels who might escape were then hunted down by patrols commanded by Ottoman captains and lieutenants. A single detachment might deal with a small cross-border raiding party or a localized revolt of a tribe or a town.

For large-scale insurrections, the Ottomans employed their regular forces, broken down into a number of tactical detachments. In the case of the Bosnian revolt, which affected almost an entire province, the Ottomans initially committed 30 infantry battalions, which grew to a total of 44 battalions over the course of the four-month counterinsurgency campaign.[34] The Ottoman forces began by wresting control of the roads and key passes in the mountains from the rebels, after which the Ottomans seized the major towns. Finally, the army drove the insurgents into the hills where they were isolated and destroyed in detail. The campaigns were bitterly contested and, in the Bosnian revolt, many Ottoman battalions lost a third of their men. The most active counterinsurgency campaign fought by the Ottomans at the end of the nineteenth century in Europe occurred in Crete in 1896, when the Third Army put down an attempted revolt supported by Greeks from the mainland. In addition to the regular army division stationed on the island, the sultan sent 12 additional infantry battalions to assist in the counterinsurgency campaign.[35]

The Macedonian insurrection of August 1903 represented a significant challenge for the Ottoman army because of its unusually large scale, estimated at 25,000 men organized and armed by the IMRO *Komitacıs* with perhaps 10,000 rifles.[36] The well-planned insurgency immediately cut provincial communications and seized the key communications centers and choke points. Initially, the Ottoman army, caught by surprise, sent 12 infantry battalions into the province commanded by Omer Rusdu Pasha. This force was clearly insufficient and the Ottomans distributed rifles to the local Muslim inhabitants to secure the towns.[37] By the end of the month, the Ottoman First, Second, and Third Armies sent an additional 40 battalions to reinforce the effort and command transferred to Nasir Pasha. On August 24, 1903, Nasir Pasha reorganized his forces into

> five detachments, which starting from outlying positions in the rebellious area headed toward its center...the soldiers encircled every zone controlled by the insurgents and hunted the revolutionary forces by surrounding them in an ever narrowing circle before crushing them...the soldiers systematically burned and destroyed Christian villages as for every shattered village there was a revolutionary center that was eliminated.[38]

It took the Ottomans several months using these brutal tactics to extinguish the insurrection and, in the end, they ended up burning several hundred villages, killing about 5,000 civilians, and forcing some 30,000 to flee into neighboring Bulgaria.[39] About 1,000 *Komitacıs* were killed as well as about 5,000 Ottoman soldiers.[40] However many soldiers the Ottomans actually lost, the ferocity and totality of their response destroyed the cohesion and effectiveness of the Macedonian revolutionary organizations, which had difficulty recovering from this defeat.[41]

By 1907, Macedonian *Komitacıs* had regained enough strength to renew their terrorist campaigns, forcing the Ottomans to again reinforce the army. The sultan formed mobile detachments and also a reinforced "special gendarmerie corps of three to four thousand men" to combat the guerrillas.[42] Characterized by a Western author as "mobile commandos," the forces totaled 12 battalions divided into 120 detachments of 30 men each.[43] The use of the term "commando" is not reflective of the modern connotation of a highly specialized individual soldier, but rather of the original use by the Boers as a self-sufficient and highly mobile independent force. Complementing the mobile commandos, the Third Army, a force that had grown to 124 infantry battalions, employed 80 battalions directly in the counterinsurgency campaign while 44 battalions sealed off the Bulgarian and Serbian borders.[44]

Over the winter of 1907–1908, the sultan's forces swept through Macedonia sealing off areas of known guerrilla activity, destroying villages suspected of harboring and supporting the *Komitacıs*, and, finally, hunting down and annihilating the survivors using the mobile columns. The campaign quickly turned into one of no quarter in which massacre, countermassacre, and atrocity became commonplace. Nevertheless, in the end the Ottomans again prevailed and ended the outbreaks of insurrection.

The Ottoman counterinsurgency campaigns in Macedonia against the Bulgarian *Komitacı* were marked by the evolution of distinct tactics that reflected the contemporary counterinsurgency practices of the Ottomans. First, the army employed large numbers of regular soldiers, who were heavily reinforced by the *jandarma*. This force was used to seal the borders and isolate the tactical area of operations, often dividing it into manageable sectors. Villages thought to support the *Komitacı* were raided and when hidden arms were found, put to the torch and the inhabitants forced to flee. Finally, the isolated guerrillas were then ruthlessly hunted down by independent and highly mobile Ottoman detachments. In the bitterly contested campaigns, atrocities on both sides were commonplace and the nature of the revolutionary committee structure insured that the army viewed the entire local populations as wholly responsible for the insurrections. Taken together, Ottoman counterinsurgency practices in the empire's European provinces can be characterized as well-organized campaigns executed by large numbers of regular forces but which were punitive and brutal.

The Evolution of Ottoman Counterinsurgency Practices in Caucasia

Unfortunately for the Ottomans, instability and insurrection by committee erupted simultaneously (1890–1912) in the eastern Anatolian and Caucasian provinces. Poorly resourced to execute a coherent counterinsurgency campaign in one theater, the Ottomans found it almost impossible to conduct counterinsurgency campaigns in a second. In turn, along the Ottoman Empire's Caucasian frontier, and within its eastern Anatolian provinces, the Ottoman army evolved a different counterinsurgency policy characterized by vastly different force structures and tactics.

This difference was brought about not by choice or sound national military policy, but by the constraints caused by the spending priority dedicated to the European front, which absorbed both financial and human resources. The origins of this began as a result of the costs of the war and indemnities imposed by the Congress of Berlin, which caused the already shaky Ottoman finance system to collapse. The creditor nations then forced the Ottoman government to create a public debt administration in 1881 that administered tax revenues with a view toward the repayment of foreign investors.[45] This reduced government revenues to a trickle and crippled the ability of the sultan to rebuild the empire's military capacity for the next decade.

Most of the available Ottoman military budget in the 1880s went toward weapons procurement and fortress construction.[46] The navy suffered terribly during this period with almost no money going to that service, and the size and force structure of the army was frozen.[47] Moreover, as previously discussed, the internal and external Balkan threats to Ottoman national security pulled a disproportionate share of the existing force structure and resources to the European armies. Likewise only 20 percent of the field *jandarma* was deployed in the six eastern Anatolian provinces.[48] This situation, in turn, created significant weakness in the empire's resource-poor eastern and outlying provinces.[49] Financial pressures increased and, in 1889, the desperate sultan ordered a study aimed at reducing the Ottoman active force from 250,000 to 130,000 men.[50] This reduction never took place as the security needs of the empire precluded its implementation, but it illustrates the severe fiscal strain imposed by financial weakness. Unfortunately for the government, the threat of armed insurrection by the Armenian *Komitacis* grew in Caucasia forcing the financially pressed Ottoman military to search for an adequate but "relatively inexpensive" solution, which it found in the resurrection of irregular light cavalry forces.[51]

In 1890, the sultan ordered the formation of the Hamidiye tribal cavalry, modeled on Russian Cossack regiments, as a standing force for internal security and border security.[52] Historians of the Hamidiye cavalry present a number of motives for the formation of the tribal force. Bayram Kodaman argued that the Hamidiye were formed to establish centralized authority, change the sociopolitical balance, benefit from tribal military power, hinder Armenian activism, protect eastern Anatolia from the Russians and the British, and carry out policies of Pan-Islamism.[53] Armenian historian Raymond H. Kévorkian argued that the Hamidiye regiments were explicitly formed to "annihilate" and oppress the Armenian inhabitants of eastern Anatolia.[54] Janet Klein asserted that the formation of the Hamidiye was something of a personal project for Sultan Abdülhamid, who famously enjoyed tinkering with his military and naval forces, but that the empire's aims became transformational, aiming at the inclusion of tribal peoples into the fabric of society.[55]

However, none of these arguments explain why the sultan or the Ottoman military chose a force structure model that was known to be inefficient, undisciplined, and riddled with problematic command and control issues. Therefore, the author believes that the most compelling motive to establish the Hamidiye regiments was simply one of expediency driven by the lack of funds necessary to field a regular armed force. Nominally organized as regiments under progovernment tribal chieftains and notables, who received a stipend from the army, the units were uniformed and well-armed, but untrained and undisciplined. The cavalrymen in the regiments received guns and equipment but received no pay until, and unless, called into service.[56] Upon mobilization, the men were paid small salaries but the money was delivered directly to the chieftains and distributed by them.

As the government was always short of cash during this period and often unable to pay salaries, it attempted to accommodate the cavalrymen with tax reductions and other compensatory methods.[57] Moreover, since the government was not saddled with the overhead costs of barracks, medical care, cantonments, and the training of conscripts, further savings were achieved. In truth, the force was expedient and inexpensive compared with the costs of maintaining an active force of similar size.[58] Janet Klein used the phrase "from tribesmen to troops and back again" to describe the process.[59] Most of the regiments were composed largely of Kurdish tribesmen, although there were Laz and Azeri regiments as well. Within four years, 30 regiments were raised with a total strength of well over 40,000 men. Although the army established a special military school for the regimental leaders, the force remained largely unresponsive to conventional military discipline, a condition that would cause great difficulty when the regiments were committed operationally in arduous circumstances.[60]

Events coalesced in August 1894, in the Bitlis province, when well-organized Armenian *Komitacıs* rose in rebellion in the town of Sason.[61] It remains difficult to pinpoint the beginning of the fighting; the Armenians blamed Ottoman persecution and massacres, while the Ottomans blamed Armenian raids on Muslim villages, which were encouraged by the Tiblisi committee, as the proximate cause. In any case, it fell to Fourth Army commander Zeki Pasha to suppress the insurrection and, for this task, his army had only the 8th Infantry Division available in the area (which under the Ottoman manning policies was maintained at less-than-half strength).[62] After subtracting fixed garrisons, and even when reinforced with local *jandarma* regiments, the Fourth Army had much less than a division to deal with the insurgency. This led Zeki Pasha to mobilize his tribal cavalry regiments and send them to assist in the suppression. Unfortunately, the undisciplined and poorly led irregulars quickly gained notoriety for excessively heavy-handed tactics that included the massacre, mutilation, rape, and pillaging of the Armenian population. It proved impossible to stop them from destroying Armenian villages thought to be supporting the *Komitacıs*.

About a quarter of the Armenian inhabitants of Sason were killed and both the rebellion and Ottoman response spread to adjacent areas. It is clear today that much of the destruction was caused by impoverished tribesmen anxious to acquire the wealth and property of their neighbors. Armenian authors have asserted that 100,000 were killed in what became known as the Hamidian Massacres but the French ambassador claimed a lower number of 40,000. In any case, eastern Anatolia became a slaughterhouse. This should not, of course, have been an unforeseen outcome given the inherent difficulty of counterinsurgency operations and the indiscipline of the tribal cavalry. Nevertheless, the willingness of the government to tolerate the atrocities of the Hamidiye cavalry damaged the reputation of the Ottoman military for the remainder of its existence.

After the suppression of the Sason rebellion, small numbers of additional regular troops were sent to the region but there were never enough to maintain security. In 1896, renewed Armenian rebellions broke out in Van and Zeytun, which were again ruthlessly put down by government forces. According to an Armenian historian, the Ottoman army sent in a division of 8,000 soldiers reinforced by 30,000 irregulars to quell the Zeytun rebellion.[63] Over the course of the four-month campaign, the Ottoman commander Remzi Pasha was replaced by Edhem Pasha for failing to subdue the insurgents, who numbered some 1,500 men.[64] A new commander, Sadettin Pasha, personally led several assaults and attempted to restrain the tribal cavalry; unfortunately, the pattern of atrocities continued.[65] As a matter of practice, the irregular Hamidiye tribal cavalry in Caucasia employed more indiscriminate tactics than those employed by the regular army in Macedonia. Over the next decade, there were a number of outbreaks of violence involving the Armenians, both as victims and as perpetrators. As late as 1909, irregular tribal cavalry regiments were used in counterinsurgency operations in Caucasia.

In the early twentieth century, Ottoman counterinsurgency practices in Caucasia evolved along fundamentally different lines from those evolving simultaneously in the empire's European provinces. In eastern Anatolia, the nearly bankrupt Ottoman state deliberately chose an underresourced approach caused by military policies that had prioritized its European fronts. As a result, the famously undisciplined irregular tribal cavalry regiments were the instrument of choice in the counterinsurgency campaigns waged against the Armenian *Komitacıs*. These campaigns were characterized by insufficient regular troops and by the inability to successfully coordinate operations between the army and the tribal cavalry. Success was gained in most cases by the indiscriminate destruction of Armenian villages and the wholesale slaughter of Armenians.

Reciprocally, atrocities committed by the Armenian *Komitacis* and committee architecture insured the transposition of responsibility to the general population making things all the worse. Although generally successful in counterinsurgency operations, the brutal excesses of the Hamidiye cavalry enraged even the most hardened Ottoman officials and, in 1911, the tribal cavalry regiments were disestablished or converted into reserve light cavalry regiments. This experiment failed miserably when the empire went to war in November 1914, as the Reserve Cavalry Corps, composed of men from the former Hamidiye regiments, was committed to conventional combat against the regular Russian army. The corps' performance was so weak and unreliable that the Ottomans immediately deactivated the entire force in December. In sum, Ottoman counterinsurgency practices in the empire's eastern Anatolian provinces can be characterized as poorly coordinated campaigns executed mostly by irregulars (rather than by regulars), which were episodic, punitive, and needlessly bloody.

The Ottoman Army at the End of the Hamidian Era

After 1878, Sultan Abdülhamid attempted a vast reformation of the army in an effort to create a viable military force capable of defending the empire. Hobbled by the lack of financial backing, his efforts were incompletely applied and, while some components of the army flourished (notably the highly trained corps of general staff officers trained at the military and war academies) other parts atrophied. The training of the army was sadly deficient as the money invested in fortifications and equipment took away from the training of line officers and soldiers, which was itself costly. In particular the new reserve system existed largely on paper and underwent almost no meaningful annual training, making it a useless tool. In the Balkan Wars of 1912–13, the army's shortcomings were ruthlessly exposed and reflected the financial priorities and military policies of the Hamidian government. Ottoman staff work was excellent as was the effectiveness of the field artillery; however, mobilization and operational maneuver and logistics were inefficient. The army's tactical performance in conventional operations, especially in leadership and battlefield coordination, was dismal and the war was a disaster.[66]

In comparison, Ottoman counterinsurgency campaigns in the core areas were notably successful. This was mostly a result of the decentralization of effort within which Ottoman officers had to learn by themselves, under very adverse conditions, how to conduct counterinsurgency operations against guerrilla organizations. Most of the academically trained officers spent several rotations (sometimes whole careers) in Macedonia fighting on their own against ideologically motivated, well-equipped, and well-led guerrilla organizations. The main problem for them was the lack of government support, as well as a lack of doctrinal tactics, to combat unconventional and irregular fighters. The officers involved were quick to recognize the evolution of traditional insurgents and social bandits into *Komitacıs*, who were ideologically motivated and highly disciplined guerrilla fighters. In a relatively short time, they understood the importance of gaining support from the population and made use not only of the potential of the Muslim population, but also of the different Christian groups, pitting them against each other.[67] Consequently, independent of the government, various practices and tactics were implemented, and more or less an unofficial, but widely accepted uniform counterinsurgency doctrine was in use after the 1890s. By making use of their academy and war college-acquired competencies in foreign languages, the Ottoman officer corps also followed developments in foreign militaries. For example, the British practice of constructing blockhouses in order to control and secure rugged terrain during the Boer War was immediately introduced under the same name (*Blokhavz*) and used widely.[68] In effect, combat units became alternative military schools and the officers' mess became clubs where army officers could discuss their ideas and tactics freely.

The counterinsurgency campaigns also played an important role in shaping the political consciousness of the officers, which was accelerated by interaction with the ideologies of their guerrilla enemies. The militant nationalism of the insurgents, particularly the continuous flow of political thoughts and their ways of propaganda and organization, greatly inspired the officers. And in the end, they applied what they had learned. Military men conducted the first political protests and formed secret organizations similar to the committees, such as the establishment of the Ottoman Union Committee (*Osmanlı Ittihad Cemiyeti*) in 1889 by Imperial Medical School cadets.[69] After 1904, more secret organizations were established and flourished at the field army headquarters and, unsurprisingly, the Third Army headquarters in Salonika became the epicenter of the most powerful group. In a relatively short time, the Committee of Union and Progress or CUP (*Ittihad ve Terakki Cemiyeti*) became the most prominent, and it absorbed the other groups into it.[70]

Despite much preparation and secrecy, the CUP's incompletely planned revolt unraveled in late April 1908. Abdülhamid immediately sent an investigation team with extraordinary powers to which the conspirators gave the alarm and reacted with disobedience and insubordination.[71] Over the summer numbers of other officers joined the rebellion, often taking up arms in the rugged Balkan mountains. The civilian population joined the cause of the officers by holding public demonstrations and sending mass petitions to the sultan. Clearly, the officers were making use of their accumulated experience in counterinsurgency by following the blueprints of the *Komitacıs*.[72] In the end, Abdülhamid gave up under intense pressure and restored the constitution that he had suspended in 1878. What came to be called the Young Turk Revolution was a remarkable victory won largely by junior officers, who were schooled in the practical art of counterinsurgency.[73] Many of the officers directly involved in these events, notably Enver Pasha, later seized control of the entire Ottoman government in 1913, while others rose to high command in the Ottoman Army. Thus, on the eve of World War I these highly politicized officers, who had built their careers fighting *Komitacıs* and guerrillas, were in positions of importance as the empire's decision-makers at the strategic and operational level.

This page intentionally left blank

CHAPTER 3

Counterinsurgency in the Periphery

*He assembled the tribes from the entire country, and they agreed to
obey him...and...to besiege the cities in which there were Turks.*

—*Mehmet Tevfik Bay about Imam Yahya,
Yemen, 1905*[1]

INTRODUCTION

The counterinsurgency campaigns in the empire's periphery were
unlike those fought in the core areas of Macedonia and Anatolia and
demonstrate another side of Ottoman counterinsurgency practices.
This was because, as Ottoman military strength was drawn to, and
concentrated in, the core areas, it became possible in the distant provinces for traditional tribal and leader-centric rebellion to take root.
Moreover, unlike the committee-led insurgencies in the core areas,
which failed to engage a majority of the respective populations, insurgencies in the periphery found broad popular support. This changed
the dynamic in favor of the insurgents and, in the end, made it impossible for the Ottomans to succeed. These hard-fought counterinsurgency campaigns in the periphery ended in military failure leading to
negotiated settlements.

Yemen was in a continuous state of rebellion from 1904 to 1911, and
the Ottoman campaigns there absorbed upward of 40 infantry battalions
fighting against very well-armed and determined enemies. In the end,
despite committing large resources, the military effort in Yemen failed
to achieve the desired effects and the Ottomans negotiated settlements
with the rebels. Likewise, in Albania, the Ottomans failed to win military
victories over the rebels and negotiated a settlement. In both cases, the
settlements resulted in near autonomy for the inhabitants. As Yemen and
Albania were peripheral to the strategic core regions of the empire, these
were acceptable outcomes for the Ottoman government.

The campaign in Libya against Italy was not a counterinsurgency at all. There, a conventional Ottoman army garrison was pushed out of the coastal cities by Italian expeditionary forces. The Ottomans then abandoned conventional operations and fought what amounted to a guerrilla campaign against the Italians. As a force multiplier, the Ottomans recruited irregular local tribes into their force structure and proceeded to wage an economical campaign against the Italians, which was designed to wear down their morale and strength. Although very successful, the Ottoman campaign collapsed in the late summer of 1912, when the Balkan League threatened attack in the empire's Balkan provinces. Arguably, the importance of the Libyan campaign for the Ottomans was that it provided a number of upwardly mobile young professional officers an opportunity to conduct a military campaign from the perspective of an insurgent.

The Constitutional period in late Ottoman history, which began on July 23, 1908, marked the point at which the professionally trained general staff officers were free to start the transformation of the Ottoman army into a modern military force. Between 1908 and the beginning of the First Balkan War in October 1912, the Ottoman army underwent a massive intellectual and physical transformation. This was accomplished while actively fighting large and difficult counterinsurgencies in Yemen and Albania, as well as fighting a war against Italy in Libya. These competing priorities placed huge demands on the already thinly stretched Ottoman military institutions.

YEMEN, 1904–1907

Tribal leaders instigated insurrection in Ottoman Yemen on a frequent basis. The most recent rebellions in 1872 and 1891 lasted several years, and required large Ottoman expeditionary forces to quell them.[2] The rebellion of 1891 was based on the influence of local tribal leaders and erupted spasmodically, and it had religious overtones.[3] Led by Imam Al-Manşur, who was both a tribal leader as well as a religious authority figure, the rebels were unable to mobilize a large centralized force, and resistance was distributed over a wide area, forcing the Ottomans to replace their system of punitive expeditions with a "grueling system of mobile war designed to hunt down and destroy the Imam's partisans."[4] The rebellion was ruthlessly suppressed by the Ottoman military governor Feyzi Pasha, who served there from 1891 to 1898. His use of hard-hitting small columns, characterized by devastating European-style firepower superiority, reflected the most current and effective counterinsurgency tactics of the age.

Nevertheless, Feyzi's policies were poorly resourced and he was never able to extinguish resistance entirely. In 1898, Hüseyin Hilmi Pasha replaced Feyzi Pasha, which led to an about-face in Ottoman policy. Hüseyin Hilmi initiated policies designed to gain the popular support of the people. These included replacing the military administration with a civil administration and reform and development programs to improve the lives of the Yemenis.[5] Unfortunately, Hüseyin Hilmi was no better resourced than Feyzi, and he was unable to fully implement his programs, which led to failure. As a result, Ottoman control deteriorated as Yemen entered the twentieth century.

The headquarters of the Seventh Army, which was the Ottoman Empire's smallest field army, was located in San-a. It was composed of the 13th and the 14th Infantry Divisions (controlling the 49th–52nd Infantry regiments and the 53rd–56th Infantry Regiments, respectively), the 7th Cavalry Regiment, and the 7th Artillery Regiment.[6] Troop strength of the Seventh Army was about 18,000 officers and men, who were garrisoned in the major towns of the province.

The accession of Al-Manṣur's son as the Imam Yaḥyā led directly to rebellion in 1904, when the new imam was forced by tradition to prove that he was spiritually and physically worthy of the position. In early October 1904, the Ottoman governor, Mehmet Tevfik Bey, estimated that 1,500 men followed the imam into taking up arms in the rural areas.[7] By the end of November, the rebels were interdicting the major roads between San-ā and Hudayda on the coast and Hajja and Ta'izz, thus isolating the provincial capital city. The imam's men cut the telegraph lines and intercepted all caravan traffic. By December 1, San-ā was under a state of siege with limited food, while the imam controlled the countryside and enjoyed lavish provisions previously stocked by his father. The Ottomans conducted limited sorties in futile attempts to break through the rebel cordon. The rebels were well-armed with modern rifles, but they had no modern artillery to overcome the Ottoman army's artillery. Although the rebels appeared to be following a strategy of starving the garrison, the presence of new pattern magazine fed military rifles in the imam's army greatly alarmed Governor Tevfik.[8]

Small Ottoman forces attempted to relieve San-ā up the road from Hudayda but were repulsed. Estimates of rebel strength ranged from 12,000 to 30,000 men.[9] The Ottoman army sent in reinforcements in the form of an expeditionary force, led by Rıza Pasha, composed of five brigades of 32 battalions drawn from the Third, Fourth, and Fifth Armies from Macedonia, eastern Anatolia, and Syria, respectively.[10] While he was gathering his 25,600 man force, Rıza Pasha launched a relief force of 3,000 men, which reached San-ā at the end of January 1905. However, the relief force could not carry enough supplies to sustain the town and the Ottomans launched an offensive in February to take the nearby town of Rawda, which held large stores of the imam's stockpiled food. A pitched battle lasting three weeks resulted but, in the end, the Ottoman regulars were unable to overcome the well-armed and motivated rebels, who had entrenched themselves into the stone houses of the town. San-ā remained more or less isolated and on the verge of starvation.

On March 10, 1905, Rıza Pasha set out with his main body of ten battalions of infantry with 14 artillery pieces. His combat forces totaled about 7,000–8,000 soldiers as well as some 700 tribal auxiliaries opposed to Imam Yahyā. Unlike the previous relief force, Rıza took a baggage train of 600 animals and 2,000 untrained conscripts, whose sole duty was to bring flour and food to beleaguered San-ā. The column was organized in classic nineteenth-century style with a vanguard, a main body, a rear guard, and flanking elements. The massive baggage train marched between the main body and the rear guard. The rebels harassed the column continuously as it made its way toward San-ā, and as Ottoman casualties mounted troop morale fell correspondingly. Disaster struck Rıza's force as it approached the Yāzil Ridge, a key terrain feature blocking the way to the plain surrounding San-ā.[11]

A rebel skirmish line on the ridge appeared to have a gap in it and Rıza's force was deployed to punch through it. However, the rebel maneuver was a feint, and while the lead Ottoman elements were attacking empty positions, rebels on the flanks captured the entire baggage train. With no resupply at hand San-ā surrendered shortly thereafter. Rıza's chief of staff was the brilliant young Ahmet İzzet, who would become the chief of the Ottoman General Staff in August 1908, and his memoirs describe why the Ottomans were defeated by the rebels. First, Rıza's force, although quite large, was hastily assembled and was neither cohesive nor particularly well trained.[12] Additionally, the men were in poor condition after an arduous sea voyage and some of the Arab soldiers were sympathetic to the rebels. Moreover, Ahmet İzzet asserted that the battalion detailed to guard the baggage train fled, rather than defending their charges. The imperative of relieving San-ā in time to avoid the starvation of its garrison drove Rıza to march up-country with a force inadequate to the task. In the end, it was logistics and sustainment that put the Ottomans in the position of having to take the tactical offensive while in a posture of being on the strategic defensive.

Faced with an enemy who not only controlled all of the major towns (with the exception of the coastal areas), but who possessed the initiative, well-disciplined troops, as well as newly captured artillery, the Ottomans were forced to take drastic methods. In this case, the government brought back the ruthless and formidable former governor Feyzi Pasha to conduct a campaign designed to win back the highlands of the interior. The government gave Feyzi 48 battalions or some 40,000 trained men, as well as 20,000 untrained conscripts, with which to reconstitute the shattered surviving battalions of Rıza's command.[13] Feyzi's forces were also more abundantly equipped with artillery. The new formations began to pour into Yemen by sea and Feyzi himself landed at Hudayda on June 1, 1905. With San-ā lost, there was no driving imperative to relieve a surrounded town; also there was no particular need to bring a heavy baggage train laden with supplies for a starving army and citizens. Feyzi knew the country, he knew his old enemies, and was supremely confident of his own ability to suppress the rebellion.

Unhampered by the need to rapidly restore order, Feyzi set about conducting a deliberate campaign that negated the previous campaign's reliance on baggage trains, which had proven to be the weak link of the Ottoman army in Yemen. He decided to reestablish complete control of the main road from Hudayda to San-ā and adopted a "two-stage system of advance."[14] The main elements of the system involved advancing a heavily armed column up the road, which then set up a base where supplies and munitions could be safely concentrated. From there, mobile columns could swing around the eastern flank to dislodge the rebel positions. Once the rebels were cleared from the roads, the mobile base column might move forward again, more or less "leap frogging" supply lines forward as the force advanced. Feyzi's offensive began on June 29, 1905, from Hudayda and he successfully staged his bases four times up into the highlands.[15]

Rebel resistance stiffened as Feyzi came closer to San-ā, and again the rebels established a strong defense on the Yāzil Ridge. The heavily entrenched rebel lines of defense incorporated fortified villages and artillery pieces and extended to the key peaks on both sides of the valley. It was a formidable position, but it committed the rebel force to a pitched conventional battle.[16] On August 19, 1905, Feyzi ordered his second in command, Şakir Pasha, to conduct a flanking maneuver at the Sinan Pass with seven infantry battalions and two artillery batteries, while a number of other Ottoman battalions frontally attacked the rebels to fix their attention away from his main effort. By the end of the day, Şakir Pasha's men had broken through the initial lines, but were stalled forcing Şakir to request reinforcements.

The next day, Feyzi sent an additional seven infantry battalions and more artillery and bitter fighting raged between the Ottomans and the rebels into August 21, when four of Şakir's battalions seized a wadi that was the key to the rebel position. This enabled Şakir Pasha to finally achieve a breakthrough on the following day, which led to the collapse of the entire rebel defense. However, it still took until August 24 for Feyzi's force to clear the plains around San-ā, which fell after token resistance at the end of the month.

Feyzi now turned his mobile columns loose in the highlands to crush the rebellion once and for all. Unfortunately, the Ottoman General Staff ordered 14,000 men home, while the replacements, eight battalions in all, failed to arrive in time to backfill the departing units.[17] The campaign lurched into December 1905, when an Ottoman force under Brigadier Rıza Pasha was caught and destroyed in the Sahahāah ravine, during which battle Rıza himself was killed. Although Feyzi captured the major fortress of Shirhā, soon after the rebels withdrew into the hills and continued to harass the Ottomans. The campaign turned into a quagmire for the Ottoman Empire and the Syrian units of the expeditionary force began to mutiny. Peace negotiations between Feyzi and the imam, combined with malnutrition and disease, further lowered Ottoman morale. The government committed itself to reinforcing Feyzi, who seemed to be capable of actually concluding the campaign on favorable terms, and it sent him an additional force of well-trained, well-equipped soldiers along with more artillery.[18] Feyzi threw them all into the fight, but the rebels could not be brought to a decisive battle. The frustrated Feyzi attempted to ally himself with the tribal enemies of the imam but this failed as well. Finally, the Ottomans concluded that even Feyzi could not defeat the insurgents, and a cease-fire was negotiated that ended the fighting on terms more or less favorable to the imam, but which restored nominal Ottoman control over Yemen.

The Imam Yahyā's rebellion was conducted in a manner that was fundamentally different from the previous Ottoman experience. The imam's campaign was conducted according to a deliberate strategy based largely on the denial of logistics to the Ottomans. Moreover, the acquisition of modern weapons, primarily magazine-fed military rifles, enabled the rebels to go toe-to-toe with the regular Ottoman army. This put the Ottomans in a position of relative weakness and enabled the rebels to engage in large-scale conventional battles. Vincent S. Wilhite asserted that the "1904 rebellion thus signaled a major transformation in the essential character of war in Yemen."[19] Previous rebellions were brought about largely by issues such as conscription and taxation, and violence was localized in pursuit of very limited objectives. Wilhite argued that the elements of transformation of the Imam Yahyā's rebellion were fundamentally larger and involved long-term campaign planning; a "total-goal" of Ottoman expulsion from Yemen, supratribal mobilization (by establishing an overarching command authority linking the previously fragmented tribes), and up-to-date weaponry.[20] The effect on the Ottomans was profound in that the empire had to commit ever-increasing levels of military power toward the suppression of rebellion in Yemen. Feyzi's 1891 campaign involved around 7,000–8,000 men, Rıza's 1904 campaign mobilized about 26,000 men, while Feyzi's 1905 campaign brought in over 110,000 Ottoman soldiers. Beyond the scale of the latest effort, unverified press reports estimated total Ottoman casualties in the 1905 campaigns at 25,000–30,000 men.[21]

Transformation, 1908–11

The Ottoman army, in 1908, comprised seven numbered field armies and fielded 13,880 officers and 273,997 men, of whom 1,342 officers and 35,196 men were actively engaged in operations against rebels, brigands, and revolutionaries.[22] The army was organized on an obsolete model into 21 infantry divisions, 6 cavalry divisions, 5 artillery divisions, and a number of independent brigades and regiments. The army had neither modern combined arms divisions nor modern corps-level headquarters. In essence, the empire's armies commanded divisions organized to fight the Crimean War (the 1855 era), and which were centered on the empire's provincial capital cities. Additionally, there was a system of reserves, but these units were similarly organized, seldom brought together for training, and poorly equipped.[23] On August 15, 1908, the minister of war, Recep Pasha, appointed Ahmet İzzet Pasha as the chief of staff of the army, and he would remain in this position until January 1, 1914. Ahmet İzzet was a general staff officer, who was an ardent advocate of modernization, and he set about eliminating the conservative and uneducated *alaylı*, or regimental officers, who were an impediment to change. As a result, the unhappy disenfranchised regimental officers led a mutiny known as the March 31st Incident (using the old calendar, but it actually occurred on April 13, 1909), demanding an end to modernization efforts. The mutiny was crushed and two laws that dramatically changed the army were passed. The first, the Law of Age Limitation on June 26 eliminated elderly officers, and the second, the Law for the Purge of Military Ranks on August 7 established educational and time in grade provisions for promotion. These actions and laws ended a patronage system that had existed for centuries and enabled the army to move forward with modernization. This also cleared the way for the school-trained officers of the army (known as *mektepli*), the preponderance of who were members of the CUP, to advance into positions of importance.

Concurrently with these actions, Ahmet İzzet was orchestrating a massive reorganization of the Ottoman army, which he had begun to think about over the winter of 1908.[24] Assisting the Ottomans, German General Colmar von de Goltz led an inspection team in the summer of 1909 that tested and assessed various experimental organizational architectures under tactical field conditions in large-scale exercises.[25] The heart of Ahmet İzzet's initial reorganization was the restructuring of the army's divisions into triangular combined arms formations composed of three infantry regiments supported by an artillery regiment. The Ottoman triangular division presaged the evolution of the modern combat division and it is notable that the armies of the major European powers adopted this particular architecture during World War I. But in 1909, this idea was a major departure from the contemporary European model in which divisions were composed of two brigades of two regiments each (often called the "square division"). In July 1910, the army published its instructions for reorganization, which deconstructed and then reorganized the entire army into triangular combined arms infantry divisions that mirrored Ahmet İzzet and von der Goltz's radical ideas.[26] The two brigade headquarters assigned to all Ottoman army infantry divisions were entirely eliminated. This was followed by further official army instructions in September, which merged the elements of the reserve, inactivated the artillery divisions, as well as reorganized the irregular Hamidiye into paramilitary Tribal Light Cavalry.[27] The new formations were subjected to large-scale field maneuvers under field army control in the fall of 1910 around Edirne (then called Adrianople by the Europeans) in the area of western Thrace. Most of these organizational innovations were structural and tactical in nature. One major exception was the restructuring, in 1909, of the Ottoman General Staff into the German model, often called the "chief of staff system," with staff directorates mirroring the Great Prussian general staff, one of which was explicitly tasked with managing the reorganization.[28]

In terms of modern command and control, however, the most significant tactical change came in January 1911, when Ahmet İzzet Pasha issued further army instructions involving the inactivation of the seven numbered field armies and replaced them with only four such armies. He then formed and activated fourteen new army corps headquarters.[29] The new architecture reflected the current practices in the major European armies and positioned the Ottoman army to conduct warfare at the operational level. Unfortunately for the army, the brand new corps headquarters lacked experienced commanders and staffs, and often, essential equipment. At the same time, a German-inspired system of army-level reserve inspectorates was created, as were the subordinate divisions required to bring the Ottoman army to its authorized wartime order of battle and combat strength. In this way, Ahmet İzzet revitalized the army's reserve by recasting it as a mirror image of the active army.

YEMEN, 1908–12

As the campaign against the Imam Yahyā began to wind down, a rival claimant to tribal leadership named Muhammad ibn Idrıs arrived in Yemen. Idrıs was a follower of the more strict Wahabı faith and presented Yahyā as a weak vessel, who had sold out to the Ottomans.[30] Idrıs was determined to raise the standard of rebellion again as a way to legitimizing his own claims to religious and secular authority over the tribes. This led to a renewal of the revolt, which was reenergized when the rival imams attracted enough followers willing to support reengaging the Ottomans. The Ottoman military responded in kind and dispatched a new force of 12,000 to combat Idrıs and, by 1910, counterinsurgency operations were again in full swing.

In January 1911, the Ministry of War mobilized 16 battalions for deployment to Yemen. Ahmet İzzet Pasha, the chief of the general staff, personally led an elite expeditionary force of 9 battalions from the premier I Army Corps. Fierce battles were fought against the rebels around Ta'izz and along the outpost lines outside San'a. While the Ottomans gained the upper hand in these battles, a further four regular and four reserve battalions were sent to Yemen. The Ministry of War ordered Ahmet İzzet to crush the imams once and for all, and ordered another 30 battalions dispatched to reinforce the newly organized XIV Army Corps in Yemen.[31] The proposed counterinsurgency force was set at 35 regular and 10 reserve infantry battalions, supported by 3 field artillery batteries and 2 machine gun companies (altogether some 50,000 combat soldiers). Additional reserve units were mobilized to provide transport and logistics services.[32] All of these forces were detached and deployed from Ottoman armies elsewhere, primarily from the manpower-rich First Army in the capitol area, and the Second Army in Macedonia; however the massive reinforcement effort also drew in substantial numbers of soldiers from Syria and even Libya.

The tempo of the fighting rose in the summer of 1911 as the Ottomans sought to regain the initiative and bring Idrıs's men to decisive battle. A pitched battle was fought at Jāzān, in which the Ottomans lost about 1,500 men altogether as well as several artillery pieces and machine guns. Once again, the Ottoman government recognized that its efforts to suppress what came to be called "the Idrıs insurrection" had failed to achieve satisfactory results. In the end, the Ottomans negotiated a settlement with the imams, which granted them favorable tax and customs concessions, judicial reforms, infrastructure improvements (telegraphs and railroads), and official apologies.[33]

Yemen was in a continuous state of rebellion from 1904 through 1911, which absorbed significant numbers of Ottoman army soldiers, as well as consumed large amounts of scarce resources. The Ottoman Seventh Army, headquartered in San-ā, was disestablished in January 1911 under Ahmet İzzet's reorganization of the Ottoman Army.[34] In its place the new independent XIV Army Corps was activated to provide operational command and control for the army's tactical units in Yemen. The XIV Army Corps was assigned three infantry divisions, the 39th, the 40th, and the 41st, which all had three of the new triangular infantry regiments as well as a nonregimental rifle battalion, for a total of 30 infantry battalions. An additional 13 regular army infantry battalions were deployed to Yemen to reinforce the XIV Army Corps, for an overall total of 43 infantry battalions.[35] When supporting arms such as artillery, engineers and cavalry, and combat support units such as baggage and ammunition trains are added to the Ottoman force committed to counterinsurgency operations in Yemen annually from 1909 to 1912, they numbered well in excess of the Feyzi's 1905 total of 110,000 men.

THE ALBANIAN REVOLT, 1908–12

It should not come as a surprise that secret revolutionary societies and committees were formed in the Ottoman provinces, which now compose modern Albania. The Ottomans responded in kind by oppressive activities that included the closing of Albanian-language schools, prohibition of Albanian nationalist publications, and repression of freedom of assembly and free speech. As the Albanian population was mostly Muslim, opposition to the government centered on taxes, conscription, and home rule.[36] The revolt began on July 3, 1908, when two young army officers simultaneously struck government targets and then retreated into the safety of the mountains. They were Captain Resneli Ahmed Niyazi Bey, an ethnic Albanian, and Staff Major İsmail Enver Bey, a CUP member who later rose to become the Ottoman minister of war during World War I.[37] Both were active Ottoman army officers, but while Resneli was a nationalist, Enver was an ardent CUP modernizer. Niyazi focused on "mobilizing the Albanian community for the revolutionary cause" while Enver was trying to drive cracks in the Hamidian regime.[38] The advent of the Constitutional Period in 1908 obviated Enver's insurgency, while Niyazi was acclaimed as an Albanian hero and neither went to prison as the new government took over.

In the democratic flush of the Constitutional period, Albanian notables and committeemen expected the new parliamentary government to accommodate political change leading to some kind of autonomy and political consolidation of the ethnic Albanian population living in the Ottoman Balkan provinces. When this did not happen, demonstrations involving around 2,500–6,000 men began to erupt in the Albanian sanjacks.[39] By the end of 1909, heavily armed Albanians began to appear in plain sight, greatly worrying the Ottoman governor, Brigadier Hasan Bedri Pasha, who had only seven infantry battalions for internal and border security tasks.[40] Active revolt soon flared up in Kosova, which was immediately crushed by the elite Ottoman 5th Rifle Battalion. Insurrections by ethnic Greeks in the Ottoman Epirus compounded the problem adding spatial and ethnic complexity.[41]

The isolated insurrections grew into a cohesive and coordinated whole in the spring of 1910, as Albanian leaders raised large bodies of men. The most immediate threat appeared in northern Albania and Kosovo where Idris Sefer led 5,000 men in cutting railway lines and communications, while Isa Boletin led another 2,000 in attacks in Firzovik and Prizre.[42] The new Ottoman military commander Şevket Turgut reacted with alacrity and violence by dispatching 15,000 Ottoman soldiers to raze houses, burn villages, conduct public floggings and summary executions.[43] The Ottomans were able to restore communications to the provincial capital of Işkodra, and even though they committed 50,000 men to the campaign, they lacked the manpower to follow the rebels into the mountains and destroy them.[44]

The rebellion continued into 1911, as Catholic tribesmen returned home to join the fight from exile in neighboring Montenegro. The Ottomans searched for a nonmilitary solution and decided to negotiate with the rebels. Although the sultan himself journeyed to Pristina to offer amnesty, large numbers of men remained defiant in rebellion. An odd bit of diplomacy broke out when King Nikola, the Montenegrin monarch, encouraged tribesmen to raid into Ottoman territory and had to be restrained by the Great Powers. The men in the mountains turned to guerrilla warfare and armed *çete*s ranging in strength from 200 to 600 rebels began marauding into the smaller towns. One clash in the Avalonya region involved a *çete* of over 800 guerrillas.[45] The guerrillas were supported by "virtually all segments of Albanian society" including "doctors, landowners, lawyers, soldiers, and peasants."[46] The Ottomans were neither able to quell the rebellion nor able to negotiate a solution and the rebellion froze into stasis.

The final and major general insurrection, which had been planned outside of the Albanian provinces, broke out in May and ended in August 1912. The proximate cause that led to this was the victory of the CUP in the parliamentary elections of April 1912, an event that sounded the death knell for the political aspirations of minorities such as the Albanians, the Armenians, the Macedonians, and other groups seeking political inclusion and reasonable representation. Moreover, the previously heavy-handed Ottoman counterinsurgency practices, which had included the burning of villages and the physical punishment of the Albanian population, served to enrage the populace and paved the way for antigovernment support.[47] Huge numbers of Albanian men were mobilized in the insurgency, some 25,000 around Pristina, and another 20,000 in southwest Kosovo.[48] Making things worse, the local regular army units, which were composed mainly of locally conscripted Albanian men, began to suffer mass desertions and mutiny. Now heavily engaged in Yemen and Libya, the Ottoman Empire was no longer able to contest control of the region, as the Albanian insurrection had metastasized into a "national uprising."[49]

The new grand vizier, Gazi Ahmet Muhtar Pasha, then began to move his government toward an actual negotiated settlement and, at the beginning of August, General Ibrahim Pasha began direct negotiations with the Albanians. A settlement granting the Albanians almost all of their demands, short of complete autonomy, was sent to Constantinople. The demands included bringing the two previous Ottoman cabinets to stand trial. On August 14, 14,000 Albanian rebels occupied the provincial capital of Üsküp. With the exception of the two trials, the government accepted 12 demands (there were 14 in all).[50] Finally, on August 18, 1912, the Albanians accepted the Ottoman government's offer and the revolt ended. Within two months, however, the attacks of the Christian Balkan League drove the Muslim Albanians temporarily back into the arms of the Ottomans, but at the end of the Balkan Wars the great powers established Albania as an independent country.

The Albanian insurrection was unique in that it was successful. In the sources available at the present time, it is unclear why this was so. A case can be, however, that the Ottoman army was badly overstretched between 1910 and 1912, with the massive reorganization efforts that overlapped the ongoing rebellions in Yemen and the Italo-Ottoman War. It may also be a factor that the inhabitants of Albania were overwhelmingly Muslim, and many families had been tightly integrated into the army and into the government for generations. This might have weakened those institutions by making them more sympathetic to, and willing to negotiate with, the Albanians. But, it is also true that these areas were located on the Ottoman periphery and none were particularly important geopolitically to the survival of the empire itself. That said, Albania's location inside the Ottoman sphere of its European possessions would seem to have attracted more substantial and serious efforts than the Ottomans employed there. Moreover, it is hard to reconcile the fact that they sent massive forces to distant Yemen, itself more of a strategic liability than anywhere in the Balkans, while allowing Albania to drift into autonomy. In truth though, what made the Albanian insurrection so different, and perhaps unwinnable, was the fact that it transitioned so rapidly into a generalized popular revolt involving most of the Albanian population. In this regard then, it was strikingly different from the internecine tribal struggles that afflicted Yemeni insurgents or the intercommittee squabbles that proved so divisive to the Macedonian and the Armenian committees.

THE ITALIAN-OTTOMAN WAR

The Italians divide this little-known war between Italy and the Ottoman Empire into three phases, the first occupation (October 1911), the establishment of bases (November 1911 through March 1912), and the intensification of the war in Libya and the Aegean (April through October 18, 1912).[51] The presence of a powerful and modern Italian fleet guaranteed the isolation of the Ottoman province and made the Ottoman campaign unwinnable from the start. Moreover, from the Ottoman perspective the war was a distraction from its primary efforts of organizational transformation and its operational counterinsurgencies in Macedonia and Yemen.

The Ottoman province of Libya (Cyrenaica), the sanjack of Benghazi (Trablusgarp Vilayeti ve Bingazi Sancağı), and the province of Arabia (Hicaz Vilayeti) were the garrison homes of independent infantry divisions, which were not assigned to either armies or corps. Moreover these were some of the largest infantry divisions in the Ottoman force pool. In Libya, the garrison consisted of the 42nd Infantry Division, which was composed of the 124th, 125th, 126th, and 127th Infantry Regiments, the 38th Cavalry Regiment, the 42nd Rifle Battalion, two field artillery battalions, and the Libyan Fortress Artillery Battalion.[52]

The military commander Colonel Neşet Bey commanded the 42nd Division, which was very short on men with a nominal strength of approximately 12,000 men on paper under his command. However, because of the ongoing counterinsurgency in Yemen, the Ottoman General Staff stripped able-bodied and trained men from units in Libya to send to Yemen.[53] While this was a general problem for the entire Ottoman army, in 1911 it affected the 42nd Division (which was considered to be one of the worst divisions in the Ottoman army) more severely since it was already in such a poor state of readiness.[54] In actuality, Colonel Neşet only had about 5,000 infantrymen and 400 cavalrymen, who were inadequately equipped and poorly trained.[55] He had another 2,500 recently conscripted men, who were untrained but he could, in theory, mobilize an additional 20,000 reserves, which were organized into 30 infantry battalions and 60 cavalry squadrons.[56] About 3,000 of the trained men and 2,000 of the conscripts were concentrated in Tripoli with the remained located in the principal coastal cities of Benghazi, Derna, Tobruk, and Solum.

War broke out on September 29, 1911, when Italy declared war on the Ottoman Empire and began a naval blockade of the Ottoman province. After a naval bombardment, the Italians landed and occupied Tripoli on October 5, followed by a similar occupation of Tobruk five days later. Resistance was minimal as Ottoman opposition consisted merely of a few cannon shots from their coastal forts, while Colonel Neşet withdrew his mobile forces to the high ground south of the towns.[57] However, the Ottomans chose to offer determined resistance at Benghazi, where the Italians fought their way ashore on October 18, 1911. Fighting inside the town claimed the lives of a dozen Europeans and destroyed the British and Italian Consulates. The Ottomans finally evacuated the city on October 29 and withdrew to the high ground east of the town.

Surprisingly, the Ottoman's poor conventional capacity turned out to be an enormous advantage. Instead of trying to resist the initial Italian amphibious landing, which would have been futile, Ottoman units moved out of the range of the naval guns at the cost of leaving heavy equipment. The majority of the local recruits (around 2,000), most of whom were of urban origin, deserted their units.[58] The acting provincial commander, Colonel Neşet, had no other choice under these conditions than to initiate unconventional warfare against the Italian invaders. The Italian military was completely unprepared for this type of war. Small bands of Ottoman soldiers easily infiltrated into Italian defense perimeters and inflicted small but humiliating defeats. The local population was encouraged by these easy victories and began to actively support the Ottoman troops.

In turn, heavy-handed Italian tactics that targeted the civilian population more than the actual fighters were counterproductive and increased the hatred of the locals. Hundreds of volunteers and tribal warriors joined the Ottoman troops. But it was the support of the Sanusiyya religious order (or, more correctly, fraternity) that dramatically changed the flow of the war.[59] The Sanusiyya was not only a religious brotherhood, but also an economic and social alliance of the tribes. It was the only effective cement within the otherwise socially fragmented tribal society of Libya (especially the Cyrenaica region). Moreover, the Sanusis were well-known fighters and had already fought against another colonial power, France, at the southern extremes of the Sahara desert.

The Ottoman-Sanusiyya alliance achieved remarkable results in terms of a dramatic increase in manpower and logistical support for the fight. But it was the arrival of Ottoman officer-volunteers that tipped the balance. The apparent failure of the government to respond to Italian aggression created a moral crisis and outburst of patriotic and religious feelings in which many young Ottoman officers volunteered to fight. The Ottoman General Staff and CUP military committee, without the authorization and support of the government, selected its best and brightest, including the hero of the Meşrutiyet revolution Enver Bey, future president of the Turkish Republic Mustafa Kemal (Atatürk) Bey, counterinsurgency mastermind Süleyman Askeri Bey, and Halil (Kut) Bey.[60] Most of them were veterans of the Balkan counterinsurgency campaigns. In addition to these men, Libyan and other officers from predominantly Arab provinces, including ardent Arab nationalist Aziz al Masri, Muhittin (Kurtiş) Bey, and Ali Sami (Sabit Bey), were also assigned.[61]

The first group of officers arrived in the conflict zone via Egypt and Tunis in the middle of October 1911, but groups and individuals continued to arrive through the summer of 1912. Their arrival immediately changed the character and tempo of the war. The theater of war was divided into four theaters of operations in which Tripoli and Benghazi were the main ones. Regular soldiers, gendarmeries, volunteers, and tribal warriors were organized into flexible, mission-oriented units under the command and control of regular officers. All operations were closely coordinated and integrated according to an ad hoc strategic plan, which simply sought to wage a campaign of long and attritional unconventional warfare.[62] As veterans of counterinsurgency campaigns themselves, the Ottoman officers were well aware that such a war would be long and bloody and, in the end, moral factors would become paramount. They were hoping to frustrate the Italians by inflicting as many casualties as possible.

In opposition to the geographic orientation of the Italians, the Ottomans were not targeting the recapture of coastal cities but choosing instead to annihilate the enemy.[63] The asymmetric nature of the conflict frustrated the Italian command and staff planners. Even though they tried several novel methods successfully, such as the use of aviation for reconnaissance and artillery forward observation, for the first time,[64] they still stubbornly stuck to conventional tactics and techniques, even if the results were disastrous and costly. The Italian infantry assault columns offered excellent targets for the elusive Ottoman combat groups and bands. They would lure Italians deep into desert valleys and, after exhausting and disorganizing them with repeated hit-and-run skirmishes and small ambushes, the main group would suddenly attack and destroy the isolated groups (sometimes whole assault columns). Even the heavily fortified coastal towns were not safe and immune from the Ottoman guerrillas. Night raids, infiltration into defensive perimeters, and the hunting of isolated guards and patrols became a continuous activity.[65]

The Italian setbacks and blunders gave the Ottoman field commanders time to reorganize and train their mostly local troops.[66] The assignment of regular officers as the superior authority for tribal forces created immense problems initially. The tribal warriors had a traditional way of war fighting, which was always anarchic and uncoordinated and which prevented performing even the simplest maneuvers. The Ottoman officers managed to overcome this serious problem by treating combat operations more or less as step-by-step training exercises and by accommodating their military priorities with the interests of the tribesmen. Interestingly, the tribal cavalry learned to evade aerial observation and attacks while the local infantry units learned to successfully employ antiaircraft fire techniques.[67] The furious Italians, who were suffering casualties at an alarming rate and were unable to fix and destroy the elusive enemy, increasingly targeted the civilian population and its livelihood. The execution of real or imaginary supporters, collective punishments, and other elements of

a scorched-earth policy became part of the daily routine. For understandable reasons, these heavy-handed and misguided actions helped
the Ottomans greatly, not only increasing civilian support in terms of
volunteers and logistics, but also providing them with a sense of moral
and ethical superiority.[68]

After several bitter experiences, the Italian expeditionary forces
decided to remain within range of naval gunnery and, instead of trying
to expand their occupation deep into the hinterlands, they preferred
to remain on the coastline. At the same time, they tightened the naval
blockade and tried to close the Egyptian and Tunisian borders. Even
though this strategic shift created enormous logistics problems for the
Ottoman side, it also gave them a free hand to transform blockades of
the Italian-occupied zones into sieges. The confident Ottoman troops
and their local allies began to launch bolder and more concentrated
night attacks and raids.[69] They also tried to solve logistics problems by
using captured spoils of war. Specially organized detachments plun-
dered the Italian depots and magazines during the night raids.[70]

At last, the Italian political leadership came to the understanding
that their proud expeditionary force would not be able to defeat the
Ottoman defenders and conquer the interior of Libya. Instead the
leaders decided to move the war to the core regions of the empire
in order to force the Ottoman political leadership to give up Libya.
Understandably, they could not risk another land confrontation with
the Ottoman military, so they decided to use only their navy. In April
1912, the Italian navy tried various tactics, including naval demonstrations and limited shelling of the Red Sea and Syrian and Aegean
coastlines, blockading the straits, and even supporting the Sheikh Idris
rebellion in Asir on the Arabian Peninsula.[71] Out of frustration, the
Italians occupied the weakly defended Dodecanese Islands between
April 24 and May 20, 1912. Understanding the occupation of the
main island of Rhodes is instrumental in explaining the aftereffects of
Ottoman success and the Italians' exaggerated sense of caution. On
Rhodes, the Italians employed an entire reinforced division against the
tiny Ottoman defensive force, consisting of a single infantry battalion
with four light artillery pieces, despite the fact that the Italians enjoyed
the popular support of the predominantly Greek population.[72]

The cost of the Libyan expeditionary forces to Italy was substantial and forced immediate military mobilization, which began before
hostilities on September 25, 1911. Many in the Italian government
had believed that Libya might be taken on the cheap with as few
as 15,000–20,000 men.[73] However, the initial two-division Italian
expeditionary force was composed of 34,000 men, 6,300 horses and

mules, and 76 artillery pieces.[74] Italy committed a second wave of two infantry divisions in October bringing Italian strength in Libya to 55,000 men, 8,300 animals, and 126 artillery pieces.[75] Defying the predictions of easy victory, relentless Ottoman attacks forced Italy to increase its troop strength again and again and by September 1912, Italy had 110,000 men in Africa.[76] Because it was impossible to sustain their army in Libya from the surrounding hinterlands the Italians were forced to supply food, fodder, ammunition, and all manner of supplies from Italy. The transport costs of supplying the expedition as well as the costs of maintaining the blockade and bombarding Ottoman ports in four seas, in turn, drained the Italian navy. One author asserted that Italy maintained its entire navy in constant operations for the course of the war (a total of 39 battleships and cruisers, 74 torpedo boat destroyers of all types, 30 auxiliary ships, and 92 transports and other vessels).[77] In contrast, the cost to the Ottoman Empire was minimal as it was able to fight the war largely with its forces in place, thus avoiding actual military mobilization.

The Ottoman administration reluctantly came to terms with Italy due to the imminent threat coming from the Balkan states. Anticipating an attack by the Balkan League, the Ottoman army began full-scale mobilization on September 30, 1912, and activated its Balkan provinces war plan two days later.[78] This effectively ended the Ottoman ability to continue the war with Italy. The Ouchy Peace Treaty, which was signed on October 15, 1912, ended Ottoman sovereignty in Libya. The field commanders received the order three days later. This was a serious blow to the Ottoman officers who were more than sure of their ability to win the war, and they encountered huge difficulties explaining why the empire had given up after so many successful engagements by their local soldiers and allies. However, the military members of the CUP decided to establish a sound base for keeping the insurgency alive in hopes of restarting the war after the end of Balkan crisis. Some officers and other ranks (overall 300 personnel) were selected to remain, and nearly all the heavy weapons and ammunition were left behind. Selected local NCOs and soldiers were passed through an intense military technical training in order to operate the heavy weapons and various devices during the three-month-long evacuation period. As a part of this scheme, more than 100 young Libyan students were transferred to military schools in Istanbul for the training of the next generation of leaders and officers who would lead the next war. Unfortunately for the empire, this bold scheme fell victim to the Balkan defeats and was only partially realized during World War I.[79]

The Hamidiye Tribal Light Cavalry

Because of more urgent reforms needed to transform the obsolete Ottoman army, Chief of Staff Ahmet İzzet Pasha did not begin reforming the Hamidiye tribal cavalry until 1909. Ahmet İzzet was committed to modernization and the undisciplined irregular Hamidiye simply did not fit into the disciplined and professional models presented by contemporary European powers—even the czar was reducing the size of his Cossack forces. The advent of the Constitutional Period enabled the reform of the Hamidiye by bringing both a reduction in antigovernment activity from the Armenian revolutionary committees, as well as encouraging positive hopes for genuine rapprochement between the government and the Armenians. Ahmet İzzet began by dissolving twelve of the Hamidiye regiments on December 6, 1908.[80] The remaining Hamidiye were organized into seven brigades and three independent regiments with a total of strength of sixty-one tribal cavalry regiments altogether. The brigades contained from six to nine cavalry regiments and were centered on tribal areas.[81]

A symbolic and significant change then followed in 1909, when the government dropped the title "Hamidiye" and adopted a new title—the Tribal Light Cavalry (*Aşiret Hafif Süvari*).[82] Janet Klein argued that this was an unmistakable sign that the new regime was firmly in control and "the change was to communicate firmly and clearly to those tribes who formed the regiments that their former patron was no longer there to oversee and protect them."[83]

An inspection tour in February 1910 by Lieutenant Colonel Mahmud Bey revealed glaring deficiencies in the regiments including the fact that many existed only as paper cadres wherein their tribal chief reported nonexistent men while collecting full pay and allowances.[84] The authorities of the 1910 transformation of the army introduced significant internal changes to the Tribal Light Cavalry as specific new regulations for the tribal regiments were established on August 17.[85] Regular army officers were assigned as tribal cavalry regimental commanders and squadron commanders and while the tribal chiefs retained their rankings, they were demoted to second-in-command status. The regulars were assigned for a period of four years. The new regulations also established a "Tribal Cavalry Inspectorate" of seven officers of the regular army led by a regular army major-general. These changes were accompanied by training instructions in 1911 that laid down methods of training the regiments for more conventional cavalry missions that included screening and reconnaissance.[86] The new regulations also fixed current regimental strength at 64 regiments but allowed for reductions.[87]

These internal administrative changes were accompanied by a complete realignment of the tribal cavalry organizational structure. Four new Tribal Light Cavalry Divisions were authorized, each of which contained from five to eight light cavalry regiments (for a total of twenty-four regiments).[88] This architecture replaced the existing seven brigades and allowed for a gradual drawdown of the number of regiments to a total of around 30.[89] Moreover the September 1910 reorganization of the army further altered the organization of the four new Tribal Light Cavalry Divisions by integrating regular cavalry regiments with tribal light cavalry regiments.[90] By 1911, the 1st Tribal Light Cavalry Division was composed of six tribal light cavalry regiments and the regular 39th Cavalry Regiment, the 2nd Tribal Light Cavalry Division, was composed of eight tribal light cavalry regiments and the regular 34th Cavalry Regiment, the 3rd Tribal Light Cavalry Division, was composed of five tribal light cavalry regiments and the regular 24th Cavalry Regiment, and the 4th Tribal Light Cavalry Division was composed of five tribal light cavalry regiments and the regular 20th Cavalry Regiment.[91] These new divisions came directly under the operational control of the Ottoman Third Army.

The remaining regiments that were not assigned to the divisions were grouped together into "Tribal District Inspectorates" and to each one, a regular army cavalry squadron was to be assigned from the Third Army.[92] The new inspectorates came under the administrative control of the Third Army Inspector of Cavalry. At the same time tribal light cavalry reserve units (*redif*) were established, which mirrored the reserve structure of the Ottoman army. Over the next several years many of the district-level tribal light cavalry regiments were disestablished until the overall number of tribal cavalry regiments was just 30.

The Constitutional period saw a complete restructuring of the Hamidiye tribal cavalry from an irregular Cossack-like force, which was largely uncontrollable, to one that was more tightly managed and commanded by regular officers. This was done by changing the nature of the force itself through the assignment of regular army officers as regimental and squadron commanders. Importantly, at no level were tribal light cavalry units unassociated with regular army cavalry units and the integration of irregular tribal units with regular units insured that the tribal light cavalry now had professional units on which to model their tactics and behavior. Each of the new divisions had a regular cavalry regiment assigned and each of the newly organized tribal districts had a regular squadron assigned as well. Moreover, at higher levels the new divisional organizational architecture transferred command and control of the tribal light cavalry regiments to the staff and headquarters of the Third Army.

Taken together these measures ended the Ottoman experiment with irregular tribal cavalry forces. While these regiments still existed in the Ottoman force structure, during the Constitutional Period the Ottoman military clearly forced them into a conventional and disciplined mold while, at the same time, drew their strength down by half. This was possible only because the Ottoman army's transformation coincided with a lull in Armenian violence that created enough time for the Ottomans to consider and implement change in their irregular forces.

Conclusion

Summarizing the counterinsurgency campaigns in Yemen and Albania it is fair to say that they failed spectacularly to suppress the rebellions in those provinces. The Ottoman effort in Yemen was extensive and lasted for over seven years and the Ottomans fought it to win. However, in the end the Ottomans recognized that due to the terrain, modern weaponry in the hands of the rebels, and the intractability of the enemy the war was militarily unwinnable. Their efforts in Albania were much smaller and the Ottoman never committed decisive forces to that conflict. In both cases, the war evolved into a struggle where the rebellion matured into a generalized insurgency supported by the majority of the population. This marked a significant shift away from traditional insurgencies in the empire, which were tribal or leader centric and which rarely involved entire populations. In opposition, the committee-led insurgencies in Macedonia and Anatolia failed to engage and involve the majority of the populations. When confronted with the changing nature of insurgency in Yemen and Albania, the Ottomans found that their traditional counterinsurgency practices failed to achieve the expected results.

The war in Libya produced a number of young professional officers who would move up into positions of importance during the Armenian insurgency of 1915. These included Enver, Halil, and Süleyman Askeri. Their experiences in an unconventional setting as guerrilla fighters gave them an understanding of the effectiveness of such methods against fixed garrisons and fixed lines of communications. Their strategy of relentlessly attacking isolated Italian garrisons and drawing conventional Italian forces into tactically unfavorable conditions in the interior followed time-honored guerrilla practices and proved very successful.

This page intentionally left blank

CHAPTER 4

A Template for Destruction

When is a war not a war?
When it is carried on by methods of barbarism...

—*Henry Campbell-Bannerman London,*
June 14, 1901[1]

INTRODUCTION

At the dawn of the twentieth century counterinsurgency policies based on the removal and relocation of civilian populations emerged as viable and acceptable practices in warfare. Three wars, in particular, set important precedents for the Western world in the way in which militaries dealt with guerrillas and irregular insurgents. These wars involved Spain in Cuba, the United States in the Philippines, and Britain in South Africa, and all three saw the evolution of similar strategic, operational, and tactical practices by the Western powers. At the strategic level, the powers sought the destruction of guerrilla and irregular military forces in order to end insurgencies and, in the case of the Boers, end a conventional war that had entered a guerrilla warfare phase. Operationally, the powers employed campaign designs that focused on separating the guerrillas from their principal sources of support, which were the friendly civilian populations, thereby enabling the military defeat of the weakened guerrilla armies. At lower tactical levels, military commanders isolated the guerrillas by establishing fortified lines that cut their operational areas into manageable sectors and then removed the civilian populations. Simultaneously, they swept the sectors clean of enemy forces by driving the guerrillas to destruction unto fixed barriers. To varying degrees these campaigns were successful with the British in South Africa, setting the standard for the complete and brutal subjugation of the Boer republics.

There were political consequences and liabilities resulting from the issues involving international practices of war-making and involving the morality of waging war so completely on innocent civilians. In all three countries there were commissions and investigations into the nature and conduct of operations and there was public outcry against the harsh treatment of civilians. In some cases, individual military commanders were put on trial for blatantly illegal and reprehensible acts. Unfortunately, however, these wars did not result in international conventions or prohibitions against such policies and practices.

While there was little that proscribed direct military operations against civilians there was little that prescribed it either. The Western armies of the early twentieth century employed field service regulations that provided commanders with instructions regarding tactics, administration, logistics, and operations. These publications were almost exclusively technical in nature. Higher level doctrines at the strategic and operational level were largely absent as official publications and understandings of these subjects evolved by reading such classical military thinkers as Clausewitz and Jomini. Unfortunately, in these kinds of works there was almost nothing on guerrilla warfare or insurgency and it may be argued that counterinsurgency policies and practices in the early twentieth century were a matter of practice rather than of theory. Indeed, the major theorists of the field, T. E. Lawrence and Mao Zedong, for example, were post–World War I authors. During the period examined in this chapter there were a number of books written about guerrilla and irregular warfare. The most well-known of these on the subject was Colonel Charles E. Callwell's *Small Wars, Their Principles and Practice*, which was first published in 1896 and which was regarded "in its day...as a minor classic of military writing."[2] Callwell's third edition appeared in 1906 and contained insights gathered directly from Britain's experiences in the Boer War.[3] Drawing on French Marshal Thomas-Robert Bugeaud's Algerian campaigns of the 1840s as well as recent British experience in South Africa, Callwell articulated the conventional wisdom of his day regarding counterinsurgency. He noted that an effective campaign against well-led guerrillas was "well-neigh impossible."[4] Callwell maintained that success depended on good intelligence and the employment of highly mobile flying columns to give the enemy no rest. This was set in a context of denying the guerrillas the support of the population, subdividing the theater of war into sectors, constructing block house lines, and employing a "happy combination of mobile columns and of defensive posts" to drive the guerrillas to destruction.[5] Although, Callwell did not mention population removal directly, he did highlight the necessity of "rendering it impossible for an enemy to exist in the country at all owing to no food or shelter being left" and he advocated the destruction of property, such as crops, homes, and livestock.[6] In Callwell's defense, he did note that such tactics are often counterproductive when the population remained in place.

It seems clear that about the time of the Russo-Japanese War (1904–1905) there existed a fair amount of uniformity in the application of counterinsurgency and counterguerrilla policies among the militaries of the Great Powers. These policies were punitive and involved the relocation of populations and the wholesale destruction of private property. The most successful example of the implementation of such policies was that of the British in South Africa, which was singularly notable for the totality of the application of the practices of population removal and sweeping sectors clean of guerrillas. While repugnant, the British war against the Boers proved beyond the shadow of a doubt that such policies, when vigorously and thoroughly employed, might transform Callwell's "well-nigh impossible" situation into a victory.

Spain: *La Reconcentración* in Cuba

The modern basis for what matured into policies of relocation and concentration began on the Spanish-held island of Cuba in the 1890s against Cuban *insurrectos*. On July 15, 1895, revolutionary nationalists proclaimed the formation of a Cuban republic. Scornfully called a "government in the woods," the insurgents organized a Cuban Revolutionary Army that numbered from 25,000 to 40,000 men at any one time.[7] Máximo Gómez commanded the army, which was armed with rifles and machetes, and there was a formal organizational architecture of regiments, divisions, and corps within the army. However, the army rarely fought along conventional lines, but Gómez launched a highly successful campaign in the western part of island, lasting from October 22, 1895, to January 22, 1896, aimed at the destruction of the Spanish sugarcane economy.[8] On the eastern part of the island, General Calixto Gárcia commanded the eastern wing or Liberating Army (the western wing was known as the Invading Army) and performed similar operations. By early 1896, the insurgent army was worn down by operations and losses and began to operate as guerrillas using hit-and-run tactics against small Spanish posts and lines of communications.

In the summer of 1895, Spain sent a distinguished general, Arsenio Martínez de Campos, to Cuba with a mission to end the insurrection. General Martínez de Campos had ended a ten-year Cuban insurrection previously and revived a strategy that he had used successfully against insurgents. His strategy sought to contain the insurgents on the eastern end of the island through the use of "*trocha*." The *trocha* cut the island from north to south by establishing a line of forts and blockhouses positioned along a military road bordered by about one hundred meters of cleared land. Although Spain poured reinforcements into the island to support the effort and, in spite of the *trocha*, Gómez and Gárcia were able to move freely through the landscape. Martínez de Campos's defensive strategy was essentially passive and resulted mainly in the decline of morale of the Spanish soldiery, which lost men to raids and languished in isolated small forts.[9] The military failure and the loss of sugar revenue in turn led to the relief of General Martínez de Campos.

On February 10, 1896, the Spanish authorities assigned General Valeriano Weyler y Nicolau, a professional soldier from Majorica of German immigrant parentage, the mission of pacifying Cuba. Weyler was determined to end the insurrection as quickly as possible with the resources at hand and his brutal methods earned him the nickname "Butcher." Weyler was a soldier of great experience fighting irregulars and rebels, and had campaigned previously in Cuba, as well as in the Philippines and Spain itself. He arrived with definite ideas about how to deal with the insurgents and he resolved to put in place a system that would end multiple problems with "one stroke."[10] Weyler's operational concept, known as "*la reconcentración*" (reconcentration), quickly became infamous and was designed to accomplish specific tactical objectives. Weyler's program was intended to 1) deprive the insurgents with the means of subsistence, 2) deprive them of information, gathered from the peasants, regarding the movement of Spanish troops, 3) limit the spread of revolutionary propaganda to those already involved in the insurgency, 4) prevent more Cuban men from joining the insurgency, and 5) demoralize the insurgents, who would have relatives in the camps and thus be influenced by their hardship to end the rebellion.[11] Reconcentration was an ambitious program which hinged upon the complete removal of the indigenous population from designated areas to what Weyler called concentration camps. Weyler issued three proclamations on February 16, 1896, which outlined his plans.

Weyler's first proclamation ordered the inhabitants of two Cuban provinces, Puerto Principe and Santiago de Cuba, and the district of Sancti Spiritus, to leave their homes within eight days and "to concentrate" in the locations of Spanish division headquarters.[12] Two additional proclamations followed on the same day that placed the island under martial law[13] and identified specific acts committed in support of the insurgents as crimes of insurgency.[14] Among these new definitions of criminality were such acts as reviling the prestige of Spain, providing cattle and horses to the rebels, communicating news to the enemy, conspiring to adulterate or alter the price of provisions sold to the army, and tolerating those who dealt with the rebels. Of course, such direct actions as providing the enemy with arms, ammunition, and explosives and spying were also included.[15] There were also accompanying proclamations regarding amnesty and specific instructions on the establishment of the new concentration camps. Of note, Weyler's directives did not differentiate between people who might reasonably be thought to support the rebels or property that might reasonably be considered to be useful to them either. His directives were notable for their totality in cleansing entire provinces of their inhabitants.

Once his troops had emptied the provinces of people, Weyler used Martínez de Campos's *trocha* system of fortified roads as a base of operations from which to drive the insurgents into destruction. There were two *trocha*, which isolated the areas of the island affected by insurrection into manageable sectors. Three thousand of Weyler's men began in the west against a rebel leader named Maceo, where they attempted to drive the insurgents like hunted beasts upon the fortified *trocha* lines. Fighting between the Spanish and the insurgents continued sporadically throughout the summer. By October 1896, Weyler himself was personally leading over 6,000 soldiers (18 infantry battalions and 6 artillery batteries) against Maceo and 153 men.[16] In late November, Maceo was pinned against the *trocha* but managed to get around the end of it successfully, by boat. Unfortunately, the Cuban leader was only able to bring 17 men with him and in early December the Spanish caught up with his band and killed him. Despite his desire for rapid results, Weyler's strategy was sequential, required a large number of soldiers, and was time-consuming. By year's end, he had to deploy substantial numbers of regular troops to hunt down most of the insurgents but he was never entirely successful and the insurgency remained alive.

The insurgency continued from January 1897 through April 1898, when the United States declared war on Spain. By that date, Weyler had over 40,000 soldiers on the island, composed of 34 infantry battalions, 4 cavalry regiments, and associated artillery, conducting counterinsurgency operations.[17] Unfortunately for the Spanish, however, many of their units and soldiers were tied down in defensive garrisons (some of which were of battalion size) or in the block houses of the *trocha* lines. The insurgents, commanded by Máximo Gómez, numbered about 3,000 men and fought 41 engagements in the field with the Spanish in this period. The main body of insurgents operated in an area of about five hundred square miles within which they were able move about freely. Even in these field engagements the Spanish were often unsuccessful against the highly motivated Cubans. In effect, Weyler controlled the major cities and towns as well as the major lines of communications but his soldiers were unable to defeat decisively the highly mobile insurgent army. Moreover, Weyler's brutal methods were counterproductive in the complete pacification of the general Cuban population, which continued to support the insurrection with funds and supplies.

There were associated problems with Weyler's strategy revolving around the relocation decision that also created enemies for Spain. The new concentration camps were hugely inadequate to the task and lacked shelter, sanitary facilities, and clean water. There was little food and almost no medical care and the Cubans died in the thousands. While Weyler focused on the military defeat of the insurgents he paid scant attention to the conditions in the camps. In truth, the Spanish had few resources and little money to devote to the camp system and their indifference to the plight of the occupants exaggerated the effects of the reconcentration. It is difficult to establish today exactly how many Cubans were forcibly removed from their land and homes and relocated to the concentration camps. Contemporary American observers claimed that 400,000 noncombatants were relocated by December 1896, but others placed the number at 500,000–600,000 people.[18] Despite humanitarian outcries in the United States, Weyler proceeded with his plan and some contemporary authors claimed that over 400,000 people died (or about a quarter of the population). However, testimony before the US Congress in 1898 placed the number of dead at 200,000[19] and a modern historian puts the true number at somewhere around 100,000 dead.[20] It is more than obvious that the initial claims were vastly exaggerated.

Much of the information about reconcentration flowed into the United States through the Department of State via the reports of American consuls and agents in Cuba. The reports were highly inflammatory and created a great deal of ill-will toward Spain. An example of such a report came from US commercial agent Barker, in which Barker said a young Spanish officer had told him that he had been ordered to "go ahead, execute every person you believe to be in sympathy with the Cubans, but make no report of your actions— the idea is to exterminate and conceal your method of doing so."[21] As a result of the gathering groundswell of American public opinion against "Butcher" Weyler, as the press named him, the US Congress conducted a number of hearings to examine and determine what was happening in Cuba. These hearing then generated a number of resolutions condemning the Spanish military campaign and urging Spain to grant independence to Cuba.[22] Ultimately, American public opinion against Weyler would act as an accelerant in the American decision to go to war with Spain in 1898.

Weyler clearly failed to end the insurgency in one stroke and the insurrection went on for over two more years ending only with Spain's defeat in the Spanish-American War. An assessment of the effectiveness of Weyler's operational design might question whether he had enough troops and resources to accomplish the task at hand. After manning the *trocha* he had few soldiers left with which to conduct active mobile field operations on the fever-ridden island. Given more time Weyler might have eliminated the insurgents; however, this was problematic in view of Spain's reluctance or inability to provide him with more forces. Unfortunately, in the end, Weyler's legacy was the creation of an operational design for the destruction of an insurgency.

The United States: The Philippine Insurrection

The American experience in the Philippines Islands began in late April 1898, when Commodore George Dewey's fleet smashed the Spanish Fleet at Manila Bay. This, in turn, caused President William McKinley to send ground troops there to take control of the archipelago. As in Cuba, the Spanish were then wrestling with a full-blown rebellion in the islands, and Commodore Dewey had actually assisted a Tagalog rebel leader named Emilio Aguinaldo by bringing him back from exile in Hong Kong to the Philippines.[23] The United States formally gained sovereignty over the entire archipelago on December 10, 1898, with the signing of the Treaty of Paris. President McKinley then moved rapidly to establish an administrative apparatus that effectively made the Philippines an American colony. Unfortunately, the United States lacked a colonial office or a ministry of the marine that was prepared to take on the mission of "benevolent assimilation" as McKinley called the process of annexation and, thus, the job of governing the Philippines fell to the US Army.[24]

The first US Army commander in the islands was Major General Wesley Merritt, who conquered Manila from the Spanish. His tenure was short lived and he was replaced in late August 1898 by Major General Elwell S. Otis, a Civil War veteran, who was known for his rigidity and poor judgment. As it became clear that the United States did not intend to liberate the Philippines, nationalist leaders such as Aguinaldo turned against the Americans and by February 1899, the US Army was at war with Filipino insurgents. Otis struck hard against them and was initially successful because Aguinaldo attempted to fight a conventional war with the Americans. Unable to fill its new overseas commitments with the tiny 65,000-man US Army, Congress authorized a 35,000-man volunteer force, which was enlisted for two years exclusively for service in the Philippines.[25] This force was very well trained and led, and began to arrive in the Philippines in November 1899. By January 1900, Otis had 63,000 men in 17 regular and 24 volunteer infantry regiments, as well as 3 cavalry regiments with which to pacify the islands. The strength of the American force caused Aguinaldo and other Philippine leaders to abandon conventional tactics and shift to guerilla warfare instead. Otis commanded the Division of the Philippines and also served as military governor. He divided the islands into four departments, Northern Luzon, Southern Luzon, the Visayas, and Mindanao and Jolo. To his credit, while simultaneously fighting the insurgents, Otis organized local government and established a fair judicial code.

From November 1899 through April 1900, the US Army fought 671 engagements and lost 196 men while 634 were wounded.[26] Many of the battles were fiercely fought and the American 1st Division commander Major General Henry W. Lawton was killed at San Mateo in December. The army claimed to have killed 3,200 and wounded 700 insurgents in the same period, while capturing 2,900 more.[27] Otis felt successful enough to request relief from his assignment and he was relieved in May 1900 by the 2nd Division commander, Major General Arthur MacArthur.

It was under MacArthur's leadership that American counterinsurgency policies in the Philippines began to gain notoriety because of his harsh methods. This began as MacArthur's continuation of Otis's policies failed to produce rapid and decisive results, which, in turn, pushed the secretary of war to pressure MacArthur. On December 20, 1900, MacArthur issued a proclamation that placed the Philippines under martial law.[28] The legal basis for the declaration of martial law lay in General Orders 100, issued by the US War Department on April 24, 1863 (also known as the Lieber Code).[29] The Lieber Code laid out specific criteria for the identification of combatants and defined allowable behavior when the army was fighting rebels and partisans. The code was a product of the American Civil War and was designed around the idea of fighting and governing occupied territory. It was quite harsh and, under certain circumstances, permitted the starvation of civilians, retaliation, summary execution, and the use of no quarter.[30]

MacArthur's declaration was nowhere nearly as specific as General Orders 100, but it defined what constituted a rebellious act and outlined the penalties for transgressions. While harsh, it is sometimes forgotten that the proclamation also extended protection to those Filipinos who chose to support the rule of law. According to historian Brian Linn, "MacArthur believed that his proclamation marked the beginnings of 'an entirely new campaign...based on the central idea of detaching towns from the immediate support of guerrillas in the field, and thus also precluding the indirect support which arose from indiscriminate acceptance by the towns of the insurrection in all its devious ramifications.'"[31] Concurrently, American troop strength rose to a peak of 70,000 men and MacArthur proceeded to put the insurgents under relentless pressure with a combination of tactics. American troops were teamed up with locally recruited military units known as Native Scouts and provinces were swept of guerillas. In some locations, the population was concentrated into camps and a system of US Army provost courts was established. Many villages came over to the Americans, especially when the locals were allowed to harvest the crops of their neighbors who had been identified as insurgents. Aguinaldo himself was captured in March 1901 and other top leaders surrendered in some numbers. By late spring, MacArthur judged that many provinces were, in fact, pacified. His tour ended shortly thereafter and MacArthur was replaced on July 4, 1901, by Major General Adna R. Chafee.

At the same time that Chafee took command, William H. Taft arrived as the new civil governor, a move that enabled Chafee to refocus the army on primarily military tasks. This division of effort was the result of MacArthur's successes, which, in combination with increasing uneasiness about the harshness of military occupation, led some in Washington to think that the Philippines was ready for civilian-led rule. Operationally, the reorganization allowed Chafee to "replace civil-military organizations with purely military ones, and thus divorce the army from civil administration."[32] Acting as an accelerant to his action was a combined attack by guerrillas and townspeople on an isolated American garrison at Balangiga, Samar, on September 28, 1901. On that day, insurgents attacked 74 American soldiers of the Company C, 9th US Infantry Regiment early in the morning in what has been termed a massacre. In hand-to-hand fighting with knives and clubs, 48 Americans were killed, including all of the company's officers. Only 4 soldiers remained unwounded and the attack shocked the American public. The massacre spurred Chafee to action and he immediately authorized local retaliation. Following this he dissolved the old geographical departments and, in October, formed two divisions and seven separate brigades. These army units were assigned sectors and given missions to eradicate the remaining resistance through military means. Meanwhile, US troop strength in the islands had steadily dropped to 48,000 men in July and to 37,349 on December 1.[33] In terms of maximizing his declining strength, Chafee's concept of untying his army from geography did much to restore the mobility of his few remaining troops.

Unfortunately, Chafee's reassignment of command responsibilities led to what many contemporary observers and later historians have terms as atrocities. Of his subordinates, two officers were particularly linked to practices that today would be considered as war crimes. They were Brigadier General J. Franklin Bell, who commanded the 3rd Separate Brigade on southern Luzon, and Brigadier General Jacob H. Smith, who commanded the 6th Separate Brigade on Samar. Both officers took up their commands in November 1901.

Bell's campaign on Luzon was methodical and was based on forcing the insurgents to want to make peace, which meant imposing drastic measures on the general population. While Bell focused on making life impossible for the insurgents and their supporters, in fairness, he also focused on fair and considerate treatment for those Filipinos who abided by the rule of law. Bell began his program on December 8 by ordering his commanders to establish "zones of protection" within the physical limits of towns into which all Filipinos had to move no later than Christmas.[34] His men then collected up all the foodstuffs in the area from December 26 to 31. Once this was accomplished, Bell's brigade began to sweep through the operational area hunting the insurgents. In essence the American strategy on Luzon rested on a basis of the reconcentration of the population in order to deny support to the rebels and his overall aim was to separate the guerrillas from the people.[35] Bell's measures were extreme—houses were burned, Filipino prisoners were executed in retaliation for the killing of American soldiers, and sometimes men found outside the zones of protection were shot at sight.[36] Nevertheless, these ruthless tactics and the relentless pursuit led directly to the surrender of the primary insurgent leader, Miguel Malvar, and his men on April 6, 1902.

Meanwhile on Samar, Brigadier General Jacob Smith instituted an even more brutal counterinsurgency regime than Bell had established on Luzon, earning him the nickname "Howling Jake" Smith. As on Luzon, Smith quickly reconcentrated the people and began to hunt down the insurgents; however the brutality of the Balangiga massacre apparently served to enrage Smith (many of the dead Americans had been mutilated beyond recognition).[37] Smith's nickname derived from his instruction to US Marine Corps major Littleton Waller to make Samar "a howling wilderness." Waller's orders, moreover, contained specific instructions to take no prisoners and burn and kill everything in sight.[38] Smith's tactics were brutally effective and he successfully pacified the island within six months. Both Smith and Waller were later tried by courts-martial for these activities, although Waller was acquitted on a technicality. On July, 4 1902, President Teddy Roosevelt declared the insurgency to be over but, in truth, the insurgency continued for years afterward. About 4,200 American soldiers of the 126,500 men who served in the islands during the insurrection died, while 16,000–20,000 insurgents died as well as about 34,000 Filipino civilians, who died as a direct result of the war.[39] Another 200,000 Filipino civilians died in the cholera epidemics that accompanied reconcentration and deprivation.[40]

The United States' suppression of the Philippine insurrection left a bitter taste in many American's mouths. Its brutality served as grist for the propaganda mills of the anti-Imperialists in the United States and American abuses were the subject of a number of congressional commissions and inquiries. Interestingly for modern Americans in the post-9/11 world, the issues of torture and a coercive practice called the "water cure," which were used to extract information from prisoners were subjects of interest to the congressional committees.[41] Independence for the islands would not come until 1946 and, ironically, at the hands of Arthur MacArthur's son, General Douglas MacArthur.

America's suppression of the Philippine Insurrection lasted about four years and, in the near term, might be classified as generally successful. The American operational design shared many features with that used by Weyler in Cuba, however, the employment of *trocha* was unnecessary in the Philippines because the islands themselves were compact enough to be treated as single subsectors. To suppress the insurrection, the United States initially deployed a substantially larger force that was well equipped and well trained. But, as American troop strength in the islands dropped, the Americans turned increasingly to harsher methods that exceeded the brutality seen in Cuba under Weyler.

BRITAIN: THE BOER WAR

Britain's defeat of the Boer republics in the Anglo-Boer War was decisive and had well-known immediate and profound effects on the

British army and on contemporary military thought. In Britain, these included the modernization of the reserve system, the establishment of a general staff, and revisions to army tactical doctrines. Relative to this study was the development of a comprehensive counterinsurgency policy by the British that led to the successful conclusion of the war. The policy was based on the full and successful implementation of a counterinsurgency strategy similar to Weyler's ideas of reconcentration in Cuba for the purpose of separating guerrillas from the population. It is important to note here that Britain's war in South Africa was not, in the technical sense, a war of counterinsurgency. It began as a conventional war that devolved into a guerrilla war fought mainly by Boer irregulars and Britain's war, after the summer of 1900, evolved into a campaign against mounted and highly mobile guerrillas. Nevertheless, the strategy and tactics used against the Boers mirrored contemporary Spanish and American operations and British operations in South Africa became a model for later counterinsurgency campaigns.

The fighting in South Africa began when the Boers invaded Natal on October 12, 1899, and Cape Colony several weeks later. The widely scattered British forces were quickly penned up inside towns while the British marshaled their field forces. Obsolete British tactics led to disastrous conventional defeats during what came to be known as Black Week in early December. However, a change of command in January 1900 and reinforcements enabled the British to reverse the tide and, by midspring, British forces had relieved the major encircled towns. The new commander responsible for restoring the situation was Field Marshal Frederick S. Roberts with General Horatio Herbert Kitchener as his chief of staff. Both men were very capable and had demonstrated records of success in colonial warfare.[42] They would reframe Britain's approach to the problem of guerrilla insurgency.

Although primarily and famously successful in conventional operations against the initially clumsy British offensives, the Boers were relentlessly pushed back. As Roberts and his army approached the Boer capital of Pretoria the underarmed and outnumbered Boers recognized that they could not stop the British using conventional military means. On March 17, 1900, the Boer leadership decided to shift the army's tactics away from conventional battles to disrupting British communications through the use of guerrilla tactics.[43] After the fall of Pretoria, Boer commander-in-chief General Louis Botha ordered his field commanders to destroy the British railways, and on the night of June 6–7, General Christiaan DeWet's commando launched several successful attacks on bridges and junctions. DeWet's raids caused over £100,000 damage and cut off Pretoria for an entire week.

This act galvanized the British into action leading to a policy of relocation. The extreme sensitivity of the British to Boer attacks on their lines of communications is evident from a proclamation by Roberts on June 16 that held local civilians accountable for aiding and abetting Boers, who destroyed or cut railway and telegraph lines.[44] Roberts authorized the burning of Boer homes and the taking of civilian residents as prisoners of war. A subsequent proclamation three days later further authorized the fining of civilians for damages, the destruction of farms, the forced placement of civilians on trains (the modern term for this is "human shields"), and placing civilians under the authority of martial law.[45] In spite of these harsh measures, Boer attacks on the railways increased in July in frequency and intensity.[46]

The mechanics of the relocation and concentration of Boer civilians began on June 18, when Roberts's chief of intelligence, Colonel Colin Mackenzie, recommended that Boer families, whose men were on commando, be "sent to be supported by their own people at Lydenburg."[47] The particular problem then facing Roberts in Pretoria was how to feed the enemy population with the railways being cut. Robert, however, was disinclined toward removal of civilians and the idea died. Later, on July 17, the military governor of Pretoria, Brigadier John Maxwell, revived the idea and ordered that families without means of subsistence "be deported to a place or places beyond the British lines to be hereafter to be determined by me."[48] The first 412 women and children were sent out of the town several days later to Boer lines rather than to camps where the British would have to feed them.

This pattern of relocation continued throughout the remainder of 1900. The exact date of the establishment of camps for Boer civilians is contested. Some accounts asserted that the earliest actual camp existed outside Mafeking as early as July 1900, but officially, the British established the first camps in January 1901.[49] Nevertheless, by July 25, David Lloyd George, speaking in the House of Commons, stated, "It seems to me that in this war we have gradually followed the policy of Spain in Cuba."[50]

This was followed on August 20, 1900, by an article that appeared in a London newspaper advocating the employment of Weyler's methods to deal with the Boers.[51] Alfred Milner, the high commissioner for South Africa, wrote to Roberts three days later recommending the establishment of camps in the Cape Colony. The impetus to establish camps supervised by the British military gathered as Roberts announced that Boers who surrendered voluntarily would be treated honorably as prisoners of war rather than as criminals. By the early winter, a number of camps were established in the Orange River Colony and in the Transvaal.

With Pretoria captured, the Boer army defeated, and the beleaguered towns relieved, the war appeared all but won. On November 29, 1900, Kitchener succeeded Roberts, who had asked to be relieved in September. Britain had about 230,000 soldiers in South Africa when Kitchener assumed command and the War Office believed that they were opposed by 8,000 Boers, who remained active in the field.[52] Unfortunately for Britain and Kitchener, the Boers ignored these odds and chose to continue fighting. Moreover, their leaders resolved to conduct guerrilla warfare in an attempt to wear out the British in the vastness of the South African veldt. In order to relieve British pressure on the commandos the Boers invaded Cape Colony on December 16, thereby expanding the scope of the war and thoroughly alarming the British. Determined to end Boer resistance once and for all, Kitchener decided upon a strategy similar to that of General Weyler in Cuba. The heart of this was the construction of barbed wire fences along railways, roads, and across the veldt with interlocking blockhouses, the construction of which began in early 1901 (Weyler had called these *trocha*). These barriers were, at first, hastily constructed and porous, but as time went on they became more comprehensive.

By the end of the war there were 3,700 miles (6,000 kilometers) of lines with 8,000 blockhouses manned by 50,000 British troops and 16,000 Africans.[53] Kitchener then reorganized his army into columns, led by aggressive young commanders, who were given the mission to drive the Boer commandos onto the blockhouse lines. In this manner, entire sectors could be cleared of guerrillas and then brought under control. At first, it was easy for the Boers to slip thorough the blockhouse lines but by mid-1901, this was becoming increasingly difficult, as Kitchener organized about 50,000 men into columns of 1,000–5,000 horsemen. These self-sufficient, highly mobile columns, often containing pom-poms and artillery, were turned loose inside the ever-increasingly restricted blockhouse lines to hunt down the Boers.

The columns were also charged with the responsibility of sweeping up Boer civilians and destroying their property, including livestock, in order to deny the commandos logistical support. By March 1901, the drives were in full swing, large numbers of Boer civilians were arriving in camps, and vast areas of the Transvaal were swept clear of livestock and people.[54] By the end of the month, there were over 20,000 Boers in camps in the Transvaal and another 2,500 in camps in Natal.[55] The scope of the sweeps was staggering and sometimes netted huge numbers of livestock. In one sweep lasting about a month the British seized 7,000 horses, 38,000 sheep (of which 15,000 had to be slaughtered as they could not be moved efficiently), and about 6,000 head of cattle.[56] Farm burning and the deliberate devastation of property turned the Boer landscape into a wasteland. Kitchener distanced himself from the devastation by encouraging the Boers to surrender and by attempting to hand over control of the camps to civilian authorities.[57]

The first use of the phrase "concentration camp" also came in March from radical MPs C. P. Scott and John Ellis, who took it from Weyler's program of reconcentration camps in Cuba.[58] Parliamentary interest accelerated and, by April, the House was demanding statistics and information about the treatment of Boers incarcerated in British camps. As more Boers were brought in from the drives, camp numbers increased to about 50,000 by May 1901. The handover of camp control to civilian authorities, who had few resources with which to manage and sustain the camps, envisioned by Kitchener went badly, and conditions inside the camps rapidly deteriorated. Rations and water supplies were inadequate, medical care was sporadic or nonexistent, and sanitary conditions were abysmal. As a result, mortality rates in the camps shot up.

By September 1901, the British had confined over 100,000 white civilians in 33 camps, most of which contained about 3,000–5,000 people. Alert to the racist policies of the Boers, the British segregated whites and blacks into separate camps and about 66,000 blacks were incarcerated by September as well. Mortality rates in the camps for both races soared as diseases such as typhus and dysentery swept through the crowded tents. Sadly, mortality rates among children were particularly high and approached 30 percent in many camps.[59] The horrific conditions inside the concentration camps became a cause célèbre in England and activist Emily Hobhouse's scathing indictments of Britain's neglect of Boer civilians scandalized the country.

> Hobhouse's reports described a catastrophe of near genocidal proportions conducted by the British Army under Kitchener. They showed that the British, incapable of protecting the health of their own troops, thousands of whom died of disease, were totally at a loss in dealing with problems of malnutrition and mass disease that spread like wildfire in the cramped and insanitary conditions of the concentration camps.[60]

As a result of this adverse publicity, and belatedly, British authorities began to improve conditions within the camps but death rates continued to rise in the white camps peaking in October 1901 and in the black camps peaking in December. British politicians frantically began to distance themselves from Kitchener's policies and called for parliamentary investigations. Kitchener, for his part, informed London that the government should not complain unless it was in a position to do better, but after December, few additional whites were sent to the camps.[61] Blacks, however, continued to be swept up and by May 1902, there were about 107,000 blacks confined to the camps. The total number of dead remains contentious. The most comprehensive estimates come from a postwar Boer government investigator, who asserted that almost 28,000 white Boers died in the camps.[62] An accurate number for black victims will probably never be known, but certainly exceeded the total number of whites.

With the destruction of the Boer farmsteads, logistical support for the Boer commandos began to constrict and many abandoned their German rifles and began to use captured British rifles and ammunition. Similarly, the capture of British food and supplies became equally important for the commandos. In spite of this, the defeat of the Boer guerrilla forces in the field took 18 months and a huge effort by Kitchener's columns. In the end, there was nowhere for the surviving Boer "Bitter Enders" to hide and most of the surviving commandos were run to ground and killed or captured. A peace agreement was signed on May 31, 1902, at which time the British held some 30,000 prisoners of war.[63] The Boer War ended and became the last of what the Victorians called the "small wars." It was, however, never a small war and might properly be classified as a protracted war that only ended when the British eliminated what Mao Zedong later called "guerrilla base areas." Indeed, Kitchener's strategy of population removal and sweeps proved remarkably effective, although success came at a huge price in manpower, effort, and money. Over 450,000 British and Imperial soldiers were sent to South Africa, of whom 22,000 died and another 80,000 became casualties.[64] The financial cost of the war exceeded anything the British army had done since the Napoleonic Wars, including the Crimean War and, additionally, they lost over 400,000 horses and mules. The Boers lost 7,000 dead from about 87,000 combatants and their country was devastated by Kitchener's policies of destruction.

It may be argued that although very costly, Kitchener's operations were ultimately successful and introduced the idea of waging total war on ethnically similar civilians in the twentieth century.[65] Kitchener's operations were technically not counterinsurgency operations but rather fall more properly under the category of counterguerrilla operations. British operations in the Boer War mirrored Weyler's operational design in every major aspect, especially in the separation of the people from the guerillas and in the sweeping of closed-off subsectors. Kitchener's war lasted about 30 months and his progress toward the subjugation of the Boers was methodical and relentless. Significantly, Kitchener enjoyed a huge numerical advantage and the resources to construct the physical means needed to employ Weyler's ideas (the blockhouse lines and concentration camps). The completeness of the British victory was mostly a result of Kitchener's successful implementation of a coherent counterguerrilla operational design, but it is important to remember that it was never a counterinsurgency campaign. The Boers were not in revolt, but were driven to guerrilla warfare after the defeat of their regular forces, and in the end, their political leaders surrendered.

CONCLUSION

The similarities between these three wars are self-evident and demonstrate a growing willingness on the part of Western powers to employ harsh methods aimed at the civilian population in order to suppress insurgents or guerrillas. What might be said about the viability of an operational design for waging counterinsurgency using such methods as described in this chapter? Several conclusions may be drawn from these wars about what is needed to successfully implement what might be termed the "Weyler method." First, the geography must be manageable in the sense of being able to isolate and divide the enemy forces. Second, adequate numbers of troops must be available and a significant number must be capable of highly mobile and independent operations. Third, the removal of the population must be complete in order to separate guerrillas from their support. Last, there must be the political will necessary to weather public criticism and sustain the effort over a protracted time period. Only Britain's conduct of the Boer War brought all four of these factors into a coherent operational focus.

Taken together, the Spanish, American, and British armies created what might be termed a template for destruction, the signature of which was the involuntary relocation of the civilian population to confined locations. While this template did not deliberately target civilians for destruction, large numbers died as a consequence of insufficient regard for their care and well-being. In many instances, this was the result of inadequate resources rather than simple neglect or deliberately destructive actions. Deaths in the concentration camps and zones of protection occurred mainly as a result of diseases caused by inadequate medical care, malnutrition, and dangerous overcrowding, which were themselves, predictable problems. Sadly, overcoming these problems was never as high a priority for the Spanish, the Americans, or the British as was the military defeat of insurgents and guerrillas. Nevertheless, after the Boer War, and absent considerations of morality and human dignity, the basic operational design of Weyler's methods appeared to be fundamentally valid in both theory and practice.

CHAPTER 5

Invisible Armies

You do not understand the kind of warfare the Turks wage. It is not such as Western Europe knows. There is no mercy shown. It would do you no good to be a non-combatant. You would be slain, just the same, if they caught you. The askares never take prisoners.

—*Arthur D. Howden Smith,*
Fighting the Turk in the Balkans, 1908[1]

INTRODUCTION

The period from 1912 to 1914 was a time of military disaster for the Ottoman Empire as war erupted in the fall of 1912. Following the failed counterinsurgencies in the periphery of the empire and the loss of Libya to Italy, the cumulative defeats of 1912 enabled the Committee of Union and Progress (CUP) to seize control of the government. This led to a brief period of strategic pause wherein the exhausted Ottoman state and the Armenian revolutionary committees recognized the possibility of a shared political future. Unfortunately, this short period of hope disintegrated rapidly as the Great Powers once again began to meddle in the affairs of the "sick man of Europe" by demanding the implementation of an intrusive Armenian reform plan. In turn, the CUP and the Armenian committees again moved in divergent directions toward an increasingly militarized capability, which essentially reset them in opposition.

The First Balkan War pitted the Christian Balkan League of Bulgaria, Greece, Montenegro, and Serbia in a war of aggression against the Ottomans. The war ended badly for the empire in the late spring of 1913, when it lost the productive provinces of Yanya (Epirus), Manastir (Macedonia), Kosovo, Salonika, and Işkodra (Albania). A second Balkan war between the erstwhile Christian allies broke out in June 1913 and lasted until August of the same year; during this period the Ottomans recovered the important city of Edirne (Adrianople). The war shattered the Ottoman army and the following year was spent in the reconstitution of the army and in retraining it in modern combat tactics. Germany renewed its defunct military mission to the Ottoman Empire and sent General Otto Liman von Sanders and about 30 officers to Constantinople to assist the Ottomans in rebuilding their army.

The CUP staged a bloody coup d'état, known as the Raid on the Sublime Porte, and established tighter control over the faltering Ottoman state. However, this failed to bring victory in the Balkan Wars. The military defeats gave rise to hundreds of thousands of Muslim and Turkish refugees, who poured into the empire's western regions from the newly conquered provinces. Moreover, defeat in the Balkan Wars brought renewed activity on the part of the European powers in establishing a supervised administrative reform package supporting the Armenian population in eastern Anatolia. Together, these events moved the Armenian committees to break off relations with the CUP, resurrect their dormant organizations, revive their military capability, and open direct channels of communication with the governments of Russia and France. As a general European war broke out in the summer of 1914, the Ottomans viewed the increasingly strident nationalism of the Armenian committees as a serious threat to the empire's security.

ARMENIAN ACTIVITIES IN 1912

The elections of 1912 were a source of much concern to the Armenians and led to a variety of outcomes, including the public break between the Armenian Revolutionary Federation (ARF) and the CUP in May. Within the ARF, there was internal disagreement over the intent and designs of the CUP between the Eastern Bureau, which was more favorably inclined to continue working with the CUP, and the Western Bureau. While the party leadership argued over its relationship with the government, the organization of the local and regional bodies deteriorated.[2] To correct this, the Western Bureau sent representatives to Samsun and Elâzığ while the Eastern Bureau sent representatives to Van and Muş. In Van, the ARF Central Committee worked directly with the governor, who agreed to implement what amounted to a local reform initiative. This was in response to a worsening security situation there, which was characterized by increasing numbers of attacks on Armenians. These measures included hiring Armenians as public officials, increasing Armenian participation in the *jandarma*, building guardhouses in especially dangerous areas, punishing perpetrators and restoring Armenian property and land, arming Armenian village guards, and returning weapons previously confiscated.[3]

In mid-September, the ARF convened a special committee in Constantinople and the "question of self-defense" was the leading item on the agenda.[4] This was the first time since 1908 that the issue had surfaced. The committee reached a consensus that the self-defense project would require far more responsible cadres in the provinces and resources than were then available, which made progress impossible in the near term. As hostilities appeared imminent, the ARF took a position opposing a general Balkan war, which placed it further in opposition to the public mood in the capital. Upon mobilization in late September 1912, thousands of Armenian men were called up for active duty in the Ottoman army and, notably, Armenian officers were especially effective in the artillery (which was a technical branch heavily dependent on educated men).[5] A small number of refugee Armenian committeemen in Bulgaria chose to take up arms against the empire; however, their actions were not reflective of the overwhelming numbers of Armenians who served the empire with distinction during the wars. Shortly after the war started, rumors surfaced that Armenians fighting together with the Bulgarians near Kavala had massacred Muslims. The ARF moved quickly to disprove these rumors by pointing out that there were no Armenian names in the list of those accused and by publishing telegrams and testimonials from survivors of the Ottoman units involved that no Armenians were responsible.[6] Rather than view the war as an opportunity or rebellion, the ARF essentially viewed it as a distraction from positive political engagement with the Ottoman state.

Unfortunately, in a startling development unconnected to the ARF, Kevork V, the Catholicos of all Armenians in Etchmiadzin, engaged in negotiations in October 1912 with the czar's viceroy for the Caucasus Count Illarion Ivanovich Vorontsov-Dashkov to discuss Armenian reforms inside the Ottoman Empire.[7] In December 1912, Kevork V formed the Armenian National Delegation and appointed Boghos Nubar Pasha as its president.[8] Nubar was an extremely influential and well-known Armenian politician, businessman, and the son of an Egyptian prime minister, who had established the Armenian General Benevolent Union in Egypt in 1905. The delegation established itself in Paris and immediately became active in advancing Armenian positions regarding an Armenian reform package for eastern Anatolia. Another member appointed to the delegation by Kevork was James Malcolm, an Armenian who became a naturalized British citizen.[9]

Malcolm, an Oxford graduate, was well connected and enjoyed a wide circle of influential friends. He resided in London and became the delegation's point man in its dealings with the British. Although it did not represent an established government, the Armenian National Delegation functioned, more or less, like an embassy by establishing formal ties to European governments thereby establishing de facto relationships between the Armenians and the Europeans.

Nearly simultaneously on December 21–22, 1912, the Armenian Political Council in Constantinople met secretly to consider how to handle the reform question. In attendance were two Russians from Saint Petersburg, Professor Nicolas Adontz and a lawyer name Sirakan Tigranian.[10] After discussions, the chamber moved to create an advisory committee to assemble information about abuses occurring in eastern Anatolia and to consider appropriate reform measures. In early 1913, the architecture of Armenian diplomacy began to emerge. Boghos Nubar and the Armenian Delegation were to be responsible for external negotiations with the European governments, while the Political Council "seconded by the Constantinople and Tiblisi Commissions" were to negotiate the reform question internally with the Ottoman and Russian governments.[11] The strong hand of the Russians is immediately apparent as their interests and agents began to appear internally and externally.

THE BALKAN WARS, 1912–1913

As background to the Balkan Wars, the composition of the Ottoman government must be examined. As mentioned previously, the CUP took control of the parliament in the spring of 1912. The grand vizier, Sait Pasha, himself a coalition compromise leader, was then forced to take more CUP members into his cabinet.[12] However, as the war against Italy in Libya and the counterinsurgency operations in Albania and Yemen began to fail, a number of high-ranking military officers, who were unhappy with the counterproductive political involvement in these wars, formed a political committee in the capital. Calling itself the Group of Liberating Officers, its members were committed to reducing the autocratic control wielded by the CUP over military operations. Supported by the Liberal Union in parliament, the Liberating Officers threatened violent action unless their demands were met. Sait Pasha resigned on July 17, 1912, and the government collapsed. A new government, led by an elderly war hero named Gazi Ahmet Muhtar Pasha, was formed and this excluded the CUP members from cabinet posts. Moreover, numbers of CUP deputies failed to retake their seats in the new parliamentary elections held in early August. The brief period of CUP dominance ended just as the Ottoman Empire stood on the cusp of renewed fighting in the Balkans.

The First Balkan War began in early October 1912 when the armies of Bulgaria, Greece, Montenegro, and Serbia attacked the Ottoman Empire.[13] The Ottoman army began mobilization at the end of September, but its forces were unready and incompletely positioned at the outbreak of hostilities. Ottoman reserves were only partially mobilized and, in any case, the empire's inefficient transportation system was incapable of delivering them to their combat positions. In spite of this, the high command determined to conduct operational offensives while standing on the strategic defensive. This resulted in the smaller and incompletely prepared Ottoman army attacking the larger and better-equipped invading armies. Of course, this led to immediate defeats at Kirkkilise in Thrace, and Kumanova in Macedonia, after which, the Ottomans retreated. In the subsequent battles of Lüleburgaz and Bitola, in Thrace and Macedonia, respectively, the Ottomans again attempted to attack the invaders with similar disastrous results. The government collapsed and Kamil Pasha, who had been grand vizier three times previously, formed a new cabinet. By the middle of November, the Ottoman army in Thrace had been pushed back to the Çatalca lines, 20 miles to the west of Constantinople, where it finally stopped the advancing Bulgarians. The counterpart Ottoman army in Macedonia was almost completely shattered and withdrew into what is now Albania. On the Greek front, the Ottomans lost the major city of Salonika but continued to hold the fortress of Yanya (Jannina) in Epirus.

The embattled Ottomans concluded an armistice on December 3, 1912, which ended the fighting in Thrace, Macedonia, and Albania, but not in Epirus (as Greece refused to abide by the terms). Thereafter, high-level negotiations to end the war formally began in London on December 12. The negotiations were contentious, with the Greeks and the Bulgarians at odds over the specifics of what the Ottomans proposed, and discussions were suspended on January 6, 1913. By this time, the ambassadors of the European powers and the British foreign minister Sir Edward Grey, worried about the intransigent positions of the belligerents, stepped in with a peace proposal that accommodated the aims of the Balkan League and badly penalized the Ottoman Empire. They presented the peace proposal to the Ottoman government as a collective démarche, which was almost immediately accepted by both the Ottoman cabinet and by an overwhelming majority of the parliament on January 22, 1913.

Unfortunately for the cabinet, the CUP regarded the terms of the proposal, which gave up the Balkan provinces to the enemy, as humiliating and also as visible evidence of bankrupt leadership in the government. As a result, the CUP conducted a coup d'état on the afternoon of January 23, which overthrew the government in what is called the Raid on the Sublime Porte.[14] The conspirators forced Kazim Pasha to resign at gunpoint and shot Minister of War Nazim Pasha to death. The sultan quickly confirmed Mahmut Şevket Pasha as both grand vizier and minister of war and Talat Pasha as minister of the interior. Ahmet İzzet Pasha, recently returned from Yemen, assumed the post of army chief of staff. Lieutenant Colonel Enver and Colonel Cemal, members of the CUP's inner circle, were participants in the coup and hoped for high cabinet positions; however, both returned to operational assignments immediately afterward. On January 31, 1913, the newly appointed acting minister of war, Ahmet İzzet Pasha, began to send out orders to the forces on the fronts in preparation for a renewal of fighting and for offensive operations. The armistice expired on the evening of February 3, 1913.

The war continued with the Ottoman army failing to regain the strategic or operational initiative and a second armistice went into effect in mid-April 1913. Most of the participants signed the subsequent Treaty of London on May 30, thus setting the western border of the Ottoman Empire on the Enos-Midia line, which forfeited the entirety of the empire's Balkan provinces including the cities of Edirne (Adrianople) and Salonika. A second Balkan war broke out when Bulgaria, which had borne the bulk of the hard fighting and which failed to gain the majority of Macedonian territory under the treaty, attacked its former allies Greece and Serbia. Romania quickly entered the war against the Bulgarians. While the Christian states were fighting among themselves, the Ottoman army took the opportunity to reclaim Edirne and pushed the border farther to the west from the Enos-Midia line. Treaties in Constantinople with the Bulgarians, and in Athens with the Greeks, formally ended the wars for the Ottomans in the fall of 1913.

An historian estimated that about 8,000 Armenian citizens were conscripted and served actively in the Ottoman army during this period.[15] In effect, this served to provide a large number of Armenian men with direct military training and experience. Moreover, a small number of exiles in Bulgaria, who had fled the empire during the Hamidian massacres, decided not to sit idle. The well-known Armenian military leader Antranig Ozanian formed 273 Armenian refugees into a volunteer company to fight alongside the Bulgarians.[16]

Antranig became the company's commander and his lieutenants were "Torgom, Nzhdeh, Arghamanian and others."[17] The well-armed and professional-appearing company was photographed in uniform displaying a banner proclaiming Freedom or Death.[18] Antranig soon led them into action and the company fought in four battles in what is now Greek Thrace (Mestanle on November 4, Uzun on November 6, Balkan Toresi on November 7, and Merhamle on November 15).[19] Little is known about Armenian participation in these battles and Antranig Chalabian's account is clearly exaggerated and contradicts both Turkish and Western histories. For example, Chalabian erroneously asserted that Antranig personally forced the defending Ottoman general M. Yaver Pasha and ten thousand men to surrender at Merhamle.[20] Nevertheless, Antranig and his Armenians were highly visible. Chalabian correctly narrated that Leon Trotsky, then a war correspondent observing the war, wrote an article about him, Bulgarian newspapers praised Antranig's gallantry, and the Bulgarians awarded him a medal. But Antranig's activities were largely symbolic and the scale of participation in the fighting by this tiny and exotic band of Armenians did not have a dramatic impact on the war. Moreover, it did not reflect, in any way, the high levels of loyalty to the Ottoman state displayed by the vast majority of its Armenian citizens during the Balkan Wars. However, the Ottoman authorities paid close attention to Antranig's exploits and would consider his 1912 war record as preparation for fighting with the Russians in 1915.

Armenian Activities and the Great Powers in 1913

Politically, in the late spring of 1913, the ARF and the Armenian National Assembly thought to use the post–Balkan War period of severe Ottoman diplomatic and military weakness to establish a reform plan for the Armenians in the Ottoman Empire, which would replace the ineffective clauses of the 1878 Treaty of Berlin. There are several versions of how the plan came to be drafted. One historian asserts that an informal committee of dragomen of the Constantinople embassies, some of whom were Armenians, drew up a draft plan and gave it to André Mandelstam, chief dragoman of the Russian embassy. The plan became the centerpiece of a proposal relayed by Russian ambassador Mikhail Giers to his British, French, German, Austrian, and Italians counterparts in Constantinople.[21] Another historian asserts that the plan was drawn up by the Armenian Political Council's Special Commission and then forwarded to Mandelstam.[22]

The plan as envisioned was aggressive and called for the unification of six provinces, the nomination of a Christian governor and religiously balanced council, the establishment of a *jandarma* commanded by European officers, the disestablishment of the Hamidiye, legalization of the Armenian language and schools, and the establishment of a special commission to examine land confiscations empowered to expel Muslim refugees, However, most contentious for the Ottoman government was a clause obligating the European powers to enforce the reforms.

The Armenian reform plan became somewhat of a political football as first the British, and then the Germans and Russians argued over the terms with the Ottoman government. A general agreement was reached in September between the Germans, who did not want Russia to increase its influence in the Ottoman Empire, and the Russians. However, the Ottomans balked at the idea of Great Power control and negotiations floundered while the powers put increasing amounts of diplomatic pressure on the Ottoman government in the late fall. Additionally, there was significant disagreement among the ARF leadership bureaus regarding how the Europeans were changing specific clauses as well.[23] The Ottomans themselves presented a counterplan centered on a network of inspectors-general with a view toward marginalizing Great Power oversight by decentralizing the implementation of the reforms. At the end of 1913, the Ottomans finally gave in and accepted the substantially revised agreement.[24] The final version of the plan was signed in February 1914. The basis of the plan placed six eastern provinces (Bitlis, Diyarbakır, Elâzığ, Erzurum, Sivas, and Van) into an administrative zone within which the Europeans would manage reforms. Map 5.1 shows these provinces and the distribution of Ottoman Armenians within the core provinces. Two European inspectors-general were to be appointed, who would supervise the reforms and, moreover, would have the authority to appoint and relieve provincial officials and bureaucrats proving obstructive to reforms.

"Most of the ARF's party work in the spring of 1913 was arms related" as a worsening situation in the provinces created an urgent need to revive the self-defense capability.[25] This drove the committee's bureaus in a number of directions. As a first order of business, fund-raising drives were initiated within the Ottoman Empire, and from Armenian expatriate groups living abroad, to bring in the sums of money needed to buy weapons. An important source of funds came from the Armenian communities in the United States. When the Armenians in Egypt failed to support the effort with contributions,

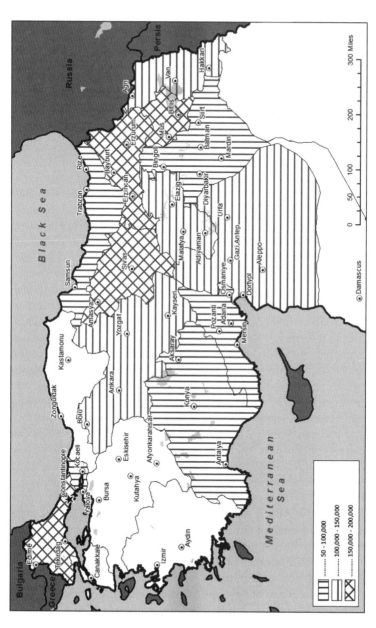

Map 5.1 Distribution of Ottoman Armenian population, 1913.

the ARF contacted Boghos Nubar and pressured him to influence the Armenians in Egypt. Although Nubar opposed the idea in public, he quietly supported the campaign in private.[26]

The end of the Balkan Wars flooded the region with surplus military weapons, which were available in bulk and at cheap prices. The ARF sent representatives to Rodosto (Tekirdağ), a hub of the illegal arms trade, to purchase military rifles in huge quantities.[27] Most of the arms purchased within the empire itself went to Erzurum for distribution to the Armenian community in the surrounding provinces. Older arms smuggling routes through Persia were reactivated as rifles and pistols from Russia began to appear in Van province.[28] A large number of armed Armenian detachments were organized in 1913 and put under the command of local commanders.[29]

In fact, the Armenians had cause for concern because during 1913 there were a number of increasingly troubling attacks on Armenians in the Ottoman Empire. The eastern provinces had been characterized as particularly dangerous and having a "tinderbox atmosphere" because of restive Kurdish tribes.[30] Armenians in Cilicia were particularly worried that reports of rebel Armenians near Zeytun might trigger Adana-like massacres. In Bitlis and Van provinces, local ARF committees reported banditry and murder perpetrated on Armenians, which were ignored by the Ottoman police and judicial authorities.[31] In April, a "potentially provocative incident" occurred in Erzincan when a home owned by an Armenian named Kazanjian exploded. In the rubble, authorities found 60 homemade bombs, hand grenades, and other armaments.[32] The local ARF and Hunchaks disavowed the man and worked hard to insure that there was not a government reaction penalizing the Armenian community. Over the summer, a number of Armenian villages were attacked directly and in strength by Kurdish tribal gangs.[33] There were incidents in the western parts of the empire as well. In Rodosto, a large number of Armenians were massacred in early July by the Ottoman army when the town was abandoned by the retreating Bulgarian army. It has been suggested that inflammatory articles by the Ottoman press against Armenians enraged the Ottoman soldiers, who reoccupied the town on July 1–3, 1913.[34]

The Seventh World Congress convened in Erzurum on August 17, 1913, was the briefest in ARF history and lasted only one week. Of 18 Armenian committees and organizations, 14 sent representatives. The decisions of the previous World Congress were confirmed and remained in effect. The ARF expressed great concern that war was an imminent probability and, with war, the probability was high that Armenians and others, including Persians and Caucasians, would be caught on opposing sides.[35] According to Dasnabedian, the Seventh World Congress "decided to prevent armed conflict—when political complexities arise—through all possible legal means and in consultation with other socialist parties"; however, should war become unavoidable, "all citizens will carry out their civic duties toward their own governments."[36] The congress affirmed the break with the CUP and also addressed Armeno-Kurdish relations and land claims. An important outcome of the Seventh World Congress was a restructuring of the organizational architectures of the committees. The congress established a separate supreme body called the Bureau of Armenia, which included the six Armenian provinces and Trabzon.[37] This restructuring effectively detached the Ottoman eastern Anatolian provinces from the Bureau in Tiblisi, thereby organizationally separating Ottoman Armenians from Russian Armenians. Moreover, the congress endowed the three bureaus with authorities previously reserved for the Responsible Bodies. Henceforth, the ARF Central Committee consisted of the three bureaus and the Central Committee of America (which had grown in strength and influence).[38] It must be noted that the establishment of a separate Armenian Bureau within Ottoman Anatolia presaged and supported the administration of the geographic area of six provinces envisioned in the proposed reform program.

The Social Democrat Hunchakian Party also convened a separate Seventh Congress in Constanza, Romania, on September 17, 1913. Entering the twentieth century, the Hunchaks had remained a weak sister of the ARF and they were almost exclusively concerned with peaceful Marxist-inspired social and economic changes. At the Sixth Congress on July 25–29, 1909, the Social Democrat Hunchakian Party endorsed the idea of self-defense but rejected the use of terrorism as a political weapon.[39] Their latest political doctrinal tract published in Constantinople in 1910 was titled *The General Statutes Governing the Ottoman Social Democrat Hunchak Organization* and concerned itself only with economic, social, and political goals.[40] In 1913, armed revolution and self-defense were not mentioned at all publically in Constanza. Indeed, a postcongress circular sent around between the committees in October suggested that the organization remained operationally dysfunctional compared to the ARF as it addressed such mundane issues as who was invited and which committees failed to attend.[41]

The Ottoman military intelligence services, however, thought otherwise considering the Hunchaks as a slumbering threat and tracking their activities. A number of Hunchaks were arrested and put on trial for subversive activities and conspiracy. The military courts-martial indictment of Samuel Tomadjian and Hrant Aghagianian stated that, after attending and returning from the Seventh Congress in Constanza, Tomadijan instigated insurgency and sent assassins to kill Minister of the Interior Talat Pasha.[42] The indictment also named Tomadjian and Aghagianian as the leaders of a secret group known as the Inter-party Freedom Organization Central Committee, which advocated separating the Armenian provinces from the Ottoman Empire by means of a general armed insurrection. Once back inside the empire, the conspirators collected money from Armenians in accordance with a financial plan devised by Boghos Nubar to support their illegal activities. The evidence against them came from a large body of testimony from Armenians, who declared that Tomadjian and his associates stored bombs in their Amasya neighborhood, as well as from physical evidence that included documents and bomb-making materials confiscated by the authorities.[43] Tomadjian and Aghagianian were found guilty of plotting to murder members of the government and sentenced to death.[44]

In another courts-martial indictment involving the Hunchaks, Ottoman intelligence reports implicated Hamparsum Boyadjia (codenamed "Murat") and Doctor Benene with targeting fellow Hunchak committeeman Arshavir Sahagian, who was said to have betrayed the organization, with assassination.[45] The indictment asserted that the conspiracy was hatched at the Constanza Congress and the individuals involved were arrested in Constantinople in August 1914. Again, there was substantial probative testimony introduced during the trial as well as confiscated revolvers, rifles, and bomb-making brochures that proved the men guilty.[46] These military courts-martial records reinforce Talat Pasha's claims that the Seventh Congress decided to renew fighting and accelerate the implementation of violent revolutionary terrorist activities in pursuit of the acquisition of rights.[47]

In fact, Talat Pasha had managed to infiltrate an agent from the Ottoman intelligence services into the Constanza Congress. The agent, Arthur Esayan, alias Arshavir Sahagian, slipped into the congress as a delegate from the Cairo committee.[48] Esayan provided the minister of the interior with "a comprehensive account of the decisions adopted by the Congress and a list of the participants."[49] Although found out, Esayan managed to survive and report. Armed with this information, Talat Pasha's intelligence services were able to keep track of the conspirators into the spring of the following year and then arrested dozens of Hunchak committeemen in July 1914.

It is fair to say that, as 1913 drew to a close, there was a general consensus among the Armenian committees that the Armenian situation inside the Ottoman Empire was growing worse by the day. It is also true that many Armenians thought war between the Ottomans and the Russians was on the horizon. From these beliefs, there arose a number of contradictory policies within the different committees and organizations. The Dashnaktsutiun committees increased the acquisition and distribution of weapons and revived their dormant military capability. But at the same time, they publically embraced a policy opposing a general war and advocating that Armenian citizens support their own particular country. The Hunchaks, on the other hand, continued to advocate peaceful Marxist-socialist change, while covertly returning to the use of violence in pursuit of achieving their aims. The only policy common to all the committees was an increased commitment to generate revenues for the purchase of weapons through internal collection or coercion and through fund-raising from Armenian expatriate communities in foreign countries.

OTTOMAN MILITARY AND POLITICAL ACTIVITIES IN 1913

Grand vizier and minister of war Mahmut Şevket Pasha was an ardent admirer of Germany and its military system, as was the army chief of staff Ahmet İzzet Pasha. Both were deeply concerned about the failures of the Ottoman military, which were ruthlessly exposed during the Balkan Wars, and both thought that political influence badly affected the army's performance. After much consultation with German diplomatic and military representatives, the Ottoman government formally asked for an enlargement of the moribund German military mission on May 22, 1913.[50] Shortly thereafter, members of a terrorist conspiracy assassinated Mahmut Şevket Pasha on June 11, 1913, an event that enabled the hard-line inner core of the CUP to take control of the government. The assassins were apprehended rapidly and included discharged army officers and a career criminal named Topal Tevfik, who was the actual assassin.[51] Apparently the conspirators had revolutionary aspirations but, to this day, their actual motives remain unclear. The assassination of Mahmud Şevket Pasha left several cabinet portfolios vacant and the CUP appointed Sait Halim as the new grand vizier. The CUP appointed Ahmet İzzet Pasha as the new minister of war on June 18, 1913, and Halil Bey, Enver's uncle, became the president of the council of state.

The Ottoman army struggled to evacuate its remaining forces from Albania to ports in Anatolia and, in August, it began to return forces from the front in Thrace to their home garrison cities. In the fall, the army began an effort to reconstitute some of the army corps and infantry divisions that had been destroyed in the Balkan Wars.[52] This effort involved not only the movement of troops, but the restationing of units in new garrisons and the cross-leveling of equipment. At the same time, the army engaged in a massive demobilization of reserves and conscripts who had been called to the colors for the war. Negotiations with the German general staff continued over the summer and the final contract between Germany and the Ottoman Empire for a five-year mission, with the possibility for an extension, was signed on October 27, 1913. Çürüksulu Mahmut Pasha became acting minister of war on November 5, so that Ahmet İzzet Pasha might focus on the vast tasks he was responsible for as army chief of staff. However, what was really happening behind the scenes was that the CUP was easing Ahmet İzzet Pasha, who was a modernizer but not a strong supporter of the CUP, out of his position of authority.[53]

Over the fall, Ahmet İzzet Pasha had the general staff working on a massive reorganization of the Ottoman army, the staff work for which was completed on December 11, 1913, and which was unveiled as the *New Organization of Active Forces according to Army, Independent Corps and Division Areas.*[54] These regulations made dramatic changes in the force structure of the Ottoman army. First, the previous corps and inspectorate areas, made obsolete by the loss of the Balkan provinces, were redrawn. However, the most sweeping change was the outright elimination of the army's organized reserve corps and divisions, which had failed catastrophically in the Balkan Wars.[55] In place of organized units, the Ottoman reserve system transitioned to a system of individual reservists, who were slotted to fill active Ottoman army infantry divisions, which were manned at cadre strength, up to war establishment. The regulations also projected the reconstruction of an active army of 38 infantry divisions.[56] Thus, Ahmet İzzet Pasha laid the groundwork for what might be termed a nonexpansible army. This flew against contemporary European reserve army doctrine, which used the German expansible army model and which enabled the mobilization of large military forces.[57] The exceptions to this model in the new regulations were the four Caucasian light cavalry divisions that were redesignated as reserve cavalry divisions. While this made the training of individual reservists easier and generally simplified mobilization, the limitations placed on expansion by this regulation would prove to have profound consequences on Ottoman counterinsurgency operations in eastern Anatolia in 1915.

German general Otto Liman von Sanders, accompanied by 41 German officers, arrived in Constantinople on December 14, 1913. Under the terms of the contract, Liman von Sanders would not command the Ottoman army but rather supervised a training mission (known as the German Military Mission). The officers were distributed as individual advisors to a single infantry division, 3 regiments, and 11 military training and educational institutions, including the prestigious Military Academy.[58]

Politically, 1913 was the year when the CUP began to construct what would become totalitarian one-party rule over the Ottoman government. The CUP's initial changes in government started in mid-March 1913, with the passing of a new provincial authority law that strengthened provincial authority by increasing the powers of the police and the *jandarma*, making them more responsive in limiting the activities of terrorist groups.[59] This was followed in April by a law that secularized the appeals courts by establishing state control over the ulema and religious courts. This law was the result of secular reform proposals made by CUP ideologue Ziya Gökalp, who was a professor and an early adherent of the CUP.[60] Gökalp began his rise to party prominence in 1909 as a vigorous advocate of Ottomanism. By 1913, he was an influential member of the CUP's Central Committee but had given up Ottomanism for a kind of Turkish nationalism called Turkism.[61] His ideas formed the intellectual bedrock for a CUP ideology that drew a Turkic identity from history and which led, in the view of some contemporary scholars, to the CUP practicing racially motivated ethnic cleansing and genocide.[62]

The Origins of the Teşkilat-ı Mahsusa, 1913

The origins and activities of the infamous Teşkilat-ı Mahsusa, or the Special Organization (SO), began in 1913. Academic opinion about what kind of an organization the SO actually was continues to rage even today and there are two basic positions on the nature of the SO.[63] The most common and well-known view on the SO originates from Armenian authors, who assert that, from the onset, the SO was the military arm of the CUP and its designed purpose was "the systematic liquidation of the civilian population."[64] This view takes the position that the SO was the primary instrument of an alleged genocide conducted against the Armenians in 1915 and also asserts that the SO was focused on counterinsurgency and population engineering. This is untrue and the opposite position, from military historians, proposes that the SO grew to become, first, an organization designed to foment insurgency and, second, an intelligence service.

The institutional origin of the SO was directly related to the unsatisfactory result of the First Balkan War and began after the recovery of

Edirne during the Second Balkan War. Under the terms of the peace treaties, Bulgaria and Greece gained portions of western Thrace on the Aegean Sea (more or less centered on Kavala and Drama, respectively), which were areas heavily populated by ethnically Turkish Muslims, many of whom refused to leave. The peace treaties themselves were unpopular among many members of the Ottoman government and the military and a few men determined to act in support of the ethnic Turks caught on the wrong side of the border. As a revolutionary organization, SO had no precedent in Ottoman history and grew directly out of the counterinsurgency experiences from Macedonia and the guerrilla experiences from Libya of a handful of Ottoman officers.

As a formally organized institution, the SO was established on November 30, 1913.[65] Opinions vary regarding whether Talat, Enver, or the inner circle of the CUP established the SO,[66] but as a matter of fact, a large number of SO files (about 40,000) from November 1913 through November 1918 are to be found today in the Turkish military archives in Ankara, giving credence that the SO was a military rather than a political organization.[67] The individual most associated with the actual establishment of the SO is Süleyman Askeri, who undertook the first mission into the Rhodope Mountains of Bulgarian-controlled western Thrace, where the SO supported the Independent Provisional Government of Western Thrace.[68] Encouraged by the Ottoman Empire's reclaiming of Edirne, the provisional government declared independence on August 31, 1913, and was composed of Turks and Pomaks, who refused to submit to the terms of the peace treaties or live under Bulgarian authority. They established a short-lived republic, which collapsed in late October 1913.

Determined to cause problems for the occupying Christian states, Talat's Ministry of the Interior charged Süleyman Askeri to command a paramilitary guerrilla force in the hope of inflaming Muslim opposition to Christian occupation. He was chosen for this mission because he had experience in irregular warfare through fighting against the Italians in Libya as a member of the Union of Patriotic Officers (other officers with similar backgrounds were Eşref [Kuşçubaşı], Halil [Kut], Enver Bey, and Mustafa Kemal Bey).[69] In the fall of 1913/14, Süleyman Askeri, Çerkez Reşit, Manastırlı Halim, and Eşref organized a number of guerrilla bands (*çete*), which began to conduct irregular attacks against the isolated outposts of the Greek and Bulgarian armies.[70] Although Süleyman Askeri departed shortly thereafter for other tasks assigned by the government, these operations continued into 1914.

Ottoman Military and Political Activities in 1914

On January 3, 1914, the CUP cabinet appointed Colonel Enver to the position of minister of war.[71] Enver was young, charismatic, a longtime member of the CUP's inner circle, and was at the center of a movement to replace Ahmet İzzet Pasha. Once in power, Enver moved immediately to consolidate his grip on the army by forcibly retiring some 1,300 officers on January 7.[72] Many of these men were elderly, some were undereducated *alayı* (or regimental officers), but others were opponents of the CUP and modernization. One historian recounted that some were confined in the war ministry basement on the day itself and that some were members of the Group of Liberating Officers, which had brought down Sait Halim's government in July 1912.[73] It was a bloodless coup and none were executed. On the same day, Enver abolished the Council of Military Affairs, which eliminated a competing source of power within the government.[74] The astonishing rapidity with which Enver carried out what amounted to a bloodless purge clearly demonstrates detailed planning and aforethought on his part. Enver's takeover of the Ministry of War completed the ironclad grip that the CUP had on the Ottoman government and Raymond Kévorkian's phrase "Ittihadist Dictatorship" accurately characterizes the Ottoman government for the following five years. Sometimes the Ottoman war cabinet is described as a triumvirate composed of Enver, minister of war; Talat, minister of the interior; and Cemal, minister of the navy. However, it was Enver and Talat who made the crucial decisions (especially after Cemal went off to Syria in early 1915). The grand vizier, Sait Halim Pasha, can only be described as a figurehead and CUP puppet.

The appointment of Enver to the critically important Ministry of War portfolio was a key ingredient in the transformation of the cabinet to a functionally militaristic government. In addition to his portfolio as minister of war (*Harbiye Nazırı*), Enver further consolidated his hold over the army by retaining the title of acting commander-in-chief (*Başkumandan Vekili*) and chief of the general staff (*Erkân-i Harbiye-i Umumiye Reisi*) as well. Holding these three offices concurrently enabled Enver to establish primacy over strategic direction and policy, supervise and direct the general staff, and to command the Ottoman army operationally. It was a staggering consolidation of power in the hands of a single person and no other individual in any country had similar authority.

Enver also moved very quickly to transform the Ottoman army into a more effective military force. General Orders Number 1, published on March 14, 1914, contained detailed guidance about how to train the army in modern combined arms tactics.[75] A month later, he accelerated and centralized the resurrection of the Ottoman army's formal training schools, which had been halted for mobilization during the First Balkan War. On May 24, 1914, Enver issued directives standardizing war diaries and the formats for combat and intelligence reports. Although he continued Ahmed İzzet's reconstruction of the army he established a contentious working relationship with Liman von Sanders of the German military mission.[76] One of the most important positions filled by a German, in the winter of 1914, was the assignment of Colonel Friedrich Bronsart von Schellendorf as the second assistant chief of the general staff. In this position, Bronsart von Schellendorf was tasked to rewrite the previous 12 versions of mobilization and war plans, which were now obsolete because of the loss of the empire's Balkan provinces. Under his direction, the Ottoman general staff replaced 12 plans, which were keyed to a variety of potential adversaries and combinations of enemies.[77] The new Primary Campaign Plan was published on April 7, 1914, and specified the potential enemy threats as Bulgaria, Greece, and Russia.[78] The plan was a single-purpose plan that concentrated the bulk of the Ottoman army in Thrace against the Greeks and the Bulgarians and along the Caucasian frontier against the Russians. The associated mobilization and concentration plans that supported the new campaign plan assembled and moved the army's divisions and corps from their home garrisons in the core areas to wartime assembly areas on the frontiers.[79] The plan stripped forces from the interior provinces and from Mesopotamia leaving those areas exposed to internal and external attacks.

The CUP's domestic focus in the spring and summer of 1914 revolved around the negotiation, the signing on February 8, 1914, and the implementation of the Armenian reform package, a major provision of which involved the arrival of the European inspectors. In accordance with the agreement, the government appointed 80 Ottoman civilian inspectors to posts in the affected provinces.[80] The actual agreement itself was between the Ottoman and Russian governments and the final compromise package left many Armenians very unhappy, including Zohrab and Garo. The Russians found five candidates to offer as inspectors and the Armenians, including Boghos Nubar, assisted in the final selection of two inspectors-general.[81] On April 14, the Ottoman government appointed Louis Westenenk, a Dutch chief administrator who had served in the Dutch East Indies, and Major Nicolai Hoff, a Norwegian army officer, as inspectors. Westenenk was assigned to the northern sector in Erzurum and Hoff was assigned to the Southern sector in Van with authority of Bitlis, Diyarbakir, and Elâzığ as well.[82]

The inspectors met in Paris, conducted meetings with Garo, Zavriev, and a representative of the patriarch, and arrived in Constantinople on May 3, 1914. There was some bickering over the contracts and the inspector's authorities between the Europeans and the government. Moreover, there were tensions between the Armenians themselves over who might be appointed to the inspector's staff.[83] Both inspectors returned to their home countries to finalize staff selections. Hoff managed to return in July and completed a tour of his assigned sector. By the time that Westenenk returned in the first week of August, however, military mobilization had begun and Talat requested that he remain in Constantinople, where Hoff shortly joined him. The outbreak of war ended the establishment of the reform package although both inspectors remained in the Ottoman Empire until the end of the year.

On June 28, 1914, Gavrilo Princip, a member of the secret Black Hand terrorist group, assassinated the Archduke Franz Ferdinand, heir to the Austro-Hungarian throne, and his wife Sophie in Sarajevo. The Black Hand was a secret Serbian nationalist committee determined to force the Austro-Hungarians to free the province of Bosnia-Herzegovina. The subsequent July Crisis ensued and Europe found itself spiraling toward war. The fascinating and failed diplomacy of this period is best told elsewhere, but it is important to note that the Ottoman Empire remained outside the crisis and was not allied with either side.[84] The Balkan Wars of 1912–1913 had battered the Ottoman economy, crippled its financial system, and all but destroyed its army. The defeated Ottomans were in no shape to go to war in 1914. Although the Ottoman Empire had strong diplomatic ties with Great Britain and strong economic ties with France, it can be argued that the Ottoman government was pro-German in 1914. It may also be argued that three wars of Russian expansion and continuous support for the Balkan Christian states created enormous enmity toward that country and helped drive the Ottomans into the arms of the Germans. Moreover, within the Ottoman government, a number of notable CUP members could be called Germanophiles, including Enver and Talat, and the army itself was strongly based on the physical and intellectual model of the German military system.

Ottoman foreign policy coalesced on August 2, 1914, when the government signed a secret treaty of alliance with Germany. Although much has been made of the treaty, when Germany declared war on Russia the previous day, it invalidated the terms of the treaty.[85] The treaty did not obligate the Ottoman Empire to enter the war, but it did serve to move the Ottoman closer toward cooperation with the Central Powers. Even so, the Ministry of War declared mobilization effective August 3, setting the empire on a course for war. Importantly, the treaty set the stage for the German battle cruiser *Goeben* and its cruiser consort *Breslau* to find refuge from their British pursuers on August 11, 1914. The arrival of these ships and their aggressive commander, German Vice Admiral Wilhelm Souchon, directly led the Ottoman Empire into the war on October 29.

THE TEŞKILAT-I MAHSUSA AND THE CUP, 1914

The SO operated under the authority of the Ministry of War from 1913 to 1918 and the proof of this is the actual organizational files of the Teşkilat-ı Mahsusa from that period, which are maintained today in the Turkish military archives in Ankara.[86] There were certainly similar predecessor institutions to the SO, such as Abdülhamid's Secret Service (*Hafive*) and Yıldız Palace Intelligence Service (*Yıldız İstihbarat Teşkilatı*), and these functions transferred to the ministry of security in 1909.[87] Stanford Shaw asserted that Enver ordered the files of these organizations burned in the garden of the Ministry of War in July 1914.[88] It is known for certain that, as soon as Enver became minister of war, he took full control over the SO and it is the view of the present author that Enver intended the SO to be used for instigating insurgency, conducting espionage in foreign countries, and counterespionage inside the Ottoman Empire.

It is important to remember that Enver himself had fought as a guerrilla with irregular tribesmen in Libya and, therefore, knew the inherent strengths and limitations of such undisciplined forces. And, through his own experiences as a guerrilla fighter in Libya and in conducting counterinsurgency operations as a conventional soldier in Macedonia, Enver also knew that a small number of regular officers might lead irregular forces and achieve effects far out of proportion to their actual numbers. Moreover, a number of officers from the Union of Patriotic Officers (*Fed'i Zabitan*), who fought in Libya, subsequently served in the SO in western Thrace. It is known today that Enver focused intensely on rebuilding the conventional Ottoman army in 1914, but it should not come as a surprise that he undertook creating a complementary unconventional capability as well.

Philip Stoddard, the most well-known Western historian specializing in the subject, called the SO "Enver Paşa's 'force special'" and compared its activities with the OSS of World War II.[89] Stoddard described the SO as a European-style organization that had "an administrative history, a headquarters, a secret budget, directors, assistant directors and field directors—in short, a complex overt and covert administrative apparatus, secret cells, and a system of recruitment, training and financing."[90] He viewed the SO as a response to the pressures of internal dissent and external encroachment. His conclusion about the organization was that it was "a most significant Unionist vehicle for dealing with the twin threats of Arab separatism and Western imperialism to the Ottoman state."[91]

There are a number of authors who assert that the Teşkilat-ı Mahsusa was formed either in 1913, or in 1914, and was designed with a dual-track architecture of command. For example, Raymond Kévorkian, writing in 2011, stated that "it would appear from late July 1914 this first Special Organization, controlled by Enver and the army had a second subsidiary structure."[92] Moreover, he asserted that this second and parallel secret structure was directly controlled by the CUP and commanded by Dr. Bahattin Şakir and Dr. Nazım for the explicit purpose of exterminating the Armenians.[93] No such files, copies of reports, or authentic documents supporting the idea of a second and secret SO exist anywhere in the world today.[94]

There is no actual evidence to support any claims of a dual-track SO architecture and the idea that it existed comes from the indictments and verdicts of 1919 military tribunals printed in the official Ottoman gazette *Takvimi Vekayi* as interpreted by Vahakn Dadrian.[95] The trials were something of a kangaroo court established by the Party of Freedom and Accord Party to appease the British occupiers and to suppress the surviving rump CUP. Neither the actual evidence itself nor the trial transcripts exist today.[96] At the tribunal proceedings, the accused were asked ten questions by the judges, one of which enquired about the relationship between the CUP and the SO.[97] All of the accused denied such an organic relationship but allowed that Midhat Pasha helped the SO recruit members early in the war.[98] The tribunal could not firmly establish any tangible relationship, but during the questioning of Yusuf Rıza Bey, commander of Batum and its environs, came to the conclusion that there was an open SO and another deeply secret SO. However, during the remainder of the interrogation, Yusuf Rıza Bey stated that the two-track system was all sensational and based on gossip.[99] The courts-martial did not attempt to deepen the enquiry to adduce probative evidence.

Correspondence in the SO files from its foundation, on November 30, 1913, through October 25, 1914, signed by Süleyman Askeri Bey, confirm that he was the head of the organization during that period.[100] Süleyman Askeri and Enver had fought the Italians together in Libya and Süleyman Askeri had been responsible for guerrilla operations in western Thrace. There was an SO central committee as well, consisting of Süleyman Askeri, Atıf Bey (Kamçıl), Aziz Bey, Dr. Bahattin Şakir Bey, and Dr. Nazım Bey, which operated out of the organization's headquarters on Nur-i Osmaniye Street in Constantinople.[101] Below the central committee, the SO staff was organized initially into four departments: the European Section headed by Arif Bey, the Caucasian Section headed by Captain Rıza Bey, the Africa and Trablusgrab (Africa and Libya) Section headed by Hüseyin Tosun Bey and Ali Başhampa Bey, and the Eastern Provinces Section headed by Dr. Şakir and Ruşeni Bey.[102] Some authors assert that two parallel SOs existed by the summer of 1914 and that Bahattin Şakir built and commanded a secret second SO in the eastern provinces.[103] However, as a matter of fact, there was no parallel organization and the unconventional and clandestine activities planned by the SO were already well under way at that time under the direct control of the Ministry of War.[104]

Convergent Ottoman and Armenian Activities, Summer 1914

The year 1914 brought renewed acts of violence against Armenians by Kurdish chieftains along the Russian border and around Bitlis. Some of the Kurdish tribes were in a state of near rebellion themselves and incited violence by conducting provocative acts and terrorism.[105] Although some improvements were made in the *jandarma*, which involved the assignment of European inspectors and trainers, the situation for many Armenians in the eastern provinces worsened. The tempo of the Armenian committees' efforts to acquire arms and rebuild military capacity increased as well. Fund-raising efforts in France, and in other countries, accelerated and the ARF was able to import significant numbers of weapons, particularly automatic Mauser pistols, which could be used as a carbine, into the villages around the city of Van.[106]

It is clear the both the Ottomans and Armenians considered the events of the dangerous summer of 1914 as a precursor to war. Although not at war itself, the Ottoman government began partial military mobilization on August 1, 1914, and full mobilization two days later.[107] This set the wheels into motion for activities that began to occur well before the actual outbreak of hostilities in November 1914. It is clear today that as early as the first week in August 1914, both the Teşkilat-ı Mahsusa and certain elements of the Armenian committees were actively planning wartime activities.

Over the spring of 1914, the ARF decided to convene its Eighth World Congress in the eastern Anatolian city of Erzurum. Rosdom coordinated the congress and it attracted a worldwide spectrum of the Armenian elite, including E. Agnouni (Western Bureau), Roupen Zartarian (Azadamard), Mardiros Haroutiunian (Eastern Bureau), Simon Vratsian (United States), Roupen Der Minisiajn (Muş), Mirhan Terlemezian (Van), Armag Okhigian (Bitlis), Hamazasb Srvantsdiants (Constantinople), Ardavazi Hamemian (Egypt), Avedis Injejikian (Beirut), and the well-known "social-revolutionary" Vahan Minakhorian.[108] The congress convened on August 8, 1914, and although World War I had not yet erupted, there was a clear understanding that war was imminent. There was a consensus to maintain the decisions of the previous congress and to continue in opposition to the CUP. Organizationally, the congress eliminated the ARF Eastern Bureau and transferred its regions to the Bureau of Armenia, which would also have a Constantinople section.[109] The most contentious episodes during the congress resulted from discussions about what the committees ought to do in the event of war between the Ottoman Empire and Russia. This split in opinion caused an actual rupture in the ARF itself.

The majority opinion within the ARF favored a continuation of the policy that citizens of each state were to fulfill their civic obligations to their state.[110] Unfortunately, it was the western Armenians who held to this view, while the eastern Armenians favored the idea that the Armenians must seize the opportunity provided by war to side with the Russians against the Ottomans. The minority who felt this way included Rosdom, Hovsep Arghutian, Armen Garo, and Simon Vratsian (Andranik, who was then in Bulgaria, would later align himself with this faction).[111] This group of eastern Armenians and the Armenian National Bureau in Tiblisi broke ranks with the ARF by deciding to support actively the Russians through military means.[112] At the end of the congress, a Commission of Nine remained in Erzurum to finalize administrative matters.[113]

It was at this time that Bahattin Şakir, Dr. Nazım, Omer Naji, and Hilmi Bey, who were all members of the SO, arrived in Erzurum.[114] "They had brought with them several scores of Caucasian and Persian agents. Their aim was to organize an anti-Russian propaganda campaign and struggle in the Caucasus and Northern Persia. Their program involved the total mobilization of the eastern provinces"[115] This observation tracks well with what Stoddard thought the purpose of the SO really was and the presence of such a group in Erzurum indicates that the Ottoman Ministry of War was actively planning unconventional activities against Russia prior to the July Crisis.[116] There were two initial meeting with the Armenians, at which the Ottomans enthusiastically assured them that war had been decided on, and that Germany was bound to win.[117] Furthermore, the SO delegation asserted that the Muslims of trans-Caucasia, the northern Caucasus and Persia and, in particular, the Georgians and the Azeris, were prepared and willing to rise in revolt against the Russians. They proposed that the Armenian committees join the Ottomans by using their cross-border connections to accomplish a general Armenian insurrection in Russian Caucasia.[118] Moreover, the SO wanted positive assurances that the Armenians would not rise in rebellion against the Ottoman Empire and they even suggested the Armenian committees organize their military units to aid in securing the Ottoman army's rear.[119] Perhaps the most surprising suggestion came when the SO delegation proposed the creation of an Armenian republic carved from lands occupied by the Russians after 1827 (which would obviously include Batum, Kars, and Tiblisi) with its center at Etchmiadzin in trade for the Armenian committees becoming "the spearhead of an anti-Russian revolution in the Caucasus, in case war broke out."[120]

The Committee of Nine found this entire affair alarming and tried to dissuade the Ottomans from going to war and from attempting such a scheme.[121] After some debate, they refused to cooperate with the SO delegation and rejected the offer. It is unclear today whether the SO delegation was acting alone or under the authority of either the Ministry of War or the CUP government. Importantly, the concrete suggestions of the SO do establish conclusively that at least some individuals in the Ministry of War, who were experienced in insurgency and irregular warfare, believed the Armenian committees had powerful military potential, both internally and externally, in Russian Caucasia. It must also be mentioned that, at the time, Ottoman intelligence firmly believed that the Eighth Congress's public proclamation that the Armenians should perform their civic obligations in their own countries was a subterfuge aimed at allaying the concerns of the government.[122]

In fact, the Ottoman intelligence services possessed information that some members of the congress actually intended, when war was declared with Russia, that Armenian soldiers in the Ottoman army would go over to the Russians with their arms and that the well-armed Armenian committees would form guerrilla bands and begin preplanned insurgent operations behind the Ottoman army's lines.[123] The Ottoman intelligence reports are contradicted by some of the memoirs of the congress' participants, but it is a fact that immediately after the conclusion of the Eighth Congress, a number of influential Armenians left Erzurum for Russia in order to form volunteer regiments to fight the Ottomans. In any case, it is clear that the Ottoman intelligence services and the SO felt that the ARF Eighth World Congress was a significant event in terms of viewing the Armenians as either powerful enemies within or as effective allies against Russia, respectively.

CONCLUSION

Ottoman defeat in the Balkan wars set the conditions for the return of the CUP to power, which in turn, created a climate of fear among the Armenian committees. Although, clearly, there were differing opinions among the Armenians about whether to endorse revolutionary activity or to loyally support the government, it is equally clear there was universal consensus that the committees ought to acquire more arms and remilitarize their base. The Ottoman intelligence services and the Ministry of the Interior knew this and tracked the committee's illegal activities. At the same time, within the Ottoman Ministry of War, Enver Pasha was rebuilding the conventional capability of the army as well as creating an unconventional capability that would give the empire parallel military capacities in the event of war. It must also be said that after the outbreak of World War I, the inner circle of the CUP committed itself and the Ottoman Empire to joining the war on the side of the Germans. In a convergence of what can only be termed as militaristic prewar mobilization both the Armenian committees and the Committee of Union and Progress prepared themselves for the coming of the war.

This page intentionally left blank

CHAPTER 6

Readiness for War

The Turkish Army is not a serious modern army...no sign of adap-tation to western thoughts and methods. The army is ill-officered, ill-commanded, and in rags.

—Colonel Sir Henry Wilson to CIGS,
Constantinople, 1913[1]

INTRODUCTION

The Ottoman Empire entered World War I in early November 1914, three months after hostilities erupted between the European alliances. The mobilization and concentration plans of the Ottoman general staff moved the entire mobile field army to the fringes of the empire in anticipation of combat operations against the Balkan states and Russia. The mobilization effort itself was slow and incomplete. As a result, the Ottoman Empire's deployed field armies were ill-equipped for the rigors of active campaigning, and yet were thrown recklessly by Enver into offensive operations.

The Ottoman general staff's appreciations of potential enemy threats in 1914 were conventional and oriented primarily on the Balkan states and Russia. The general staff's view was exclusively focused and fixed on neighboring external nation-states. As a result of these appreciations the six most well-trained and well-equipped army corps of the thirteen available in the army deployed to Thrace and western Anatolia to support a campaign plan oriented against Bulgaria and Greece. There they sat idle while weaker army corps were sent against the Russians and the British. Importantly, the Ottoman general staff's concentration plan deployed the army to the frontiers and totally denuded the interior provinces of combat forces. This left the Ottoman army very poorly positioned to respond to internal threats such as terrorism and insurgency.

THE OTTOMAN ARMY IN 1914

At the apex of the Ottoman military structure was the Ministry of War, which had been established in 1826 after the suppression of the Janissaries. Within the ministry there were offices for procurement, combat arms, peacetime military affairs, mobilization, and for promotions. From January 3, 1914, through October 4, 1918, Enver served as the minister of war (*Harbiye Nazırı*) as well as the army's chief of staff (*Genelkurmay Başkanı*). The titular commander-in-chief of the Ottoman military forces was the sultan. However, the minister of war fulfilled this role as well by commanding all forces under the title of acting commander-in-chief (*Başkomutan Vekili*).[2]

The Ottoman general staff was patterned on the German general staff. The general staff fulfilled the classic staff duties then in use by all major European powers and was staffed by trained general staff officers, who were selected and trained in staff procedures at the War Academy in Constantinople. After completion of the War Academy, graduates were advanced in grade over their nongraduate contemporaries and immediately assigned to key billets in the army. The staff was supervised by a chief of staff and was composed of various divisions, which specialized in a variety of military fields.[3] The most influential staff division was the First Division (or the Operations Division). There was also an Intelligence Division, and like the Germans, the Ottomans had separate divisions for railroads and communications, and a variety of additional staff divisions to administer and supply the army. To help the chief of the general staff, or to run the staff in the absence of the chief, in the summer of 1914 there were two assistant chiefs of staff, Colonel Bronsart von Schellendorf and Ottoman Staff Colonel Hafız Hakkı. In the absence of Enver, who was often engrossed in diplomacy, Bronsart von Schellendorf and Hafız Hakkı began immediate preparation of mobilization and war plans.

The active regular army force of 36 infantry divisions was divided up among the army corps of four numbered inspectorates, which became field armies upon mobilization.[4] Ottoman army corps comprised, on paper, three infantry divisions, an artillery regiment, and a cavalry regiment. The triangular Ottoman infantry divisions were composed of three infantry regiments and an artillery regiment. All of these forces were mobile and were capable of sustained combat operations. Reserve forces were distributed throughout the empire and constituted a reserve manpower and small unit pool, which would be used to augment and to bring the regular forces up to their wartime strength. There were four fortress area commands: the western border city of Edirne, the Dardanelles, the Bosphorus, and the eastern border city of Erzurum. A fifth fortress area was established at Çatalca during the First Balkan War to protect Constantinople, and although it was maintained in readiness, it was inactive for most of the war.

Among the remainder of Ottoman military strength were the Light Reserve Cavalry Regiments. These units were the successors to the irregular Hamidiye cavalry formations, which were disestablished on August 17, 1910.[5] These new regiments were formed into seven cavalry brigades and three independent regiments and were composed mainly of Kurds, some rural Ottomans, and an occasional Armenian. Conventional-style military discipline had always been a problem with these irregular units and the Ottoman General Staff was determined to end this with the establishment of the new reserve formations. After 1912, these brigades and regiments were consolidated into four reserve cavalry divisions placed in wartime under the control of the Third Army.

An important addition to the war time strength of the army was the paramilitary *jandarma*. Formed after the disastrous Russo-Ottoman War of 1878 under a French training mission, the *jandarma* was a powerful force. Its mission was primarily internal security and preservation of the borders. It was deployed throughout the empire. Most of the provinces had a mobile *jandarma* battalion, many large cities had mobile *jandarma* regiments, and there were substantial numbers of local static battalions as well. The mobile regiments contained 2,371 officers, 39,268 men, and 75,395 animals, but total *jandarma* strength including staffs, border guards, and support personnel may have exceeded a hundred thousand men. Under mobilization, control of this substantial force transferred from the Ministry of the Interior to the Ministry of War.

The strengths of the Ottoman army were primarily at the extreme ends of its rank structure.[6] At its highest echelons, its highly trained general staff officers were aggressive and well trained. At the bottom end, its rank and file were tough and capable of great feats of endurance, and were famous throughout Europe for their tenacity. However, it was in the middle ranks that the Ottoman army was the weakest. Unlike the British or the Germans, the Ottomans had no long service corps of professional noncommissioned officers (sergeants), and there was no tradition of such service in the Ottoman forces. In peacetime, this made the effective and rapid training of recruits difficult. In combat, as junior officers were killed, this lack of professional depth meant that there were no leaders to step up and assume leadership responsibilities. This particularly hurt the Ottoman army when engaged in the highly attritional battles, which characterized World War I.

War Plans

On April 7, 1914, Bronsart von Schellendorf completed the staff work on the Primary Campaign Plan for the Ottoman army, which would move the army from its peacetime garrisons in the interior, as shown in map 6.1, to the frontiers. This plan was prepared prior to the events of the summer of 1914, and reflected the then-current strategic situation. The Ottoman general staff estimated that Ottoman Empire would simultaneously oppose both a renewed Balkan coalition of Bulgaria and Greece, and Russia. The mobilization plans subsequently developed supported this intelligence estimate. The Primary Campaign Plan specified that three basic tasks were to be initially accomplished by the military. These tasks were: first, the army had to secure key terrain along the frontiers; second, the army had to bring a majority of forces to decisive points; and third, the army had to insure that enough time was available to complete mobilization and concentration. The plan specifically forbade units being committed piecemeal as had happened in the Balkan Wars of 1912–13.[7]

According to Bronsart von Schellendorf's plan, the Ottomans would field an army of observation on the Greek and Bulgarian frontiers. Although this army was prepared to fight, it would not act provocatively, nor would it engage in offensive operations. In the east against Russia, the Ottomans would attempt to gain the tactical initiative by conducting limited attacks should favorable operational conditions exist in Caucasia. The plan recognized the supreme strategic importance of Constantinople and the Ottoman Straits by prioritizing the establishment of the Çatalca Fortified Zone, covered by the fortress city of Edirne and an army of observation.[8] Additional forces from Syria and Mesopotamia were earmarked for transfer to the Ottoman Thrace to support this deployment. The principal weaknesses of the plan were perennial shortfalls in artillery and technical units. In order to increase combat potential against the Russians, the Ottomans increased their *jandarma* strength in the east and, additionally, planned to mobilize their entire reserve cavalry force of four divisions there, as well.

After the calamitous events of July 1914, the Ottoman Empire found itself bound to Germany in a Secret Treaty signed on August 2, 1914.[9] She then found herself tied to neighboring Bulgaria in a second secret treaty. These two treaties essentially negated the strategic principles that Bronsart von Schellendorf had formulated in the spring by eliminating Bulgaria and potentially adding the Entente powers as opponents. Responding to these rapidly changing conditions,

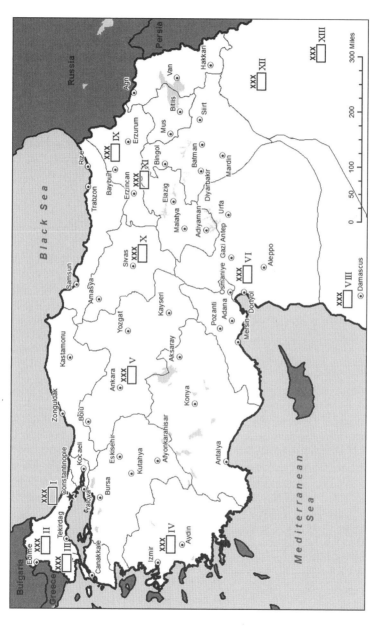

Map 6.1   Locations of Ottoman army corps in August 1914.

Bronsart von Schellendorf began to adapt the Primary Campaign Plan on August 20, 1914. Certainly the possibility of a direct attack on Ottoman Thrace had receded with the signing of a Secret Treaty of Alliance with Bulgaria. However, Ottoman forces would continue to concentrate in Thrace, but with an eye toward conducting possible operations with the Bulgarians against either the Romanians or the Serbs.

Although Russia maintained strong forces on the Caucasian front, the Ottomans thought that they would not be inclined to attack, since Russia was already heavily engaged against Germany and Austria-Hungary. As a result, the idea of a large-scale Ottoman offensive using the Ottoman Third Army against the Russians in Caucasia began to be seen as a viable option, in spite of the deplorable logistical and communications difficulties involved. Since eventual hostilities against Great Britain were likely, the Ottomans also began to consider the possibility of an offensive against Egypt and the Suez Canal. With the continuing security of a friendly Bulgaria and with the increasing likelihood of a neutral Greece, staff work and estimates continued supporting these twin offensives.

On September 6, 1914, the Primary Campaign Plan was formally and significantly changed.[10] In Syria, the Fourth Army was ordered to plan an attack on the Suez Canal with forces from the VIII and the XII Corps. In the absence of a Russian attack, the Third Army was ordered to plan for offensive operations toward Ardahan and Batum. Furthermore, it was decided that a wing of the Third Army would maneuver from a base formed by the fortress city of Erzurum and crush Russian forces in the area of Sarıkamış. The Ottoman forces remaining in Mesopotamia would guard Basra and also menace Afghanistan and India. In addition to the planned attack on Egypt, the VII Corps in Yemen would observe and threaten Aden.

Although the Ottoman Empire was not immediately a belligerent in World War I, the events of late July and early August 1914 were sufficient to cause the Ottoman Empire to mobilize. By August 1, 1914, the major European powers and several minor powers were mobilizing their forces for war. Ottoman Empire followed suit by issuing partial mobilization instructions to the I Corps, in Thrace, and to the VII Corps, in Arabia. On Friday afternoon, August 2, the Ottoman general staff ordered general mobilization effective from 9:00 AM that day. For planning purposes, the following day, August 3, would be the first "numbered" day in the mobilization schedule. In theory, the army could be mobilized in about 22 days; however, the general staff expected that delays and mismanagement would extend the mobilization window to about 40–45 days.[11] In addition to the missing regiments, battalions, and companies in the cadre strength Ottoman divisions, the peacetime army had significant shortfalls in cavalry, communications, field bakery, and combat engineer detachments. Ottoman divisions had no munitions reserves or depots. At corps level, severe shortages existed in animal depots, bakery detachments, telegraph detachments, and field hospitals. Only one corps had its allotted howitzer battalion, only one corps had a full strength telegraph battalion, and only one corps had its assigned cavalry regiment.[12] Crippling shortages of all kinds characterized the logistical capability of the Ottoman Army to carry out mobilization. Thus, instead of delivering capable forces with timetable precision to battle positions on the frontier, the Ottomans simply lurched forward trying only to assemble major forces in army areas. The offensives sought by Enver and Bronsart von Schellendorf were delayed indefinitely until the major commanders in the field reported their readiness.

By the middle of September, or over 45 days into mobilization, the army was still not prepared for war. The I Corps reported that it was not ready and had severe shortages of artillery horses and transport. In addition, the reserve manpower the corps had received would not be ready "for a long time." The II Corps was short 2,000 cavalry and had never received its infantry depot battalion. The III Corps was short uniforms, did not have enough soldiers and officers, and also had never received its infantry depot battalion. The IV Corps had similar shortages.[13] These four army corps were stationed in the western and most highly developed parts of the empire.

The Third Army's three army corps, located in eastern Ottoman Empire and unserviced by railroads, were in even worse shape. The IX Corps was missing officers and mountain equipment. It was also missing 1,823 horses, 1,324 oxen, uniforms, and equipment. The X Corps was missing 229 horses and 130 wagons, 1,552 oxen and 779 ox-carts, and 448 camels. The Fortified Zone of Erzurum was short 150 infantry, 157 artillery, and 31 combat engineer officers. The fortress was short 9,000 rifles and for its 80-mm Krupp artillery, it was short 2,896 fuses and 14,728 shrapnel shells. The situation for its critical 120-mm artillery was in a similar state and fuse and shrapnel shortages were 444 and 8,700, respectively. The fortress was short 28,000 uniforms.[14] This was the army that Enver would order to go over to a winter offensive in December 1914.

Critical shortages were even worse in units that were farther away from the Anatolian heartland, and the units in Mesopotamia, Syria, and Yemen suffered accordingly. While the general staff received reports outlining these shortages, there was little it could do to alleviate the problem. There were simply no war reserves, beyond limited munitions stocks, available to fall back on. In fighting the Balkan Wars of 1912 and 1913, the Ottoman Empire had used up what little reserves it possessed, and in the intervening year, the nearly bankrupt empire was unable even to restock partially its war reserve of military equipment. In due time, the army reported itself mobilized. The actual time required to mobilize the corps exceeded even the most pessimistic predictions with mobilization lasting as long as two months in the army corps stationed in the distant provinces of Mesopotamia and Yemen.[15]

THE READINESS OF THE OTTOMAN ARMY

In terms of human resources, the general staff believed that the empire had a mobilization potential of about 2 million men.[16] However, this ambitious figure was, in fact, never achieved during the course of the war. In the summer of 1914, the classes of 1893 and 1894 (each age cohort was about 90,000 men) had been called to the colors and the army enjoyed a peacetime operating strength of about 200,000 men and 8,000 officers. Unlike other European powers, the Ottoman Empire did not employ first-line formations in peacetime at war establishment, preferring instead to field a higher number of reduced establishment formations. This policy was systematically carried out by reducing all units below division level; every Ottoman infantry regiment was short a battalion, and every battalion was short a company. The average strength of Ottoman infantry divisions, in the summer of 1914, was 4,000 men out of a war establishment of 10,000 personnel. In order to bring the field army to war establishment the Ottoman army required a total of 477,868 men and 12,469 officers to completely fill out its divisions. This use of a reduced establishment or cadre structure (a lean and understrength organizational framework designed to be heavily augmented) was intentional and reflected a deliberate decision taken by the army after the Balkan Wars. There were no reserve artillery or reserve technical formations. In any case, the general staff believed that approximately 1,000,000 men and 210,000 animals were easily available for recall and that, immediately upon full mobilization, the mobile field army would have an effective strength of 460,000 men, 14,500 officers, and 160,000 animals.[17] To this must be added the heavily armed and trained *jandarma* of 42,000 men (25,000 gendarmes, 12,000 frontier guards, and 6,000 mule-mobile troops).[18] Altogether, the Ottoman army planned to field about 500,000 men in mobile operational units, the remainder serving in fortress garrisons, coastal defenses, and in servicing the lines of communications and transportation.

In material terms, the army was ill-equipped to fight a modern war. Most divisions had 21 or fewer of the 75-mm field guns they were authorized out of an establishment of 36 pieces. This artillery force was a mixed bag of French Schneider, German Krupp, and Austro-Hungarian Skoda pieces[19] and numbered about 900 field pieces. At corps level, most of the 105-mm howitzers, 12 in number, required for the three batteries of corps artillery were available. Overall, the army needed 280 field artillery pieces to bring itself up to war establishment. Additionally, in the fortresses of Edirne, Erzurum, the Bosporus and Gallipoli, and Çatalca, there were an additional 900 fixed or semifixed coastal and fortress artillery pieces, which were ill-placed for immediate use. The machine gun situation was worse. Each Ottoman infantry regiment was authorized four machine guns. Some regiments were short and the army needed 200 to equip the regimental force to standard. At battalion and company level, there simply were no machine guns and the army estimated that it needed 20,000 more to fill all requirements. At 1,500,000 in hand, rifles were a less critical shortage but the army still needed 200,000.[20] Ammunition stockage was low and the Ottomans were unable to meet anticipated wartime demands. There were 150 cartridges available per rifleman, a further 190 available in corps depots, and for the entire army there were 200 million cartridges in reserve. For the Ottoman artillery, there were about 588 shells available per gun; the European standard, at the time, was 1,500 per artillery piece.

In service support, the Ottoman army suffered terribly. Each division was authorized a field medical unit, and each corps was authorized four field hospitals; however, these were never filled at established strengths. This deficiency was compounded by chronic shortages of doctors, medicines, and medical supplies. The total Ottoman hospital capacity was 37,000 beds, of which 14,000 were located in the city of Constantinople. Transportation was a critical bottleneck; especially short were supply wagons and draft animals. Motorization and aviation were almost nonexistent in the army. Mobilization planning was based on peacetime conscription, which provided a flow of trained individuals from the active army into the reserve forces. Active service in the peacetime Ottoman army was for a period of two years for the infantry and three for the artillery and technical services.[21] Likewise, animals served for a period of four years and, in turn, were returned to civilian use carrying a lifelong obligation for national service. Non-Muslims had previously been excluded from military service but by the Balkan

Wars were conscripted to the colors as well. The extremely heavy losses in trained leaders suffered during the Balkan Wars dramatically affected the ability of the forces to train replacements adequately.

All men were liable for military service and were drafted as a group according to their chronological age as a class or cohort. This usually occurred annually in the late summer. Liability for service began on March 1 in the year when a man turned 20 and ended 25 years later. The Ottoman military was divided into an active force (*Nizamıye*), a reserve force (*Ihtiyat*), and a territorial force (*Müstahfız*). The two youngest classes provided the manpower for the active army, the next sixteen classes provided the trained manpower for the reserve, and the oldest seven classes comprised the territorial forces.[22] The previous reserve system of the *Redif* (organized reserve units), begun in 1886, was discontinued in 1913. Some reservists and territorials were organized into units of battalion size or smaller and had local depots designated as mobilization stations; however, after 1913, almost all were assigned individual replacements. The Ottoman Empire was not wedded to the idea of military units reflecting local character (as were the British or German armies), but in 1914, Ottoman army units were mainly composed of locally recruited men. This changed as the war progressed, and men were sent as individuals or in levies to whatever units needed them the most.

Unlike all other major European powers, the Ottoman Empire did not have a large-unit reserve system, which could field intact reserve corps composed of reserve divisions.[23] The use of permanently established reserve infantry divisions stationed in major cities had been discontinued in 1913 with the end of the Balkan Wars. Consequently, there was no major increase in the raw number of formations available to the Ottoman Army immediately upon mobilization. There were several exceptions, those being the XII Corps (Independent), the 38th Infantry Division (Independent), and 1st, 2nd, 3rd, and 4th Reserve Cavalry Divisions. Later in the war, as the Ottomans needed more combat infantry formations, they simply mobilized more regular divisions. The identification of Ottoman divisions mobilized after August 1914 as "reserve divisions" is erroneous. Likewise, the identification of some wartime Ottoman divisions as "bis" or paired divisions by British intelligence was in error. The probable culprit in both cases was likely to have been a misunderstanding of how the *Redif* changed in 1913.

There was also a residual volunteer system, called the *Gönüllü Sistemi*, which encouraged men to volunteer to fight together. While the last major use of this system was during the Russo-Ottoman War, it remained in existence and there was some use of it in the Caucasus and in Thrace. However, the *Gönüllü Sistemi* was used mainly in attempts to recruit from the many groups of Muslim refugees harbored in the empire. These Muslim volunteer groups would see action in the Sinai, in Persia, and in the Caucasus.

Between July 1913 and August 1914, the Ottoman Army was undergoing an enormous reorganization and reconstruction effort as a result of the devastating losses suffered in the Balkan Wars. Compounding this huge task was Enver's determination to rid the army of older and less active officers, which he felt were an obstruction to modernization. Over 1,100 officers were involuntarily retired during this period.[24] The scale of this effort to rebuild the army must be explained in some detail because this reorganization of the Ottoman forces provides the basis for understanding both the offensive failures of 1914 and the defensive successes of 1915.

In the Balkan wars of 1912 and 1913, most of the Ottoman First and Second Armies were destroyed or broken apart. The Ottoman army lost 14 infantry divisions out of a beginning total of 43 and the corps-sized fortress garrison of Adrianople was also lost.[25] Additionally, 22 Ottoman army reserve divisions were destroyed or surrendered as well. Eight regular infantry divisions and 15 newly mobilized infantry divisions of reservists and territorials had been deployed to European Ottoman Thrace to serve in the freshly formed Çatalca and Gallipoli Armies. Several infantry divisions and a corps headquarters had been dissolved to provide replacements. Only six of the infantry divisions of the pre-Balkan War regular Ottoman army were spared the trauma of combat. In another context, 90 percent of Ottoman infantry divisions mobilized participated in the Balkan Wars. Casualties from the wars exceeded 250,000 men.[26] This was a military disaster of unprecedented magnitude for the empire, which all but destroyed the regular Ottoman army as an effective fighting force.

At the conclusion of the Balkan Wars, the condition of the Ottoman army demanded attention. Complete armies had been shattered, corps had been deliberately dissolved, and there were huge disparities in the fighting strengths of infantry divisions. There was a large number of ad hoc reserve divisional formations (named after their city of origin) composed of older reservists and territorials that had been mobilized to replace the lost regular formations. Training was at a standstill, as was weapons procurement. Finally, and not the least worrisome, almost the entire Ottoman field army was deployed in Ottoman Thrace. These strategic and operational imperatives forced the Ottoman Empire immediately to engage itself in a massive military reorganization effort in the aftermath of the Balkan Wars.

The reorganization of Ottoman forces in 1914 was comprehensive, and was designed to return the army back into its pre-Balkan War garrison locations, and also to rebuild the divisional and corps base of the army. This was a gigantic undertaking and was incomplete on the eve of World War I. In the reconstituted First Army, only the III Corps survived the war intact and retained its original organic pre-Balkan War divisions. The II Corps and I Corps lost a division each and each was rebuilding a new division. It is significant, and no surprise, that the combat hardened and intact III Corps was selected to defend the strategic Gallipoli Peninsula in 1915. Facing the Russians in Caucasia, of the Third Army's nine infantry divisions, three were being rebuilt from scratch and four were deployed there from Thrace that year. This hastily assembled and cobbled-together army was hurled against the Russians in December 1914, with predictably disastrous results. The Second Army was reconstituted in Syria and Palestine and was rebuilding two divisions while absorbing two more that were redeployed from Thrace. Altogether, 14 of 36 Ottoman infantry divisions organized in August 1914 were in the process of being entirely rebuilt and 8 divisions of the 36 had conducted a major redeployment from combat zones within the year. The overall effectiveness of these 22 new or redeployed infantry divisions was low and would inevitably take time to remedy. However, events overcame preparation time and 12 of these divisions were involved in the early Ottoman offensive disasters of 1914–15. Reciprocally, the single organizationally intact corps—the III Corps with its organic 7th, 8th, and 9th Infantry Divisions—successfully defended the Gallipoli Peninsula in the spring of 1915. It could be argued that defeat in the Balkan Wars, and subsequent Ottoman reconstitution and restationing efforts, set the stage for Ottoman success or failure in the initial phases of World War I.

MOBILIZATION

Immediately after the signing of the Secret Treaty of Alliance with Germany, the Ottoman leadership took several important diplomatic decisions, the most important of which were the decisions of August 6 and 9, which established the direction of Ottoman foreign policy.[27] Meanwhile, in the military arena, Enver ordered mobilization on August 2, 1914. The important point about this was that instead of ordering a limited mobilization, which supported the diplomatic framework envisioned by Sait Halim, Enver ordered general mobilization. This measure was widely misinterpreted by the Entente as overtly hostile to allied interests.

Unlike the 12 complicated mobilization plans of 1912, the war-weary and overtaxed Ottoman general staff had but one mobilization plan in the summer of 1914. Bronsart von Schellendorff approved the staffing of this single plan on June 7, 1914.[28] The plan recognized the supreme strategic importance of the Ottoman Straits and Constantinople and, once again, brought the bulk of the regular army back into European Ottoman Thrace. Under the plan, of thirteen regular army corps in the Ottoman Army, five deployed directly to either Thrace or the Marmara region. A further army corps went to Smyrna in western Anatolia. Three army corps deployed against the Russians, and the remaining three went to Mesopotamia, Palestine, and Yemen, respectively. None of the corps received offensive missions and, like the 1912 plans, all were ordered only to defend Ottoman territory.

Even though the weight of the army appeared to threaten Bulgaria, the Ottoman general staff had no plans for cross-border operations or offensive operations oriented toward the west. This mystified the Entente attaches in Constantinople, who had observed the mobilization of 1912 and, moreover, confused reports emanated from the allied embassies throughout the Balkans. The British thought that the Ottomans were preparing to attack Russia on the Asiatic frontier, while trying to ally themselves with Bulgaria for an attack on Serbia.[29]

Because of their disastrous experiences with the mobilization plan of 1912, the Ottoman general staff realized that the underdeveloped railroads and lines of communications could not support timetable-based deployment schemes. As a result, completion of mobilization schedules became very problematic. It made no sense, for example, to plan on the VI Corps (which deployed from Aleppo to San Stefano) being ready to assume an operational role at the thirtieth day of mobilization, if substantial elements on the corps were still on the road. As a result, the Ottomans now viewed mobilization as event-driven rather than timetable-driven. Units were not assumed to arrive at the scheduled times and were only counted in the line when physically reported as being ready. Bronsart von Schellendorff simply had no real idea of exactly when Ottoman units would arrive from their peacetime mobilization stations at their wartime operational positions. Consequently, the military began to push the diplomats for breathing time during which the slowly evolving mobilization plan could sort itself out.

Compounding these problems was the fact that the Ottoman army was engaged in a large unit reconstitution program that was rebuilding the 12 divisions and the 3 corps headquarters lost during the First and Second Balkan Wars. This was further reason to delay the entry into the war for as long as possible. Because of all of these difficulties, mobilization proceeded slowly and was not complete until well into early November 1914. Even when completed, the mobilization plan of the Ottoman Army resulted in the least concentrated deployment scheme of any of the major combatants.

Within the Entente capitols, there were mixed feelings about the direction in which the Ottoman Empire was headed. The British felt that the alliance with Germany and the presence of a German naval squadron in Constantinople made dialogue with Ottoman Empire impossible. The Russians also believed that the Ottoman Empire was not serious about a renewal of constructive dialogue. France almost ignored the Ottoman question and concentrated her efforts on bringing Greece into the war on the side of the allies. Winston Churchill felt that, of all the intelligence pouring into Whitehall, the British were the most uninformed about the situation in the Ottoman Empire.[30]

As the months progressed, Bronsart von Schellendorff received minor instructions to fine-tune the developing mobilization plan. On September 4, 1914, Enver ordered him to adjust the mobilization and deployment plan to accommodate a potentially hostile Greece.[31] Additionally, mobilization of many Ottoman army corps dragged on for 25–40 days, which was well beyond projections and making detailed planning difficult. By the middle of October 1914, Bronsart von Schellendorf received further instructions to begin planning for a strategic attack aimed at seizing the Suez Canal. Unfortunately, the single-use mobilization plan of June 1914 had delivered the most proficient fighting divisions of the army to European Ottoman Thrace. In retrospect, the military deployment and concentration of forces available to the Ottoman Empire did not align well with the overall diplomatic situation, nor was the defensive nature of the empire's mobilization clearly understood by the allies. Thus, as either a useful tool for the diplomats or as an unsheathed sword for the generals, the Ottoman army's mobilization failed to meet the needs of the empire.

The means for the Ottoman Empire's entry into the war lay with the weak and ineffective command relationship between Vice Admiral Wilhelm Souchon, commander of the German squadron, and the Ottomans. Throughout early October 1914, Sait Halim continued to press for Ottoman neutrality, and for a time, Talat seemed to be with him. Enver, operating almost unsupported, secured several million Ottoman pounds in gold from Berlin and continued to plan the opening move, which was designed to force the Ottoman Empire into the war.[32] By late October 1914, however, Talat had swung back to Enver's interventionist clique. In spite of the agreed-upon prohibitions, Souchon took his heavily flagged and bedecked ships out into the Black Sea again. Unfortunately for the empire, Sait Halim failed to act decisively to put an end to such excursions. Seizing this chance to overturn the prohibition, Enver issued instructions on October 25 to Vice Admiral Souchon authorizing him to conduct maneuvers in the Black Sea and to attack the Russian fleet "if a suitable opportunity presented itself."[33] Importantly, Enver's orders called for an incident at sea and were based on the assumption that the Russians would rise to the bait of German ships steaming in the Black Sea. This abrogation of authority to Vice Admiral Souchon was the proximate cause of the Black Sea raids, which brought the Ottoman Empire directly into the war.

On October 26, 1914, the Ottoman navy received orders directing preparations for a reconnaissance exercise and was also provided with sealed orders from Souchon.[34] The fleet weighed anchor and departed Hyderpaşa the next day for its concentration areas. On October 28, 1914, the Ottoman fleet reorganized for combat by splitting itself into four task forces steaming for separate targets along the Russian coast. Vice Admiral Souchon with his flagship the ex-SMS *Goeben* and several Ottoman destroyers opened fire on shore batteries at Sevastapol at dawn on October 29, 1914. Other Ottoman naval task forces bombarded Feodosia, Novorossiysk, and Yalta.[35] As a result of these attacks, the allies severed relations with the Ottoman Empire and delivered ultimatums. Several days later, on November 2, 1914, Russia declared war on the Ottoman Empire. Outfoxed by Enver and facing an aroused Entente, Sait Halim was overcome by events as Britain, and France, in turn, declared war against the Ottoman Empire.

Thus, in the course of a three-month period, the Ottoman Empire drifted from a position of neutrality to that of full-fledged belligerence. With the exception of its partially mobilized armies, the empire was no more prepared to wage modern war than it was when the archduke was gunned down in Sarajevo. In a case unique among the major powers, the Ottomans had no definite or finely tuned war aims, which reflected national policy objectives. The Ottomans did not covet the return of lost provinces (with the minor exception of some small Greek islands), nor did they expect to receive new lands. While they hoped for some financial remuneration and relief, this was not, of itself, a rational justification for going to war. The Ottomans simply tried to walk a neutral path for as long as they could and, with the exception of Enver, the Ottoman Empire went unwillingly to war.

THE CONCENTRATION OF FORCES

To support the Primary Campaign Plan, the Ottoman general staff wrote a Concentration Plan. It is important to distinguish this plan from the Mobilization Plan, which dealt with force generation and force readiness. The purpose of the Concentration Plan was to task organize the command and control of the Ottoman army and to position it to execute the Primary Campaign Plan.[36] In the planning endeavors of the more sophisticated armies of the major powers, these plans tended to merge into one nearly simultaneous effort. However, in the poorly developed Ottoman Empire, these plans were three distinct procedures separated in time, scope, and intent.

After mobilization, the Concentration Plan shifted major forces to European Ottoman Thrace for the protection of the Ottoman Straits, to Caucasia for the Third Army's winter offensive, and to Palestine for the attack on the Suez Canal. The Second Army Headquarters deployed with the VI Corps to Constantinople and assumed responsibility for the defense of the Çatalca Fortified Zone and the Bosporus Straits. The V Corps was also deployed north from Izmir (Smyrna) and was reassigned to the Second Army as well. The XIII Corps was slated to reinforce the Third Army and deployed northward from Mesopotamia. All of the reserve cavalry divisions, and the mobile Van Jandarma Division, were also assigned to the Third Army.

For the offensive into Egypt, a new Fourth Army Headquarters was formed in Damascus on September 6, 1914, and the XII Corps transferred to it from Baghdad for the attack. As economy of force measures to support these deployments, both Mesopotamia and the Smyrna region were literally stripped of regular corps and divisions and were converted into Area Commands. The Concentration Plan put a severe strain on the already overtaxed railway system and, like the Mobilization Plan, huge delays unavoidably afflicted the execution of the Concentration Plan. In particular, the XIII Corps, traveling by barge up the Tigris and Euphrates Rivers and then foot marching into the Anatolian hinterland, failed to arrive in the Third Army area in time to participate in the winter offensive.

How realistic and how effective were the Ottoman plans and the subsequent execution of those plans? The Ottoman general staff only had a single year to adapt itself to the loss of Ottoman Empire-in-Europe and to a reconfigured, and possibly more threatening, strategic situation. The former plans of 1912, a dozen in all, were hopelessly outdated and were replaced by a single mobilization plan. While this did not speed up mobilization, it certainly streamlined the planning parameters and made subsequent staff work much easier. This would seem to have been a sound decision. Any further assessment of the effectiveness of the Ottoman Mobilization and Concentration Plans must return to the Primary Campaign Plan, since that document was the engine of the deployment scheme. Bronsart von Schellendorf's Primary Campaign Plan delivered the preponderance of Ottoman fighting strength to Thrace. Given the uncertainties of the Balkan situation in April 1914, in August 1914, and even as late as November 1914, this was a prudent strategic decision.

It must also be remembered that the loss of Edirne, and the near loss of the Çatalca Line and Constantinople in 1913, was branded into the minds of the Ottoman officer corps. This legacy and burden drove all strategic decisions for the Ottoman general staff in 1914.[37] While the Ottoman Empire could trade space for time in all other theaters, she had no strategic margin for retreat in Thrace. Any possible campaign plan had to address this imperative before considering anything else. Although the deployment of six out of thirteen active corps to sit idle in Thrace and western Anatolia seems conservative beyond belief, it reflected the absolute necessity to defend, at all costs, the strategic center of gravity of the Ottoman Empire.

Bronsart von Schellendorf's final variant of the Primary Campaign Plan orchestrated simultaneous offensives on two widely separated fronts. For the opening offensives, only three Ottoman corps attacked in Caucasia and only a single corps attacked in the Sinai. No other belligerent contemplated conducting operational offensives with such weak forces. The only other power even attempting such dispersed operations as its opening campaign strategy was Austria-Hungary, which suffered similar disasters at the hands of the Serbs and the Russians. It is questionable whether the Ottoman Empire possessed the military resources to conduct a single main effort offensive in late 1914, and it is beyond doubt that the Ottoman Empire could not reasonably expect success from two weakly resourced offensives, which were not mutually supporting.

The Concentration Plan itself seemed to be fairly simple in transferring the centrally positioned corps, which were located in the interior of Anatolia, in Syria, and in upper Mesopotamia, to concentration positions on the frontiers. However, again movements were delayed and the plan proved slower to execute than expected. The IV, V, and VI Corps traveled over separate routes to Thrace but were still arriving in December 1914. The routes taken by the XII Corps actually overlapped, and conflicted with, the routes taken by the XIII Corps. This affected the deployment of the XIII Corps and delayed its deployment to the Caucasus for the Third Army's winter offensive. These slow movements presaged future problems with Ottoman Empire's inadequate infrastructure and weak transportation system.

Becoming convinced that the Ottomans would enter the war sooner or later against them, the British and the Russians used the time generated by the slow Ottoman concentration to prepare measures against them. Both allied countries prepared to take the offensive immediately upon commencement of hostilities and both countries proved more capable than the Ottomans in their ability to position and to direct forces for immediate use. On October 31, 1914, several days prior to the official start of hostilities, Russian army units began cross-border operations near Doğubeyazit and on the same day, Russian ambassador Giers departed Constantinople. British operations began the following day in the Persian Gulf with the landing of troops near Fao and in the Mediterranean with a Royal Navy bombardment of Gaza. A major Russian attack on the Third Army's defensive lines at Köprüköy began on November 5 and two days later major British forces landed at Basra in Mesopotamia. By November 19, 1914, the Ottomans had lost Basra and the Russians began larger operations aimed against Saray and Van. It is evident that the allies considered a hostile Ottoman Empire to be a likely outcome of the complex diplomatic maneuvering of the fall of 1914 and prepared accordingly.

Thus, the time gained by delaying the entry of the Ottoman Empire into the war still had not been sufficient to insure that the Ottoman Empire would gain the initiative. As late as December 5, Enver was sending his final attack order to the Third Army and, on the next day, he offered command of that army to General Otto Liman von Sanders. Liman von Sanders, a trained general staff officer himself, wisely refused, thereby rendering his informal opinion on the potential success of Enver's offensive plans in Caucasia. Instead of remaining in the capital to direct the overall coordination of the Ottoman Empire's widely scattered war fronts, now numbering three in December 1914, Enver decided to travel to the Third Army's area of operations to personally supervise operations there. In any case, by mid-December 1914, partially mobilized forces, with which to begin offensive operations, were in position in the Caucasus. Longer distances and the change in Ottoman headquarters arrangement from the Second Army to the Fourth Army in Syria delayed the Sinai offensive for another two weeks.

Conclusion

In 1914, the Ottomans attempted to seize the strategic initiative with offensives in the Caucasus and in the Sinai with the limited forces in place under an outdated campaign plan. In their initial attacks, the Ottomans used 9 infantry divisions in the Caucasus and parts of 3 infantry divisions in the Sinai, thereby committing only 12 of their 36 infantry divisions to combat. Additionally, many of these were newly raised infantry divisions with very limited experience. This was serious mistake but one that was not easily overcome given the realities of the Concentration Plan.

Certainly, the most preventable and serious mistake that the Ottomans made in the early days of the war was the failure to provide an adequate defensive force in Mesopotamia. The decision to leave the Shatt al Arab poorly guarded opened the door for a British presence in Mesopotamia, which lasted the entire war. Although the British ultimately sent almost double the number of men that the Ottomans had in that theater, this was a dangerous situation, which created competing strategic priorities for the empire for the rest of the war. While there remained a huge number of Ottoman divisions in Thrace, there was a growing body of reports from Egypt that the British were bent on seizing the Dardanelles. Therefore, the First and Second Armies were maintained at nearly full strength and were retained in the vicinity of Constantinople. This decision would prove to be fortuitous in the coming spring of 1915.

In assessing the operational effectiveness of the Ottoman operational plans, the dispersion of Ottoman strength appeared as the most critical determinant of failure. In attempting to conduct simultaneous offensives on widely separated fronts, the Ottoman general staff failed to achieve a decisive concentration of strength in any single theater. The poor condition of the Ottoman lines of communications further complicated this dispersion and the Ottomans were unable to take full advantage of their favorable geographic interior position. As a result, the Ottoman general staff was left with inconclusive results on three active fronts.

As this chapter has demonstrated the Ottoman war plans, both prewar and as adapted by contingencies, were based on conventional appreciations of the military situation vis-à-vis the empire's neighbors and the European powers. It is a fact that Enver and Bronsart von Schellendorf moved the entire mobile combat power of the Ottoman army to concentration areas on the fringes and borders of the empire. These deployments left no combat formations in the interior of the empire's heartland, except for recruit training regiments and depots and a handful of formations traveling en route to the fronts. Every bit of the Ottoman army's combat power was focused outward toward external enemies. It is evident that through early 1915, the Ottoman general staff's planning processes did not consider the likelihood of internal insurgency to be a serious possibility. As a result the empire's military planners were almost completely unready when the "enemy within" metastasized in the spring of 1915.

CHAPTER 7

Irregular War in Caucasia and in the Levant

It is not in the nature of things for Turkey to proceed on an even and progressive path; debts, massacres, rebellions, and revolutions will provoke crises in the future as in the past, and once again when the moment is ripe the question of partition will arise.

—Report of the Committee in Asiatic Turkey,
April 8, 1915[1]

INTRODUCTION

The newly created Ottoman irregular forces, and the revived and remilitarized Armenian committees, saw advantages in making preparations for operations in eastern Anatolia and the Caucasus. Both Ottomans and Armenians recognized that the coming of war would place the Ottoman Empire in a position of grave weakness thereby creating a window of opportunity for a successful insurrection by the Armenian committees. In August 1914, the Armenian committees convened the Eighth World Congress in Erzurum, which the Ottomans viewed as a threshold event that presaged an Armenian insurrection in eastern Anatolia. While there is no question that some members of the Armenian committees wanted to rebel against the Ottomans, it is equally true that other committeemen were opposed to such action. As the Ottoman army deployed to its wartime concentration areas along the frontiers in the fall of 1914, a power vacuum appeared in the fabric of Ottoman control of eastern Anatolia. This encouraged members of the Armenian committees, as well as the Ottoman SO, to commence irregular war before hostilities formally began.

There is no "smoking gun" evidence proving that the key leaders of the Armenian committees sat down somewhere and decided to raise rebellion. In fact, this would seem impossible because of the geographic dispersion of the Armenian leadership. This begs the question of how a rebellion actually began and whether a series of similar incidents over time constitutes what might be termed a regional insurrection.

This chapter presents the idea that the Armenian committees responded positively to overtures from the allied powers, which bought the committees into alignment with allied interests opposing those of the Ottoman Empire. Early, and very tentative, Armenian support for cooperating with the allies grew dramatically after the Ottoman defeats at Sarıkamış, Basra, and on the Suez Canal. Over the fall of 1914, and into the spring of 1915, violent incidents by members of the heavily armed Armenian committees escalated inside the Ottoman Empire. From the Ottoman perspective these had the appearance of cohesive and coordinated insurrectionary activity.

Armenian and Russian Military Activity in the Caucasus

The nexus of Armenian insurrectionary activity was undoubtedly the Georgian city of Tiblisi, where the Armenian bureaus had been operating since the 1890s. The Armenian committee infrastructure in Tiblisi was extensive and by the summer of 1914, committees had established a new "central recruitment bureau" to enlist Ottoman Armenian volunteers in the Russian army.[2] Hampartsum Araklyan, editor of *Mshak*, the leading Armenian-language newspaper in the Caucasus, supported this endeavor.[3] As early as August 5, 1914, the Russian high command discussed the idea of arming the Armenians and encouraging them to rise in rebellion against the Ottomans.[4] On August 29, General Nikolai Yudenich, chief of staff of the Russian army group in the Caucasus, composed a memorandum titled "On the Arming of Ottoman Armenians," in which he advocated arming the Armenians as a fifth column (to use a modern term) inside the Ottoman Empire.[5] Moreover, he proposed that covert weapons depots be established along the border and that trustworthy Armenian couriers smuggle the weapons into Ottoman territory. Two days later, Yudenich followed his suggestions by requesting that the Russian high command (the *Stavka*) provide 25,000 rifles and 12 million rounds of ammunition with which to arm the Armenians.[6]

In September, the Russian viceroy in Tiblisi, Count I. I. Vorontsov-Dashkov, worked out a "careful step-by-step strategy...that aimed to give the Russians as much control as possible over events."[7] According to one historian, "Small Armenian guerrilla cells (less than 100 men each) would be created in the frontier towns on the Russian side of the border, including Oltu, Sarıkamış, Gizman (Kâğıman) and Igdyr (Iğdır)."[8] In addition to each guerrilla carrying a rifle, each cell had an additional 250 rifles and money, which it would smuggle across the border into the Ottoman Empire. Cumulatively, the cells had the potential to arm a force of about 1,000 men. A Russian assessment of the willingness and the readiness of the Ottoman Armenian population to support armed insurrection stated that the Armenians possessed adequate hidden weapons caches but would "not likely risk launching the uprising until the Russians are right on their doorstep."[9] Likewise, the Russians actively courted the Laz, the Greeks, and the Kurds to form similar armed guerrilla bands that would also strike the Ottomans.[10]

The ARF's Armenian National Bureau initially formed the Ottoman Armenians, who enlisted to fight for the Russians, into four military formations known as *druzhiny* in the Armenian language.[11] The exact organizational structure of the *druzhiny* is unclear from the available sources in the English language and, unlike the revolutionary cells, they had a nonstandardized structure. They are sometimes called "legions" in the literature and the author feels that this is a very appropriate term. The Armenian hero and military leader Antranig arrived on October 19, 1914, at the Tiblisi railway station to throngs of cheering Armenians.[12] Antranig desired to centralize and command all of the volunteers, about 3,100 men altogether, but the Russians sent the legions in different directions.[13] The First Legion, composed of 1,200 men, led by Antranig personally, deployed to the Persian border immediately while the Second Legion of 500 men, led by Dro, followed to Igdir on October 20, 1914.[14] Hamazapsp's Third Legion and Kéri's Fourth Legion, each of 500 men, marched toward Sarıkamış on November 1 and 6, respectively.[15] A message from Yudenich to General Nikolayev confirmed that Dro was positioned near Igdir for operations against Doğubeyazıt and Van.[16] A Fifth Legion under Vardan set off toward the frontier opposite Van. These movements mirror the deployments envisioned by Vorontsov-Dashkov. In spite of opposition from the ARF's Tiblisi bureau the Hunchaks belatedly formed a Sixth Legion of 1,500 men, under Grigor Avsharian, as well as an independent troop of 350 men under Pandukht.[17]

The Ottoman intelligence services quickly discovered what was happening in Russia and the Ottoman government became aware of the formation and arming of the Armenian *druzhiny*. The Erzurum Jandarma reported the movement of Armenian families into Russia.[18] Russian deserters reported the distribution of arms in mid-August.[19] The Ottoman ambassador in Tehran reported on September 7 that the Russians were distributing arms to Armenians in the Caucasus.[20] On September 19, the Ottoman general staff warned the commander of the Erzurum fortress that the Russians were organizing Armenian regiments and conducting war training exercises in the Caucasus for operations against the empire.[21] Enver alerted the Third Army in late September that the Armenian committees and the Russians agreed to provoke the Ottoman Armenians to rebel.[22]

In early October, the Third Army warned the Ottoman general staff that Russian-born Armenians, who had military experience in the Russian army, were crossing over into the empire with money, maps, and weapons.[23] On October 20, the 4th Reserve Cavalry Regiment patrolling from its lines in Köprüköy uncovered a cache of Russian rifles hidden in Armenian homes in Hasankale.[24] A frontier security battalion reported that aggressively nationalist Armenians were gathering in large numbers.[25] On October 23, the Third Army staff informed the Ottoman general staff that large numbers of armed Armenians were moving into Muş, Bitlis, Van, and Erivan.[26] Thus, on the eve of hostilities, the Ottoman government and its military staffs were very aware of the activities of the Armenian committees.

OTTOMAN MILITARY ACTIVITY IN THE CAUCASUS

On their side of the border, the Ottomans were not idle and, in the fall of 1914, the Special Organization (SO) conducted an aggressive countercampaign against the Russo-Armenian build-up.[27] Responding to the dangerous situation developing along the Russian-Ottoman frontier in October, the SO established an "East Anatolian Operations Office" in Trabzon under Rıza Bey and Nail Bey.[28] About the same time, Bahattin Şakir and Ömer Naci arrived in Erzurum.[29] Rıza began to organize several types of SO detachments, including coastal defense units (*Sahil Muhafaza Birlikleri*) and raiding columns (*Akıncı Kolları*) but was prohibited from interfing with the ongoing mobilization of the Ottoman army.[30] Unable to compete with the army in recruiting men eligible for the war effort, Rıza famously recruited men for his organization from prisons, immigrant and refugee camps, and from tribal groups; nevertheless, by the end of the month he had raised about a thousand men.[31]

Similarly, the SO responded to imminent hostilities against the Entente by launching a number of clandestine expeditions to distant locations to encourage rebellion and conduct guerrilla warfare when war broke out. These included expeditions to Persia and Afghanistan, as well as missions to Arabia, Libya, Egypt, the Sudan, and India. These expeditions and missions were closely coordinated with, and included, the Germans. Interestingly, when war actually broke out, the sultan, at the instigation of the German Kaiser, declared a *Cihad* or holy war against the allied combatants. Many well-known individuals participated in these clandestine missions, including the Ottoman naval hero Rauf Bey, Wilhelm Wassmuss, and Oskar von Niedermayer.³² With the exception of Libya, these expeditions were notably unsuccessful and encouraged the allies to counter with their own versions, illustrated very well by the later efforts of Colonel T. E. Lawrence in raising the Arab Revolt in 1916.

In the latter part of October 1914, the chief of the SO, Süleyman Askeri, who was increasingly concerned about the rift between Enver and Talat, unified the SO contingents in eastern Anatolia by designating Şakir as the overall operational commander. At an SO organizational meeting in Bayburt, Şakir drew up new regulations forming the Caucasus Revolutionary Society (*Kafkas İhtilal Cemiyeti*).³³ There were growing pains as Rıza's gathering force was brought under Şakir's control but, in the end, there was a coordinated SO command architecture operating out of Erzurum. According to Turkish historians, the society's mission was to "prepare a general revolt against Russia in the Caucasus and to work to insure the defeat of Russia in the war."³⁴ Şakir directed that the new eastern Anatolian SO apparatus establish itself with a cell-like internal component and an external component, in effect, making it a mirror image of its Armenian opponent.³⁵

The general headquarters of the society maintained its administrative component in Erzurum, where it worked in close cooperation with the German and Austro-Hungarian consulates to coordinate the departure of, and the support of, the clandestine expeditions into Georgia, Persia, and Afghanistan. Rıza Bey maintained his office in Trabzon and a Van district committee, led by Cevdet Bey and Kâzım Bey, was put in charge of organizing revolutionary activity inside Russia in the cities of Kars, Ardahan, Baku, and in Georgia.³⁶

THE QUASI WAR ON THE FRONTIER

It is fair to say that in September and October of 1914, the irregular forces of Russia and the Ottoman Empire were in an undeclared, but active, state of war in the Black Sea frontier provinces of their empires. The area of conflict on the northeast frontier ran from the Black Sea coast near Batum southeast to Sarıkamış. This area encompassed the town of Artvin in the Çoruh River valley and the nearby towns of Ardahan and Oltu. The province belonged to the Ottomans until the Russo-Turkish War of 1877, when the Russians seized the territory. While many fled the area in 1878, in 1914, a large number of Muslims still lived in the region and these people were the SO's target audience as potential guerrillas. The region lay between the Ottoman Empire and Georgia, where the SO also hoped to raise rebellion. Reciprocally, inside the Ottoman Empire a large number of Armenians lived in the cities of Erzurum, Bayburt, and Trabzon and the frontier region lay in their path to raising an Armenian rebellion in these cities. Thus, the geography of the plans of the opposing forces drew them to this region.

Certainly Rıza Bey was the most active of the SO commanders in the immediate prewar period.[37] He organized 600 men and 5 Ottoman officers into groups, which he launched in October 1914 into the Caucasus to raid as well as carry arms to the Muslims of Azerbaijan and Georgia.[38] Rıza was well supported in these endeavors by the navy, which provided small motor boats. By the end of October, he was able to report that the Georgians and the Muslims in the Caucasus were ready to revolt in support of an invasion by the Ottoman army. Inside the Ottoman Empire itself, Rıza's SO squadrons engaged Armenians guerrillas (classified by the Ottoman intelligence services as *çete*) in combat in the area around the Ottoman town of Hopa.[39] On October 5, 1914, the local Ottoman authorities in Hopa estimated the size of enemy guerrilla force as 800 Russian and Armenians armed with Russian weapons.[40] Further to the south, around Erzurum, SO forces under Dr. Şakir and Yakup Cemil battled Russian-organized Armenian guerrillas.[41] Similarly, the SO launched raids from Erzurum across the border Russia.[42] A report to Süleyman Askeri from Dr. Şakir noted that the cross-border SO raids gained experience for its troops as well as having captured 1,400 sheep and cattle.[43]

The excesses long associated with the employment of irregular forces in the Caucasus manifested themselves during this period. Some authors highlight the massacres and pillaging of Armenian villages on both sides of the border.[44] However, it must be noted that hard facts regarding the actual numbers and locations of atrocities are hard to establish. It is fair to say that both the Armenian committees and the SO committed atrocities in his period but it is speculative to suggest that these were part of an orchestrated plan on either side or that they were frequent occurrences. Likewise, the scale of the guerrilla activities along the Black Sea frontier is greatly exaggerated with Armenian authors asserting the SO employed 10,000 deliberately released criminal felons in its ranks and Turkish authors asserting the Armenian *druzhiny* and internal committees fielded 15,000 men.[45]

Similarly, both sides engaged in a quasi war in northwest Persia as well, with both sides encouraging Kurdish tribes to violence to support their own interests.[46] Both the SO and the ARF were very active in smuggling weapons through to, and recruiting, surrogate forces in northern Persia.[47] Once again, the geography of the SO's and the committee's plans dictated that northern Persia would become a zone of

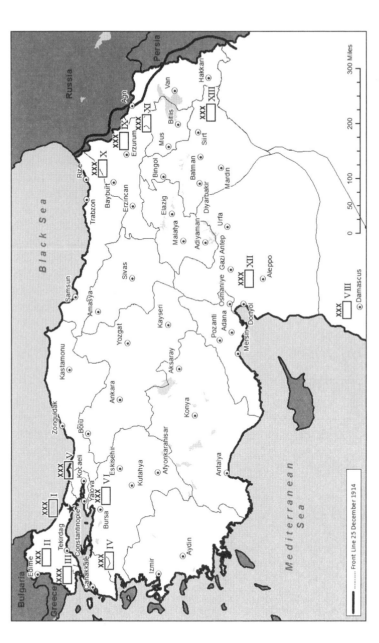

Map 7.1 Locations of Ottoman army corps in December 1914.

confrontation. The cities of Van, Malazgirt, and Muş, which were heavily populated with Armenians, lay directly to the west of the Persian frontier. Van, in particular, was a center for ARF activity, including military cells and large arms caches, and the ARF hoped to raise insurrection there. Reciprocally, the road to Azerbaijan, where the SO hoped to raise a Muslim insurrection, went directly through the Persian towns of Kotur and Dilman. Compounding the situation, local Kurdish inhabitants, organized in bandit gangs, already inflamed by the Ottomans and Christian Assyrians and now encouraged by the Russians, terrorized and massacred villagers of all kinds in pursuit of regional dominance.[48]

Most of the Ottoman Third Army's concentration of forces was completed by the end of September 1914 in the center sector of the Ottoman-Russian border. By September 29, the 17,000 officers and men of Mehmet Fazıl's Reserve Cavalry Corps established a cavalry screen immediately behind the frontier guard battalions (*hudut tabur*).[49] The Ottoman XI Corps and the IX Corps moved to assembly areas with their headquarters in Hasankale and Erzurum, respectively. The headquarters of the X Corps remained well behind the border in Sivas to guard the Black Sea coast.[50] Other major forces in the area included the 2nd Cavalry Division, which was positioned north of Erzurum, while behind the Persian border lay the Van Reserve Cavalry Brigade and the newly activated Van Jandarma Division.[51] Reinforcements from Mesopotamia, the XIII Corp headquarters, and the 37th Infantry Division were en route but would not become available until the end of the year. The heavily defended fortress city of Erzurum was the logistical and command hub of the Third Army headquarters. Almost no combat forces remained in the garrison cities in the interior of the vast Third Army area. Map 7.1 shows the wartime concentration of the Ottoman army away from the core provinces.

OPERATIONS IN THE ÇORUH VALLEY

Despite the concentration of Ottoman forces in the Caucasus, it was the Russians who struck first and very heavily at the Ottoman lines at Köprüköy. In many ways, this was a result of the extensive railway system that the Russians had built in Caucasia since 1878. Like the German and French rail systems, the Russian government subsidized railroad construction to accommodate military mobilization by constructing lines and spurs that led to mobilization areas on the frontiers. The poverty-stricken Ottoman Empire, on the other hand, depended on foreign entrepreneurs to build its railway system. The result of this was that the Ottoman railroads connected cities that fed the economic interests of foreign companies, while the Russian railways supported military campaign planning. A Russian railroad ended at Sarıkamış, about 50 kilometers from the border, while the Ottoman railroads terminated 600 kilometers from the frontier at Ankara and Adana. Consequently, the Russians amassed more rapidly a much better-prepared and well-supplied army poised to attack the Ottoman Empire.

Minor combat between regular Russian and Ottoman forces occurred on October 30–31, 1914, and was followed on November 1–4 by a major Russian attack across the border, which ran over the border guard battalions and the cavalry screen. The Russians then launched a major offensive toward Erzurum known today as the Battles of Köprüköy and Azap, fought between November 5 and 23.[52] These battles were bloody and, at the end of them, the front lines stabilized about 20 kilometers inside the Ottoman frontier.

According to the original Ottoman war plan, the Third Army was ordered to stand on the defensive in the Caucasus, while the bulk of the Ottoman army concentrated in Thrace. However, in early September 1914, a revised campaign plan directed the Third Army to conduct offensive operations in the event of war. When war formally broke out between Russia and the Ottoman Empire on November 2, the Ottomans were actively planning a winter offensive in the Caucasus. The plan called for the Third Army's three army corps to encircle the Russian army at Sarıkamış with a supporting operation on the Black Sea flank between Batum and Ardahan.[53] There were no regular Ottoman army combat units on the Turco-Russian frontier from the Black Sea south for about 100 kilometers for this supporting attack.

The only forces available for the supporting attack were Rıza's SO units and the Hopa border guard battalion. Nevertheless, Rıza pushed aggressively across the frontier and, on November 22, closed in on the Russian town of Artvin.[54] The attacks were very successful, with local Muslims assisting the SO and the Hopa battalion, capturing 140 Russians and 4 artillery pieces.[55] At the same time, Rıza infiltrated his SO units near Batum forward to foment an uprising among Laz and Turkic peoples inside the Russian Empire. In addition to this mission, Dr. Şakir ordered Ziya Bey, an army artillery major, commanding the SO detachment already inside Russia, to encircle and destroy Armenian guerrilla forces.[56] The SO also attacked regular Russian army units, capturing 4 officers and 63 Russian soldiers in late November.[57] One Turkish source also shows a large force of volunteers operating in the Çoruh River valley under Yakup Cemil Bey.[58] Another Turkish source asserts that Yakup Cemil's detachment was a SO force composed of irregulars or guerrillas (*çeteler*).[59] In this bitter internecine fighting, many Muslims civilians, Armenians, and other local ethnic groups were massacred indiscriminately.[60]

On December 6, the Ottoman general staff ordered the Third Army to push the irregular forces onward toward Ardahan.[61] To assure the success of this endeavor, the Third Army ordered the newly arrived 8th Infantry Regiment, two artillery batteries, and the Çoruh Border Security Battalion into the attack.[62] This newly organized force was designated the Stange Detachment and ordered to take Artvin while the rest of the army moved toward their main objective at Sarıkamış.[63] Captain August Stange, a Prussian officer, who was a member of the German Military Mission, commanded the detachment.[64] Against light opposition, Stange pushed forward and took the town on December 21.

With so many different units and organizations operating in the area, there was bureaucratic wrangling over how to unify the command as the Sarıkamış campaign approached. In the end, Stange took command of the entire force—regulars, border security battalions, volunteers, and the Special Organization. However, the SO and volunteers continued to receive their orders from Şakir and Rıza, who wanted to retain independent control of the operation, while Stange answered to the X Corps commander, in whose sector he operated.[65] On December 22, the X Corps and Third Army ordered Stange, the SO, and the volunteers to converge separately on Ardahan. The SO, now locally commanded by Captain Halit Bey, cooperated and joined the advance.[66] Despite bad winter weather, these forces began to encircle the city on December 29. Because Stange controlled neither the Special Organization nor the volunteers, he sent coordination copies of his own detachment orders to Halit, who passed these on to the adjacent volunteers.[67] This was a clumsy arrangement, and there is no indication that the SO or the volunteers reciprocated. The result was an uncoordinated attack on Ardahan. Stange's detachment suffered heavy casualties, while the SO and volunteer losses were light.[68]

The Ottomans failed to hold the city for long. In early January 1915, the Russians retook the city with bayonet assaults. Over the next month, the Ottomans conducted a fighting retreat back toward Artvin. At the end of January 1915, Şakir consolidated some of the SO units into a Special Organization Regiment (*Teşkilat-ı Mahsusa Alay*) commanded by Halit.[69] This regiment was assigned 9 officers and 671 men and Halit also gained control over a group of volunteers known as the Baha Bey Şakir Force.[70] Subsequently, and because of the deteriorating tactical situation, Şakir ordered the SO regiment to cooperate with Stange in defensive operations along the border. Additionally, a smaller SO detachment commanded by Rıza Bey conducted operations around Murgal, northwest of Artvin. Although Stange received some 1,600 replacements to fill his depleted ranks, he was pushed back to the border in hard fighting.

OTHER MILITARY OPERATIONS IN THE CAUCASUS

The southern wing of the Russian army, the Erivan Group, pushed south into the Elişkirt River valley on November 7, 1914, and rapidly took the border towns of Doğubayazıt and Diyadin.[71] Included in the Erivan Group's forces were a number of Armenian *druzhiny*, including Dro's legion, which were very important in assisting the advance.[72] The Ottoman Van Jandarma Division was drawn north to contain these advances but remained near the Persian border. A report from the division commander, Kazım Pasha, on November 17 noted that the Van Reserve Cavalry Brigade was engaged with Armenian and Kurdish guerrillas advancing on the road from Kotur.[73] To combat this threat, the 37th Infantry Division was rerouted toward the area.

By December 1, 1914, Russian columns were advancing toward Van near Hoşop and Dir. This situation greatly concerned the governor of Van, who feared an Armenian uprising.[74] The Van Jandarma Division was sent forward to block these advances, which the Ottoman general staff felt were oriented toward seizing Malazgirt. In turn, the incoming XIII Corps headquarters and the 37th Infantry Division were ordered to concentrate there. The Van Jandarma Division pushed the Russo-Armenian force back and by December 19, won a battle with them near Kotur.[75] Andranig's legion, coming out of Persia, was involved in these actions.[76] Relieved of the need to guard the city of Van, the Ottomans launched an invasion of Persia of their own on January 4, 1915. The main forces involved in this offensive were the Van Jandarma Division and the irregular SO forces of Ömer Naci and, by mid-January, they had taken Dilman and Hoy.[77] These operations pushed thousands of refugees ahead of the Ottoman forces as the advance sowed panic among the Persian Christians, who feared retribution for supporting the Russians.[78]

Another event of significance occurred earlier on November 21, 1914, which was the inactivation of the Reserve Cavalry Corps. The reasons were based on the indiscipline and the poor levels of training of the irregular Kurdish tribesmen, who made up the bulk of the men in the reserve cavalry regiments. The corps had been in continuous combat since November 1 and its performance was uneven and sporadic.[79] The details of the inactivation itself are contained a Third Army operations order and may be found in the modern Turkish official history. [80] They are worthy of note. The first order of business in the order concerned the corps' animals, which were to be turned over to the regular 2nd Cavalry Division and the Erzurum remount depot. Likewise, the surviving men were to report to the replacement depots in Erzurum. The 2nd Cavalry Division commander was also given the authority to request cavalry officers from the corps, by name, for transfer to his division. The next day, the greatly reinforced 2nd Cavalry Division began redeployment to take a key role in the forthcoming Sarıkamış offensive.

The inactivation of the Reserve Cavalry Corps reflected the unhappiness of the conventional Ottoman military establishment toward irregular Cossack-style cavalry forces that dated back to the days of the Hamidiye tribal cavalry. In these early conventional operations, the reserve cavalry regiments failed to be operationally effective. There were several outcomes of this, which are relevant to future Ottoman military operations. First, the 2nd Cavalry Division was brought up to strength and saturated with experienced cavalry officers and men. In turn, this formation became the Third Army's fire brigade. Second, this concentration of combat power in a single division eliminated four weaker, but highly mobile, formations, which might have been used in counterinsurgency operations in the spring and summer of 1915. Last, the author feels that it is unlikely that many of the unhorsed Kurdish cavalrymen actually reported to the Erzurum replacement depots for reassignment to other combat units. Their demonstrated undisciplined behavior makes it more than probable that they either returned home or turned to banditry, in effect, creating armed gangs of hardened combat veterans in eastern Anatolia.[81]

THE SARIKAMIŞ CAMPAIGN

The details of the infamous Sarıkamış campaign are well told elsewhere, and this section will detail only the basics, which are relevant to building an understanding of its effect on the Ottoman counterinsurgency campaign of 1915.[82] Enver conceived the campaign after learning about the great Cannae-like German campaign of annihilation at Tannenberg in East Prussia, fought in late August 1914. In that campaign, smaller German forces encircled a larger Russian army and forced its surrender. After the battles of the frontiers in November 1914, Enver believed that the Russian army in Caucasia had overextended itself and lay in a vulnerable position. His plan involved concentrating the IX and X Corps into a Left Wing and the XI Corps and the revitalized 2nd Cavalry Division into a Right Wing. The Right Wing would fix the Russian army with a strong demonstration attack. Meanwhile, the Left Wing would swing rapidly around the Russian right flank through Oltu and Badız and seize the railhead at Sarıkamış. With their lines of communications cut off in the dead of winter, Enver believed that the Russians would panic and that their command and control would collapse. Once that happened, surrender would inevitably follow as it had at Tannenberg.

Enver launched the operation using 75,000 men on December 22 and six days later, the hard marching forward elements of the X Corps stood on the high ground overlooking the town of Sarıkamış and the road to the f rontier. Although criticized as reckless and foolhardy by most military historians, it must be noted that the operation came very close to succeeding, but failed primarily because Enver's assumption that the Russians would panic did not happen. Instead, in a brilliant display of operational art and professionalism, General Yudenich kept his nerve to hold his ground and rapidly shifted Russian forces to inflict a disastrous defeat on the Ottomans.

The campaign was a catastrophic defeat for the Ottoman Third Army. Total casualties amounted to 33,000 dead, 7,000 prisoners, and 10,000 wounded, the bulk of which came from the combat divisions of the IX and XI Corps.[83] However, the subsequent exaggeration, by early Western historians, of the number of Ottoman dead to 90,000 have led later authors to assert that the excessive losses of the Sarıkamış campaign made it a "threshold event" for "the extermination of the Armenians."[84] This line of argument asserts that Ottoman losses gravely weakened the Ottoman army's strategic posture in eastern Anatolia and, more importantly, that a politically weakened Enver needed a scapegoat (the Armenians) to blame the disaster on.[85] This is untrue and the effect of these losses on the operational posture of the Third Army, as well as the military reasons for the relocations, will be discussed later in this work. Other authors today assert that Armenian participation in the campaign was a significant factor in the Ottoman defeat.[86] This is untrue as well.

It is a fact that Armenian *druzhiny* participated in the Sarıkamış campaign; however, their location and mission prevented meaningful participation at the culminating point of the battle. On December 22, 1914, Third Legion (Hamazapsp) and the Fourth Legion (Kéri) were in contact on the front with the Ottoman 2nd Cavalry Division near the villages of Ardı and Alağoz, some 50 kilometers southwest of the town of Sarıkamış.[87] Both of these *druzhiny* remained along this portion of the front at least through December 26, when regular Russian infantry formations were pulled off the line and sent north.[88] While the two *druzhiny* participated in the campaign, they were not involved in Yudenich's dramatic counterattack on January 4, 1915, which was the decisive turning point in the Ottoman failure.[89]

FRENCH AND BRITISH OPERATIONS IN CILICIA AND SYRIA

In addition to the Russians, in the fall of 1914, the French and British governments also encouraged and supported Armenian operations against the Ottoman Empire. The most vocal advocate of the Armenian cause in the western allied capitals was Boghos Nubar, the president of the Armenian National Delegation in Paris. As early as October 1914, the British consul at Aleppo noted the obvious by reporting that "all the Christians sympathise with England and France and would welcome with joy a swift British or even French occupation."[90] Confirming this, Boghos Nubar told British military planners in Egypt in November the Armenians had volunteered to "support a possible disembarkation at Alexandretta, Mersina or Adana" and, moreover, promised "valuable assistance could also be provided by the Armenians of mountainous districts, who, if supplied with arms and ammunition, would rise against Turkey."[91] A British historian asserted that Nubar and the delegation promoted the use of volunteer units from the diaspora and that "the units were envisaged to help form an Entente bridgehead and precipitate a general rising by militants within key Cilician communities."[92] At the same time, ARF theoretician Mikayel Varandian made similar overtures to the allies that the Cilician Armenians be given "the opportunity to take part in the war against Turkey."[93]

Early allied operations in the Mediterranean were primarily naval. On December 13, 1914, Vice Admiral R. H. Peirse (commander-in-chief East Indies on board HMS *Swiftsure*) ordered Captain Frank Larkin of HMS *Doris* to patrol off Alexandretta and to interdict supplies on the Hedjaz railway for a period of about ten days.[94] Performing similar operations, at the same time in the same area, were the Russian cruiser *Askold* and the French cruiser *Requin*. Of note, Peirse sent an intelligence officer from his staff, Lieutenant H. Pirie Gordon, RNVR (who was something of an Ottoman specialist), to accompany the *Doris*.[95] As will become apparent, Pirie Gordon's job was to investigate landing sites for large-scale operations near Alexandretta. Between December 14 and 19, HMS *Doris* raided up and down the Leventine coast.[96] Larkin sent a landing party ashore, which destroyed over two miles of telegraph line (wire, insulators, and posts), and then six miles north of Alexandretta, he sent another landing party ashore that pulled up the rail sleepers; moving the railway tracks a bit out of true. This caused a railway train of 35 wagons to derail.[97]

On December 19, Larkin bombarded the railway bridge at Payas with shells making it impassable. The *Doris* sailed off the next day

to find a large steel girder railway bridge close by the railway station at "Duert Yol" (Dörtyol). Larkin decided to blow up the bridge
and landed a large party that was opposed by rifle fire, which was in
turn suppressed by shells from the *Doris*. Nevertheless, the bridge was
destroyed at the cost of one man wounded. The landing party then
occupied the railway station to destroy the telegraph lines, whereupon
they cut the wires while assisted by "the Armenian railway officials
themselves smashing the electric batteries on the lines with particular
satisfaction."[98] The three officials then asked for protection and were
taken onboard *Doris* to be questioned by Pirie Gordon, who obtained
"useful information" for his intelligence report.[99]

On December 22, Pirie Gordon went ashore for direct talks with
the American consul, who acted as a sort of intermediary between
Larkin and the Turks. This time, Larkin reduced his demands to the
destruction of railway locomotives. After the passing of notes, the
Turks agreed to allow Larkin to demolish some locomotives, which
had been trapped in the city by the downed bridge anyway. Finally, at
day's end, the British blew up two locomotives as the ship departed.
The following day, the ship exchanged salvos with a Turkish field gun
with no apparent effect. The next several days saw *Doris* patrolling the
coast and she pulled into Famagusta, Cyprus, on December 26, so that
Pirie Gordon might secure the services of a Mr. Lukach, who was to
be taken aboard as an Ottoman translator. Unfortunately, Mr. Lukach
could not be located and *Doris* departed for a final pass around the
Beirut coast, where Pierie Gordon secured further intelligence from
some French Dominican friars, before the ship returned to Egypt.[100]

Early on New Year's Day 1915, Larkin and HMS *Doris* sailed from
Port Said. Returning to Cyprus, the errant Mr. H. C. Lukach was
embarked on January 5, after which *Doris* sailed to Mersina (Mersin) to
destroy an important railway bridge. Because of strong Ottoman opposition Larkin could not land men so *Doris* closed on the shore and bombarded the bridge with shells. *Doris* left for Alexandretta, anchoring off
the Jonah's Pillars.[101] While, observing a previously blown up railway
engine, Larkin saw a supply of timber adjacent to the bridge he had
destroyed on his previous voyage. He sent two landing parties ashore on
January 7, 1915, which destroyed the timber and the railway embank-
ment, as well as cutting the telegraph lines. One party was attacked by
Ottoman infantry but suffered no casualties. Mr. Lukach accompanied
one party and questioned an Armenian man on the road. *Doris* then
sailed to nearby Dörtyol to reinspect the destroyed bridge there.

Larkin received wireless orders on January 7 to prevent the enemy
from sending troops and supplies to Alexandretta and thence to Aleppo

by way of Beilan Pass. At Dörtyol, Larkin saw that the Ottomans had bypassed the destroyed bridge using a temporary road and he once again decided to land a demolitions party. The party encountered sniping, which forced it to withdraw, suffering one dead.[102] Larkin then bombarded the bridge successfully but found it "a matter of no satisfaction in view of the regrettable death of Corporal Warburton."[103] Plans to bury the corporal were interrupted by the arrival of the French armored cruiser *Dentrescasteaux*.

It is unclear from the records available today why, when, and how the *Doris* came to have a party of spies aboard. In any case, we know that Larkin persuaded the French captain to "land the Egyptian spy at Sheik Jabar near Tripoli, on the Syrian coast, this he readily agreed to undertake, accordingly the spy with his three native boatmen in their boat were transferred to the *Dentrescasteaux* as also was Doctor Scrymgeour to act as interpreter in Arabic."[104] *Doris* then spent two days shelling a number of vehicles and freight wagons on the roadway and destroying a hitherto unseen bridge, making it Larkin's fifth destroyed bridge.

On January 10, 1915, *Doris* rendezvoused again off Jonah's Pillars with the *Dentrescasteaux*, whose captain paid Larkin a visit to explain why he had been unable to persuade the spy to land. Larkin re-embarked the spy, as well as Doctor Scrymgeour, onboard *Doris*.[105] Later that day, *Doris* shelled a mule train on shore and bombarded some trenches on January 11, and a camel caravan the following day. By January 13, *Doris* was again cruising off Mersina and shelled a small blockhouse. The next day Larkin "proceeded to sea with the intention in the first place of endeavoring to land and re-embark the Egyptian spy at Sheik Jabor near Tripoli, and afterwards of preceding along the coast with a view to distributing the proclamation received from you by the *Requin*."[106]

However, bad weather, high seas, and low coal bunkers forced Larkin to return to Port Said without landing the spy. Larkin set off again on January 20, joined by Lukach, the doctor, and a Mr. Dupuis, bound for Alexandretta.[107] Larkin cruised off Beirut, making contact with the Ottoman governor there, and on January 24, *Doris* sent a landing party ashore and discharged Lukach and the doctor.[108] Another landing party went ashore the next day and, on January 26, yet another landing party went ashore near Alexandretta. On January 30, Larkin's landing parties seized five Ottoman soldiers defending a trench as prisoners of war.[109] The next day, landing parties took three more POWs before returning the lot to Port Said. Three Armenians were among the eight prisoners. Although the facts remain unclear, the Ottoman Fourth

Army reported on February 3, 1915, that sixty enemy soldiers landed near Adana and captured an additional two Armenians, who abandoned their weapons and voluntarily fled to join the allied force.[110]

In February, the massing of the fleet for the attempts to force the Dardanelles, and the subsequent Gallipoli invasion, took Larkin and the *Doris* away from the Alexandretta coast. What could be said about the ship's operations? While HMS *Doris* certainly performed missions of importance interdicting Ottoman troops and equipment destined for the impending Ottoman invasion of Egypt, there were obviously other missions of great importance attached to her voyages as well.[111] A report on January 7, 1915, with sketches of the beaches, obstacles, and enemy fortifications, prepared by Pirie Gordon and Lukach detailed "possible sites for a large-scale landing at Alexandretta."[112] The presence of spies and interpreters additionally reveals an active search for useful intelligence and a letter reveals Mr. Dupuis of the "Soudan Civil Service" to have been lent to *Doris* as an interpreter of Arabic.[113] In the same letter, Larkin also detailed gathering intelligence from three Armenian refugees who were dragomen to the consuls at Aleppo, who he then collected, and passed on, to the Military Intelligence Department in Cairo.

The story of the British plans and efforts to seize the Dardanelles in 1915, which resulted in the failed Gallipoli campaign, are widely known. However, other British plans to invade amphibiously the Ottoman Empire near Alexandretta are less well-known. By January 1915, it was evident to the British War Council that Britain's navy might exercise significant strategic effect using its amphibious capability to break the growing deadlock on the western front. Many ideas were considered including Admiral Jackie Fisher's schemes to land on the Baltic coast and Winston Churchill's plan for seizing the island of Borkum as a prelude to landing in Schleswig-Holstein. Fresh from an assignment in India, Field Marshal Lord Horatio Kitchener emerged as an advocate of staging a landing in the Alexandretta area with a view toward severing Anatolian Turkey from Syria, Palestine, and Egypt.[114] Strategically, Kitchener's plan would end the Ottoman threat to the Suez Canal and exploratory planning had already begun under the hand of Lieutenant General Sir John Maxwell in Egypt, an idea previously presented by Boghos Nubar in 1914.[115] The intelligence operations involving the maritime insertion of agents, or spies as they known then, conducted by HMS *Doris*, as well as other allied ships such as the *Requin* and the *Philomel*, were designed to support these efforts with fresh tactical and geographic information.[116] As late as March 1915, Kitchener continued to advocate for the occupation of Alexandretta.[117]

CONCLUSION

A modern military analysis of the prewar conditions would note the strategic posture of the opposing forces in the Caucasus, which mirrored each other in many ways. The Ottoman and Russian general staffs concentrated large conventional military forces along the Kars-Sarıkamış-Erzurum axis and prepared them for offensive operations. Separate from this conventional concentration, both sides planned to employ irregular forces to raise rebellion among their ethnic and religious brethren inside enemy territory. Ottoman and German planning envisioned employing local Muslims, in the border regions, to assist conventional Ottoman forces supporting Georgian and Azeri rebellions in Russia. Armenian and Russian planning envisioned employing Armenian revolutionary committees, in the border regions, to assist Russian and Armenian conventional forces supporting Armenian rebellions in the eastern Anatolian cities of the Ottoman Empire. It is fair to state that the Ottoman irregular effort, in this regard, was much more ambitious, and that the formal organizational structure of the SO far outpaced its Armenian and Russian counterparts.

Once formal hostilities erupted, first the Russians and then the Ottomans conducted large-scale conventional offensive operations. Both sides failed and, by mid-January 1915, the front had stabilized more or less along the original Ottoman-Russian border. The Ottomans, however, were quick to take advantage of the opportunities created by the Russian failure to guard their Black Sea frontier, particularly the regions around Ardahan and Artvin, as well as the Russian failure to send conventional forces rapidly into Persia. The combined offensive by the Stange detachment and the SO that drove deeply into Russian territory, as well as the Van Jandarma Division's drive into Persia, showcase the cohesiveness of Ottoman command and control.

Finally, Captain Larkin's operations were highly and dramatically visible, and had an operational effect that was significantly out of proportion to their cost and purpose. When reports of the *Doris* and her depredations reached the intelligence staff of the Ottoman Fourth Army, they were combined with internal reports about Armenian committee activities, which reinforced the notion that a significant threat existed to the vulnerable southeastern coast. This nexus of information will be explained fully in the following chapter, as well as the effect that it had on the threat-based analysis leading to Ottoman strategic decision-making.

CHAPTER 8

Enemies Within

What is perceived as real is real in its effect.

—*Professor John Hall, Saint Lawrence*
University, 1982[1]

INTRODUCTION

The uprising in the city of Van, in April 1915, was orchestrated by the Dashnaks in conjunction with a simultaneous offensive by the Russian army, which itself included Armenian legions of expatriate Ottoman Armenian citizens. It was carefully planned; the small Ottoman force in the area quickly lost control of the city, and then failed to prevent the relief of the Armenians by the advancing Russian army. The loss of the city in this manner, to internal revolt supported by well-coordinated Russian military offensives, was immediately viewed by the Ottoman high command as a template for future enemy operations. Moreover, in the Alexandretta and Dörtyol regions, the Ottomans expected an amphibious invasion by the British and French to link up with, and support, the heavily armed Armenian committees in that area as well. Today, there is no doubt that the allies encouraged and supported the Armenian committees to revolt against the empire in the spring of 1915, and that the Ottomans believed that what happened in Van was about to be repeated elsewhere.

The location of the Armenian population and areas of insurgency are critical to understanding the nature of the existential threat that it posed to the national security of the Ottoman state. The Ottomans were fighting the Russians on the Caucasian frontier, and the British in Mesopotamia and Palestine. The lines of communications supporting those Ottoman fronts ran directly though the rear areas of the Ottoman armies in eastern Anatolia that were heavily populated by Armenian communities and, by extension, by the heavily armed

Armenian revolutionary committees. Importantly, none of the Ottoman armies on the fronts in Caucasia, Mesopotamia, or Palestine were self-sufficient in food, fodder, ammunition, or medical supplies and all were dependent on the roads and railroads leading west to Constantinople and Thrace for those supplies. Moreover, none of these forces had much in the way of prepositioned supplies available and all required the continuous flow of war material. The Armenian revolutionary committees began to attack and cut these lines of communications in the spring of 1915. Ottoman army messages regarding the interdiction of the roads and lines of communications, in the spring of 1915, clearly demonstrate both alarm and concern for the acute danger presented by the Armenian insurgents. The cutting of the road networks for more than a period of several days had a severe impact on the amount of material getting through to the armies on the active fronts thereby denying them the means to fight. Thus, the Armenian insurrection was a genuine security imperative requiring an immediate solution, and it was an existential threat to the survival of the empire's armies.

OTTOMAN INTELLIGENCE AND THE ARMENIANS

The intelligence services of the Ottoman general staff (the staff's 2nd Division) provided the government a wide range of comprehensive information about foreign and domestic affairs. It is important to review some of these reports and to examine what kind of picture they portrayed to the government and general staff. This section focuses on the intelligence picture regarding the activities of the Armenian revolutionary committees and their interaction with the enemy powers.

Throughout the rest of 1914 and into January 1915, many reports to the Ottoman general staff outlined the danger posed by armed Armenians in the Third and Fourth Army areas. Incidents of terrorism increased, particularly bombings and assassinations of civilians and local Ottoman officials.[2] The Third Army reported that the local Armenians were supporting Armenian guerrilla operations in Bitlis and Van provinces.[3] The areas around Erzurum were hotbeds of activity, and Ottoman intelligence tracked the local Armenian committee leaders and the villages that hid and supported them, for example, Bogos Boyaciyan from Toti and Ohannes Kokasyan from Velibaba.[4] There were minor revolts in Bitlis and areas near Van in early February.[5]

In Armenian villages on the road between Sivas and Erzincan, Ottoman officers found illustrated bulletins and posters advocating resistance and massacre of Muslims.[6] These incidents were especially disturbing to the Ottomans because they indicated a higher degree of organization, which also included the cutting of communications lines and the interdiction of roads.[7] Pitched small-scale battles became common across eastern Anatolia. A three-day battle took place near Hizan and it left seven soldiers and gendarmes dead.[8] Gendarmes near Muş were attacked in a battle that lasted several hours. An eight-hour battle at Kümes village of Akaan Buçağı left nine soldiers dead, while similar encounter near Arın left more soldiers dead.[9] Whether the Armenian activities were acts of self-defense or acts of revolt remains controversial and inconclusive even today.[10]

One of the most significant documents from this period was a ciphered cable the Operations Division of the Ottoman general staff sent on February 25, 1915, to the field armies directing them to take increased security precautions.[11] In this cable, Enver directed an increase in surveillance and security measures, and he established the operational architecture that the army would use for dealing with the Armenian committees. He directed that the Third and Fourth Armies and the Iraq Command would be the highest authorities for establishing surveillance, security measures, and precautions in their respective areas.[12] In the remaining army areas, the numbered army corps headquarters were to be responsible for establishing similar measures in their areas as well (in the First Army: I-IV Corps and Second Army: V and VI Corps). The reason for this was simply the army corps on the First and Second Armies were not in combat and occupied provincial-sized areas, while the army corps in the Caucasus, Palestine, and Mesopotamia were fighting on the front lines. In essence, the non-engaged army corps in the west had the capacity to manage internal threats in their areas of operation, while those in the east did not.

The directive also alerted the armies to increased dissident Armenian activity in Bitlis, Aleppo, Dörtyol, and Kayseri, and, furthermore, identified Russian and French influence and activities in these areas. In particular, secret encoding books in French, Russian, and Armenian were discovered in Armenian homes in the city of Kayseri. Moreover, commanders were ordered to disarm Armenian soldiers, and remove them entirely from important headquarters staffs and command centers. The final measure fits a report that the Armenian Patriarchate in Constantinople was transmitting military secrets and dispositions to the Russians.[13]

The timing of Enver's orders corresponded with information provided to the Russians from the Armenian committee in Zeytun that 15,000 Armenians there were ready to take up arms and attack lines of communications of the Ottoman army in Erzurum.[14] The Third Army notified Enver on February 27 that although there had been outbreaks of violence in Muş and Bitlis, things were in hand and that it was redeploying some *jandarma* back to the provinces to maintain security.[15] This message, in turn, generated a cipher from Enver to the provincial governors and the army commanders reminding them of the importance of speedy intelligence and prompt action.[16]

In early March 1915, the intelligence picture of Armenian activities grew worse and the Third Army expressed renewed concern about the activities of the Armenian patriarch.[17] The insurgent situation in the Doğubeyazıt-Van region had considerably worsened. The governor of Van reported numerous massacres of isolated Muslim villagers by armed groups of Armenian guerrillas.[18] The governor sent a report containing the names of over one hundred villagers who were killed, raped, or maimed in these attacks.[19] On the other hand, the local Armenian community accused the governor of unprovoked massacres of Christians and there were similar reports of the killing of Armenians.[20] Regardless of cause, by this time, the staff of the Third Army was sufficiently concerned by the possibility of armed insurrection to begin shifting *jandarma* and army units into the area to meet the threat. Far to the west, the 2nd Infantry Division near Constantinople reported that Armenians in Tekirdağ (Rodosto) were storing guns and ammunition for use in arming deserters.[21] Similar reports from the Fourth Army reinforced the gathering pattern of Armenian activities.

In the Fourth Army area, Armenian activity in Zeytun caused army commander Cemal Pasha to move a battalion from the 22nd Regiment to that area.[22] About the same time, Armenian deserters from Maras resisted arrest, killed six gendarmes, and then fled to Zeytun, where they led an uprising on March 12.[23] They and 150 other Armenians then broke out of the Ottoman cordon and went into a monastery in the mountains on March 23.[24] Short, but violent, skirmishes between the army and the Armenians broke out several times. Nevertheless, the army successfully forced the surrender of some 130 army deserters on March 29, 1915, ending the outbreak.[25]

Mahmut Kamil, the commander of the Third Army, sent a report to the general staff on March 23, 1915, noting that similarly to the Armenians, rebellious Kurdish tribal leaders were returning via Persia to raise rebellion.[26] The X Corps sent a report on March 27 to Third Army that the well-armed Dashnak committee of Sivas was organizing to "cause turmoil in the regions behind the Ottoman lines and thus ease the advancement of the enemy."[27] A 19-page packet of reports was put together by the governor of Van covering the period of March 1–31, which contained mostly old information, but which did outline some new activities, such as an Armenian plan to start the rebellions beginning in Van, Bitlis, Erzurum, and Şabin Karahısar, as well as Armenian personal correspondence revealing arms and money smuggling.[28] This report also outlined a number of massacres of Muslim villagers in the Van province by Armenian guerrillas.

In April 1915, Fourth Army commander Cemal Pasha notified the intelligence directorate that small bands of Armenian guerrillas were operating in Kilis near Aleppo and in Maraş.[29] To the north, there were renewed reports of heavily armed Armenian bands near Sivas and Erzincan.[30] A First Army report corroborated previous information regarding the activities of armed Armenian volunteers traveling through Azerbaijan to Bayburt and Kayseri.[31] On April 8, Cemal sent an additional report adding the city of Konya as an area of Armenian activity.[32] A follow-up report the next day also noted suspicious activities sponsored by the Armenian patriarch in his army area as well.[33] A simultaneous report from Mahmut Kâmil in Third Army noted rebellion brewing in Van province, treasonous Armenian activity and weapons seizures in Bayburt and Sivas, and requested the government to ask the Armenian patriarch to urge the Armenians toward compliance and patriotism.[34] An important ciphered message from Cemal on April 14 alerted the general staff to the dangers posed by Armenians in the Pozantı Gap.[35] This was a strategic chokepoint where the Berlin-Baghdad railway passed through a very narrow mountain pass.

Intelligence reports from early April indicated that the Armenian villages of Çatak and Gevaş, astride the key roads south and west from Van, were in a state of rebellion, and that the local Ottoman police stations had come under fire.[36] This report also identified that Armenians in Sivaş were making, and training with, bombs. Of note, Armenian bands began to cut the telegraph lines and interdicted the Bitlis road that connected Van with the outside world.[37] German diplomatic and consular reports indicated that the insurgency was expanding from Zeytun into neighboring areas.[38] An alarming report followed on April 16 from Kâzim Bey, the commander of the Van Jandarma Division, stating that Armenian insurgents at Çatak had cut the roads and telegraphs there as well. Moreover, Kâzim reported he had sent troops there but that they were unable to have much effect. [39] The battles around Çatak and Gevaş raged for two days as the Ottomans unsuccessfully attempted to restore their lines of communications.

The province governor, Cevdet Bey, tried to disorganize the gathering rebellion by ambushing and assassinating the leaders of Van's Dashnak committee. His efforts killed three of the top four men, but also served to inflame the rebellion rapidly.[40] He then arrested local Armenian leader Arshag Vramian, who was actually trying to quell the violence. Cevdat then made things worse by demanding that the Armenian community turn over its young men for induction into the army's labor battalions. In fact, the local Ottoman response to the outbreaks of violence near Van can be characterized as inflammatory and counterproductive rather than effective.

THE INSURRECTION AT VAN

The Armenian insurrection metastasized in late April 1915 when Armenians in the city of Van launched an uprising simultaneously with a Russian offensive. It is unclear today whether the uprising was spontaneous or previously coordinated with either the Russians or the *druzhiny*. An early report dated April 20, 1915, from Cevdat Bay informed the Third Army that Armenian rebels held the Akkilise Monastery in Van and the villages of Atalan and Peltensi as strongholds, and that fighting was heavy in the Armenian and Garden quarters of the city.[41] The Van Jandarma Division immediately sent back its Erzurum and Erzincan Mobile Jandarma Battalions (*seyyar jandarma*) along with some artillery from the 28th Division on April 23 to quell the rebellion.[42] Meanwhile, the staffs alerted the training depot in nearby Muş to prepare for action. The Ottomans maintained their grip on the citadel in Van but the rebels were able to burn down the large Hamid Ağa Barracks. Fighting raged in the city as the Armenians burned down the post office, the Ottoman bank, the Public Debt Commission, and the Tobacco Monopoly.[43]

Led by Aram Manukian, the resourceful surviving Dashnak leader from Cevdat's assassination plots, the rebels put into practice their well-rehearsed tactical plans and made excellent use of their previously hidden stockpiles of weapons. Ottoman reports accurately identified the Dashnaks as the core of the rebellion.[44] The fighting lurched into early May, when more of the Van Jandarma Division was pulled off the front lines in Persia and sent back to the city in a forlorn attempt to suppress the rebellion.

Venezuelan soldier of fortune Rafael De Nogales observed the battle and noted that "the Armenians of the Vilayet of Van rose *en masse*, were heavily armed and fought with courage and determination."[45] Ottoman army intelligence estimated the rebels in, and around, Van numbered about 2,000 trained men.[46] In late May 1915, the American ambassador in Constantinople sent a confidential report to Washington elaborating the nature and the large scale of the insurrection:

> It would seem as if an Armenian insurrection to help the Russians had broken out at Van. Thus a former deputy here, one Pastormadjian who

had assisted our proposed railway concessions some years ago, is now supposed to be fighting with the Turks with a legion of Armenian volunteers. These insurgents are said to be in possession of a part of Van and to be conducting guerrilla warfare in a country where regular military operations are extremely difficult. To what extent they are organized or what successes they have gained it is impossible for me to say; their numbers have been variously estimated but none puts them at less than ten thousand and twenty-five thousand is probably closer to the truth.[47]

While Morgenthau's figures seem high, the Armenian National Defence Committee (ANDC) reported in July that the British could "rely on 25,000 Armenian insurgents in Cilicia and could rely on 15,000 more from nearby provinces."[48] There is no question that the Russians supported the Armenians, inside and outside the Ottoman Empire, with money, weapons, and encouragement.[49] What remains unproven is the extent to which the Russians and the Armenian committees waged a joint and coordinated campaign to seize the city of Van.

The premier historians of the Caucasian campaigns W. E. D. Allen and Paul Muratoff noted, "Well informed by Armenian agents of the situation at Van, Yudenich (the Russian theater commander) determined to take advantage of it. Since March, four of the Armenian *druzhiny* had been concentrated at Bayazit" with a Cossack brigade.[50] Another historian asserted that the Armenians demanded urgent action to assist their beleaguered brethren and that the *druzhiny* at Bayazit were specifically formed into the Ararat Unit, composed of the Second, Third, and Fourth *Druzhiny*, which was assigned to capture the city of Van itself.[51] Several Armenian writers describe meetings in early April between Armenian military leaders from the *duzhiny* and the Armenians of Van.[52]

Yudenich planned to move the Armenians with the Russian army toward Van in May 1915. To the east, the Russian army entered Persia and heavily engaged Halil's 1st Expeditionary Force at Dilman, which was forced to withdrawn from Persia at the beginning of May. Antranig's First Legion served under the Russians in this battle and then was shifted to assist in the Russian offensive toward Van.[53] There were no reinforcing Ottoman army units available within reach of Van and Cevdat's men fought a losing battle for control of the city. Between May 7 and 12, the city's Muslim inhabitants were evacuated from Van and on May 16, Cevdat gave up the struggle and withdrew his surviving men from the citadel.[54]

By mid-May, the Russian northern force from Bayezit had reached Bargiri, on the northern rim on Lake Van, while the Russians from

Persia took Kotur and seized Başkale on May 7. The Ottoman Third Army now determined that the campaign for Van province was lost and withdrew the battered remnants of the Van Jandarma Division and Halil's force, southwest toward Bitlis. The Russians and the Armenian *druzhiny* entered Van on April 20 to find a Dashnak government in place led by Aram Manukian. After the fall of the city, *druzhiny* legions under Antranig, Dro, and Hamazasp cleared the Ottoman rear guards from the southern shores of Lake Van, as well as seizing Çatak and Müküs on the road to Siirt.[55]

The Van uprising acted as a catalyst and uprisings broke out in other cities in the Third Army's area of responsibility. Making things worse for the Ottomans, Armenian *çeteler* or guerrilla bands (this word may be translated as guerrilla, insurgent, or bandit depending on context) began to interdict the vulnerable Ottoman lines of communications by cutting telegraph wires and conducting road sabotage in other locations to cut and block roads (notably along the Erzurum-Sivas logistics corridor).[56] Along the front lines northeast of Erzurum, Armenian volunteers assisted the Russians in pushing the Stange Detachment back from the area around Artvin and were supported by Armenian insurgents (*çeteler*) operating behind Stange's lines.[57] The governor of Sivas reported several times in late April that large numbers of armed Armenians in the mountains posed a security problem for unguarded Muslim villages.[58] The Third Army corroborated the reports from Sivas and noted that the Armenians were cooperating with the Russian enemy.[59] Diyarbakır (situated on the southern logistics corridor) erupted in a rash of bombings later in the month[60] and another uprising broke out in Zeytun.[61] German cables from Constantinople reported that Armenian clubs in Erzurum committed a series of political murders, and that Armenians were serving as guides for the Russian army.[62] The Germans also confirmed some of the Ottoman intelligence reports concerning Armenian arms caches, noting that bombs and bomb-making materials had been discovered in Kayseri.[63]

It is important to note here that the Ottomans, the Russians, the Germans, the Americans, the Armenians themselves, and even an independent Venezuelan observer indicated that a large number of Armenians, who possessed large numbers of weapons, revolted in the eastern provinces of Anatolia in support of a Russian offensive. This point is often overlooked in examinations of what happened to the Armenians in 1915. In any case, the Ottomans did not have adequate forces in position to deal with the problem. In spite of months of tension, the Ottoman army was largely unprepared for outbreaks of violence on the scale of the Van rebellion. There were pitched battles between the insurgents and the *jandarma*, Ottoman army paramilitary volunteer units, and the few regular army units in the area. Beginning in mid-April, the Ottoman general staff began to shift reinforcements into the region in order to suppress the insurgents at Van.[64] These forces were inadequate to the task and, as a consequence, the loss of Van ruptured the entire Ottoman strategic posture in southeast Anatolia by forcing the front back hundreds of kilometers to Bitlis.

Dörtyol and the Fourth Army

The Ottoman general staff and army were particularly sensitive to their railway lines of communications leading east from Constantinople, all of which ran directly through the Ottoman Fourth Army area. Sometimes called the Berlin to Baghdad Railway because of German investments, the railway split at Dörtyol with the pilgrimage route leading south to Mecca and an uncompleted spur leading east for about 30 miles. In truth, the railway system was the empire's military "Achilles Heel" because it serviced almost the entire logistics needs of the three Ottoman field armies in the Caucasian, Mesopotamian, and Palestinian theaters of operations (the Third, Sixth, and Fourth Armies, respectively).[65]

None of these theaters of war were self-supporting logistically and Caucasia and Palestine even lacked the food crops and fodder to sustain large numbers of men and animals.[66] A tight allied naval blockade that began in November 1914 forced almost all logistics traffic onto the fragile single-track railway leading from Constantinople to Alexandretta and Aleppo. Making things worse for the Turks, there was also an acute shortage of engines and rolling stock and, moreover, the line was incomplete leading through the rugged Toros and Amanus mountains.[67] Of particular concern were the tracks and bridges near Dörtyol that lay close by the Mediterranean Sea, making them tempting targets for allied interdiction. Unfortunately for the Turks, the mobilization and concentration plans of 1914 stripped the Levantine coast of all regular forces and, from mid-October 1914 through mid-April 1915, there were no Ottoman army combat units of battalion size or larger in either northern Syria or near Alexandretta.[68] With few forces available, other than depot battalions and the local gendarmerie, the Ottoman Fourth Army, under Cemal Pasha, was poorly prepared to deal with any threat north of the staging areas near Gaza of the Egyptian invasion force.[69]

The activities of Captain Larkin and HMS *Doris*, as well as those of the French and Russian navies, alerted the Ottomans to the profound operational weaknesses in their Levantine coast strategic posture. Ottoman reactions were both predictable (military reinforcement) and unpredictable (population relocation) and had profound outcomes for the local Armenian population, in particular. As a result of the escalating allied activities in the Alexandretta area, Ottoman authorities elevated the watchfulness of their scant security forces along the coast, especially around Dörtyol, and soon intelligence reports began to arrive in Constantinople.[70]

A report from the Governor of Adana to the national police directorate in the Constantinople Ministry of the Interior on February 26, 1915, noted that three Armenians were caught on February 12 as they attempted to take refuge on an "enemy battleship" off Dörtyol.[71] The same report identified a man named Agop hiding in the reeds on shore, who was also caught, and who testified that the three Armenians were conveying information about Ottoman army positions. Continuing the report, the governor noted that a "heliostata device" (a signaling machine that used mirrors) was discovered in the reeds near Payas (along the railway 34 kilometers from Alexandretta). This information was forwarded to the headquarters of the Fourth Army in Damascus on March 5; however, the army staff was already aware of the situation and had previously, on February 26, begun to reinforce the region with a detachment of troops from the 8th Infantry Division.[72]

As if this were not enough, the flow of information upward to the Ministry of the Interior from the Adana region now came back downward from the Ministry of War.[73] A security alert bulletin was issued from the operations division of the Ottoman general staff warning all army commands and army areas that Armenians were a serious threat.[74] In this alert, the problems in Dörtyol and Aleppo took priority of place in the first paragraph. Worried about the security situation in Dörtyol, and short of available troops to adequately secure the area, the Ottomans began in early March to relocate the local Armenian population from there to prevent further incidents.[75] A cable from Interior Minister Talat Pasha to Fourth Army commander Cemal Pasha on April 11 identified Dörtyol again, as well as Alexandretta and Adana, as locations from which Armenians must be relocated for security reasons.[76]

German consular officials also began to report activities around Dörtyol, noting on March 7 that Armenian gendarmes had surrendered without resistance to the landing parties of the cruiser HMS *Doris*, and also that antigovernment activities were increasing there as well.[77] Another consular report the following week titled "The unrest in Dörtyol" outlined more problems in the village and that "several times after the bombardment of the Turkish harbors by the English warships, the British came on land without any difficulty and went to the Armenians in Dörtyol to do their shopping."[78] Moreover, the report identified an Armenian deserter named Saldschian, who was recruiting locals "for foreign service" and that he had returned to an "English war-ship" before the police could arrest him.[79] The report continued with the information that another Armenian named Koschkerian had come ashore from the English warship carrying money to organize a conspiracy or revolution. In turn, the German ambassador forwarded these reports, along with many others documenting dissident Armenian activities in the Ottoman Empire, to the Foreign Ministry in Berlin.

The area north of Dörtyol was particularly sensitive to Ottoman authorities because the railway from Adana to Osmaniye came to within ten kilometers of the sea near Ceyhan. A raid on an Armenian house next to the railway bridge at Ceyhan on April 17 netted the authorities 50 kilograms of dynamite.[80] Simultaneously, armed attacks by Armenian guerrillas using guns and bombs began in the rear areas of the Fourth Army.[81] An interesting letter exists from the Armenian National Defense Committee of America to Sir Edward Grey outlining a plan to send American Armenian volunteers to fight and raise insurrection in the Caucasus and urging the British to invade Cilicia, where the local Armenians were prepared to rise in revolt.[82]

The sensitivity of the Ottomans to threats to their railway lines of communications, as the dangerous spring of 1915 arrived, is illustrated by further message traffic from Constantinople. In a ciphered message to the Fourth Army, which had operational control over the Alexandretta and Dörtyol areas, Talat Pasha specifically requested that relocated Armenians from the towns and villages of the Alexandretta and Bilan districts, within which lay Dörtyol, be managed in a particular manner. Talat proposed guidelines for the resettlement of displaced Armenians in temporary villages, but directed that the relocated Armenians from these areas "be definitely resettled at least twenty-five kilometers away from the Baghdad railway lines running to the frontier as well as away from other railway lines"[83] The message contained no rationale for the specified distance, but the author believes that a standoff distance of 25 kilometers from a railway line made it all but impossible for a terrorist (in the era before motorization) to travel to and from a target safely under the cover of darkness. In any case, this proviso indicates the high priority that the Ottomans placed on their railways.

The Ottoman Army Rear Area and Logistics

The operational areas of the armies of World War I were character-ized by two zones, the forward area and the rear area. The forward area ran from the front of the front lines to the rear of the army corps areas of operations. This area was physically dangerous and was almost entirely under enemy artillery fire and aerial observation. The rear areas lay behind the forward area and were not normally particularly dangerous; often the army rear area was inside the belligerent's own country as in the case of France and the Ottoman Empire. Militarily, lines of communication connecting the forward and rear areas and the Ottoman Empire's principal lines of communications are shown in map 8.1.

The Ottoman army of 1914 patterned itself, its doctrines, its operational thought, and its approach to war on the German army. Logistically the Ottomans separated their operational field armies from supporting logistics infrastructure by creating lines of commu-nications inspectorates (LoCIs) in the rear areas upon mobilization (and mirroring the German system).[84] These "formed the conveyor of the army" and were "the middleman between home and army."[85] In military doctrinal terms, the LoCIs were a service support organiza-tion (as opposed to a combat or combat support formation) and had no intrinsic combat capabilities. This system enabled combat com-manders at the front to focus their energy on operational and tactical matters while logisticians handled supply matters.

As its capstone logistics command element the Ottoman general staff activated the General Lines of Communications Inspectorate (*Menzil Genel Müfettişliği*) on August 5, 1914, in Constantinople.[86] This organization exercised command authority over the logistical lifelines of the empire at the strategic level.[87] High-level logistical planning and coordination remained a function of the general staff's Fourth Division, while the GLC Inspectorate coordinated daily move-ments and logistical functions through lower-level subordinate num-bered army inspectorate commands.[88]

In eastern Anatolia the Third Army Lines of Communications Inspectorate (*3ncü Ordu Menzil Müfettişliği*, hereafter referred to as 3 LoCI) supported the Ottoman Third Army. The 3 LoCI head-quarters became operational on August 26, 1914, in Erzurum using officers from the Ottoman X Corps and moved to Erzincan a week later.[89] Colonel Fuat Ziya assumed command[90] of the 3 LoCI, which was assigned a variety of army support units, including ammunition depots and trains, transportation units, field hospitals, remount and

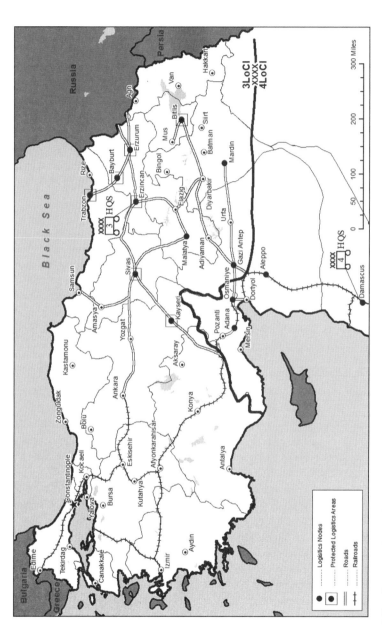

Map 8.1 Ottoman lines of communication.

veterinary stations, basic training depot battalions, bakeries and repair shops, supply depots, and labor battalions.[91] Its area of responsibility began at the rear edge of the combat corps areas and stretched 800 kilometers westward and southward to the railway servicing eastern Anatolia. Fuat Ziya exercised command through subordinate local commanders called post or node commanders (*nokta komutanlık*). After a month of operations the 3 LoCI had stockpiled 30 of the minimum 45 days of rations and supplies required by war regulations for the Third Army.[92] Likewise, ammunition and medical supplies were in very short supply.[93] This was a slim margin for war and the situation was aggravated by the huge losses of equipment and supplies suffered by the Ottoman army in the recent Balkan Wars.

By September 26, 1914, the Third Army reported 168,608 men and 53,794 animals (horses, camels, mules, and oxen) assigned to its rolls.[94] The following month reports from the 3 LoCI indicated that it had stockpiled two and a half months of bread and meat, thirteen days of oil and dried vegetables, eighteen days of barley, twenty days of rice, and five months of sugar for a planned force of 200,000 men and 70,000 animals.[95] Ammunition was a particularly difficult challenge because of the wide variety of rifles and cannon used by the Ottoman army, but there were about 1,000 rounds of rifle ammunition per rifleman and about 850 shells per cannon.[96] This was about half as many shells as the Western powers considered as adequate stocks for war, which averaged about 1,500 per mobile field-gun or howitzer.[97]

Bringing food, ammunition, and supplies forward challenged Colonel Fuat's organization to its fullest because of the vast distances to the front. Unlike the great powers of Europe, which built railway nets to accommodate mobilization and supply armies, the Ottoman Empire's railways were built by foreigners for economic profits. Consequently, none ran to the eastern Anatolian theater of operations, and the Ottoman front-line units there found themselves over 900 kilometers from railheads. This situation was compounded by a tight Allied naval blockade that forced all logistics traffic onto the two macadamized all-weather roads (*Bellibaşlı karayolları*) that led into eastern Anatolia. Thus, the 3 LoCI supported a force approaching a quarter of a million men and animals 900 kilometers from railheads using animal-drawn transport on two avenues (Sivas-Erzincan-Erzurum in the north and Diyarbakır-Bitlis-Van in the south).

War broke out on the Caucasian frontier on November 1, 1914, and after a month of combat operations, the logistical situation was already strained. Altogether the 3 LoCI had 70 days of rations on hand, but front-line units were reduced to 20–25 days on hand, while the fortress of Erzurum had 40–45 days on hand. The provinces of Trabzon and Van had 3–4 months on hand, but the logistics command lacked the transport to transfer supplies rapidly over the abysmal road system.[98] The battles on the frontiers also depleted ammunition stocks and sent about 6,000 wounded into the 3 LoCI hospitals at Hasankale and Erzurum.[99]

In Syria and Palestine, the Fourth Army formed on September 6, 1914. It activated the Fourth Army Lines of Communications Inspectorate (*4ncü Ordu Menzil Müfettişliği*, hereafter referred to as 4 LoCI) on November 12, 1914, with the headquarters in Damascus.[100] The activation of 4 LoCI, which was commanded by Major Kazim, occurred after the declaration of war, and there was no opportunity to stockpile munitions or supplies. Unlike the Third Army, Fourth Army was responsible for the security and maintenance of the railway line that led from the Pozantı Gap to the Euphrates River and south through Palestine to Medina. The railway posed particular problems because it was constructed by European entrepreneurs rather than by military planners. There were two uncompleted gaps in rugged mountains at Pozantı (54 kilometers) and Osmaniye (36 kilometers), different gauge tracks (e.g, 100 centimeters wide from Remleh to Jerusalem but 105 centimeters wide from there to Damascus), and the entire line was in an extremely poor state of repair.[101] Compounding the difficulties all supplies for the Mesopotamian theater were shipped through the 4 LoCI area and competed for the inadequate transportation resources.

The Fourth Army began combat operations against the British in late January 1915 when it invaded Egypt in an attempt to block the Suez Canal. As at Sarıkamış, on the Caucasian front, this operation ended in failure, but casualties were very light and did not affect the combat capability of the Fourth Army. No major combat operations happened on this front during the spring and summer of 1915. However, disaster struck the adjacent Sixth Army, which lost all of inhabited Mesopotamia below Nasiriya on the Euphrates River by April 1915.

The Effect of the Sarikamiş Campaign on Ottoman Logistics

In late December 1914, the Ottoman Third Army conducted an unsuccessful full-scale envelopment operation aimed at the destruction of a major part of the Russian army in Caucasia. The effect on 3 LoCI was immediate as the previously wounded men were shifted rearward from Erzurum and Hasankale to hospitals in Sivas and Narman.[102] As the wounded went back, munitions, uniforms, food, and supplies were moved frantically forward. Several thousand replacements were also rushed forward from depots in Sivas, Giresun, and Tokat to the Köprüköy lines.[103] On January 18, 1915, further drafts from Elaziğ (1,500 men) and Tokat (2,000 men) arrived at the front. Senior officer replacements were in very short supply and available officers were spread out between the infantry divisions. Thousands of reserve rifles were dispatched to make up for the losses as well.[104]

By February 8, the Third Army reported 59,226 men and 14,833 animals available for combat duty and 10,074 men and 8,277 animals assigned to the 3 LoCI.[105] North of Erzurum, supply stocks were down to about 40 days of rations and 17 days of fodder, while stocks in the army rear areas were sufficient for 60 and 16 days, respectively.[106] In March 1915, stock levels rose to 39 days of rations and 14 days of fodder in the combat zone, and 129 days of rations and 37 days of fodder in the army rear area. April brought a Russian offensive toward the lakeside city of Van and Malazgirt. Renewed fighting in May witnessed a Russian offensive in the Tortum valley, which was barely halted. Ottoman losses in these months were severe and approached those of Sarıkamış (58,000 men killed and wounded). The fighting quickly consumed accumulated supplies, and by May 30, 1915, stocks were down to critical levels of 41 days of rations and 7 days of fodder in the combat zone and 25 days of rations and 4 days of fodder in the army rear area.[107] It is apparent from these figures that resupply, especially of fodder (a critical commodity for an animal-drawn army), was not keeping up with the demands of campaigning.

Munitions were also in short supply in the Third Army during this period, and this was compounded by the variety of weapons in use. For example, the army used five models of rifle, two models of pistol, and four models of machine gun.[108] Supplies for small arms and artillery are difficult to establish because these munitions were reported as cases of ammunition rather than as "days of supplies."[109] However, the modern official Turkish history notes that losses of weapons and munitions in eastern Anatolia in the spring of 1915 exceeded the totals of incoming quantities.[110] Likewise, personnel replacements, especially trained officers, were also desperately short, and the depot system could not draft and train men fast enough to keep up with losses. In late May 1915, the infantry divisions of the Third Army, which should have contained over 9,000 infantrymen each, were worn down to an average strength of around 2,000 infantrymen each.[111]

While the Sarıkamış campaign is commonly seen as the proximate cause of Ottoman operational weakness in Anatolia in the spring of 1915, it is clear that the 3 LoCI was able to restore much of the Third Army's logistical posture and effectiveness in the following months.[112] However, such capacity as existed was quickly exhausted, and it was the Tortum-Van-Malazgirt battles that wore the Third Army down to ineffectiveness. The idea that the losses and aftermath of Sarıkamış somehow "fuelled the zeal for exterminating the Armenians" has no basis in fact.[113] In any case, by late May 1915, the logistics situation of the Ottoman Third Army was unsatisfactory, and any interruption of the supply chain would further degrade the army's effectiveness.

CHARACTERISTICS OF OTTOMAN LOGISTICS SECURITY

The Ottoman logistics system was a conveyor or pipeline that moved men and supplies from rear areas to forward depots for storage and further distribution to front-line corps and infantry divisions. Although 279 officers, 119 doctors, and 12,279 men were assigned to the 3 LoCI on April 14, 1915, few of these were available for point or area security.[114] Most of them were needed to care for the 7,924 draft animals and the thousands of various carts and wagons assigned to the inspectorate and to move supplies. Motorization was almost nonexistent, for example, there were only 12 automobiles available in the 3 LoCI area, mainly for use by high-ranking officers in the Erzurum area.[115] Along the routes, node commanders were responsible for the security of the roads and for coordinating movements and convoys.

Protection and self-defense were major concerns for the army: Third Army weapons reports from early May 1915 reveal that the soldiers assigned to the 3 LoCI were issued with a mere 1,231 rifles and 82 cases of rifle ammunition (for a force of over 10,000 men).[116] Significantly, this reflected organizational weapons authorizations, rather than theater weapons shortages, as the logistics inspectorate system was designed to operate in friendly territory (the soldiers were supply and services men and not fighting men). In early March 1915, the 3 LoCI ordered selected node commanders to establish "protected logistics areas" (*toplama muhafaza*) that provided security for both convoys and for fixed facilities such as hospitals and magazines.[117] These improvised protected logistics areas were fortified hastily and reflected an immediate reaction to security problems. They were established notably along the Sivas-Erzurum corridor, which carried the bulk of the Third Army's supplies. They were also established along the Trabzon-Erzurum corridor, which contained the bulk of the army's magazine capacity. This was because most of the army's ammunition was shipped through the port of Trabzon in peacetime and the magazines were built to accommodate munitions movements from there to Erzurum. The establishment of these improvised fortified camps along what should have been secure rear-area lines of communications shows that the Ottoman logistics command reacted to an actual internal threat by adjusting its organizational architecture in a nondoctrinal way.

Adding to Ottoman vulnerability, the weak road network within the Third Army area was rapidly deteriorating as a result of extraordinarily heavy use. The inability of the provinces to maintain the few all-weather roads in operational condition forced the military to assume this burden. This required the army to build up its labor services, which were organized into unarmed labor battalions (*amele taburu*).[118] The Third Army was unprepared for this upon mobilization in 1914, and only had six road construction battalions (*yol inşaat taburu*) on strength.[119] In 1915, these were reorganized and expanded into 30 *amele (yol) taburu*, or labor (road) battalions, of which 11 were deployed on the Erzincan-Erzurum-Hasankale-Tortum corridor.[120] These units were not penal battalions, but much of the manpower required for the increase in the number of battalions came from Armenian soldiers that the Ottomans forced out of combat units in the spring of 1915.

Some authors suggest that the labor battalions were really penal battalions specifically designed for the intentional killing of Armenian soldiers assigned to their ranks.[121] In fact, the labor battalions were an essential part of the Ottoman logistics architecture and were an absolute requirement to keep the roads operational. Attrition wore them down, and in the summer of 1916, the surviving 28 labor battalions were reorganized into 17 battalions because of severe shortages of men.[122] These battalions had been weakened severely in the disastrous retreat from Erzurum and Trabzon, sustaining heavy casualties, which caused the merging of some battalions to bring others up to strength.[123] Regardless of the composition of the labor battalions, maintaining them at peak strength was a priority for the Third Army, in order to keeps the roads open.

To the south, the railway ran directly through the Fourth Army's 4 LoCI to the front, but that inspectorate, likewise, remained heavily reliant on human and animal labor. The 4 LoCI had 10,280 animals on hand in early 1915[124] and about 18,000 men assigned.[125] Much of this capacity was deployed south of Damascus and is not relevant to the Armenian rebellions. In the area north of Damascus, the 4 LoCI was involved mainly in the movement of supplies rather than stockpiling rations or munitions for combat. This was because the fronts and associated supply and munitions depots were much farther to the south in Palestine. From the records examined, it does not seem that the 4 LoCI fortified protected logistics areas, as did the 3 LoCI. However, there is evidence in the message traffic that army staffs were concerned about this problem. For example, a top priority message to the Fourth Army from the Ottoman general staff on April 22, 1915, outlined the operations of the Armenian committees in Karahisar (in Sivas province), which particularly threatened telegraph lines and roads.[126] Of note is the fact that, within the Fourth Army staff, this information was passed immediately for special action and attention to the railroad inspectorate, the transportation inspectorate, and the railroad troops detachments inspectorate (the *3 Şube Şimendifer Müfettişliği*, 6 *Şube Menzil Umum Müfettişliği*, and 8 *Şube Şimendifer Kitaatı Müfettişliği*, respectively), with instructions to increase immediately security measures and protective troop detachments. This indicates the Fourth Army's sensitivity to the Armenian threats to the army's transportation networks.

Taken as a whole, the Ottoman army modeled its LoCI system on a German organizational architecture that was designed to operate within the context of a regular army's friendly rear areas. Neither Ottoman nor German LoCIs were staffed or equipped to do much more than coordinate logistics and transport supplies. In both 3 LoCI and 4 LoCI areas there were very long stretches of undefended roads through which logistical convoys constantly moved. The convoys had extremely limited numbers of small arms and convoy guards, and they were very vulnerable targets that could be easily isolated by insurgents or bandits, although the improvised "protected logistics areas" offered some relief in the 3 LoCI. Moreover, there were no combat forces assigned to the LoCI as reserves or as quick reaction forces in case convoys had trouble. In summary, when the LoCI architecture operated in a high-threat environment it was fragile and dangerously vulnerable to interdiction and destruction.

The Armenian Threat and the Beginnings of a Counterinsurgency Strategy

The definitive study of the Caucasian campaigns assessed Kayseri as the critical "nodal point" and "most important cross roads in Asia" because the Ottoman Third Army was supplied through there via Sivas to Erzurum.[127] By mid-April 1915, the Ottoman army possessed convincing and genuine intelligence that Armenians had hidden weapons, including rifles, bombs, pistols, and military explosives there and in many of the key cities that lay astride or adjacent to the northern line of communications in Anatolia.[128] Ottoman reports also indicated that almost 5,000 rifles and tons of explosives were hidden in the cities of Aşkale, Bayburt, Elazığ (Harput), Kayseri, Erzincan, Erzurum, Malatya, and Sivas, all of which contained sizeable Armenian populations.[129] In the Bayburt and Erzurum areas, large bands of insurgent Armenian guerrillas operated and actively assisted the Russian army. In the vicinity of Sivas, there were very large numbers of guerrilla bands in the mountains, which were attacking Muslim villages. There is no question that insurgents in the Third Army's area of responsibility, armed by the Armenian revolutionary committees, possessed the military potential to interdict or to destroy the 3 LoCI's primary supply route.

The Fourth Army's southern route was equally threatened by armed insurgency. In the Adana-Alexandretta (Dörtyol)-Aleppo area, Armenian bands were in direct contact with the British and French fleets. The prospect of an amphibious invasion was an ever-present concern. Since the autumn of 1914, there had been frequent clashes between Ottoman paramilitary forces and Armenian terrorist and guerrilla groups in the areas of Adana, Bitlis, Malatya, Maraş, and Urfa. There was a large insurrection at Zeytun. Moreover, there was a major insurrection at Van that was closely coordinated with the Russian army and with the Armenian committees.[130] The insurrection at Van turned into a significant defeat for the Ottoman army and opened the strategic back door to Diyarbakır and Malazgirt. Again, there is no question that heavily armed insurgents possessed the capability to interdict, or destroy, both the 4 LoCI's southern lines of communications and the army's supply routes.

The Armenian military capability in key locations was considered in the calculations of security for the Ottoman army. It is certain today that the Van insurrection provided the worst-case paradigm for Ottoman army planners and commanders.[131] At Van, the Armenian committees quickly distributed large quantities of prepositioned weapons and rose up in concert with a Russian offensive. The insurgents were in direct contact with fellow committeemen in the *druzhiny* fighting alongside the Russians. There were too few Ottoman forces available to crush the Armenians and the Ottomans lost the city. By late May 1915, the Ottoman staffs were advancing the idea that what had happened at Van was in the process of happening in other strategic locations.

Taken together, the acts of violence and Armenian military capability came to be seen as a genuine and identifiable threat to the security of the Ottoman state in 1915.

The intelligence reports, and associated message traffic, in the first four months of 1915 between the Ministry of the Interior, the Ministry of War, and the staffs of the Third and Fourth Armies show a joint appreciation that Armenian rebellion, terrorism, and weapons collection had erupted into a full-blown insurrection. A recent article by noted German historian Hilmar Kaiser rejects this notion and asserts that "Turkish and pro-Turkish historians interconnected these events to prove an alleged master plan coordinated by Armenian revolutionaries located in Constantinople and abroad."[132]

It is true that, to date, no historian has been able to produce authentic evidence of a coordinated Armenian master plan for revolution. However, what is perceived as real is real in its effect. The message traffic shows that coordinated past activities of the revolutionary committees, combined with rising numbers of violent incidents and the irrefutable evidence of allied encouragement and support, convinced the Ottomans that such a plan existed. The Ottoman government and military staffs believed it and that was all that mattered. Exaggerating and accelerating Ottoman military appreciations about the Armenians and Van was the certain knowledge of an impending allied invasion at Gallipoli.[133] In turn, there was a policy shift within the Ottoman government, which the German ambassador attributed to these circumstances.[134] Two of the most significant policy documents to emerge from this period, which reflect this shift, were directives published on April 24, 1915, by the Ministry of the Interior and the Ministry of War. Together, these directives laid the foundations for what would evolve into a counterinsurgency strategy of relocation coordinated between the two ministries.

Talat ordered the arrest of the leaders of the Armenian committee leaders in Constantinople and elsewhere on April 24.[135] He justified this by stating the recent troubles in Zeytun, Bitlis, Sivas, Kayseri, and Van were caused by the revolutionary Armenian committees that had gathered "to incite upheavals in the regions in the army's rear areas and to threaten the Ottoman Army at every opportunity through their attempts, organizations and publications."[136] Continuing, Talat ordered the immediate shutdown of both the Hunchak and Dashnak committees.

Talat also sent a secret cipher to the governors of the provinces and cities explaining his actions in the capital.[137] Again, his thoughts were explicit, asserting that the Armenian committees "have dared to carry out treacherous activities which could affect the very existence and the future of our country, especially at the present when our state is at war. The incidents that took place in Zeytun, Bitlis, Sivas and Van have revealed the aims of the Armenian committees." It should be remembered that the Ottoman general staff was expecting the imminent arrival of a massive allied amphibious force, which landed on the Gallipoli peninsula on April 25.

Enver and the Ministry of War also issued a directive on April 24 to begin localized evacuations of Armenians in the areas, where the Armenians were actually in rebellion.[138] The directive also noted that "the Armenians were a great danger to the war effort, especially in east Anatolia."[139] This directive empowered the commanders of the Third and Fourth Armies to relocate Armenians that they designated as dangerous, but only from areas where they actually were engaged in rebellion. Interestingly, the implementation of the evacuations, as they were initially called, was not centralized and was left up to the discretion of the army commanders. Two days later, Enver reinforced Talat's directive by ordering all subordinate military commands to shut down the Armenian committees within their respective areas.[140]

The importance of these joint ministerial directives is threefold. First, they demonstrate the willingness of Talat and Enver to cooperate and work together to find joint and reinforcing solutions to the empire's security concerns. Second, Talat's explanation of the danger to the rear areas of the army explicitly demonstrates the government's awareness of the particular nature of the Armenian threat. Third, Talat defined the Armenian insurrection as an existential threat to the Ottoman Empire. Enver, who was a trained general staff officer, and a highly experienced guerrilla fighter himself, took the initiative to put into place a limited and localized evacuation policy. Taken altogether these government policy positions laid the foundations for a counter-insurgency strategy of relocation.

CHAPTER 9

A New Course of Action

The choice of explanation determines the nature of the problem's resolution.

—*Lieutenant General Paul Van Riper, USMC (Ret.),*
Quantico, Virginia, August 5, 2011

INTRODUCTION

To say that the Ottoman army was unprepared to deal with an insurrection in its rear areas understates greatly its strategic dilemma in the spring of 1915. The prewar general staff anticipated renewed war against the Balkan states but not against any of Europe's Great Powers. This left the Ottomans badly positioned for a multifront war against the Entente, particularly against Russia in Caucasia and Britain in Mesopotamia. Since the Ottomans did not anticipate war against the Great Powers, likewise they did not make plans to deal with an Armenian insurrection, which was itself an outgrowth of alliance warfare. Consequently, no significant combat forces were positioned within the interior core area containing the empire's critical lines of communications. Moreover, a centrally located strategic reserve did not exist, nor did the means exist to deploy such a force rapidly if it was needed, further limiting military options. This strategic posture constrained a coherent Ottoman military response to rear-area security concerns in eastern Anatolia, in effect forcing the army toward a resource-driven counterinsurgency "strategy of poverty" employing relocation, which was itself a new course of action.

An understanding of the relocation decision as a resource-driven strategic outcome requires an examination of the Ottoman government's assessments of the security situation, as it existed in May 1915, and the directives themselves. The partial relocation directives from the Ministry of War in April 1915 evolved into a regional program of population removal a month later. By late May 1915, government policy crystallized in formal relocation measures promulgated by government decree. These government instructions explicitly outlined the reasons for the relocation of Armenians from specified areas as well as presented the idea that these policies were a new military course of action. The army's part in this was to forcibly remove any Armenians who resisted relocation. This dynamic provided the framework for a reactive counterinsurgency campaign using units of the Third and Fourth Armies.

OTTOMAN STRATEGIC POSTURE AND REACTION

To summarize Ottoman concerns, armed hostile Armenian revolutionary committees working in concert with the Russians actively threatened both the rear areas of front-line units of the Third Army and the army's lines of communications. Additionally, there was a gathering threat to the Fourth Army lines of communications and there were strong suspicions that an Allied amphibious invasion, supported by Armenians, was imminent in the Alexandretta-Dörtyol area.[1] These potential disruptions to the lines of communications also constituted an indirect threat to the logistics posture of the Sixth Army in Mesopotamia. Map 9.1 shows the concentration of large Ottoman Armenians communities along the principal lines of communications in 1915.

The localized, and exclusively tactical, reactions of the Ottomans in April and May 1915 were increasingly ineffective as the tempo of the insurgency accelerated. Reports detailing the disaster at Van began to circulate throughout the Ottoman military establishment. The success of the Armenian committees in seizing Van were attributed to their high degree of organization and their ability to isolate the city by cutting the telegraph lines and road networks.[2] Moreover, intelligence indicated that after taking Van, the Armenian revolutionary committees and the Russians intended to execute similar operations against Başkale and Saray.[3] The Ministry of Finance joined in the accusations by stating that "a large part of Armenian officials are indeed committee members acting with the aim of realizing their national aspirations" and ordered the governances to dismiss them.[4] In Diyarbakir, "a great amount of explosives, 50 bombs, plenty of ammunition and weapons" were discovered in searches of Armenian houses.[5] The Third Army uncovered evidence of increasing levels of Armenian committee offensive preparations in six provinces, including Erzurum, Van, Bitlis, Mamüretülaziz, and Diyarbakır.[6] The evidence

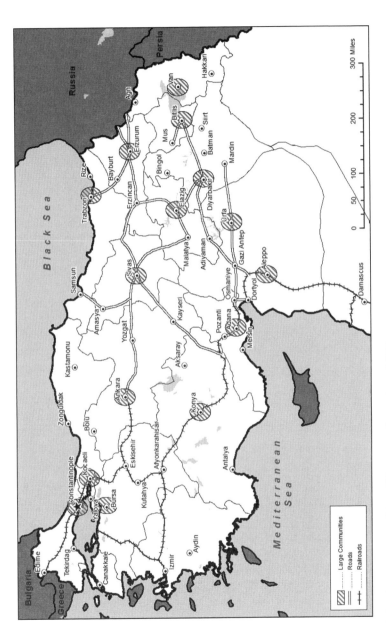

Map 9.1 Large communities of Ottoman Armenians, 1915.

involved bomb-making, developing plans for attacks, and a plot to take over the town of Karahisar.[7] Other messages reported the massacre of Muslim civilians by Armenian armed bands along the Black Sea coast[8] and the collaboration of "Christian traitors who supported the enemy."[9]

The Van rebellion and the events of April and May 1915 caught the Ottoman army without the regional combat strength necessary to deal effectively with the Armenian insurgency.[10] The Van Mobile Jandarma Division and part of the 1st Expeditionary Force (then transiting the area en route to the front) were sent into action in mid-April at Van, along with several light cavalry regiments. Additionally, the 36th Infantry Division, en route to the Caucasian front from Mesopotamia, was diverted briefly to the area as well.[11] These divisions were all short of artillery, engineers, and ammunition trains. Nevertheless, they represented the sum total of Ottoman army divisions available to quell the Armenian insurrection; three divisions out of a total of forty-six then in the Ottoman army's order of battle. Reacting to this, the army activated three new, but understrength, infantry divisions (the 41st, 43rd, and 44th) in March and June from depot battalions in the Adana-Aleppo region.[12] Composed mostly of older reservists, these new divisions were unfit for combat until late summer. Effectively, the strategic deployment of the Ottoman army concentrated combat forces at the fringes of the empire where the army was in contact with its Allied enemy and not in its center core areas where an insurgency was likely to occur.[13]

Almost counterintuitively, as the military situation in Gallipoli, the Caucasus, and Mesopotamia (Palestine was relatively stable at this time) grew increasingly desperate, the Ottoman general staff began to strip the interior core areas of trained men and formations to send to the fighting fronts. On April 20, 1915, the Ministry of War noted that it was undesirable to take regular army units and mobile field *jandarma* from the front for operations against insurgents.[14] Furthermore, the ministry directed that field commanders were to use the local *jandarma* against the Armenians and Greeks, who were forming insurgent bands. In fact, the experienced Van Field Jandarma Division and 1st Expeditionary Force were soon relieved from counterinsurgency duties and returned back to the front in mid-May 1915 to participate in offensive operations. The 36th Infantry Division followed them back to the front lines in mid-June. The Ottoman general staff maintained this military policy over the summer of 1915 and, as late as July 28, the Ottomans were arming civilian Kurds and Cizre tribesmen to suppress the Armenians.[15] These measures had the effect of further denuding the interior of fighting strength with which to confront the Armenian committees.

The historical antecedents of Ottoman military policy and counter-insurgency strategy as discussed in previous chapters, likewise, offered no real solutions to the contemporary problem of the suppression of an Armenian insurrection. Previous Ottoman experiences, in the period 1890–1911, involved sending thousands of soldiers organized into well-armed conventional armies against rebel armed forces. Moreover, the Ottoman experience in combating the well-organized revolutionary committees in the core areas also involved committing large-scale military forces. Finding a strategic solution became even more problematic because the stark reality was that the empire's enemies, in the midst of a global war, were actively encouraging and assisting the Armenian committees. In the absence of the military forces necessary to deal with insurgency in traditional ways, the Ottomans turned to a strategy of population relocation.

There is no direct evidence that the Ottoman decision-makers modeled their actions against the Armenian committees on contemporary Western military thinking. However, it is a historical fact that the Ottoman military modeled its strategic, operational, and tactical practices almost exclusively on those of the German and European armies. Therefore, the existence of Western counterinsurgency practices, such as relocation, cannot be discounted in the equation of a strategic solution to the Armenian threat.

In Cuba in the 1890s, the Spanish general Weyler devised a relocation-based strategy called "reconcentration" that relocated a population involved in insurgency to protected enclaves. The Americans conducted similar operations in the Philippines. Later the British army relocated most of the civilian Boer population to concentration camps specifically to isolate the commandos from their sources of supply. This brutal method proved to be the most successful counterinsurgency strategy of the early twentieth century and, when combined with cordon and search tactics, decisively broke Boer resistance. The Boer War notably generated intense public interest and scrutiny across Europe, especially in the newspapers of Britain, France, the Ottoman Empire, and Germany (where pro-Boer sentiment was rampant)[16] and became a cause célèbre of the age. While this strategy and its associated tactics were never formally embedded in the formal military doctrines of any army of the period it became a template for the destruction of guerrillas and insurgents in the twentieth century.

Relocation as a counterinsurgency strategy would reappear in various forms over the next 70 years. In the 1950s, the British in Malaya relocated over 500,000 ethnic Chinese into New Villages under the auspices of the Briggs Plan.[17] The French relocated 800,000 Algerians in the 1950s to Regroupment Centers under the infamous *Quadrillage* system.[18] The Americans employed the same principle in Vietnam, in the 1960s, by relocating thousands of villagers into what they called "protected hamlets."[19] In a different context, in 1942, the United States removed Japanese American citizens from California to relocation camps in the Nevada deserts in order to deal with a perceived Fifth Column threat to national security. Whether the process was called relocation, deportation, or detention and the destinations defined as concentration camps, regroupment centers, relocation camps, protected hamlets, or new villages—the basic strategy of relocation remained the same.

Although the Ottoman army did not include the subject of counterinsurgency in the war college curriculum, it is known that officers of the Ottoman Army intensively studied the lessons of the Boer War, most notably Pertev Pasha of the Ottoman general staff, who maintained an active correspondence with Colmar von der Goltz regarding the war.[20] It is also known that, despite the absence of formal counterinsurgency training at the war college, student officers and military faculty conducted informal discussions on this subject in the prewar years.[21] While there is ample evidence of Ottoman awareness of contemporary counterinsurgency practices, like the Western practitioners of counterinsurgency, the Ottomans themselves had no actual formal counterinsurgency doctrines using relocation or otherwise.

Even without formal doctrines, the strategy of relocating a potentially hostile population was exercised several times during the Balkan Wars of 1912–13 by the Ottoman army. The best-known relocation occurred in Thrace when the Ottomans moved thousands of Christians, who were ethnic Bulgarians and Greeks, across the Bosporus to Asia because they were thought to be in sympathy with the Christian Balkan League and potentially hostile.[22] These citizens returned to their homes after the war. In early April 1915, the Ottomans relocated the Christian population from the Gallipoli peninsula, about 22,000 mostly Greek citizens, because it was thought to be a rear-area threat to security.[23] Most of these Ottoman Greeks never returned home and were caught up in the massive population exchanges of 1922–23. In both cases, however, the relocated population survived because the concentration camps were located in the resource-rich western provinces. Thus, by 1915, in theory and in practice, relocation and internment were military tactics applied in a wide context of both counterinsurgency and counterguerrilla applications, by the Europeans, the Americans, and the Ottomans.

The Evolution of a Counterinsurgency Policy of Relocation

The Ottomans reacted vigorously, on a variety of levels, to these actual and potential Armenian threats. A modern historian characterized the Ottoman state's political response in this period as moving "from regional measures to general policy."[24] Likewise, the development of the Ottoman government's military policy toward the Armenian rebellion can be characterized as moving from a localized response of relocation to a general counterinsurgency campaign based on relocation.

It is difficult today to separate the effect of ideologically driven fears from actual security concerns but certainly security concerns played into the hands of the ideologically hard-line CUP, which has been accused of wanting to alter the eastern Anatolian demographic situation. In addition to the measures discussed in the previous chapter, on April 24, 1915, Enver ordered that the localized relocations should result in a new demographic in which Armenians were less than 10 percent of the total population in the affected areas.[25] Enver followed these orders on May 2, 1915, with a recommendation to the Ministry of the Interior to drive what he called "Armenian insurgents" away from the borders and resettle the areas with Muslim refugees from the Balkans.[26] These directives did not order the extermination of the Armenians but they do indicate the existence of a policy of population engineering that has a range of interpretations from simple relocation to ethnic cleansing.[27] The extant record does not reveal whether ideology or security concerns predominated, but in the military sense, Enver was clearly determined to insure that large concentrations of Armenians would not affect the operational situation.

It is known that large numbers of Armenians were relocated from the immediate tactical rear of the Third and Fourth Armies in April and May 1915. Beginning on May 16, for example, the first convoys of Armenians were relocated away from the Plain of Erzurum. One historian asserted that some 30,000 people were moved away from the Third Army's headquarters at Hasenkale in this particular relocation.[28] Moreover, the April 24 the directive to shut down the Armenian committees and apprehend the leaders was vigorously enforced in the eastern provinces, with the imprisonment of hundreds of prominent Armenian officials and professionals.[29] It is also known that in May 1915, the Ottoman staffs were advancing the idea that what had happened at Van was in the process of happening at other strategic locations as well.[30] A prominent Armenian concurred with this assessment, writing to Boghos Nubar that after the fall of Van and as the attacking Russian army approached Bitlis, "the Armenians there would have been of great assistance."[31] German diplomats also believed that the Armenian movement was "more widespread than was presumed up to now and that it [was] being encouraged from abroad with the help of the Armenian Revolutionary Committee."[32]

At the political level, Talat now joined Enver in applying policies centered on relocation. On May 24, 1915, a message went out from the Ministry of the Interior to the headquarters of the Fourth Army outlining a plan to relocate Armenians.[33] The ministry identified the provinces of Erzurum, Van, and Bitlis, as well as a number of other cities and sanjacks, as locations from which the Armenian population would be relocated. Talat established the architecture of command by appointing regional inspectors, who would manage the removal and the resettlement.

As he had directed previously, Talat once again affirmed that the resettled Armenians "shall be definitely located a minimum distance of twenty-five kilometers from the lines connecting with the border of the Baghdad Railway and other railways."[34] At that time, most of the Armenians already in the pipeline were clustered around Konya and Aleppo. However, Cemal Pasha made the decision to move them father southeast.[35] The ultimate destinations for most of the relocated Armenians were camps located downstream from Aleppo, along the Tigris River near Der Zor (modern Dayr az Zawr in Syria). The decision to send the Armenians to these destinations has a range of interpretations, ranging from a deliberately constructed and centralized CUP "death sentence" decision,[36] to a local decision by Cemal Pasha to solve the problem of how to sustain so many people.[37] In terms of national security, and in accordance with the relocation directives, Cemal based his decision on the idea that "in order to avoid new concentrations, Armenians had to be settled in places without an Armenian population."[38]

Talat sent the prime minister a classified memorandum on May 26, 1915, that restated the relocation decisions and locations, which he had already sent to the armies. Of note, Talat explicitly outlined the reasons behind his actions by stating that

> some of the Armenians living in places close to the battlefields have recently become involved in activities aimed at creating difficulties for our army in its fight against the enemy to protect the Ottoman borders. Those Armenians did everything to obstruct the operations of the army against the enemy, prevented delivery of supplies and munitions to the soldiers on the battlefronts, collaborated with the enemy and

some of them joined the enemy's ranks. Within the country they carry out armed attacks against the military forces and innocent civilians.[39]

He followed this with an outline of recommended measures for state security essentially based on relocation.[40] It is important to note that Talat did not accuse the entire Armenian population, referring only to "some of the Armenians," and also that he reaffirmed the danger to the army's lines of communications. The next day, the cabinet ratified the relocation decision and the Ottoman parliament passed a provisional law directing the army to crush Armenian resistance and to begin to round up Armenians in response to military necessity.[41]

On May 31, 1915, the Sublime Porte issued the now infamous public decree to relocate the Armenian population of the eastern provinces.[42] Much of what the sultan's decree contained was a restatement of the previous confidential military and cabinet documents. However, it is worth noting the following language:

> The conduct of such rebel elements rendered it necessary to remove them from the areas of military operations and to evacuate the villages serving as bases of operations and shelters for the rebels. To achieve this, a different course of action has begun to be implemented. Within that framework, the Armenians living in the provinces of Van, Bitlis, Erzurum, with the exclusion of the centers of Adana, Sişs, and Mersin; the sanjaks of Adana, Mersin, Cebel-i Bereket and Kozan; the sanjak of Maras with the exclusion of the center of Maras; the towns and villages of Inkenderun, Bilan, Cisr-i Sugur and Antakya of the province of Aleppo; with the exclusion of the central district of Aleppo have begun to be rapidly transferred to the southern provinces.

This decree demonstrates that the removal of the Armenians was based on the same rationale that the Americans, British, and Spanish used to remove insurgent populations in the Philippines, the Boer Republics, and Cuba. Moreover, it illustrates that the government was shifting its counterinsurgency strategy to something that was "a different course of action" from what it had done previously. Finally, the decree demonstrates that the relocation of Armenians was tailored to address known areas of Armenian insurgency, within a particular region, that directly threatened national security. These were not simply random cities and areas as all figured heavily in the ministries' message traffic from the previous months regarding the Armenian peril. It is evident from the timelines, however, that the decisions to relocate people were made largely by Talat, with some help from Enver, and they were a de facto accomplishment before the full cabinet and the sultan were aware of them.

An examination of the elaborate government policies regarding the safeguarding of the Armenian's real and personal property as well as for their safety during convoy to relocation camps are outside the framework of this book.[43] Suffice it to say that the difference between what the Ottoman government stated as its intentions, in this regard, and what actually happened over the course of the summer of 1915 was huge. Similarly, the tragic looting and massacres of Armenians, which became common as the eastern provinces were drained of the Armenian population, are also outside the military history of the Ottoman counterinsurgency campaign.

As the relocations began in earnest, however, there were important changes to the relocation policy over the course of the summer, which excluded a number of categories of Ottoman Armenians from movement. In early July 1915, Talat ordered that tradesmen and artisans, who were not committeemen, or who were not involved in harmful activities, remain in their home provinces to continue working, under the provision that they move to another town other than the one they currently lived in.[44] On August 3, Talat called an immediate halt to the relocation of Catholic Armenians, many of whom had been converted to Catholicism by German missionaries.[45] Two weeks later, Talat ordered the exclusion of Protestant Armenians, who had been largely converted by American missionaries, from relocation.[46] Subsequent messages from the Ministry of the Interior created additional categories and indicated Talat's continuing interest in excluding Ottoman Armenians who posed no threat to the state or who were valuable to the war effort in some way.

On August 15, Talat ordered that Armenian deputies and their families were not to be relocated.[47] On the same day, he directed that "the families of army members, officers, and medical officers of the Armenians subject to removal...will not be transferred."[48] On August 17, 1915, Talat directed that Armenian officials who were working in the railway administration and their families were not to be deported either.[49] The exclusion of Armenian railway officials shows the sensitivity of the government to the increasingly dysfunctional Ottoman railway system, which was vital to the empire's military lines of communications. On that day Talat also sent a message to the governor of Antalya directing that the Armenians of Antalya be left outside the scope of the relocations "as they are a small population, for the time being there is no need for the transfer of Armenians living there."[50]

Talat's exclusions particularly affected the Armenians in the Fourth Army area, which had been a hotbed of Protestant and Catholic missionary activity and which contained the Baghdad railroad. The

Third Army area, which was more heavily populated with Orthodox Armenians and through which no railroads passed, was less affected. Overall, these exclusions greatly reduced the number of Ottoman Armenians subject to relocation and made the army's job easier, while easing its worries about the maintenance of its logistical lines of communications.

The government's regional relocation order replaced the existing Ministry of War directives authorizing selective localized relocations around the Lake Van and Erzurum areas as the government reacted to the growing insurgencies in a larger area. Over the coming summer, Ottoman military and security forces began to concentrate the Armenians in the identified region for relocation. Many chose resistance, which in some cases was interpreted by the Ottomans as insurgency, making it difficult to determine the real reasons for the fighting in many locations.

Additions to Ottoman Force Structure in the Affected Areas

In August 4, 1914, the Ottoman general staff ordered the organization of the Halep Jandarma Division as a part of the ongoing military mobilization of the armed forces in Halep (Aleppo).[51] This division's 1st, 2nd, and 3rd Provisional Regiments were composed of battalions of the professional mobile gendarmerie (*seyyar jandarma*). The men were trained to military standards and were armed and equipped like the active Ottoman Army. On October 16, the *jandarma* division was deactivated and its regiments transferred elsewhere. However, a provisional infantry division was maintained in its place and it was assigned the depot battalions of the 72nd, 76th, and 78th Infantry Regiments. In this reduced role, it continued to conduct military training for new conscripts that included marching, marksmanship, and maneuvers.[52] In effect, from mid-October 1914 through mid-April 1915, there were no Ottoman Army combat units, of battalion-size or larger, in northern Syria and the Alexandretta area (modern Iskenderun), capable of either coastal defense or counterinsurgency operations.

On April 9, 1915, the provisional division was reorganized and was activated as the regular Ottoman army's 41st Infantry Division, composed of the 131st, 132nd, and 133rd Infantry Regiments.[53] These three regiments were built around the nucleus of the depot battalions and were made up of reservists and recruits. The new infantry division was assigned a tactical area, named the Alexandretta Area or *Iskenderun Bölgesi*, within the Ottoman Fourth Army's area of operations. Cemal Pasha commanded the Fourth Army and was responsible for road, area, and coastal security operations, as well as the operational front along the Suez Canal.[54] Lieutenant Colonel Hüseyin Hüsnü Abdullah commanded the division, which was given the mission of coastal and area defense for Iskenderun and the coast, and road security against bandits and insurgent Armenians.[55] Colonel Hüseyin assigned the 131st and 132nd Infantry Regiments to internal security duties in Zeytun and Urfa (Şanliurfa) and the 133rd Infantry Regiment to coastal defense duties near Alexandretta.

The activation of the 41st Infantry Division was taken in reaction to a pattern of dissident Armenian and allied naval activity in the Iskenderun area. Despite the threat and importance of its ongoing missions, the 41st Infantry Division was ordered to send two infantry battalions (of nine in the division) to assist in training the newly formed 53rd Infantry Division. Moreover, the Ottoman general staff ordered the division to send the 2nd Battalion, 131st Infantry Regiment and the 3rd Battalion, 132nd Infantry Regiment to Iraq to reinforce the faltering military situation there.[56] These battalions never returned to their parent division and the 41st Infantry Division was forced to activate two provisional infantry battalions of poorly trained recruits and reservists to replace them. The division also had a small field artillery force assigned to support its infantry, which was composed of a battery from the 22nd Mountain Artillery Regiment and a battery from the 35th Artillery Regiment.[57] Finally, the Ottoman general staff assigned an irregular volunteer cavalry troop to the division for reconnaissance and security operations (*Humus Gönüllü Süvari Bölüğü*).[58] In comparison with other Ottoman Army infantry divisions, the 41st Infantry Division was underequipped with artillery, engineers, and medical support. Moreover its infantry battalions were 20 percent understrength and contained numbers of older reservists.[59] This reflected the overall low priority given to the Ottoman Fourth Army by the general staff.

As the Armenian insurgency increased in scale and spread southward, the 41st Infantry Division found itself being drawn into the conflict. Within the division's tactical area, Armenian insurrections broke out in the mountainous areas near Maras and Urfa in June and July of 1915. Cemal's Fourth Army staff believed that the Urfa insurgency was instigated and supported by the French.[60] To better accommodate this expanding mission, Cemal modified the tactical areas of his army by tailoring them to better fit the reported threats of insurgency.[61] The 41st Infantry Division was assigned a revised tactical area known as the Second Area (*IInci Bölge*) and a new commander, Lieutenant Colonel Mehmet Emin.[62] The new tactical area was smaller than the Iskenderun Bölgesi and coincided very closely with the areas identified by Ambassador Morgenthau in May.[63]

The other Fourth Army division, which must be examined, was the 23rd Infantry Division, which was stationed in 1915, in Der'a, Palestine. This division was a prewar formation from Homs but had been forced to give up battalions to other divisions.[64] Its commander was Lieutenant Colonel Refet (later Bele) and by June 1915, the depleted division was composed of the 68th, 69th, and 130th Infantry Regiment (the first two of which had only one battalion on hand, rather than their full complement of three battalions, while the 130th Regiment had two battalions). Somewhat making up the shortfall, the 130th Regiment had the 4th Der'a Mobile Jandarma Battalion attached to it. Artillery was notably weak with the 3rd Battalion, 35th Artillery Regiment for fire support. In early July 1915, the newly formed and understrength division was concentrated in Nablus and shipped to Adana where it reformed on July 14 in the Fourth Army's Inci Bölge (First Area).[65]

It should be noted that in July 1915, the Fourth Army was significantly weaker overall than it had been in April. This was caused by the allied campaigns in Gallipoli and Mesopotamia, which as they gathered momentum and strength, compelled the Ottoman general staff to strip combat strength from Cemal's Fourth Army and send it to those fronts. On April 28, 1915, three days after the allies landed at Gallipoli, Enver ordered Cemal to send the 8th and 10th Infantry Divisions and the XIV Corps headquarters to the Ottoman Fifth Army on the peninsula.[66] Making the operational situation even worse for Cemal on June 2, the Ottoman general staff also ordered his 25th Infantry Division and the VIII Corps headquarters to Gallipoli as well. Map 9.2 shows the increasing concentration of Ottomna forces on the Gallipoli Peninsula in the summer of 1915, which stripped further forces away from the interior core provinces.

Moreover, as the British pushed up the Tigris River and deep into Mesopotamia, the general staff took a number of Cemal's smaller formations as well. Between May 30 and August 10, 1915, Enver ordered an additional nine artillery batteries, two infantry battalions, two cavalry regiments, and a machine gun company to the newly forming Sixth Army in Mesopotamia.[67] This left Cemal's Fourth Army with a single full strength and experienced division (the 27th Infantry Division) remaining on the Sinai front. The loss of so much combat strength crippled the Fourth Army's operational offensive capability and ended any thought of renewing the Suez Canal campaign in 1915. Although the Fourth Army gained the three newly activated infantry divisions in the spring, these were formed from preexisting

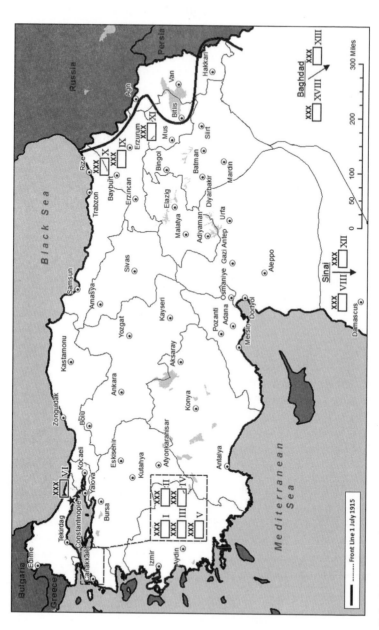

Map 9.2 Locations of Ottoman army corps in July 1915.

tactical assets and formations in the army's area of responsibility and there were no net increases in strength.

THE RELOCATION POLICY AND THE COUNTERINSURGENCY CAMPAIGN

If one were to conduct a military campaign analysis at one of the world's professional war colleges, the discussion might start with a consideration of "ends" (what they sought to accomplish), "ways" (how they intended to accomplish the operation), and "means" (the resources that were available for the operation). Success or failure in military operations almost always devolves to the proper balancing of these three considerations. In this case, at the end of May 1915, the Ottoman government committed itself to a different course of action from its previous counterinsurgency campaigns, and a brief examination of the campaign design and its ends, ways, and means are necessary to understand what followed in the summer of 1915.

There was no single unified government campaign plan to accomplish the relocation of the Armenians; however, the government messages discussed previously provide a sense of how the government intended the ministries to cooperate to relocate the Armenians. The strategic end sought by the Ottoman government was to eliminate the threat to the Third, Fourth, and Sixth Armies' rear areas caused by the actions of the Armenian committees. The way that the Ottoman government intended to accomplish this was through the compliant relocation of Armenians from designated areas to locations where they were not a threat, and when and if the Armenians resisted, to remove them by force. Once this was accomplished, the army and *jandarma* deployed their scarce resources to mop up the rebel elements. The means available were the resources of the Ministry of the Interior, the Ministry of War, and the local Ottoman governors. The concept of the operation involved local officials gathering up the Armenian population in designated areas, as rapidly as possible, and moving them to assembly points. There convoys were formed under the supervision of Ministry of the Interior officials, who were responsible for transit to, and billeting in, relocation camps that were mostly in what is now Syria. In the cases of noncompliance or resistance, the Ministry of the Interior asked the Third and Fourth Army commanders to intervene with the army to force the Armenians into submission and compliance.

Was there an actual Ottoman counterinsurgency plan or campaign plan? The answer is that there was not in the classic military sense of having an overall written master plan. The plans were cumulative and coordinated at provincial governor level. The relocation effort hinged on compliance with the law and with Ottoman Armenian citizens peacefully submitting to what many feared amounted to permanent deportation. In turn, when the Armenians resisted relocation the army was called in to enforce compliance. Ottoman counterinsurgency operations in 1915 against the Armenians were, therefore, fundamentally different than previous campaigns and can be characterized as reactive, localized, and of short duration. Without the thousands of soldiers necessary to blanket or saturate an operational area for an extended time, the Ottoman army responded to incidents of noncompliance with relatively small forces for short periods of time. This was truly, as the Sublime Porte indicated on May 30, a different course of action.

The relocation processes, which were previously localized under the Ministry of War, now turned into a regional effort under the Ministry of the Interior. The underresourced relocations were conducted very rapidly, which led to crimes of commission and crimes of omission. It is evident that thousands of Armenians chose noncompliance and were massacred in their villages.[68] The first three convoys departed Bayburt on June 4, 8, and 14, while the Armenian convoys left Erzurum on June 14, 18, and 29.[69] The convoys departed Harput on July 1, 2, and 4.[70] The rounding up of Armenians in Sivas began on June 23 and 14 convoys left the city between July 5 and 18.[71] Attacks on these convoys began immediately and the provincial governors were ordered to protect those whom the Ottomans called "deportees."[72] Episodically, in both of these circumstances, some security officials, local inhabitants, and tribal bandits committed atrocities and acts of criminality against the helpless evacuees. Moreover, many more died from episodic acts of intentional and unintentional neglect resulting from inadequate food, medical care, and shelter. Up until this point, most of the relocations, as well as enforcement of the decrees over those who choose resistance to relocation, were handled by local security forces, which, it must be remembered, were not resourced to either guard properly or care adequately for the evacuated persons. On top of these sad events, the first large-scale encounters between the Armenians and the Ottoman army were about to erupt.

ŞABIN KARAHISAR, JUNE 6–JULY 4, 1915

The town of Şabin Karahisar lay in Sivas province northeast of Sivas toward the Black Sea. Sivas province had been a hotbed of Armenian revolutionary committee as well as a haven for army deserters since the beginning of the war. Throughout the spring of 1915, the governor, Muammer Bey, had repeatedly sent warnings to the army and to the government about the situation there. Indeed, the governor had been ruthless in the suppression of the committees and the apprehension of the committeemen. In May, many prominent local Armenians were arrested, some of whom were murdered and tortured.[73] These incidents were followed by mass arrests of Armenian men in the second week of June, and on June 15, an Armenian band unsuccessfully attacked a jail where they were being imprisoned. The next day, the Armenians "spontaneously barricaded themselves in their neighborhoods" as news of the Armenian Primate's death and further arrests spread.[74] Ottoman reports painted a different picture with Armenian "soldiers" attacking Muslims in Karahisar and burning homes.[75] The surviving Armenian notables formed a military council on June 17 for the purposes of organizing resistance.[76] They then assaulted and captured the citadel and entrenched themselves, while the Muslims set fire to and destroyed the Armenian sections of the town.[77]

Ottoman army units arrived in the city on June 20–21, 1915, and began to pound the citadel, and the Armenian positions, with artillery. They launched an assault on the citadel on June 25, which failed and enabled the Armenians to recover military weapons from the dead Ottoman soldiers. Letters from Antranig to the defenders promising support were intercepted and provided to the Ottoman provisional commander, Neşet Pasha, who was commanding the battle.[78] The Ottomans reinforced their effort to three regiments from Sivas and several army battalions. However, it must be noted that some of these units were drawn from the training depots located around Sivas and cannot be characterized as combat-ready battalions. One historian asserted that the Ottoman force numbered 6,000 men while the Armenians scarcely numbered 500.[79] A major Ottoman assault on July 4 failed with over 300 casualties. However, the defenders had little food, and even less water, and they attempted a desperate sortie out of the citadel four days later, which also failed.[80] On the twenty-seventh day of the siege, July 11, the surviving defenders surrendered. Accounts about what happened then to the survivors vary, but at least a handful of them were shot on the spot.[81]

BITLIS AND MUŞ, JUNE 16, 1915

Because of Armenian operations and threats, the Third Army deployed the Reşadiye and Kop detachments of the Bitlis Jandarma into the field on June 18. These weak and poorly trained provisional detachments were composed of depot battalions from training bases.[82] An artillery battery from the 1st Expeditionary Force was sent to reinforce them. Additionally, the Erzurum Jandarma Battalion and units of the Van Jandarma Division were sent to Muş to reinforce the provisional detachment in fighting the Armenians. In early July, operations against the Armenians around Muş began with the Ottoman units pursuing the *çete* into the mountains.[83] On July 13, 1915, the commander of the Ottoman units involved sent his congratulations to the Van Jandarma Division for "cleaning the Armenians from Muş."[84]

ARMENIAN ACTIVITY ALONG THE LINES OF COMMUNICATIONS

Through June and into July, there continued to be concerns about the security of the lines of communications and road networks.[85] Mahmut Kâmil, Third Army commander, reported that Armenians from Erzurum, Van, and Bitlis were forming gangs and pillaging and plundering logistics depots.[86] The Ministry of the Interior sent out warnings to the Ministry of War about the Armenian threat to logistics columns and vehicles in the Fourth Army area on June 23, 1915.[87] Colonel Fuat Ziya, the commander of 3 LoCI, reported on July 11 that gangs of Kurds were interdicting Armenian relocation convoys near Bayburt.[88] The colonel noted that the Bayburt logistics node commander had deployed troops from the local static *jandarma* company to guard the lines of communications and protect the convoys.

In some areas, the massive number of Armenians in convoys themselves disrupted the flow of military supplies. In the Sivas area, 510 carts of 600 used for the movement of military supplies to the Third Army were allocated to Armenian convoys.[89] Armenian guerrillas attacked a detachment in Kiği on July 12.[90] Later that month, Armenians in one of the labor companies attacked their officers with shovels and pickaxes and then deserted. This caused the 4 LoCI in Aleppo to consider that the 3,000 Armenians assigned to labor battalions might be a threat to the construction projects vital to keeping the roads open and, consequently, 4 LoCI requested 800 rifles and adequate ammunition on August 10 for protection.[91] A plea from their headquarters on August 28, 1915, indicated that the 4 LoCI had received only 200 of the requested rifles.[92]

The British staffs in Cairo were especially energized with the idea of conducting an amphibious landing near Dörtyol and Alexandretta, in conjunction with a large Armenian uprising in the Zeytun region, for the purposes of cutting the Ottoman railway lines. One of the personalities behind this was Lieutenant Colonel Sir Mark Sykes, an expert on the Ottomans and the Near East, who was sent from London to Egypt to study and coordinate the idea with Armenian expatriates. On July 14, 1915, Sykes met with Sourene Bartevian, editor of the Armenian newspaper *Houssaper* and a prominent Dashnak party member, who tried to persuade Sykes to the viability of an autonomous Armenia.[93] Letters between Sykes and Major General Charles E. Callwell, author of the already well-known *Small Wars*, then a senior staff officer at the War Office and Sykes's superior, indicated that the Armenians hoped to be in possession of Muş very soon.[94] Two days later, Sykes reported to Callwell that the Armenians were prepared to provide 5,000–6,000 men for a landing, if the British would provide weapons and ships.[95] What is interesting about this particular exchange of correspondence is the fact that, subsequently, Sykes helped orchestrate the Arab Revolt in 1916, as well as coauthor the infamous Sykes-Picot Agreement that divided the Ottoman Middle East into independent states and European protectorates. It should also be remembered that C. E. Callwell was the renowned author of *Small Wars*, the subject of which was insurgency and counterguerrilla warfare (see previous chapters).

On July 22, 1915, a delegation from the Armenian National Defense Committee approached Sir John Maxwell, British commander-in-chief in Egypt, to reinforce the offer of coordinated Armenian rebellions, and to offer positive internal military assistance to the British. Boghos Nubar, a member of the delegation, claimed that the British could "rely on 25,000 Armenian insurgents in Cilicia and 15,000 from nearby provinces" to support an allied landing in the Alexandretta area, which would sever the Ottoman lines of communications leading to the Sinai front.[96] Maxwell decided not to pursue the scheme largely because the ongoing Gallipoli campaign absorbed almost the entire British effort in the Mediterranean. The details of the Armenian committee's plan were transmitted to the Foreign Office by Sir Henry McMahon, British high commissioner in Egypt, who was at the same time engaged in a famous exchange of letters with the Arabs encouraging them to revolt.[97] Belatedly, McMahon followed up in the fall with messages to the Foreign Office pointing out that an "unexpected descent" on Alexandretta would cut off the Ottoman armies in Arabia, Mesopotamia, Palestine, and Syria.[98] Conversations between McMahon, Sykes, and the Armenians continued through October before the British War Council, within which ardor toward operations in the eastern Mediterranean were cooling rapidly, called the scheme off.[99]

Although the British never landed at Alexandretta, it should be noted that these particular personalities were heavily involved in Britain's subsequent, and successful, effort to start an Arab revolt against the Ottomans. The McMahon-Hussein letters (1915) encouraged the Arabs to revolt, while the Sykes-Picot Agreement (1916) promised them independence. The instrument of British support, Lieutenant Colonel Thomas E. Lawrence (later famously known as Lawrence of Arabia), was launched into the Arabian desert with arms and gold by General Maxwell. Unsurprisingly, Lawrence's guerrilla-style hit-and-run tactics mirrored those described by C. E. Callwell in *Small Wars*. It is fair to say that the British were instigating very actively both Armenian and Arab rebellions in mid-1915.

German consular reports from Constantinople and Damascus reveal that the Ottoman Ministry of War was aware of these schemes. On August 6, 1915, the German naval attaché in Constantinople recorded a conversation with Enver Pasha noting that Enver was "aware of conspiracy, whereby 30,000 Armenians in the area around Adapazar-Ismid wanted to support a Russian landing at Sakaria."[100] Baron Max von Oppenheim also sent reports to Berlin from Damascus noting that an accumulation of evidence had aroused the fear of the Ottoman authorities that a landing was expected near Alexandretta.[101]

MARAŞ, JULY 29, 1915

The governor of Adana reported on July 29, 1915, that Armenians on the Ayvajik plateau were resisting relocation, and that Armenians from Zeytun and Hadjin were gathering there as well.[102] He noted that they were burning Muslim villages and that the 132nd Infantry Regiment had sent a cavalry unit, but no contact had yet been made. Resistance stiffened on August 1 when 400 Armenians, who had been burning villages and killing Muslims, fortified the village of Fendejak.[103] Cemal ordered the 132nd Infantry Regiment to destroy them and reinforced the regiment with a mountain artillery platoon and a regular infantry battalion.

DIYARBEKIR, JULY 17–AUGUST 4, 1915

The Diyarbekir Stationary Jandarma Regiment and the Midyat Seyyar Jandarma Battalion reported the suppression of 500 rebels, who had taken shelter in Ziyor Village, and who had been under siege since July 17–18.[104] Artillery was required to take the fortified village.

Sivas, August 2–3, 1915

In some locations, the absence of Ottoman army units compelled the staffs to resort to desperate measures. On July 27, 1915, the training depot of the 89th Infantry Regiment was ordered to dispatch 300 partly trained conscripts to reinforce the army's counterinsurgency efforts around Sivas.[105] In early August, clashes occurred in the village of Dendil between soldiers and rebels, who had fortified themselves inside caves.[106]

Musa Dağ, July 30–September 12, 1915

On July 29, 1915, the 1st Battalion, 133rd Infantry Regiment was sent to Antep (Gaziantep) to fight insurgents.[107] The 132nd Infantry Regiment (composed of three infantry battalions) was ordered, likewise, to suppress "five hundred Armenian guerrillas" (*cete*) near Zeytun.[108] The town of Zeytun itself was a hotbed of insurgent activity and in the words of American consul and missionary Reverend J. E. Merrill, "It is said that there were thirty-seven previous attempts at rebellion and this time the place was provisioned for it."[109] Merrill continued and confirmed guerrilla activity by noting that "a real danger of attacks by Armenian outlaws on Mohammadan refugees who have replaced Armenian villagers in Zeytun" existed in the region. The fight to subdue Zeytun was costly and was only resolved by a direct assault on the town.[110]

On July 30, 1915, the 3rd Battalion, 131st Infantry Regiment was sent to Antakya (Antioch), where it went into action against 500–600 insurgents.[111] The Ottoman battalion attacked the insurgents, who had constructed a well-built trench system. The Armenian fortifications were so strong that they fell only to a direct bayonet assault, in which the battalion lost 4 people and 18 were wounded. Contemporary Ottoman observers also noted that the only way to root out the rebels was at the point of a bayonet.[112] These operations in Antep, Zeytun, and Antakya were characterized by direct assaults on known points of Armenian resistance.

One of the most famous engagements of the Armenian Rebellion occurred southwest of Antioch on Musa Dağ (or Musa Dagh), a mountain in modern Hatay province.[113] In military terms, the Musa Dağ engagements provide a detailed exposition of the Ottoman Army's application of counterinsurgency warfare at the tactical level. The battle was immortalized in Franz Werfel's novel titled *The Forty Days of Musa Dagh*.[114] Although a work of historical fiction, Werfel

based his book on interviews with survivors and much of his contextual information is very specific and therefore probably accurate.
Using information from Werfel's book and Ottoman sources it is possible to examine the Ottoman military response on Musa Dağ at the
tactical level. The Armenians on Musa Dağ lived in six villages and
numbered about 5,500, of whom 1,556 were males over 14 years of
age.[115] According to Werfel, they had initially 50 Mauser rifles and 250
Greek military rifles, which were carefully buried and hidden in graves
until they were needed.[116] The Armenians on Musa Dag˘ organized
themselves into "three main divisions; a fighting-formation; a big
reserve, and a cohort of youth."[117] The fighting men numbered some
860 fit Armenian males, the reserve was composed of 1,100 older
or unfit men, and there were 300 boys, who were used as scouts.[118]
Werfel noted that every fighting man had either a military rifle (of
which there were 300) or a hunting rifle. Sixty Armenian deserters
from the Ottoman Army soon joined the insurgents. They and the
men of the area, many of whom had served in the army (some were
combat veterans of the Balkan Wars), trained the Armenian villagers
in fighting methods.

The Armenians used their time well as the Ottomans began to move
their thinly stretched combat forces into the area. By mid-July, the
Armenians were hard at work fortifying their villages and the entire
population was put to work in this endeavor.[119] This involved the dig-
ging of trenches, the clearing of fields of fire, and the emplacement of
obstacles including thorny scrub. Positions were also prepared in the
high mountains into which the villagers could retreat. Sentries were
posted along the likely avenues of approach to alert the defenders to
the approach of the Ottomans.[120]

On August 7, 1915, the recently formed 41st Infantry Division
began its counterinsurgency operations against the Armenian villages on the mountain of Musa Dağ. The daily war diary of the 41st
Infantry Division on that day reported that many Armenian children
had joined in the fighting as had numbers of Armenian deserters
from the Ottoman Army.[121] There was sporadic fighting for several
days as the Ottomans marshaled their forces and attempted to locate
and fix the points of resistance. Werfel described the first encounter
at the village of Bitias in which 400 Ottoman soldiers conducted a
poorly coordinated frontal attack on the well-camouflaged and well-
entrenched Armenians (numbering about 400 men in two trench
lines).[122] The Armenians routed the overconfident Ottomans and captured several Ottoman rifles, which were left on the field. However,
once the Ottomans were alerted to the strength of defenses and the

determination of defenders, they immediately changed their tactics. The Ottomans soon identified the location of the Armenian defenses and maneuvered around the flank of the village, making the position untenable for its defenders.[123]

The Armenians were pushed southeast and 1st and 2nd Battalions, 131st Infantry Regiment, altogether about 870 infantrymen, began a large operation against insurgent Armenians in the village of Hacıcıbılı Köyü on August 9.[124] In the village were some 1,500–1,800 Armenians, heavily armed and determined to resist.[125] This time, the two Ottoman battalions conducted better reconnaissance and carefully encircled the village. The regimental commander then brought up his artillery. After a brief bombardment, the Ottomans assaulted and carried the village with a bayonet attack. More than 1,000 weapons of various types were found in the village (while this number of weapons seems unusually large it conforms to Werfel's descriptions). The survivors and their families were rounded up and sent into temporary camps for movement out of the area. The regiment received congratulations from the corps commander for its victory.[126]

On August 13, 1915, the 41st Infantry Division received orders to take several villages in the sector and to disarm the remaining Armenian villagers who lived there. Preparation and movement for these operations went on for several days, and by August 15, the division had encircled the village of Ermeni Köyü.[127] The villagers refused to disarm themselves and the division was forced to assault the village. The Ottomans took Ermeni Köyü on the next day and also produced large numbers of captured weapons. This battle was described in Werfel as occurring on August 14 at the "North and South Bastions" and, moreover, he noted that the Ottoman force again split into two divisions of equal strength supported by artillery.[128] Clearly, the Ottomans learned quickly to respect their enemy and adjusted their tactics accordingly. In these operations, the 131st Infantry lost 6 men, 26 were wounded, and 25 went missing in action.[129] The regiment reported the expenditure of 20,353 rifle bullets, 30 shrapnel shells, 47 high explosive shells, and also reported the loss of 8 rifles and 3 pistols.[130] These operations illustrate that the 41st Infantry Division understood the importance of isolating and sealing the insurgents inside their villages.

Five days later, the local Armenians fled their villages, which had become death traps, and moved into the high mountains. In two more days of search-and-destroy operations, from August 18 to 19, nine insurgents were killed. On August 20, 1915, the division reported that "no Armenians remained in nearby Antakya."[131] After an operational pause, the 41st Infantry Division began pursuit operations and again went into action against the "Canakkale Armenians' (Çanakklık Ermeniler) near the summit of Musa Dağ on August 31st."[132] Fighting was heavy and resulted in the fall of the mountain. Pursuit operations were renewed against the fleeing survivors. The division war diary for August 1915 noted that the Armenians had paid bandit gangs of actual criminals to fight with them against the army.[133] Furthermore, the diary noted that many older Armenians were responsible for the coordination of joint guerrilla operations between the Armenian villages. In the minds of the Ottomans, when combined with the active participation of children as fighters, this appeared as evidence of an insurgency that was widely supported by the Armenian population. In spite of these volatile issues, the Fourth Army continued to coordinate the evacuation of the surviving Armenians from the area of operations.[134]

There were reports of atrocities committed against the Armenians, which were received and investigated by the 41st Infantry Division. Reports reached the division on August 13, 1915, that severe unprovoked massacres of Armenians had occurred near Musa Dağ.[135] The division also received a report on August 15 of a massacre of over 30 Armenians in Alaaddın Köyü. A detachment was sent there to investigate and confirmed that the village was burnt.[136] Moreover, the detachment found seven burnt bodies as well and made a complete report to the XII Corps headquarters. These reports, as well as others from throughout Anatolia, resulted in a three-member commission being dispatched in the fall of 1915 to investigate reports of atrocities and abuses against the Armenians.[137]

Operations continued against insurgent Armenians in September 1915. On September 7, the division reported its concern about French agents who were in contact with the insurgent groups. The agents had come ashore from French naval vessels, which included the French battleship *Victor Hugo*.[138] The division staff of the 41st Infantry Division was very concerned about the possibility of the Armenians insurgents supporting a French amphibious landing in the Gulf of Iskenderun.[139] However, the anticipated landing never occurred, although a number of French naval demonstrations were staged in the gulf, including the evacuation of some of the survivors of Musa Dağ by the French cruisers *Guichen* and *Jeanne d' Arc*.[140] By late fall 1915, the 41st Infantry Division gained the upper hand on the insurgency in its sector of responsibility and combat operations drew down by November 1915. Thereafter, the 41st Infantry Division remained on coastal and internal security duties in the Iskenderun vicinity for the remainder of the war.

In the 41st Infantry Division's tactical area in 1915, the Ottoman Army fought a very successful counterinsurgency campaign against Armenian guerrillas and insurgents. It appears from the records examined in this study that the division was ordered to eliminate rebellious activity in its assigned operational area. There is no indication that the division received orders for the general killing of the Armenian population. Nevertheless, the 41st Infantry Division eradicated the insurgency in its sector by killing or displacing the majority of the local Armenian population and, as a matter of historical fact, by 1916 very few Armenians remained in the 41st Infantry Division's tactical area. A modern label associated with operations of this severity and magnitude is "ethnic cleansing." However, it must be noted that when incidents of the deliberate massacre of Armenians were reported, the division investigated the circumstances and submitted reports to the Fourth Army. Within six months, the 41st Infantry Division completed its mission and restored stability and civil order to its assigned area. Other Ottoman Army infantry divisions participated in counterinsurgency operations against the Armenians in tactical areas to the north (the 36th Infantry Division) and the northwest (the 44th Infantry Division) of the 41st Infantry Division. These divisions produced similar successful results.

Urfa, September 28–October 23, 1915

Urfa had been a center of known Armenian revolutionary committee activity throughout 1915. The Fourth Army apprehended and placed 349 Armenians, who had been involved in fighting, under military arrest in early June.[141] On August 9, 1915, Armenians staged an uprising in the nearby village of Germüş.[142] The uprising quickly spread and within ten days had become what the Ottomans called a "large uprising."[143] In late August, the Ministry of the Interior directed the governor to Urfa to relocate within the sanjack "those Armenians who are sowing discord among the people and seen to have a tendency to perform vicious acts, as well as those who are thought to be involved in activities to stage revolts and uprisings."[144] On September 16, Armenians opened fire on a gendarme patrol killing two and wounding eight.[145] The Fourth Army noted that insufficient forces were available to suppress the Armenians and that forces from the garrisons were required to be sent to assist. The *jandarma* forces were unable to assault successfully the Armenian houses because they had been so strongly fortified and because of this the governor asked for "the dispatch of a military force with artillery."[146] Lack of military success incited angry Muslim mobs to assault the unfortified sections of the Armenian quarter as well. Reinforcing Ottoman army units arrived in the city on June 20–21, 1915, and began to pound the citadel and the Armenian positions with artillery.

Mid-September saw an increase in the tempo of operations against Armenians in the Urfa area and the Fourth Army was forced to send in reinforcements to assist the 41st Infantry Division. The 3rd Battalion, 130th Infantry Regiment was dispatched from the 23rd Infantry Division in Syria, arriving in Urfa on September 30, 1915.[147] Columns of regular Ottoman army troops arrived on October 5 and 6 and attacked the Armenian quarter from three sides.[148] Accompanying the Ottoman troops was a German captain named Eberhard Count Wolffskeel von Reichenberg, who recorded his observations in a diary. He noted that "the entire defense is very well prepared and led. The band is well provided with weapons and ammunition."[149] He also noted that while the Ottoman infantrymen were not particularly brave, or tactically proficient, when artillery was brought forward for direct fire, it proved decisive. Another infantry battalion and two artillery batteries reinforced the Ottomans on October 12.[150]

Wolffskeel von Reichenberg described his tactics as putting two infantry companies on line to lay down a base of fire while maneuvering a third around to flank the Armenians. The buildings, especially the churches, were so solidly constructed of stone that Wolffskeel von Reichenberg had to bring in heavy artillery of 120-mm caliber for direct fire to break through the walls.[151] In its largest battle against the insurgents on October 18, this battalion lost 13 men and 31 officers and men were wounded.[152] A bitter struggle ensued with the Ottoman finally overcoming resistance on October 23. After the battle, Wolffskeel von Reichenberg expressed surprise at the extensive and elaborate system of tunnels, used in the defense, which the Armenians had constructed under their quarter. The surprising combat effectiveness and resilience of the Armenian committeemen in Urfa could only have come from long military training and extensive preparations before the battle, which reinforced what the Ottomans had previously experienced at Van and Zeytun.

MERSINA AND TARSUS, OCTOBER 28, 1915

In September 1915, the Fourth Army began to relocate the Armenians of Mersin and Tarsus where "accusations of spying and insurrection were again being bandied about."[153] Upward of 8,000 people were put on the road in convoys through late October, although over a thousand skilled Armenian workers and their families were exempted from relocation.[154] Toward the end of these relocations, resistance broke out and a second battalion from the 23rd Infantry Division deployed on October 28 to fight guerrillas around the city of Tarsus.[155] Kévorkian asserted that a lesser percentage of Armenians were deported from the Adana region because Cemal was favorably inclined toward them.[156] However, in this regard, consideration must also be given to Talat's August 17 instruction exempting critical railway workers, who maintained the continuous railway connections through the Taurus Mountains, especially around the difficult Pozantı choke-point, and the Amanus Mountains.

THE END OF THE CAMPAIGN

The Ottoman counterinsurgency campaign against the Armenian committees evolved into an operational existence over a six-month period in the spring of 1915. Similarly, it ended by a drawn-out process as the six provinces and crucial transportation nodes were emptied of Armenians. In many locations, the relocations were accomplished by early summer and the provincial governors made periodic reports to the Ministry of the Interior regarding the numbers of Armenians sent into the relocation pipeline. For example, the governor of Izmit Sanjack reported that 58,000 Armenians had been sent from his province and that, as of September 17, 1915, none remained.[157] Likewise, the governor of the Eskişehir Sanjack reported the next day that all of the Armenians within the district, "who needed to be expelled,"[158] had been sent away, while the governor of Diyarbakır reported that 20,000 had been relocated from his province.[159] The reports were nuanced in reporting information about which Armenians had not been sent; for example, in accordance with the August 15 directives, the small town of Niğde sent 220 Armenians away, but no Catholic or Protestant Armenians were among them.[160] Sadly and unsurprisingly, these situation reports were often accompanied by reports from the governors of criminal actions and atrocities committed against the relocated Armenian groups as well. A large number of authentic documents exist in the Ottoman archives, many of which may be found in the published document collections, and they attest to the fact that while the Armenians were being relocated, they were being attacked in significant numbers as well.[161]

Talat Pasha and the governors were alert to the widespread criminality perpetrated against the relocated Armenians, but were unable to intervene effectively. In one of more misquoted ciphered messages from the Ministry of the Interior, Talat cautioned the governor of Ankara to exercise particular caution by insuring that the transfer of Armenians "be carried out in an orderly and practical manner, should henceforth never be left to individuals having fanatical feelings of enmity and that...Armenians, will be definitely protected."[162] It is in this message that Talat stated, "The Armenian issue pertaining to Eastern provinces has been solved."[163] This single sentence is often used out of context as explicit evidence "that the aim of the government's policies towards the Armenians was annihilation."[164] In fact, Talat's message was neither a statement of intent to annihilate nor was it a statement that the counterinsurgency campaign had concluded; rather the message was a direct criticism of the local officials, who had allowed attacks on Armenians. In context, the sentence alluded to the relocation decision having solved the problem of rebellious Armenian in the eastern provinces, and the subsequent sentences strictly warned officials to treat the Armenians humanely, and ordered them to punish officials attacking or neglecting the relocated persons. As the relocations progressed, Talat maintained a personal record of the numbers of Armenians remaining in the provinces under Ottoman control (this subject will be examined in detail in the following chapter). Throughout the fall of 1915, Ministry of the Interior messages to provincial governors and officials continued to stress that decision to relocate the eastern Armenians was the result of "military reasons and maintaining public order."[165]

The success of the army's counterinsurgency operations in the fall of 1915 enabled the Ministry of the Interior to consider slowing the tempo of relocations, by which time the ministry reports showed that over 100,000 Armenians had been relocated or were in the relocation pipeline.[166] As a result, the Ministry of the Interior began deliberately to slow down the relocation flow from selected locations. Talat ordered the governor of Kastamonu on October 23, 1915, to stop removing any additional Armenians, except those who were found with weapons.[167] Four days later, Talat ordered a complete halt to evacuations from Bursa, Ankara, Aleppo, and Adana provinces as well as Maras, Afyon, Eskişehir, Kütahya, Izmit, and Nigde sanjacks.[168] The governate of Konya was ordered to stop the relocations on November 12, 1915. In January 1916, the Ministry of the Interior reaffirmed its directive to maintain the protected status of Armenian railway workers outside the scope of the relocations. The relocations slowed to all but a trickle and, on March 15, 1916, the Ministry of the Interior dispatched explicit instructions to all provincial and sanjack governors that "no more Armenians shall be relocated for any reason on any grounds."[169] Although there was some residual shifting around of Armenians still trapped in the relocation pipeline, this can be seen as a conclusive ending date for the counterinsurgency campaign against the Armenian revolutionary committees in eastern Anatolia.

CONCLUSION

Beginning in July 1915, what were regarded by the Ottomans as coordinated and full-blown insurgencies erupted in Antep, Antioch, Karahisar, Maras, Urfa, and Zeytun. This forced the Ottomans to move into actual large-scale (regimental- and divisional-level) counterinsurgency operations using mostly inexperienced forces. The newly formed 41st Infantry Division was diverted from coastal and area defense duties to counterinsurgency missions to deal with these and later participated in the famous assaults on Musa Dagh. The following month the equally inexperienced 23rd and 44th Infantry Divisions would join in attacks on Zeytun, Urfa, and Tarsus. Later, troops were sent to Karahisar to quell an uprising there. By autumn the Ottoman army had its local defense and *jandarma* forces and three understrength infantry divisions committed to the suppression of the eastern Anatolian insurgency. This was less than seven percent of the army's operational combat strength. Nevertheless, by the early winter the Ottomans had forcibly relocated almost the entire Orthodox Armenian population of the six eastern provinces. Thousands of well-armed Armenians were killed while fighting in this process and many more thousands of innocent Armenians were massacred or died of disease while in transit.

At the operational level, the Fourth Army assigned tactical areas that clearly defined missions and responsibilities. Although the available units were understrength in infantry and artillery, they aggressively executed their assignments by bringing the fight to the enemy. The Fourth Army employed contemporary counterinsurgency tactics that included the encirclement and destruction of insurgents in villages, search-and-destroy missions to isolate and destroy guerrillas in mountainous terrain, and weapons searches and confiscation. Often these tactics resulted in the destruction of Armenian villages and were accompanied by large numbers of insurgent casualties. Objectively, however, these tactics were the result of the necessity to clear pockets of resistance with the bayonet. The presence of artillery was especially important when the army needed to assault the well-fortified Armenian quarters in urban combat environments. In terms of how the armies of the day dealt with counterinsurgency, the Ottoman army employed a very conventional approach that reflected contemporary de facto Western practices. Although overshadowed by the horror of the Armenian massacres and forced relocations, the Ottoman army was arguably very effective in its counterinsurgency campaign against the Armenian insurgencies of 1915.

The extent to which these uprising were coordinated by the Armenian revolutionary committees and the Entente, in support of allied offensives, remains controversial today. The fact that they were sequential, rather than simultaneous, argues against the idea of coordinated effort. Reciprocally, the depth and resilience of the well-armed and well-organized Armenian military cells and organizations, as well as their known links to external Armenian groups fighting with the allies, argues for the idea of coordinated effort. Moreover, the Ottoman intelligence services had genuine intelligence regarding the Entente's numerous and continuing attempts to encourage and generate an insurgency inside the Ottoman Empire. The Ottoman state's response to this situation evolved in an escalating trajectory, which was continuously modified as the decision makers refined their understandings of what they believed the nature of the threat to be.

CHAPTER 10

Aftermath

*The measures taken by the Government regarding the Armenians
have entirely resulted from the necessity to safeguard and protect the
security and order of the country and, in defending this fact, it is
stated that these measures have never been implemented implying a
general policy of annihilation by the government of the Armenian
element in the Empire.*

*—Ismail, General Directorate of Security,
on behalf of the minister of the interior*[1]

INTRODUCTION

The decision to relocate the Armenians was an evolving counterinsurgency response that began with localized population removal but
which, by late May 1915, escalated to a region-wide relocation policy
involving six provinces. There was little else that the thinly stretched
Ottomans could have done. A large-scale kinetic military response,
as they had employed from 1890 to 1912 involving the application
of force, was impossible. The Western model of population relocation had worked for the Spanish, the Americans, and the British. It
is, therefore, understandable why the Ottoman government turned
to this counterinsurgency policy, which could be operationalized
using minimal military resources, in order to deal effectively with the
Armenian insurrection. As the relocations progressed into the summer and fall of 1915, it became progressively easier for the Ottoman
military forces committed to eradicating the insurgency to mop up
the battered survivors. In 1915, for the Ottoman state, relocation was
an effective strategy borne of weakness rather than of strength.

As to the question of whether the relocation was necessary for reasons of Ottoman national security in World War I. From the perspective
of what the Ottoman government believed was happening—the answer
is yes. In fact, there was a direct threat by the insurgent Armenian

revolutionary committees to the lines of communications upon which the logistics of the Ottomans armies on three fronts depended. The consequences of failing to supply adequately its armies in contact with the Russians, in particular, must have led to the military defeat of the Ottoman Empire. The Ottoman high command simply could not take that chance. Pressed by the compelling requirements of a world war to implement an immediate counterinsurgency policy and operational solution, in the absence of traditionally available military and paramilitary forces, the Ottoman government chose a strategy based on relocation—itself a highly effective practice pioneered by the Great Powers. The relocation of the Armenian population, and the associated destruction of the Armenian revolutionary committees, ended what the Ottoman government believed was an existential threat to the Ottoman state, and the empire survived to fight on until late 1918.

The Aftermath of the Relocations

How many Ottoman Armenians died? The most commonly used number for the death toll of Ottoman Armenians in the period 1914–23 is 1 to 1.5 million people.[2] However, there are no figures that are acceptable to all interested parties. There has been only a single scholarly attempt to capture the total numbers of Armenians who were killed. In the most comprehensive attempt to report the numbers of Ottoman Armenians who were relocated or killed, Raymond Kévorkian, in *The Armenian Genocide*, presented subtotals of Armenians from each separate Ottoman province and sanjack; however, he made no attempt in his conclusion to tally the cumulative totals and his numbers sometimes exceeded the known numbers of the local Armenian populations. In truth, advocates of the Armenian position tend to report higher total numbers while advocates of the Turkish position tend to report lower numbers. For example, Turkish historian Yusuf Halaçoğlu asserted that 56,610 Armenians died during the first phase of the relocations, while Peter Balakian, an American literature professor, maintained that "by the end of 1915 three-fourths of the Ottoman Armenians were extinct."[3] These are minimalist and maximalist positions and, it is important to note, that exact numbers simply do not exist.

Unfortunately, the problem with counting the dead, the relocated, or those who remained behind really begins with the population baseline of the Ottoman Empire in the summer of 1914. Once again these numbers are just as contentious as trying to tally the number of Armenians who died. Justin McCarthy, a specialist in Ottoman demographics, asserted that based on known demographic data, there were roughly 1.5 million Armenians in Ottoman Anatolia in 1912.[4] This is larger than an estimate made in 1930 by Ahmed Emin that the Ottoman Armenians numbered 1.3 to 1.5 million people.[5] An Armenian historian suggested numbers as large as 1.9 million,[6] while a Turkish historian asserted that the total number of Armenians in the empire was between 600,000 and 800,000.[7] Readers must establish their own understandings of the total but an estimate of 1.5 million resident Ottoman Armenians is not unreasonable.

Likewise, the number of Ottoman Armenians who remained behind, who were not relocated, remains in dispute as well. The numbers controversy flared up in 2008 with the publication of Murat Bardakçı's *Talât Paşa'nın Evrak-ı Metrûkesi* (commonly referred to as Talat Pasha's *Black Book*).[8] A newspaper journalist characterized the book as a "bombshell" showing that "972,000 Armenians disappeared from 1915–1916."[9] According to the publisher, Ara Sarafian, the handwritten journal "documents his (Talat's) campaign of race extermination, 1915–1917."[10] Sarafian then offered the conclusion that "we will assume the vast majority of 'missing Armenians' in 1917 were killed or died during deportations."[11] In actuality, this conclusion is an assumption but, moreover, it is worth noting that Sarafian's conclusions rest on his own tabular information that he calls "generated data," which is composed of the following four elements: the number deported, the deported missing in 1917, the percentage deported, and the percentage of deported who were not accounted for in 1917.[12] Basically, Sarafian conflates the number of Armenians unaccounted for with the idea that they must have died.

Without question, the journal records the numbers of Armenians relocated from various locations, as well as the number who arrived at relocation destination. However, whether it was Talat himself, who recorded the data, or someone else, is contentious, as the handwriting does not appear at all similar to known authenticated documents written by him.[13] It is fair to say that Talat had possession of the journal at the time of his death in 1921.

In fact, the journal did not attempt to document what happened to these people, and only recorded that they had gone somewhere else. Sarafian's conclusions that all the missing must have perished by 1917 conflicts with the fact that significant numbers of Armenians turned up later. Nevertheless, it is important to note also that Talat's own reports of the total number of missing Armenians contradicts the idea that only small numbers of Armenians were moved, broadly supporting Armenian claims that the relocations affected a large number of people. It must also be mentioned that the journal was not exclusively concerned with Christians and also included extensive tabular information on the relocation of Ottoman Muslims from the Balkans. Significantly, the journal does not record Talat's intent, or his design for the relocation process, or its outcome.[14]

In 2011, Sarafian published an English translation of Bardakçı's book, which even contained his own introduction to the material.[15] Sarafian's interpretations of the material are debatable; however, he does not dispute Talat's tabular data, which reported that, of approximately 1,500,000 resident Ottoman Armenians (excluding Protestant Armenians), 350,000–400,000 Armenians remained in 23 Ottoman provinces in 1917.[16] Importantly, Talat's journal recorded the spatial characteristics of the Armenians remaining in 23 provinces in 1917. Table 10.1 presents Talat's data.

Table 10.1 Distribution of Armenians remaining in 1917

Western Provinces	Percentage Remaining*
Izmit	28
Bursa	22
Karesi	41
Kutahya	98
Eskisehir	28
Aydin	60
Karahisar	50
Konya	57
Central Provinces	
Bolu	53
Kastamonu	40
Ankara	39
Nigde	15
Kayseri	28
Adana	62
Ichil	72
The Six Eastern Provinces	
Erzurum	3
Trebzond	1
Bitlis	1
Diyarbakir	3
Mamuretul Aziz	3
Sivas	9

*The "percentage remaining" of Armenians in the province includes both the original Armenian inhabitants and Armenians from outside the province who were physically present there in 1917.

Source: Ara Sarafian, *Talaat Pasha's Report on the Armenian Genocide, 1917* (London: Gomidas Institute, 2011).

For reasons unknown today, Talat excluded the capital of Constantinople and the European provinces of the Ottoman Empire from his tallying. Like other estimates of the number of Armenians who were relocated, these numbers are in contention. However, it is not in doubt that the majority of Armenian inhabitants of the capital, and its hinterlands, remained in their homes and were not relocated. Moreover, it must be noted that Talat's journal is not direct evidence of how many Ottoman Armenians were relocated forcibly, how many left voluntarily to join the Russians and French, or how many were killed. It only provides direct evidence that somewhere around a million Ottoman Armenians no longer resided in their home provinces in 1917 and that 350,000–400,000 Armenians remained in their homes.

However, the actual number of Ottoman Armenians who perished from whatever cause is outside the scope of this work. This book focuses on counterinsurgency and the number of relocated Ottoman Armenians is germane to this study as a metric, which pertains to whether the Ottoman government set out to accomplish the mission that it carved out for itself. In this case, the metrics are useful in analyzing a counterinsurgency strategy of population relocation in a six-province regional area. It is apparent from the numbers recorded in the journal found among Talat's possessions that the six eastern provinces were subjected to a different relocation strategy than elsewhere. This conforms to the military and domestic policies evolved during the spring of 1915.

Russian Counterpoint

The Ottomans were not the only combatant nation to employ the forced relocation of minorities in the interests of national security during World War I. In January 1915, or about the same time as the Ottomans began to relocate the Armenians, the Russian army began a coordinated large-scale forced relocation of Jews living near the frontline area of the Eastern Front. The Russian "army command convinced itself that Russia's Jews were unreliable, that they had close ties to their kin abroad, that they were more attracted to the Austrian and German cultures than to the Russian, and that Jews shirked military service and engaged in spying and espionage on a broad scale."[17] One historian noted that about 100,000 Jews from 40 towns in the vicinity of Warsaw were forced to migrate.[18] Another historian called these "a continuous series of massive, arbitrary, wholly unnecessary expulsions of the civilian Jewish population-now predominately composed of women, children, the elderly and the infirm."[19]

After the Austro-German offensive broke the Russian Third Army at Gorlitz in April 1915, entire eastern provinces of the Russian Empire were emptied of their Jewish populations in an expanded area west of a line running north-south from Riga to Kovno. On May 15, Ivan Goremykin, chairman of the Council of Ministers, told a colleague that the recent deportation order applied to 300,000 Jews.[20] In addition to forced relocation, the Russian army began officially sanctioned hostage-taking in order to insure compliance. As in the Ottoman Empire, the relocated persons became prey for brigandage, notably by Cossacks. The scale of the forced expulsions was unprecedented in the Russian Empire and the area of Poland and White Russia known as the Pale was emptied of its Jewish population. As many as 100,000 Jews died in the process.[21] The Russian army often used accusations of sabotage or espionage as a reason to move "unreliable Jews"[22] en masse to the interior.

In addition to the relocation of Jews suspected of collusion with the enemy, thousands of Russian-subject Muslims in the Caucasus were likewise relocated to places in the interior.[23] Tatars in the Crimea and ethnic Germans in the Ukraine, both groups of which were Russian citizens but not ethnically Russian, were subjected to similar treatment. The historians working in this area have not tabulated the death toll of these relocated persons; however, the similarity of these relocations to those of the Ottoman Armenians should not be lost on the reader.

ENEMIES WITHIN?

It is clear today that a large number of Ottoman Armenians were not relocated in 1915, with estimates of their numbers ranging from 350,000 to 500,000 people. Given that observation what can be said about the patterns of relocation? First, the Armenian inhabitants of the Ottoman eastern provinces were almost entirely relocated. Second, in the Ottoman central and western provinces large percentages of Ottoman Armenians remained in place (at least until the end of the war). To what extent do these facts correspond to the arguments advanced in this book?

It is a matter of historical record that Ottoman relocation policies toward the Ottoman Armenian population were tailored to specific eastern provinces, which were designated as a war zone of special interest to the military and national security. Moreover, the acute vulnerability of the fragile Ottoman lines of communications to interdiction is not in question. There is also evidence of uneven treatment.[24] It is a matter of record that, in the summer of 1915, the Ottoman government excluded certain categories of Ottoman Armenians from relocation, including Catholic and Protestant Armenians, as well as Armenians and their families, who were working in the railway system or who were involved in working on the critical lines of communications. And, it is a fact that the Ottoman army successfully suppressed Armenian insurgencies in all of the eastern provinces affected by the relocation directives. It is equally clear from the record that the Ottoman government did not regard or characterize all Ottoman Armenians as "enemies within" and, in fact, was very cognizant that many Ottoman Armenians were loyal citizens. Given these assessments, it is to be expected that the Ottoman eastern provinces would have been emptied of their largely Orthodox Armenian inhabitants, but that small numbers of Armenians would remain in place. Map 10.1 reflects this by showing the percentages of the original 1914 Ottoman Armenian population remaining in the empire in 1917.

How do the numbers of Ottoman Armenians relate to an enhanced understanding of the relocation policies? This book presents the idea that the relocation policies and associated military strategies were the direct result of threat-based beliefs about the danger presented by the Armenian revolution committees. Not all Ottoman Armenians were considered as "enemies within" by the Ottoman government, but enough were thought to be in this category to generate a coordinated interministry response in May 1915. The objective of the response was to remove the danger to the military lines of communications in certain designated areas. Talat Pasha's tallies of Ottoman Armenians remaining in the central and western provinces illustrate the successful application of the relocation policies and military strategy. Rightly or wrongly, the Ottoman government reacted to its own beliefs about an existential threat to national security in wartime by implementing a coherent and effective response.

The consequences of the relocation were significant. Like the American, British, and Spanish experiences, the number of relocated persons immediately overwhelmed the capacity of the state to care for them. The Ottoman relocation camps established in the Euphrates valley to house displaced Ottoman Armenians unintentionally became death camps characterized by malnutrition, disease, and neglect. Making the problem far worse, of course, were the numerous unprovoked massacres of Ottoman Armenians perpetrated in their home villages or while in convoy en route to the camps. Arguably, these horrific events were an unintended consequence of government policies and military strategies designed to end a threat to national security from "enemies within." Even today, after a century of wars of

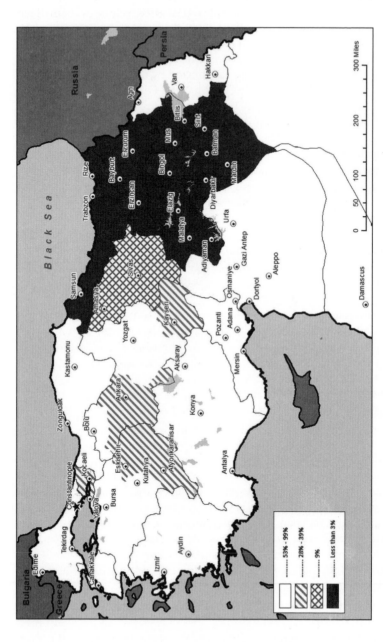

Map 10.1 Distribution of Armenians remaining in Ottoman provinces, 1917.

insurgency and counterinsurgency, it remains extremely difficult to identify the "enemies within" and to deal effectively with them. That the Ottoman government encountered great difficulty dealing with this problem in 1915 should not surprise anyone.

CONCLUSION

This book presents the thesis that the Ottoman government developed an evolving 35-year, empire-wide array of counterinsurgency practices that varied in scope and execution depending on the strategic importance of the affected provinces. Within the core areas of the Ottoman Empire, and in the empire's outer periphery, Ottoman counterinsurgency campaigns in response to insurrection were kinetic and involved large-scale combat operations. In these different places and circumstances, the Ottomans employed a wide variety of government policies, military forces, and counterinsurgency tactics to suppress insurrection and rebellion.

After 1890, the powerful revolutionary committees were both a political and a military force in being, and were an active presence in Ottoman affairs. As world war approached, both the Armenian committees and the Ottoman Special Organization developed significant irregular warfare capabilities in anticipation of conflict. In 1914, the outbreak of World War I created conditions that again brought the Ottoman state into direct conflict with the Armenian revolutionary committees. This was largely a result of the machinations of the allied powers, which encouraged and supported the eastern Anatolian Armenian revolutionary committees to commit acts of terrorism and minor insurrections in early 1915. These small and localized, but widespread, acts of Armenian violence appeared to metathesize during a major Armenian insurrection at Van in April 1915, which drove the Ottoman government into the belief that the Armenian insurrection was an imminent and existential threat to Ottoman national security.

With almost the entire Ottoman army deployed on the active fronts, the Ottomans did not have the force structure available to deal with the Armenian committees as they had done over the previous 30 years in other circumstances and places. In the late spring of 1915, the Ottomans turned to a Western-style policy of regional population relocation designed to separate the insurgents from their base of popular support. The resulting counterinsurgency campaign was, effectively, a resource-driven strategy of poverty, within which was nested a monumental failure by the state to protect and sustain the deportees.

Arguably, the 1915 Ottoman campaign against the Armenian revolutionary committees was the last major counterinsurgency campaign waged by the Ottoman Empire prior to its collapse. Ottoman army operations against the Arab Revolt of 1916–18 are more accurately characterized as counterguerrilla or counterirregular, because these were oriented against armed military groups, rather than against the Arab tribes themselves. Finally, the Ottoman counterinsurgency campaign against the Armenian revolutionary committees presaged the greater, and more lethal, counterinsurgency campaigns of the twentieth century, and it served notice on the world that only a small proportion of a population, if actively encouraged and armed by outside nations and forces, is necessary for the conduct of an insurgency.

Appendix A: The Relocation Antitheses

This is the forest primeval; but where are the hearts that beneath it Leaped like the roe, when he hears in the woodland the voice of the huntsman? Where is the thatch-roofed village, the home of Acadian farmers—Men whose lives glided on like rivers that water the woodlands, Darkened by shadows of earth, but reflecting an image of heaven? Waste are those pleasant farms, and the farmers forever departed! Scattered like dust and leaves, when the mighty blasts of October Seize them, and whirl them aloft, and sprinkle them far o'er the ocean.

—Longfellow, Evangeline,
A Tale of Acadie[1]

Protracted urban terrorism waged by small, independent cells requires little or no popular support It is difficult to counter.

—Counterinsurgency, US Army Field
Manual 3–24, 2006[2]

INTRODUCTION

Many American students read Henry Wadsworth Longfellow's epic poem *Evangeline* in high school and his dramatic opening phrase "This is the forest primeval" seems to stick in the memory of most of them. However, Americans read Longfellow's epic poem for its literary contribution to American literature and not for its historical value. In truth, the story of the Acadian expulsion or "exile without end" was an early and pragmatic variant of counterinsurgency by relocation. After the British conquest of French Acadia in 1710, which later became the Canadian Maritime Provinces, the restive French inhabitants resisted British occupation. Together with local Indian tribes, the French Acadians periodically waged guerrilla war against the British and helped supply the French fortress at Louisbourg with food and resources. In addition to irregular warfare, some Acadians formed military units and even bested the British in conventional battles. As a military solution to what had turned into a persistent insurgency, the British chose a counterinsurgency strategy of what was then called "expulsion" and, on August 10, 1755, began the first of a series of permanent relocations.

Over the next few years, around 12,000 French Acadians were forcibly expelled to destinations that included the Thirteen Colonies, England, and France. Longfellow's *Evangeline* is, of course, a part of this saga when the French inhabitants of Acadia were seized and sprinkled "far o'er the ocean." Americans will be most familiar with the cultural and linguistic legacy of the Acadians, who reappear as Cajuns in Louisiana. Unlike the relocation campaigns detailed in this book, the British had no intention of allowing the Acadians to return to their homes, making expulsion fundamentally different from relocation. Although the outline of the story of *Evangeline* is well-known in America, it is read as a literary epic of tragedy and is not generally understood by Americans to be part of the global history of counterinsurgency. I was only reminded of this linkage during a recent trip to Ottawa, Canada, where this was brought to my attention by Mr. Jamie Nicholls, member of parliament representing Vaudreuil-Soulanges in Quebec province. To my regret, I found myself asking the obvious, "Who remembers the Acadians?"

THE ANTITHESES

There will be readers, and reviewers, who will read this book and label it an apologia for the Turks. Part of this labeling will involve the idea that the author has "not engaged the entire range of archives" and/or has "ignored the extant field of scholarship available." I would like to bring to the attention of the informed reader that I am aware of the complete narrative and I have weighed it carefully. There is a considerable body of work suggesting a variety of other explanations for why the Ottomans relocated the Armenians. I have not included these in any great detail in the main text of this book.

In addition to my own position stated in this book, there are five major positions and points of view about the Armenian relocations of 1915. In scholarly terms, these amount to the antitheses against my arguments and I will present them, in no particular order, in this appendix.

Position 1—The Ethnic Homogenization of Anatolia: This advances the idea that the Young Turks, fueled by the ideological ideas of Zia

Gökalp, intended to racially purify Anatolia by removing the Armenians (and others) while replacing them with ethnic Turks (or Muslims). Moreover, this idea became embedded in secret Young Turk political platforms as early as 1909. The argument is based on the writings of Gökalp, combined with the evidence of Young Turk population engineering schemes involving Muslim refugees from the Balkans, as well as the authentic ministry cables outlining percentages and ratios of relocated Armenians. The main idea is that Armenians were relocated deliberately in order to achieve an ethnically pure Turkish Anatolian core. The argument is persuasive and the most prolific advocate of this position is Professor Taner Akçam. Recent work by Turkish historians Uğur Ümit Üngör and Fuat Dündar also support this position. In my opinion, the evidence for this has strength and some authenticity, but it fails to explain why the relocations stopped in the winter of 1915–16.

Position 2—Intent to Destroy: This advances the idea that, as early as 1911, the inner circle of the Young Turk party decided to exterminate the Armenian population of the Ottoman Empire by intentionally killing them in situ or in death camps. To accomplish this, the Young Turks established secret dual-track architecture of command using the Special Organization to direct, by word-of-mouth, the operation of an empire-wide death machine. The rationale for this position is that the Young Turks were ideologically, economically, and politically motivated to eradicate the Armenian population of the Ottoman Empire. The most ardent advocates of this position are Vahkan Dadrian and Raymond Kévorkian, while many Western authors also support this view. Moreover, Dadrian further asserts that the Germans encouraged and supported the Ottomans in the extermination of the Armenians, although this claim has lost almost all of its adherents. There is almost no authentic evidence to support this position, which is based on hearsay, the selection of facts out of context, and overt speculation.

Position 3—Cumulative Radicalization: This advances the idea that limited regional measures, brought about by the exigencies of war, led to a process of cumulative radicalization of Ottoman polices toward the Armenians. Moreover, the Armenians were encouraged to violence and rebellion by the Allies, which set them on a collision course with the Ottoman government. In effect, the Armenians were, partly, the engineers of their own destruction. The author of this position is Professor Donald Bloxham and recent work by Yücel Güçlü and Michael Gunter conforms to this position. Bloxham differs from Güçlü and Gunter in asserting that, although there was no a priori blueprint for the extermination of the Armenians, a subsequent genocide did happen as an outcome of policy radicalization. This is a very solid position with which to approach and explain the relocations, but its extension into the genocide allegations substantially weakens it.

Position 4—Retaliation and Justification: This position advances the idea that the Armenians willfully massacred helpless and innocent Muslim villagers by the thousands. Driven to desperation, the Ottoman state, as well as criminally motivated gangs, responded in kind and retaliated by killing the Armenian perpetrators. This occurred simultaneously with the relocations, which were driven by state security and military necessity. Advocates of this position tend to be exclusively Turkish and include Enver Konukçu and Türkkaya Ataöv. It is true that large numbers of Muslims, as well as Armenians, Kurds, and Greeks, were killed in eastern Anatolia during World War I in what amounted to an internecine civil war. In my opinion, these events were never causal in the relocation decision.

Position 5—State Security and Insurgency: This position rests on the idea that a large Armenian insurgency occurred in 1915, which presented an immediate and real danger to the security of the Ottoman state. It advances the idea that the Ottoman Armenians, encouraged by the Armenian revolutionary committees, which were themselves the willing accomplices of Great Power schemes and machinations aimed at the destruction of the Ottoman Empire, rose in rebellion with the purpose of establishing an independent Armenia. The modern official Turkish version of the relocations and many Turkish historians follow this line of thinking. Twenty years ago, I believed this explanation was the most reasonable. However, today, I believe that this argument breaks down in the face of the fact that only a tiny portion of the total Ottoman Armenians were actively engaged in insurgent or guerrilla activities, while most Armenians were either passive bystanders or loyal citizens. My own turnabout is a direct result of my increased understanding of, and personal involvement in, America's counterinsurgency wars of the past decade.

MY POSITIONS

I wrote this book because I was not persuaded that any of the aforementioned positions were entirely plausible. Certainly there is some truth in all of them. The position that I advance in *Ottomans and Armenians* is most congruent with the work of Professor Donald Bloxham. I too believe that there was cumulative radicalization in Ottoman policies, from regional to national level, particularly with regard to military counterinsurgency policies. I maintain that the relocations themselves were the outcome of a rapidly escalating and deliberately tailored regional counterinsurgency campaign. I would also agree with Professor Bloxham that there were no a priori decisions to commit the mass extermination of Armenians. I would also side with the recent work of Hilmar Kaiser, which suggests that Ottoman archival material indicates that Cemal Pasha went to substantial lengths to safeguard the lives and property of displaced Armenians, thereby casting doubt on the entire concept of premeditated state-sponsored extermination, during or after the fact of relocations.

As the reader is aware, I advance the idea that the Armenian revolutionary committees, although small in numbers, achieved an unintended effect, out of proportion with their actual capability. It is a fact that the Armenian revolutionary committees and rogue insurgent groups, acting proactively and reactively, respectively, interdicted the vulnerable Ottoman lines of communications leading to the front-line armies in the east. After the Van rebellion, the cumulative intelligence in the hands of the Ottoman authorities persuaded them that the empire was poised on the cusp of well-coordinated Armeno-Entente combined irregular and conventional offensives. Moving from a local to a regional military policy, and determined to find a solution to this dilemma, the resource-poor Ottomans chose a Western-style counterinsurgency campaign of relocation. The design of this campaign separated the Armenian insurgents and guerrillas from their bases of support, after which small Ottoman military forces could easily defeat them in detail.

I should also provide an explanation of why I came to the particular conclusions that I have regarding the Armenians relocations. And I first ask the reader to consider the troubling questions that puzzled me for two decades. These are:

Why isn't there a "smoking gun?" There are no authentic documents anywhere today that establish either an order to exterminate the Armenians or an order to relocate them for ideological or political reasons. In a nutshell, there isn't a paper trail documenting these things and we should ask why. The Ottomans were obsessive about paper and bureaucratic filing. In fact, almost nothing happened in the highly centralized and "top-down" Ottoman bureaucracy without written and stamped official directives and orders. The British, when occupying Constantinople for over four years, searched vigorously for evidence of state-sponsored war crimes and found none. It is simply inconceivable that 100 percent of such directives and orders, distributed empire-wide to provincial governors over the course of a global war would not have survived.

How do we explain the fact that so many Ottoman Armenian citizens were not relocated? In particular, why were as many as

350,000 Armenians in the western reaches of the Ottoman Empire left in their homes? If the goal was extermination, why weren't the western Armenians relocated as well? Moreover, why were the relocations halted at all, especially after the spring of 1916, when, arguably, the Ottomans were winning their war?

Why do words and phrases such as "probably," "it is likely," "undoubtedly," "it would seem that," "no doubt explain," "it is obvious," "are indicative of," and "we can assume" consistently appear in the work of so many authors writing on this subject? This methodology of speculation and assumption must lead a critical thinker, at some point, to ask whether the argument is constructed according to a predetermined design rather than proven on the merits of the evidence. If you dispute this, pick up any of the books by the proponents of the positions listed earlier and go through them page by page, circling these phrases.

How do we reconcile the massive evidentiary trail of communications and close contacts between the Armenian revolutionary committees and the Entente powers (Russia, Great Britain, and France) encouraging insurgency in support of allied offensive operations with the idea of the Armenians as helpless victims?

Why is it that all of the evidence regarding the Special Organization's alleged "dual-track" architecture rests on either hearsay or the "textual analysis of the indictments," and the verdicts printed in government gazettes of the 1919 show trials of Ottoman war criminals in Constantinople? Why is there no authentic evidence that such an apparatus existed? How is it that no paper trail, or even partial documentation, exists anywhere supporting this claim? How is it possible that such an organization ran for four years on orally transmitted orders?

Why is it that nobody seemed to connect the obvious similarities between the Great Powers' counterinsurgency policies of relocation of 1895–1901 and the relocation of the Armenian population? Moreover, other than Professor Bloxham, why hadn't anyone placed the relocations within the context of a global war?

Why would the Ottomans, in the worst days of an existential struggle with three of the Great Powers for the very survival of the empire, decide, in the spring of 1915, to attempt to relocate about a half million people? Ottoman strategic policy and military priorities, at that point in time, were consistent and rational. A decision to allocate scarce resources to the relocation of so many people weakened the efforts on the fighting fronts and ran counter to any known war plans or strategic priorities of the Ottoman state.

Unrelated to the writing of this book, but of importance, why is it that the Turkish archives are open to scholars today and those of Armenia, the ARF in Waltham, Massachusetts, and the Armenian Patriarch in Jerusalem closed?

My conclusions advanced in this book establish a context for understanding what happened to the Armenians as a result of the activities of the Armenian revolutionary committees over a sustained period. From the perspective of a military historian, the evidence I collected led to the unfolding of the story as I have written it. I made an effort not to speculate or make assumptions and I made an effort to base my analysis on complete documents in context, rather than to extract and cherry-pick quotes and information. Finally, my conclusions (including my personal translations of Turkish and German documents) are my own.

Does this book negate or deny the notion of an alleged Armenian genocide perpetrated by the Young Turks? I would side with Professor Guenter Lewy by pointing out that it is difficult to prove the negative. Professor Lewy pointed out in 2005 that there is a vast body of authentic evidence proving conclusively that the Nazi state carried out an intentional genocide of Europe's Jews. He also pointed out that, at the end of the day, there is no such corresponding body of authentic evidence proving the actuality of an intentional Ottoman state-sponsored extermination of the Armenians. Lewy further argued that although provable genocide remains absent at the state level, at the individual level, there were numerous provable instances of localized genocidal acts, including mass murder, ethnic cleansing, and associated crimes against humanity. He also noted that there is substantial authentic evidence remaining today that the Ottoman state was aware of these crimes and intervened ineffectually, but ultimately sent hundreds of individuals for trial to account for their actions. Lewy pointed out the obvious—that correlation is not causation and because something looks a lot like genocide does not make it so. I would agree.

This leads me to conclude with the broad question, "If the Armenian relocations of 1915 were not genocidal...then...what were they?" The counterinsurgency argument is the only narrative that makes sense to me and it is a narrative that fits all of the facts known today. However, I do not exclude the possibility that as my own position has changed over a 20-year period, it may change yet again in the future, as scholars expose new information. Finally, I encourage those interested in these events to read widely and deeply before coming to any particular conclusions of their own.

This page intentionally left blank

NOTES

INTRODUCTION

1. Sublime Porte to Ministry of War, 842, May 31, 1915, ATASE, archive 401, record 1580, file 1–36; and Department of Critical Affairs Document No. 63 to Ministries, May 31, 1915, BOA, 3267598, Siyasi: 53 reproduced in Hikmet Ozdemir and Yusuf Sarinay (eds.), *Turk-Ermeni Ihtilafi Belegeler* (Ankara: Egemenlik, undated), document 17b.

2. See Daniel Marston and Carter Malakasian (eds.), *Counterinsurgency in Modern Warfare* (Oxford: Osprey Publishing, 2008), 13–18, for an explanation of what the term "counterinsurgency" has come to mean today. See also Max Boot, *Invisible Armies, An Epic History of Guerrilla Warfare from Ancient Times to the Present* (New York: Liveright Publishing Corporation, 2013), for a splendid journey into the world of insurgency and guerrilla warfare.

3. See Donald Bloxham, *The Great Game of Genocide; Imperialism, Nationalism, and the Destruction of the Ottoman Armenians* (Oxford: Oxford University Press, 2005), for a comprehensive explanation of this idea.

4. In one of the first Western assessments of the relocations, the Armenians were seen as "a great military danger" and that "some measures of precaution were certainly justified; but the actual action taken has been challenged on the Turkish side as well as on that of the Western Powers as not being commensurate with military necessity." Ahmed Emin Yalman, *Turkey in the World War* (New Haven: Yale University Press, 1930), 219. This theme became embedded in the extant Western literature; see the following notes for examples.

5. See, e.g., Taner Akçam, *The Young Turk's Crime against Humanity, The Armenian Genocide and Ethnic Cleansing in the Ottoman Empire* (Princeton: Princeton University Press, 2012), 203; Peter Balakian, *The Burning Tigris: The Armenian Genocide and America's Response* (New York: Harper Collins, 2003), 209; Donald Bloxham, *The Great Game of Genocide, Imperialism, Nationalism, and the Destruction of the Ottoman Armenians* (Oxford, 2005), 208–10; and Vahakn Dadrian, "The Secret Young Turk Itthadist Conference and the Decision for the World War I Genocide of the Armenians," *Holocaust Studies and Genocide Studies* vol. VII (1993), 173–201.

6. See, e.g., Hüseyin Çelik, "The 1915 Armenian Revolt in Van: Eyewitness Testimony," in Türkkaya Ataöv (ed.), *The Armenians in the Late Ottoman Period* (Ankara: Turkish Historical Society Printing House, 2001), 87–108; Yücel Güçlü, *Armenians and the Allies in Cilicia 1914–1923* (Salt Lake City: University of Utah Press, 2012), 35–55; Justin McCarthy, Esat Arslan, Cemalettin Taşkıran, and Ömer Turan, *The Armenian Rebellion at Van* (Salt Lake City: The University of Utah Press, 2006), 176–91.

1 INSURGENCY BY COMMITTEE

1. Memorandum by Mr. Fitzmaurice, Constantinople, August 10, 1913, Inclosure in No. 576 (Marling to Edward Grey, August 27, 1913), FO 4017o/19208/13/44, reproduced in G. P. Gooch and Harold Temperley, *British Documents on the Origins of the War, 1898–1914, Volume X, Part I* (London: HMSO, 1936), 509.
2. Max Boot, *Invisible Armies, An Epic History of Guerrilla Warfare from Ancient Times to the Present* (New York: Liveright Publishing Corporation, 2013), 226–39.
3. Ibid.
4. Whether these insurrections were designed to liberate subject peoples or to provoke the Ottomans into heinous behavior remains contested today.
5. The modern connotation of a country called Macedonia with a discrete ethnolinguistic identity had little relevance in the pre-1914 world when the area was the epicenter of conflicting claims advanced by armed groups of Bulgarians, Serbs, Albanians, and Greeks.
6. Mesut Uyar and Edward J. Erickson, *A Military History of the Ottomans, From Osman to Atatürk* (Santa Barbara, CA: Praeger, 2009), 214–16.
7. Reşat Kasaba (ed.), *The Cambridge History of Turkey, Volume 4, Turkey in the Modern World* (Cambridge: Cambridge University Press, 2008), 54.
8. Hratch Dasnabedian, *History of the Armenian Revolutionary Federation, Dasnaktutiun 1890/1924* (Milan:OEMME Edizioni, 1990), 25–33.
9. Nilüfer Hatemi, "Unfolding a Life; Marshal Fevzi Çakmak's Diaries," unpublished PhD dissertation, Princeton University, November 2000, 44. See also Jeffrey W. Stebbins, "Bell and Banner: Armenian Revolutionaries at the End of the Ottoman Empire," unpublished MA thesis, US Naval Postgraduate School, December 2011, 65–68.
10. K. S. Papazian, *Patriotism Perverted, A Discussion of the Deeds and the Misdeeds of the Armenian Revolutionary Federation, the So-called Dashnagtzoutune* (Boston: Baikar Press, 1934), 11–13.
11. Dasnabedian, *History of the Armenian Revolutionary Federation*, 22.
12. Ibid.
13. Ibid., 25.

14. Louise Nalbandian, *The Armenian Revolutionary Movement* (Berkeley: University of California Press, 1963), 97.
15. Ibid., 98.
16. Ibid., 101.
17. Ibid.
18. Ibid., 108.
19. Papazian, *Patriotism Perverted*, 19.
20. Nalbandian, *Armenian Revolutionary Movement*, 110.
21. Ibid., 110
22. For a counterargument that these kinds of tactics were defensive rather than offensive or deliberately provocative, see Gerard J. Libaridian, "What was revolutionary about Armenian revolutionary parties in the Ottoman Empire?," Ronald Grigor Suny, Fatma Müge Göçek, and Norman M. Naimark (eds.), *A Question of Genocide, Armenians and Turks at the End of the Ottoman Empire* (New York: Oxford University Press, 2011), 99–10.
23. Ibid., 111.
24. A. Nicolson to Earl of Rosebery, No. 22, Constantinople, January 12, 1894, Inclosure 2 (Jewett to Fitzmaurice, Sivas, December 17, 1894), FO 424/178, 17/22, reproduced in Bilâl N. Şimşir, *British Documents on Ottoman Armenians, Volume III (1891–1895)* (Ankara: Turkish Historical Society, 1989), 298–299.
25. Nalbandian, *Armenian Revolutionary Movement*, 112.
26. Ibid., 121. See also Vahakn N. Dadrian, *The History of the Armenian Genocide* (Providence: Berghahn Books, 3rd revised edition 1997), 114–16; and Kamuran Gürün, *The Armenian File, The Myth of Innocence Exposed* (Nicosia: Rustem, 3rd edition 2001), 139–42.
27. See Nalbandian, *Armenian Revolutionary Movement*, 122. The commission asserted that the Armenians were guilty of very few crimes other than sheltering Murat and his band, occasional brigandage, and resisting under conditions that were not entirely clear.
28. Vahakn N. Dadrian, *Warrant for Genocide, Key Elements of Turco-Armenian Conflict* (New Brunswick: Transaction Publishers, 1999), 85–90.
29. Dadrian, *History of the Armenian Genocide*, 127–31.
30. Nalbandian, *Armenian Revolutionary Movement*, 127.
31. Dadrian, *History of the Armenian Genocide*, 127–31.
32. Ibid.
33. Nalbandian, *Armenian Revolutionary Movement*, 127.
34. Ibid., 122.
35. Ibid., 123.
36. Dadrian, *History of the Armenian Genocide*, 119–21; and Gürün, *The Armenian File*, 142–47.
37. Nalbandian, *Armenian Revolutionary Movement*, 126.
38. The story of the Armenian revolutionary parties in Czarist Russia, while often intersecting with this work, is distinct from that of the

Armenian revolutionary parties in the Ottoman Empire and outside the scope of this book. See Nalbandian, *Armenian Revolutionary Movement*, Chapter VI, 132–50, for further discussion.

39. Papazian, *Patriotism Perverted*, 11.
40. Nalbandian, *Armenian Revolutionary Movement*, 154.
41. Ibid., 155.
42. Ibid., 157; and Papazian, *Patriotism Perverted*, 9–10.
43. Nalbandian, *Armenian Revolutionary Movement*, 159; and Papazian, *Patriotism Perverted*, 19.
44. Papazian, *Patriotism Perverted*, 21.
45. Nalbandian, *Armenian Revolutionary Movement*, 159.
46. Ibid., 167.
47. It is worth noting here that this list was translated and complied from original source material by Dr. Louise Nalbandian, the primary historian of early Armenian revolutionary parties and activities.
48. Manuel Hassassian, *A.R.F. as a Revolutionary Party, 1890–1921* (Jerusalem: Hai Tad Publications, 1983), 5–6.
49. Nalbandian, *Armenian Revolutionary Movement*, 168. See also the same platform in Gürün, *The Armenian File*, 125; and Papazian, *Patriotism Perverted*, 14–15.
50. Hassassian, *A.R.F. as a Revolutionary Party*, 7.
51. Nalbandian, *Armenian Revolutionary Movement*, 173.
52. Ibid., 174.
53. Dasnabedian, *History of the Armenian Revolutionary Federation*, 45–47.
54. Ibid., 39.
55. Ibid., 51.
56. Feride Çavdar Uslu, *Armenians of Adana (1914–1918)*, unpublished masters thesis, Afyonkarahisar Kocatepe University, May 2007, 32. The information regarding the revolts of September–December 1895 comes from these pages of Unlu's thesis and Gürün, *The Armenian File*, 150–51.
57. Dasnabedian, *History of the Armenian Revolutionary Federation*, 51.
58. Gürün, *The Armenian File*, 154–56.
59. Justin, McCarthy, Esat Arslan, Cemalettin Taşkıran, and Ömer Turan, *The Armenian Rebellion at Van* (Salt Lake City: The University of Utah Press, 2006), 61. McCarthy cited British consulate reports to the foreign office detailing the killings.
60. Ibid., 62.
61. Ibid. McCarthy cites British consulate reports as the source of this information.
62. Ibid., 64.
63. Dadrian, *History of the Armenian Genocide*, 131–34.
64. McCarthy et al., *The Armenian Rebellion at Van*, 64. McCarthy's narrative of this incident and the Ottoman response, led by Sadettin Pasha, is worth reading. The event demonstrates how difficult it was

for the Ottomans to deal effectively with the problem of lawlessness in the remote and hostile terrain of eastern Anatolia.

65. Ibid., 65.
66. Dadrian, *History of the Armenian Genocide*, 135.
67. McCarthy et al., *The Armenian Rebellion at Van*, 67.
68. Dadrian, *History of the Armenian Genocide*, 138–42; and Papazian, *Patriotism Perverted*, 20.
69. Gürün, *The Armenian File*, 156–59.
70. Nalbandian, *Armenian Revolutionary Movement*, 176–77.
71. Ibid., 177–78.
72. Dasnabedian, *History of the Armenian Revolutionary Federation*, 47.
73. Ibid.
74. Papazian, *Patriotism Perverted*, 21. Papazian asserts that the Russians were behind the idea in order to sow "political unrest and turmoil" in the region.
75. Dasnabedian, *History of the Armenian Revolutionary Federation*, 49.
76. Ibid., 50.
77. Hassassian, *A.R.F. as a Revolutionary Party*, 14.
78. Dasnabedian, *History of the Armenian Revolutionary Federation*, 59.
79. Ibid., 57.
80. Ibid.
81. Ibid., 58.
82. Ibid., 62.
83. Ibid.
84. Ibid., 60.
85. Ibid., 66. See Dasnabedian's map on this page for an understanding of these arms smuggling routes.
86. Ibid., 67–68; and Gürün, *The Armenian File*, 159–60.
87. Ibid., 68.
88. Ibid., 71.
89. Ibid., 72.
90. Papazian, *Patriotism Perverted*, 22–23.
91. Dasnabedian, *History of the Armenian Revolutionary Federation*, 73.
92. Ibid., 77.
93. Gürün, *The Armenian File*, 160.
94. Dasnabedian, *History of the Armenian Revolutionary Federation*, 77.
95. Ibid., 77–79; and Papazian, *Patriotism Perverted*, 23.
96. Ibid., 79.
97. Ibid., 85.
98. Ibid., 85–86.
99. Duncan M. Perry, *The Politics of Terror, the Macedonian Liberation Movements 1893–1903*, (Durham, NC: Duke University Press, 1988), 36.
100. Nadine Lange-Akhund, *The Macedonian Question, 1893–1908: From Western Sources* (New York: Columbia University Press, 1998), 36. Duncan Perry's earlier work asserted the founding date was November 3, 1893. Often this group is known as the Internal

Macedonia Revolutionary Organization (IMRO) because it functioned inside the Ottoman Empire.

101. Perry, *The Politics of Terror*, 46–47.

102. Ibid., 54–56.

103. Lange-Akhund, *The Macedonian Question*, 48–50.

104. Ibid., 119–24.

105. Ibid., 123–24.

106. Ibid., 125–30. This is the best concise description of the 1903 revolt
in the literature.

107. Austria and Russia forced the Ottomans to submit to the Mürzsteg
Agreement of October 22, 1903, which established a European
supervised gendarmerie in the affected provinces. See Lange-Akhund,
The Macedonian Question, 141–46, for text and commentary.

108. The definitive work on the originals and formation of the Young Turk
movement is M. Sükrü Hanioğlu, *Preparation for a Revolution, the
Young Turks 1902–1908* (Oxford: Oxford University Press, 2001).

109. Hanioğlu, *Preparation for a Revolution*, 132, 136–41, 143–57,
161–72.

110. See Dikran Mesrob Kiligian, *Armenian Organization and Ideology
under Ottoman Rule 1908–1914* (New Brunswick, NJ: Transaction
Publishers, 2009), 2, for an excellent discussion of the competing
agendas.

111. Hanioğlu, *Preparation for a Revolution*, 196.

112. Ibid., 197–209.

113. Practically speaking, however, intense Russian pressure on the
Caucasian ARF committees in Russia sent many ARF members over
the border to the dubious haven of the Ottoman Empire.

114. Kiligian, *Armenian Organization and Ideology under Ottoman Rule*, 17.

115. Ibid.

116. McCarthy et al., *The Armenian Rebellion at Van*, 133.

117. Kiligian, *Armenian Organization and Ideology under Ottoman Rule*,
30. Kiligian noted that the arms smuggling work remained dangerous
and also that the preferred weapon for illegal importation was the
Mauser automatic pistol.

118. See, e.g., Gürün, *The Armenian File*, 166–70.

119. See, e.g., Kiligian, *Armenian Organization and Ideology under
Ottoman Rule*, 43–48, for a pro-Armenian viewpoint and Yücel
Güçlü, *Armenians and the Allies in Cilicia 1914–1923* (Salt Lake City:
University of Utah Press, 2010), 40–50, for the pro-Ottoman view-
point. Interestingly, both authors are extremely persuasive in present-
ing their arguments and it is difficult to reconcile the narratives.

120. Dadrian, *History of the Armenian Genocide*, 179–84.

121. Güçlü, *Armenians and the Allies in Cilicia*, 49.

122. Kiligian, *Armenian Organization and Ideology under Ottoman Rule*,
45–47.

123. Dasnabedian, *History of the Armenian Revolutionary Federation*, 91.

124. Ibid.
125. Kiligian, *Armenian Organization and Ideology under Ottoman Rule*, 59.
126. Ibid., 96.
127. Ibid., 99–100.
128. Ibid., 130.
129. Dasnabedian, *History of the Armenian Revolutionary Federation*, 100–101.
130. See Uyar and Erickson, *A Military History of the Ottomans*, 214–19, for a discussion of this topic.
131. Naci Çakın and Nafiz Orhon, *Türk Silahlı Kuvvetleri Tarihi, IIIncü Cilt 5nci Kısım (1793–1908)* (Ankara: Genelkurmay Basımevi, 1978), 502–68.
132. Ibid. Many of the insurrections were known by the name of the leader, e.g., the Ali Pasha Insurrection and the Mehmet Ali Pasha Insurrection.

2   COUNTERINSURGENCY IN THE EMPIRE'S CORE

1. Sir Phillip Currie to the Earl of Kimberley, Constantinople, March 28, 1894, Inclosure 226, FO 424/178,, Pp 1, No. 64, reproduced in Bilâl N. Şimşir, *British Documents on the Armenians, Volume III (1891–1895)* (Ankara: The Turkish Historical Society, 1989), 332.
2. Mesut Uyar and Edward J. Erickson, *A Military History of the Ottomans, From Osman to Atatürk* (Santa Barbara, CA: Praeger, 2009), 213.
3. Naci Çakın and Nafiz Orhon, *Türk Silahlı Kuvvetleri Tarihi, IIIncü Cilt 5nci Kısım (1793–1908)* (Ankara: Genelkurmay Basımevi, 1978), Map 8.
4. Niall Ferguson, *The War of the World, Twentieth Century Conflict and the Descent of the West* (London: Penguin Books, 2006), 10–11.
5. The remaining armies were the Fourth in Erzurum, the Sixth in Baghdad, and the Seventh in Sana (there was no Fifth Army).
6. Of 36 infantry regiments, 20 were stationed in Europe.
7. Çakın and Orhon, *Türk Silahlı Kuvvetleri Tarihi*, p. 213; and Document 2 (Ottoman Armed Forces, March 1881).
8. The remaining armies were the Fourth in Erzincan, the Fifth in Damascus, the Sixth in Baghdad, and the Seventh in Sana.
9. Çakın and Orhon, *Türk Silahlı Kuvvetleri Tarihi*, 215–17; and Organizational Chart 5 (1891 Reserve organization and mobilization areas).
10. Çakın and Orhon, *Türk Silahlı Kuvvetleri Tarihi,*, 215.
11. Stanford J. and Ezel K. Shaw, *History of the Ottoman Empire and Modern Turkey, Volume II* (Cambridge: Cambridge University Press, 1977), 156. See also Table 3.5, "Changes in Ottoman Departmental Budgets between 1880 and 1907," on p. 225, which show that the army budget increased from 547 million kuruş in 1880 to 898 million kuruş in 1907.
12. Ibid., 234–36. In 1907, the Ottoman field armies deployed the following numbers of infantry regiments, First Army, 8; Second Army,

16; Third Army, 24; Fourth Army, 12; Fifth Army, 8; Sixth Army, 8; Seventh Army, 8. See also Merwin A. Griffith, "The Reorganization of the Ottoman Army under Abdülhamid II, 1880–1897," unpublished PhD dissertation, University of California, Los Angeles, 1966, 36. Griffith stated that the army devoted 50 percent of is strength to the Balkans; however, this would appear to be on the low side.

13. Edward J. Erickson, *Defeat in Detail, the Ottoman Army in the Balkans, 1912–1913* (Westport, CT: Praeger, 2003), 15–33.
14. Selahattin Karatamu, *Türk Silahlı Kuvvetleri Tarihi, IIIncü Cilt 6nci Kısım (1908–1920)* (Ankara: Genelkurmay Basımevi, 1971), 147–75.
15. Çakın and Orhon, *Türk Silahlı Kuvvetleri Tarihi*, 251–53.
16. Ibid., 1888, Organized Jandarma and Zaptiye Forces, Appendixed Chart 9 (Ek 9).
17. Karatamu, *Türk Silahlı Kuvvetleri Tarihi*, Appendixed Chart 3 (Ek 3). See also Çakın and Orhon, *Türk Silahlı Kuvvetleri Tarihi*, 235, for a complete list of the fortresses.
18. Griffith, "The Reorganization of the Ottoman Army," 67–70.
19. Şadi Sükan, *Türk Silahlı Kuvvetleri Tarihi, Osmanlı Devri, Balkan Harbi (1912–1913), II Cilt 3ncü Kısım Edirne Kalesi Etrafındaki Muharebeler* (Ankara: Genelkurmay Basımevi, 1993), 2–3. By 1912, e.g., the Edirne fortress contained 247 permanent artillery pieces fixed in 18 forts and 11 artillery battalion positions (see Erickson, *Defeat in Detail*, 140–43 for details about the Edirne fortress).
20. See Jonathan Grant, "The Sword of the Sultan: Ottoman Arms Imports, 1854–1914," in *The Journal of Military History* (January 2002), 66: 1, 9–36, for an excellent summation of the Ottoman budget during these years and the decisions to purchase German weapons.
21. Uyar and Erickson, *A Military History of the Ottomans*, 205.
22. See Erickson, *Defeat in Detail*, 11–15, 21–33, 55–59, and 61–62, for varied commentary about the effect of the German military mission and Colmar von der Goltz in particular.
23. Stanford J and Shaw, *History of the Ottoman Empire and Modern Turkey, Volume II*, 245.
24. Çakın and Orhon, *Türk Silahlı Kuvvetleri Tarihi*, 228.
25. Reşat Kasaba (ed.), *The Cambridge History of Turkey, Volume 4, Turkey in the Modern World* (Cambridge: Cambridge University Press, 2008), 57, 84–86, and 92–93.
26. Justin McCarthy, Esat Arslan, Cemalettin Taşkıran, and Ömer Turan, *The Armenian Rebellion at Van* (Salt Lake City: The University of Utah Press, 2006), 44.
27. See Vincent S. Wilhite, "Guerrilla War, Counterinsurgency, and State Formation in Ottoman Yemen," unpublished PhD dissertation, The Ohio State University, 2003, for detailed discussions of how resources affected the Ottoman counterinsurgency campaigns in Yemen.
28. These wars included the Spanish in Cuba, the Americans in the Philippines, and the British in South Africa. The definitive theorist of

"small wars" as these came to be known was Britain's C. E. Callwell, who produced *Small Wars* in 1896.

29. H. Erdogan Cengiz (ed.), Enver, *Enver Paşa'nın Anıları* (Constantinople: İletişim Yayınları, 1991), 48–51.

30. Pertev Demirhan, *Generalfeldmarschall Colmar von der Goltz: Das Lebensbild eines grossen Soldaten* (Göttingen, 1960), 74–77. See also Feroz Yasamee, "Colmar Freiherr von der Goltz and the Boer War," Keith Wilson (ed.), *The International Impact of the Russo-Japanese War* (London: 2001), 193–210.

31. Yavuz Abadan, *Mustafa Kemal ve Çeteçilik* (Constantinople: Varlık Yayınevi, 1972), 53–56; Asim Gündüz, *Hatıralarım* (Constantinople: Kervan Yayınları 1973), 29–32; and Uyar and Erickson, *A Military History of the Ottomans*, 221–22.

32. Mesut Uyar and A. Kadir Varoğlu, "In Search of Modernity and Rationality, The Evolution of Turkish Military Academy Curricula in a Historical Perspective," *Armed Forces & Society*, vol. 35, no. 1 (October 2009), 185–89. See also Erickson, *Defeat in Detail*, 56–57, for a discussion of the war college curriculum.

33. Çakın and Orhon, *Türk Silahlı Kuvvetleri Tarihi*, 582.

34. Ibid., 585.

35. Ibid., 216 and 594–95.

36. Nadine Lange-Akhund, *The Macedonian Question, 1893–1908 From Western Sources* (New York: Columbia University Press, 1998), 124–25.

37. It is unclear whether the Ottomans considered its Muslim citizens more reliable than Christians but it is true that the *Komitacıs* targeted Muslims in terrorist attacks. This led, over time, to more cooperative relations between the army and the local Muslim populations.

38. Lange-Akhund, *The Macedonian Question*, 128.

39. Ibid., 130.

40. Duncan M. Perry, *The Politics of Terror, The Macedonian Liberation Movements 1893–1903* (Durham, NC: Duke University Press, 1988), 140.

41. Ibid., 139.

42. Lange-Akhund, *The Macedonian Question*, 259.

43. Ibid., 260.

44. Ibid.

45. Stanford J and Shaw, *History of the Ottoman Empire and Modern Turkey, Volume II*, 222–24.

46. See Griffith, "The Reorganization of the Ottoman Army," 85–87; and Annex IV (Income vs. Military Expenditures, 1886–1895) for detailed discussions of military expenditures.

47. Stanford J and Shaw, *History of the Ottoman Empire and Modern Turkey, Volume II*, 225.

48. Çakın and Orhon, *Türk Silahlı Kuvvetleri Tarihi*, 1888 Organized Jandarma and Zaptiye Forces, Appendixed Chart 9 (Ek 9).

49. McCarthy et al., *The Armenian Rebellion at Van*, 58.

50. Griffith, "The Reorganization of the Ottoman Army," 87.
51. Ibid., 119–22. See also Uyar and Erickson, *A Military History of the Ottomans*, 202–204. The tradition of locally organized irregular cavalry dated back to the earliest days of the Osmanli dynasty; see 53–61, for details of the Timariot Cavalry and associated frontier units.
52. Çakın and Orhon, *Türk Silahlı Kuvvetleri Tarihi*, 223.
53. Bayram Kodaman, "The Hamidiye Light Cavalry Regiments: Abdülhamid II and the Eastern Anatolian Tribes," M. Hakan Yavuz with Peter Slugglett (eds.), *War and Diplomacy, The Russo-Turkish War of 1877–1878 and the Treaty of Berlin* (Salt Lake City: University of Utah Press, 2011), 388.
54. Raymond H. Kévorkian, *The Armenian Genocide, A Complete History* (London: I.B. Tauris, 2011).
55. Janet Klein, *The Margins of Empire, Kurdish Tribal Militias in the Ottoman Tribal Zone* (Stanford, CA: Stanford University Press, 2011), 1–19.
56. Griffith, "The Reorganization of the Ottoman Army," 122.
57. Correspondence with Dr. Mesut Uyar, Turkish Military Academy, Ankara, March 23, 2010.
58. It is important to note here that the Russians gradually decreased the size of their Cossack forces as 1914 approached and that no other Great Power chose an irregular force model for their standing armies. This speaks to the generally held idea at that time that irregular forces, and the Cossacks in particular, had limited utility on the battlefield.
59. Klein, *The Margins of Empire*, 34.
60. Stanford J. Shaw, *The Ottoman Empire in World War I, Volume 1, Prelude to War* (Ankara: Turkish Historical Society, 2006), 84–86 and 145.
61. Hratch Dasnabedian, *History of the Armenian Revolutionary Federation, Dasnaktutiun 1890/1924* (Milan:OEMME Edizioni, 1990), 51–53.
62. Çakın and Orhon, *Türk Silahlı Kuvvetleri Tarihi*, 602–603.
63. Vahakn N. Dadrian, *The History of the Armenian Genocide* (Providence: Berghahn Books, 3rd revised edition 1997), 127–31.
64. Çakın and Orhon, *Türk Silahlı Kuvvetleri Tarihi*, 602–603.
65. McCarthy et al., *The Armenian Rebellion at Van*, 64–68.
66. Uyar and Erickson, *A Military History of the Ottomans*, 208–11.
67. Nurer Uğurlu (ed.), Resneli Niyazi, *Hürriyet Kahramanı Resneli Niyazi Hatıratı* (Constantinople: Örgün Yayınevi, 2003), 148–52.
68. Enver, *Enver Paşa'nın Anıları*, 52–57; Faruk Özerengin (ed.), Kazım Karabekir, *Hayatım* (Constantinople: Emre Yayınları, 1995), 379–83, 407–11, 468–75, and 503–18; Rahmi Apak, *Yetmişlik Bir Subayın Anıları* (Ankara: Türk Tarih Kurumu Basımevi, 1988), 16–23.
69. Military schools (especially the Military Academy) were the real cauldrons of dissidence and dissemination of ideologies and thoughts. See Halil Kut, *Ittihat ve Terakki'den Cumhuriyete Bitmeyen Savas*

(Constantinople: 7 Gün Yayınları, 1971), 9–17; Karabekir, *Hayatım*, 247–349.

70. Enver, *Enver Paşa'nın Anıları*, 57–69 and 75–76; Niyazi, *Hurriyet Kahramanı Resneli Niyazi Hatıratı*, 162–63; Kudret Emiroğu (ed.), H Cemal, *Arnavutluk'tan Sakarya'ya Komitacılık: Yuzbası Cemal'in Anıları* (Ankara: Kebikeç Yayınları, 1996), 9–13.

71. Enver, *Enver Paşa'nın Anıları*, 79–90; Niyazi, *Hürriyet Kahramanı Resneli Niyazi Hatıratı*, 165–71.

72. Enver, *Enver Paşa'nın Anıları*, 77 and 90–121; Bekir Fikri, *Balkanlarda Tedhis ve Gerilla: Grebene* (Constantinople: Belge Yayınları, 1978), 17–28. See also M. Şükrü Hanioğlu, *Preparation for a Revolution, The Young Turks, 1902–1908* (Oxford: Oxford University Press, 2001), 217–30.

73. Cemal, *Arnavutluk'tan Sakarya'ya Komitacılık*, 21–24.

3 COUNTERINSURGENCY IN THE PERIPHERY

1. Vincent S. Wilhite, "Guerrilla War, Counterinsurgency, and State Formation in Ottoman Yemen," unpublished PhD dissertation, the Ohio State University, 2003, 377.

2. For example, the Ottoman punitive expedition in Yemen of 1891 required 6,000–7,000 men.

3. Wilhite, "Guerrilla War," 303–13.

4. Ibid., 370.

5. Ibid., 304.

6. Karatamu, *Türk Silahlı Kuvvetleri Tarihi (1908–1920)*, Kroki 2 (Map 2) and Kuruluş 5 (Organizational Chart 5).

7. Mehmet Tevfik Bey, *Bir Devlet Adamının, Mehmet Tevfik Beyin (Biren) II, Abdülhamit, Meşrutiyet ve Mütareke Devri Hatıraları Cilt 2* (Istanbul: Arma Yayınları, 1993), 284.

8. Ibid., 281; and Wilhite, "Guerrilla War," 382–84.

9. Wilhite, "Guerrilla War," 389.

10. Ahmed İzzet Pasha, *Feryadım, Cilt I* (Istanbul: Nehir Yayınları, 1992), 27.

11. Ibid., 31.

12. Ibid., 30–33.

13. Wilhite, "Guerrilla War," 402–404.

14. Ibid., 404.

15. Ibid., 405.

16. The following paragraph summarizes Wilhite, "Guerrilla War," 405–408.

17. Caesar E. Farah, *The Sultan's Yemen, Nineteenth-Century Challenges to Ottoman Rule* (London: I.B.Tauris, 2002), 226.

18. Ibid., 229.

19. Wilhite, "Guerrilla War," 411.

20. Ibid.

21. Farah, *The Sultan's Yemen*, 227.

22. Turkish General Staff, *Balkan Harbı (1912–1913), I Cilt, Harbin Sebepleri, Askeri Haıirlıklar ve Osmanlı Devletinin Harbe Girişi (Ikinci Başki)* (Ankara: Genelkurmay Basımevi, 1993), 86.
23. See Edward J. Erickson, *Defeat in Detail, the Ottoman Army in the Balkans, 1912–1913* (Westport, CT: Praeger, 2003), 15–24, for detailed information on the Ottoman army in this period.
24. Ahmed Izzet Pascha, *Denkwürdigkeiten des Marschalls Izzet Pascha* (Leipzig, Germany: Verlag von K.F. Koehler, 1927), 165–712.
25. Ibid., 130–42. See also Erickson, *Defeat in Detail*, 24–33, for a complete summary of the plans and tests that were conducted in 1909 and 1910.
26. Erickson, *Defeat in Detail*, 27–28.
27. Ibid., 29
28. Ibid., 55.
29. Ibid., 32–34.
30. Ibid., 240.
31. Ibid., 242.
32. Ibid.
33. Ibid., 247–70.
34. Ibid., 29–32.
35. Ibid., See Appendix B, "Ottoman Regular Army Order of Battle, 1911," 371–84, for complete listings of where units were garrisoned in Yemen and where the 13 battalions came from in other army areas. See also Metin Ayışığı, *Mareşal Ahmet İzzet Paşa (Askerî ve Siyasî Hayatı)* (Ankara: Türk Tarih Kurumu Basımevi, 1997), 33–46.
36. George W. Gawrych, *The Crescent and the Eagle: Ottoman Rule, Islam and the Albanians, 1874–1913* (London: I.B. Tauris, 2006), 140–49.
37. Ibid., 149; and Karatamu, *Türk Silahlı Kuvvetleri Tarihi (1908–1920)*, 30–33.
38. Gawrych, *The Crescent and the Eagle*, 150.
39. Ibid., 158–61.
40. Ibid., 160–61.
41. Ibid., 176–77.
42. Ibid., 177.
43. Ibid., 178–79.
44. Owen Pearson, *Albania and King Zog; Independence, Republic and Monarchy 1908–1939* (London: The Centre for Albanian Studies, 2004), 12.
45. Gawrych, *The Crescent and the Eagle*, 188.
46. Ibid.
47. James N. Tallon, "The Young Turks and Ottoman Counter-Insurrectionary Operations," Unpublished conference paper, Society for Military History Annual Conference, Lisle, IL, June 9–12, 2011, unpaginated.
48. Gawrych, *The Crescent and the Eagle*, 190–93.
49. Pearson, *Albania and King Zog*, 26.

50. See Gawrych, *The Crescent and the Eagle*, 194–95, for a complete list of the Albanian demands as well as an engaging summary of the evolution of them.

51. Renato Tittoni, *The Italo-Turkish War (1911–1912)* (Kansas City, MO: Franklin Hudson Publishing Company, 1914), 25.

52. Karatamu, *Türk Silahlı Kuvvetleri Tarihi (1908–1920)*, 159.

53. Şükrü Erkal, *Birinci Dünya Harbinde Türk Harbi, VIncı Cilt, Hicaz, Asir, Yemen Cepheleri ve Libya Harekatı 1914–1918* (Ankara: Genelkurmay Basımevi, 1978), 6.

54. Hamdi Ertuna, *Türk Silahlı Kuvvetleri Tarihi, Osmanlı Devri, Osmanlı-İtalyan Harbi (1911–1912)* (Ankara: Genelkurmay Basımevi, 1981), 49–57.

55. William H. Beehler, *The History of the Italian-Turkish War, September 29, 1911 to October 18, 1912* (Annapolis, MD: The Advertiser-Republican, 1913), 18.

56. Ibid.

57. Ibid., 20–25.

58. Ertuna, *Osmanlı-İtalyan Harbi (1911–1912)*, 159–79.

59. Ibid.

60. Yavuz Abadan, *Mustafa Kemal ve Çetecilik* (Istanbul: Varlık Yayınları, 1964), 30–35

61. Cemal Kutay, *Trablus-Garb'de Bir Avuç Kahraman* (Istanbul: Tarih Yayınları, 1963), 14–51, 86–111; and Ertuna, *Osmanlı-İtalyan Harbi (1911–1912)*, 152–58.

62. Hamdi Ertuna, *1911–1912 Osmanlı-İtalyan Harbi ve Kolağası Mustafa Kemal* (Ankara: Genelkurmay Basımevi, 1985), 95–122.

63. Halil Kut, *İttihat ve Terakki'den Cumhuriyete Bitmeyen Savaş: Kutülamare Kahramanı Halil Paşanın Anıları* (İstanbul: 7 Gün Yayınları, 1972), 83–114; and Ertuna, *Osmanlı-İtalyan Harbi (1911–1912)*, 171–77, 184–85, 188–213.

64. Beehler, *History of the Italian-Turkish War*, 31–34, 54; and Ertuna, *Osmanlı-İtalyan Harbi (1911–1912)*, 187, 192, 199, 273.

65. Beehler, *History of the Italian-Turkish War*, 34–36, 48–50; and Ertuna, *Osmanlı-İtalyan Harbi (1911–1912)*, 219–51.

66. Abadan, *Mustafa Kemal ve Çetecilik*, 39–44.

67. Ertuna, *Osmanlı-İtalyan Harbi (1911–1912)*, 289, 331–33; and Kutay, *Trablus-Garb'de Bir Avuç Kahraman*, 154–201.

68. Ertuna, *Osmanlı-İtalyan Harbi (1911–1912)*, 181–83.

69. Beehler, *History of the Italian-Turkish War*, 64–66, 70–78, 83–86; and Ertuna, *Osmanlı-İtalyan Harbi (1911–1912)*, 282–88, 290–349, 404–10.

70. Ertuna, *Osmanlı-İtalyan Harbi (1911–1912)*, 220, 310, 324–27, 432–34, 446–47.

71. Beehler, *History of the Italian-Turkish War*, 50–52, 56–60, 68–70, 87–90; and Ertuna, *Osmanlı-İtalyan Harbi (1911–1912)*, 278–80, 353–68, 372–83.

72. Beehler, *History of the Italian-Turkish War*, 73–76; and Ertuna, *Osmanlı-İtalyan Harbi (1911–1912)*, 127–29.
73. Timothy W. Childs, *Italo-Turkish Diplomacy and the War over Libya 1911–1912* (Leiden, NE: E.J. Brill, 1990), 59.
74. Tittoni, *The Italo-Turkish War*, 12–13.
75. Ibid.
76. Beehler, *History of the Italian-Turkish War*, 96.
77. Ibid., 98.
78. Erickson, *Defeat in Detail*, 80–82.
79. Ertuna, *Osmanlı-İtalyan Harbi (1911–1912)*, 411–21; and Kut, *İttihat ve Terakki'den Cumhuriyete Bitmeyen Savaş*, 116.
80. Turkish General Staff, *Balkan Harbı (1912–1913)*, 90–91.
81. Bayram Kodaman, "The Hamidiye Light Cavalry Regiments, Abdülhamid II and the Eastern Anatolian Tribes," Yavuz, M. Hakan and Peter Sluglett (eds.), *War and Diplomacy, The Russo-Turkish War of 1877–1878 and the Treaty of Berlin* (Salt Lake City: University of Utah Press, 2011), 23.
82. Janet Klein, *The Margins of Empire, Kurdish Tribal Militias in the Ottoman Tribal Zone* (Stanford, CA: Stanford University Press, 2011), 107.
83. Ibid.
84. Ibid., 108.
85. Kodaman, "The Hamidiye Light Cavalry Regiments," 421.
86. Ibid., 422.
87. Karatamu, *Türk Silahlı Kuvvetleri Tarihi, (1908–1920)*, 132.
88. *New Regulations for the Tribal Light Cavalry of August 1910* (English Translation of *Aşiret Süvari Alayları Nizamnamesi*, 1326) from Janet Klein, "Power in the Periphery: The Hamidiye Light Cavalry and the Struggle over Ottoman Kurdistan, 1890–1914," PhD dissertation, Princeton University, 2002, 385.
89. Klein, *The Margins of Empire*, 109. Klein states that the "official number of enrolled regiments would be reduced by a predicted half."
90. Turkish General Staff, *Balkan Harbı (1912–1913)*, 139.
91. Karatamu, *Türk Silahlı Kuvvetleri Tarihi, (1908–1920)*, Kuruluş 9D (Organizational Chart 9D).
92. *New Regulations for the Tribal Light Cavalry of August 1910*, Chapter 1, Paragraph 5.

4 A TEMPLATE FOR DESTRUCTION

1. John Wilson, *CB, A Life of Sir Henry Campbell-Bannerman* (London: Constable and Company Limited, 1973), 349.
2. Douglas Porch, "Introduction to the Bison Books Edition," of Colonel C. E. Callwell, *Small Wars, Their Principles and Practice* (Lincoln, NE: University of Nebraska Press, 1996), v.
3. Callwell, *Small Wars*, 140–44.

4. Ibid., 126. Callwell's Chapter XI is titled "Guerrilla Warfare in General."
5. Ibid., 135–49.
6. Ibid., 133.
7. David F. Trask, *The War with Spain in 1898* (New York: Macmillan Publishing Company., Inc, 1981), 5–7.
8. The value of Spanish sugar exports dropped from $62 million dollars to $13 million dollars in one year. Ibid., 3.
9. Ibid., 7.
10. Philip S. Foner, *The Spanish-Cuban-American War and the Birth of American Imperialism 1895–1902*, Volume I: 1895–1898 (New York: Monthly Review Press, 1972), 110.
11. Ibid.
12. Proclamation by General Valeriano Weyler, Havana, February 16, 1896 (dealing with concentration), Congressional Record, 54 Congress, 1 Session, Senate Report, 883.
13. Proclamation by General Valeriano Weyler, Havana, February 16, 1896 (dealing with martial law), Congressional Record, 54 Congress, 1 Session, Senate Report, 884.
14. Proclamation by General Valeriano Weyler, Havana, February 16, 1896 (dealing with criminality), Congressional Record, 54 Congress, 1 Session, Senate Report, 885.
15. Ibid.
16. Foner, *The Spanish-Cuban-American War*, 89.
17. Ibid., 120.
18. Ibid., 115. The author feels that 400,000 is a reasonable number given that substantial numbers of the white Cuban population of 800,000 and black Cuban population of 200,000 lived in the major cities and towns, which were unaffected by reconcentration.
19. Foreign Relations, Congressional Record, 55 Congress, 2 Session, Senate Report, 885.
20. Trask, *The War with Spain in 1898*, 9.
21. Barker to Rockhill, May 5, 1896, US Consular Dispatches, Sagua la Grande, Department of State, USNA, quoted and cited in Foner, *The Spanish-Cuban-American War*, 117.
22. French Ensor Chadwick, *The Relations of the United States and Spain, Diplomacy* (New York: Russell & Russell, 1909), 427–50.
23. Brian McAllister Linn, *The U.S. Army and Counterinsurgency in the Philippine War, 1899–1902* (Chapel Hill, NC: The University of North Carolina Press, 1989), 5–6.
24. Ibid., 9.
25. These forces were known as US Volunteer formations and comprised twenty-five regiments of infantry and one of cavalry. See ibid., 13–14, for an excellent summary of the raising of these forces.
26. Robert D. Ramsey III, *Savage Wars of Peace: Case Studies of Pacification in the Philippines, 1900–1902* (Fort Leavenworth, KS: CSI Press, 2007), 22.

27. Ibid.
28. For a complete copy of MacArthur's proclamation of December 10, 1900 (which was issued ten days later), see ibid., Appendix C, 159–62.
29. For a complete copy of General Orders 100, April 24, 1863, see ibid., Appendix B, 135–57.
30. Ibid.
31. Linn, *The U.S. Army and Counterinsurgency in the Philippine War, 1899–1902*, 24. Linn cited US War Department correspondence between Brigadier General Thomas H. Berry and the commanding general, Division of Northern Luzon, for this quotation.
32. Ibid., 26.
33. Ramsey, *Savage Wars of Peace*, 96.
34. Ibid., 97–98.
35. Linn, *The U.S. Army and Counterinsurgency in the Philippine War, 1899–1902*, 165.
36. John J. Tierney Jr., *Chasing Ghosts, Unconventional Warfare in American History* (Washington, DC: Potomac Books, Inc., 2006), 132.
37. Ibid., 131.
38. Ibid., 132.
39. Ramsey, *Savage Wars of Peace*, 103.
40. Ibid.
41. Henry F. Graff (ed.), *American Imperialism and the Philippine Insurrection (Testimony taken from Hearings on Affairs in the Philippine Islands before the Senate Committee on the Philippines-1902)* (Boston: Little, brown and Company, 1969), 64–88. The testimony of Robert Hughes, Charles Riley, and Daniel Evans regarding the "water cure" make interesting comparative reading with regard to the contemporary American practice of "water boarding" in order to extract information from prisoners.
42. For biographies and context, see André Wessels (ed.), *Lord Roberts and the War in South Africa* (Stroud, Gloucestershire: Sutton Publishing Limited, 2000), xiii–xx; and André Wessels (ed.), *Lord Kitchener and the War in South Africa 1899–1902* (Stroud, Gloucestershire: Sutton Publishing Limited, 2006), xvii–xxi.
43. S. B. Spies, *Methods of Barbarism? Roberts and Kitchener and Civilians in the Boer Republics January 1900–May 1902* (Capetown: Human & Rousseau, 1977), 101.
44. Ibid., 102.
45. Ibid., 103.
46. Ibid., 106. For example, on July 3, 1900, the Boers destroyed a third of a mile of track near Greylingstad and one mile of track near Valkfontein.
47. Ibid., 128.
48. Ibid., 129.
49. See ibid., 144–45, for commentary on this subject. Emily Hobhouse, an early British woman's rights advocate, who did not arrive until

December 1900 maintained that the Mafeking camp existed from a number of eyewitness testimonies.

50. Ibid., 148.

51. Ibid. Kitchener's strength rose to 240,000 by May 1901, however, thousands were locked into garrison and lines of communications duties leaving Kitchener with less than half for active operations in the field.

52. Keith Terrance Surridge, *Managing the South African War, 1899–1902* (Woodbridge, Suffolk: The Boydell Press, 1998), 113.

53. Eversley Belfield, *The Boer War* (London: Archon Books, 1975), 132. Belfield's chapter on "Blockhouses and Drives" (129–39) contains valuable information on the construction and manning of the blockhouse lines. For a map of the mature blockhouse lines, see Leopold Scholtz, *Why the Boers Lost the War* (Basingstoke, Hampshire: Palgrave MacMillan, 2005), 120.

54. Spies, *Methods of Barbarism*, 233–34.

55. Ibid., 193.

56. Byron Farwell, *The Great Anglo-Boer War* (New York: W.W. Norton & Co., 1976), 355.

57. Kitchener to Broderick, March 7, 1901, in Wessels, *Lord Kitchener and the War in South Africa*, 79–82.

58. Thomas Pakenham, *The Boer War* (New York: Random House, 1979), 535.

59. Spies, *Methods of Barbarism*, 215. Spies asserted that in a number of localized camps the per annum mortality rate for children exceeded 100 percent.

60. Kenneth O. Morgan, "The Boer War and the Media (1899–1902)," *Twentieth Century British History*, vol. 13, no. 1 (2002), 11.

61. Spies, *Methods of Barbarism*, 258.

62. Ibid., 265.

63. Farwell, *The Great Anglo-Boer War*, 441. The mortality rates of Boer POWs are almost inconsequential and about 24,000 of the 30,000 were imprisoned outside South Africa in locations such as Bermuda, Ceylon, India, and St. Helena

64. Pakenham, *The Boer War*, 607.

65. Some historians assert that American Civil War generals William T. Sherman and Phillip Sheridan began the Western practice of destructive war on civilians; however, neither of these commanders developed or conducted policies of population removal.

5   Invisible Armies

1. Arthur D. Howden Smith, *Fighting the Turk in the Balkans: An American's Adventures with the Macedonian Revolutionists* (New York: G.P. Putnam's Sons, 1908), 25.

2. Dikran Mesrob Kaligian, *Armenian Organization and Ideology under Ottoman Rule 1908–1914* (New Brunswick: Transaction Publishers, 2009), 132.
3. Ibid., 133.
4. Raymond Kévorkian, *The Armenian Genocide, A Compete History* (London: I.B. Tauris, 2011), 135.
5. Ibid., 137.
6. Kaligian, *Armenian Organization and Ideology*, 149.
7. Kévorkian, *The Armenian Genocide*, 153–54.
8. Vatche Ghazarian (trans. and ed.), *Boghos Nubar's Papers and the Armenian Question 1915–1918* (Waltham: Mayreni Publishing, 1997), ix.
9. Yair Auron, *The Banality of Indifference: Zionism & the Armenian Genocide* (New Brunswick: Transaction Books, 2000), 218.
10. Kévorkian, *The Armenian Genocide*, 153–54.
11. Ibid., 154.
12. Stanford J. Shaw and Ezel K., *History of the Ottoman Empire and Modern Turkey, Volume II* (Cambridge: Cambridge University Press, 1977), 290–91.
13. See Erickson, *Defeat in Detail, The Ottoman Army in the Balkans, 1912–1913* (Westport, CT: Praeger, 2003), for information regarding Ottoman military operations in the Balkan Wars of 1912–13.
14. Ibid., 246–48.
15. Roderick Davidson, "The Armenian Crisis: 1912–1914," *American Historical Review*, vol. 53, no. 3 (April 1948), 491. See also Fikret Adanır, "Non-Muslims in the Ottoman Army and the Ottoman Defeat in the Balkan War of 1912–1913," Ronald Grigor Suny, Fatma Müge Göçek, and Norman M. Naimark, *A Question of Genocide, Armenians and Turks at the End of the Ottoman Empire* (New York: Oxford University Press, 2011), 113–25.
16. Antranig Chalabian, *General Andranik and the Armenian Revolutionary Movement* (USA: First Edition, 1988), 199–200; and Kaligian, *Armenian Organization and Ideology*, 240.
17. Ibid., 200.
18. Ibid., 201.
19. Ibid.
20. Şadi Sükan, *Türk Silahli Kuvvetleri Tarihi, Osmanlı Devri, Balkan Harbi (1912–1913) IInci Cilt 3ncu Kisim, Edirne Kale Etrafındaki Muharebeler (Ikinci Başkı)* (Ankara: Genelkurmay Basımevi, 1993), 341–46. See also Erickson, *Defeat in Detail*, 146–53, for information in English regarding the operations of the Kircaali Detachment's operations.
21. Kaligian, *Armenian Organization and Ideology*, xx.
22. Kévorkian, *The Armenian Genocide*, 155.
23. Kaligian, *Armenian Organization and Ideology*, 201–204.
24. The most comprehensive explanation of the reform negotiations may be found in Kévorkian, *The Armenian Genocide*, 153–65.

25. Kaligian, *Armenian Organization and Ideology*, 187–88.
26. Ibid., 189–90.
27. Ibid., 188–89.
28. Justin McCarthy, Esat Arslan, Cemalettin Taşkıran, and Ömer Turan, *The Armenian Rebellion at Van* (Salt Lake City: The University of Utah Press, 2006), 163–64.
29. See, e.g., ATASE Archive 392, Dosya 1554, File1–5, Records and Reports of the Hunchak Committee, Kilkis Branch, dated January 9, August 25, and November 3, 1913, reproduced in Arş.Ş.Mud.lüğü (ATASE staff), *Arşiv Belgeleriye Ermeni Faaliyetleri 1914–1918, Cilt I* (Ankara: Genelkurmay Basımevi, 2005), 17–25.
30. Kaligian, *Armenian Organization and Ideology*, 181.
31. Ibid., 183–84.
32. Ibid., 185.
33. Ibid., 186.
34. Kévorkian, *The Armenian Genocide*, 145.
35. Hratch Dasnabedian, *History of the Armenian Revolutionary Federation, Dasnaktutiun 1890/1924* (Milan: OEMME Edizioni, 1990), 101.
36. Ibid. See also Kaligian, *Armenian Organization and Ideology*, 193–94.
37. Ibid., 103.
38. Ibid.
39. ATASE Archive 1–2, Dosya 1036, File 5–22, Circular Number 3, Central Committee, Social Democrat Hunchakian Party, December 23, 1909, reproduced in Arş.Ş.Mud.lüğü (ATASE staff), *Arşiv Belgeleriye Ermeni Faaliyetleri 1914–1918, Cilt IV* (Ankara: Genelkurmay Basımevi, 2006), 453–57. Hereafter *Arşiv Belgeleriye Ermeni, Cilt IV*.
40. ATASE Archive 1–2, Dosya 1052, File 1, *The General Statutes Governing the Ottoman Social Democrat Hunchakian Organization*, reproduced in Arş.Ş.Mud.lüğü (ATASE staff), *Arşiv Belgeleriye Ermeni, Cilt IV*, 439–47.
41. ATASE Archive 1–2, Dosya 1036, File 5–151, Circular Number 7, Central Committee, Social Democrat Hunchakian Party, October 8, 1913, reproduced in Arş.Ş.Mud.lüğü, *Arşiv Belgeleriye Ermeni, Cilt IV*, 449.
42. ATASE Archive 1–134, Dosya 1035a, File 1–85, Courts-Martial Indictment, October 6, 1915, reproduced in Arş.Ş.Mud.lüğü, *Arşiv Belgeleriye Ermeni, Cilt IV*, 469–78.
43. ATASE Archive 1/134, Dosya 33, File 2–3, Testimony of Taiaq's son Ohannes, July 16, 1914, reproduced in Arş.Ş.Mud.lüğü, *Arşiv Belgeleriye Ermeni, Cilt IV*, 493 and ATASE Archive 1/134, Dosya 33, File 2–4, Testimony of Taiaq's son Karnik, July 16, 1915, reproduced in Arş.Ş.Mud.lüğü, *Arşiv Belgeleriye Ermeni, Cilt IV*, 291. See pages 498–511 for additional testimony from Department of Intelligence and police officials.
44. ATASE Archive 1–134, Dosya 1035a, File 1–84, Courts-Martial Verdict, October 8, 1915, reproduced in Arş.Ş.Mud.lüğü, *Arşiv Belgeleriye*

Ermeni, Cilt IV, 480–89 and ATASE Archive 1–134, Dosya 1051, File 9–1, Courts-Martial Note 2290, December 18, 1915, reproduced in Arş.Ş.Mud.lüğü, *Arşiv Belgeleriye Ermeni, Cilt IV,* 490.

45. ATASE Archive 1–134, Dosya 1035, File 1–36, Courts-Martial Indictment, May 25, 1915, reproduced in Arş.Ş.Mud.lüğü, *Arşiv Belgeleriye Ermeni Faaliyetleri 1914–1918, Cilt III* (Ankara: Genelkurmay Basımevi, 2006), 337–40. Hereafter *Arşiv Belgeleriye Ermeni, Cilt III.*

46. See, e.g., ATASE Archive 1–134, Dosya 1035a, File 1, Testimony of Agop Hazarian, August 10, 1914, reproduced in Arş.Ş.Mud.lüğü, *Arşiv Belgeleriye Ermeni, Cilt III,* 345 and ATASE Archive 1–134, Dosya 1035, File 1–2, Testimony of Vahan Boyadjian, August 11, 1914, reproduced in Arş.Ş.Mud.lüğü, *Arşiv Belgeleriye Ermeni, Cilt III,* 348. Substantial corroborating testimony follows in this volume.

47. Mehmet Talât Pasha, *Talât Paşa'nın Anıları* (ed. Alpay Kabacalı) (Istanbul: İletşim Yayınları, 1984), 63–67.

48. Kévorkian, *The Armenian Genocide,* 174.

49. Ibid. Kévorkian questions the weight of the evidence presented in the courts-martial proceedings but it must be noted that the nature of the conspiracy conforms to the agenda set forth by the Constanza Congress.

50. Jehuda L. Wallach, *Bir Askeri Yardımın Anatomisi* (Turkish edition of *Anatomie einer Miltaerhilfe*), trans. Fahri Çeliker (Ankara: Genelkurmay Basımevi, 1977), 118–22; and Ahmed İzzet, *Feryadım,* (Istanbul: Nehir Yayınları, 1992), 157–58.

51. M. Naim Turfan, *Rise of the Young Turks; Politics, the Military and Ottoman Collapse* (London: I.B.Tauris, 2000), 327–30.

52. Erickson, *Defeat in Detail,* 317–45. The Second Army and its subordinate divisions began to reconstitute in the area around the city of Konya.

53. Turfan, *Rise of the Young Turks,* 348–50; and Metin Ayışığı, *Mareşal Ahmet İzzet Paşa (Askeri ve Siyası Hayatı)* (Ankara: Türk Tarih Kurumu Basımevi, 1997), 108–14.

54. Selahattin Karatamu, *Türk Silahlı Kuvvetleri Tarihi, IIIncü Cilt 6nci Kısım (1908–1920)* (Ankara: Genelkurmay Basımevi, 1971), 209–20.

55. Ibid.; and Edward J. Erickson, *Ottoman Army Effectiveness in World War 1, A Comparative Study* (Abingdon, OX: Routledge, 2007), 8–10.

56. Tufan, *Rise of the Young Turks,* 310–13.

57. In comparison in 1914, Germany mobilized 31 reserve divisions, France mobilized 25 reserve divisions, and even Britain, with no tradition of a mass army, mobilized 14 territorial divisions.

58. Mesut Uyar and Edward J. Erickson, *A Military History of the Ottomans, From Osman to Atatürk* (Santa Barbara, CA: Praeger, 2009), 237–38.

59. Shaw, *History of the Ottoman Empire and Modern Turkey, Volume II,* 306.

60. Ibid.

61. Turfan, *Rise of the Young Turks,* 305–307.

62. See, e.g., Taner Akçm, *The Young Turks' Crime against Humanity, The Armenian Genocide and Ethnic Cleansing in the Ottoman Empire* (Princeton: Princeton University Press, 2012), 157–285; Peter Balakian, *The Burning Tigris: The Armenian Genocide and America's Response* (New York: Harper Collins, 2003), 175–96; Raymond H. Kévorkian, *The Armenian Genocide, A Complete History* (London: I.B. Tauris, 2011), 167–206..

63. For the most comprehensive review of the literature about the SO, readers should refer to Polat Safi, "The Ottoman Special Organization—Teşkilat-ı Mahsusa: A Historical Assessment with Particular Reference to its Operations against British Occupied Egypt (1914–1916)," unpublished MA thesis, Bilkent University, 2006, 6–23.

64. Kévorkian, *The Armenian Genocide*, 38. In much of the literature, the Ottoman SO is presented as a model for the Nazi SS deportation and concentration camp apparatus of World War II. This is untrue and, in many ways, the SO was a proginator for modern special forces, which specialize in guerrilla and counterinsurgency warfare.

65. Safi, *The Ottoman Special Organization*, 15. Some historians assert that the SO has direct antecedents that are traceable to the period 1908–1909. For these assertions, see Stanford J. Shaw, *The Ottoman Empire in World War I, Volume 1 Prelude to War* (Ankara: Türk Tarih Kurum Basımevi, 2006), 356; and Kévorkian, *The Armenian Genocide*, 37–38.

66. See Philip H. Stoddard, *The Ottoman Government and the Arabs, 1911–1918, A Premininary Study of the Teşkilât-İ Mahsusa*, unpublished PhD dissertation, Princeton University, 1963, 53, asserting Enver's involvement; and Kévorkian, *The Armenian Genocide*, 175, for CUP involvement.

67. Safi, *The Ottoman Special Organization*, 25.

68. Shaw, *The Ottoman Empire in World War I, Volume I*, 382–83.

69. Arif Cemil Dunker, *Birinci Dünya Savaşında Teşkilât-İ Mahsusa* (Istanbul: Arma Yayınları, undated), 272, 308–15.

70. İsmet Görgülü, *On Yıllık Harbin Kadrosu 1912–1922, Balkan-Birinci Dünya ve İstiklâl Harbi* (Ankara: Türk Tarih Kurum Basımevi, 1993), 43–44. See also Stoddard, *The Ottoman Government and the Arabs*, 53–55.

71. Karatamu, *Türk Silahlı Kuvvetleri Tarihi*, 242–43.

72. Ibid., 52. The total number of officers who were forcibly retired were astonishing: 2 field marshals, 3 lieutenant generals, 30 major generals, 95 brigadier generals, 184 colonels, 236 lieutenant colonels and majors, and some 800 captains and lieutenants. See also Kévorkian, *The Armenian Genocide*, 168.

73. Kévorkian, *The Armenian Genocide*, 168.

74. Tufan, *Rise of the Young Turks*, 293.

75. Karatamu, *Türk Silahlı Kuvvetleri Tarihi*, 405–11. See Erickson, *Ottoman Army Effectiveness in World War I*, 10, and Appendix A for a summarized translation of this order.

76. Otto Liman von Sanders, *Five Years in Turkey* (Nashville: The Battery Press, 2000, reprint of the 1928 edition), 8–9.

77. Karatamu, *Türk Silahlı Kuvvetleri Tarihi*, 336–40. See also Erickson, *Defeat in Detail*, 61–67, for a comprehensive explanation of the earlier 12 plans.

78. Cemal Akbay, *Birinci Dünya Harbinde Türk Harbi, 1nci Cilt, Osmanli Imparatorlugu'nun Siyası ve Askeri Hazırlıkları ve Harbe Girisi* (Ankara:Genelkurmay Basımevi, 1970), 212–13. See also Erickson, *Ordered to Die*, 37–39 for a comprehensive explanation of the new war plan.

79. Ibid., 231–33. See also Edward J. Erickson, *Ordered to Die, A History of the Ottoman Army in the First World War* (Westport, CT: Greenwood Press, 2001), 40–47, for a comprehensive explanation of the mobilization and concentration plans.

80. Kévorkian, *The Armenian Genocide*, 170.

81. Ibid., 171.

82. Kaligian, *Armenian Organization and Ideology*, 206–207.

83. Ibid.

84. Erickson, *Ordered to Die*, 19–47; and see also Mustafa Aksakal, *The Ottoman Road to War in 1914: The Ottoman Empire and the First World War* (Cambridge: Cambridge University Press, 2008), for the definitive comprehensive treatment of this subject.

85. See Erickson, *Ordered to Die*, 25–28, for a summary of the specific clauses and the time lines; and Aksakal, *The Ottoman Road to War in 1914*, 102–18.

86. Safi, *The Ottoman Special Organization*, 28. Safi noted that there are estimates of over 40,000 SO files maintained at ATASE. For information on the Turkish military archives, see Edward J. Erickson, "The Turkish Official Military Histories of the First World War: A Bibliographic Essay," *Middle Eastern Studies*, vol. 39, no. 3 (2003), 190–98.

87. Shaw, *The Ottoman Empire in World War I, Volume I*, 355.

88. Ibid., 356. This was probably because the files contained incriminating or embarrassing evidence about the revolutionary activities of Enver and the CUP inner leadership.

89. Stoddard, "The Ottoman Government and the Arabs, 1911 to 1918: A Preliminary Study of the Teşkilat-ı Mahsusa," unpublished PhD dissertation, Princeton University, 1963, 1–2.

90. Ibid.

91. Ibid., 8.

92. Kévorkian, *The Armenian Genocide*, 180.

93. Ibid. See also, e.g., Taner Akçam, *A Shameful Act, The Armenian Genocide and the Question of Turkish Responsibility* (New York: Metropolitan Books, 2006), 161–66; and Peter Balakian, *The Burning Tigris*, 179–82.

94. Some historians have expressed doubts that a dual-track SO existed. These include Donald Bloxham, *The Great Game of Genocide:*

Imperialism, Nationalism,and the Destruction of the Ottoman Armenians (Oxford: Oxford University Press, 2005), 69–71.

95. In fact, 100 percent of all accounts of the SO two-track system base their assertions on the work of Vahakn Dadrian, who published several articles in 1991 about the organization. See Vahakn N. Dadrian, "A Textual Analysis of the Key Indictment of the Turkish Military Tribunal Investigating the Armenian Genocide," *Armenian Review* vol. 44, no. 1/173 (Spring 1991), 1–36; and Vahakn N. Dadrian, "The Documentation of the World War I Armenian Massacres in the Proceedings of the Turkish Military Tribunal," *International Journal of Middle East Studies* vol. 23 (1991), 549–76.

96. However, Vahakn Dadrian stands accused of mistranslating, misquoting, and using phrases out of context to support his claims. See Erman Şahin, "Review Essay: The Armenian Question," *Middle East Policy*, vol. XVII, no. 1 (Spring 2010), 144–62, with particular attention to "On Yusuf Rıza Bey's Testimony," 153.

97. Stoddard, "A Preliminary Study of the Teşkilat-ı Mahsusa," 47.

98. *Takvim-I Vekayi*, H. 20, Şaban 1337, Nr. 3554, s. 89. The author is indebted to Polat Safi for providing this information. Polat Safi maintains that the two-track SO is a fabrication of the courts-martial judges. It must also be mentioned that unlike the trial records and statements of the 1915 Hunchack conspiracy trial, which exist today in the Turkish military archives, the actual trial records of the 1919 Yozgat courts-martials have been destroyed, leaving researchers with only the publically printed and published indictments and verdicts.

99. *Takvim-I Vekayi*, H. 28, Şaban 1337, Nr. 35614, s. 124–25. Provided by Polat Safi.

100. Safi, *The Ottoman Special Organization*, 122.

101. Ibid.

102. Ibid., 127–28.

103. For example, Akçam, *A Shameful Act*, 160–170; Dadrian, "The Role of the Special Organization in the Armenian Genocide during the First World War," passim; Kévorkian, *The Armenian Genocide*, 182–83.

104. Michael A. Reynolds, *Shattering Empires, the Clash and Collapse of the Ottoman and Russian Empires 1908–1918* (Cambridge: Cambridge University Press, 2011), 121.

105. Kaligian, *Armenian Organization and Ideology*, 214–15.

106. Ibid., 217.

107. Erickson, *Ordered to Die*, 40.

108. Dasnabedian, *History of the Armenian Revolutionary Federation*, 107.

109. Ibid.

110. I am indebted to Garabet K Moumdjian for providing information from Hratch Dasnabedian, *History of the Organizational Structure of the Armenian Revolutionary Federation and Other Studies* (ed. Yervant Pampukian) (Beirut: Hamazkayin Press, 2009), 374–75.

111. Moumdjian, comments to author regarding the Eighth World Congress, May 28, 2011.
112. Dasnabedian, *History of the Organizational Structure of the Armenian Revolutionary Federation*, 375.
113. Dasnabedian, *History of the Armenian Revolutionary Federation*, 108.
114. Rupen Der Minasian, *Rememberences of an Armenian Revolutionary, Vol. 7* (Tehran, 3rd edition, 1982), 126–27. I am indebted to Garabet K Moumdjian for providing this information.
115. Simon Vratzian, *The Republic of Armenia* (Paris, 1928), 8. I am indebted to Garabet K Moumdjian for providing this information.
116. The author concludes this based on the idea that recruiting and organizing dissident Caucasian and Persians and then transporting them from Constantinople to Erzurum was a process that was impossible to conduct in a period of under 30 days.
117. Vahan Minakhorian, *The Year 1915* (Venice: St. Ghazar Press, 1949), 70. I am indebted to Garabet K Moumdjian for providing this information.
118. Vratzian, *Republic of Armenia*, 8.
119. Minakhorian, *The Year 1915*, 70.
120. Minasian, *Rememberences of an Armenian Revolutionary*, 127.
121. Dasnabedian, *History of the Armenian Revolutionary Federation*, 108.
122. See McCarthy et al., *The Armenian Rebellion at Van*, 182.
123. ATASE Archive 4, Dosya 528, File 2061, *Intelligence Reports*, reprinted in *Documents on Ottoman Armenians, Vol. II* (Ankara: Prime Ministry Directorate of Press and Information, 1982), cited in McCarthy et al., *The Armenian Rebellion at Van*, 222.

6 Readiness for War

1. John Gooch, *The Plans of War, The General Staff and British Military Strategy c. 1900–1916* (New York: John Wiley, 1974), 271.
2. Selahattin Karatamu, *Türk Silahlı Kuvvetleri Tarihi, IIIncü Cilt 6ncı Kısım (1908–1920)* (Ankara: Genelkurmay Basımevi, 1971), 242.
3. Görgülü, *On Yıllık Harbin Kadrosu 1912–1922, Balkan-Birinci Dünya ve İstiklâl Harbi* (Ankara: Türk Tarih Kurum Basımevi, 1993),53.
4. Fahri Belen, *Birinci Cihan Harbinde Türk Harbi, 1914 Yılı Hareketleri* (Ankara: Genelkurmay Basımevi, 1964), 39–40.
5. Karatamu, *Türk Silahlı Kuvvetleri Tarihi, (1908–1920)*, 130.
6. See Edward J. Erickson, *Ottoman Army Effectiveness in World War I, A Comparative Study* (Abingdon, OX: Routledge, 2007), 7–15, for an examination of the strengths and weakness of the Ottoman in the prewar period.
7. Cemal Akbay, *Birinci Dünya Harbinde Türk Harbi, 1nci Cilt, Osmanli Imparatorlugu'nun Siyası ve Askeri Hazırlıkları ve Harbe Girisi*, (Ankara: Genelkurmay Basımevi, 1970), 157.
8. Belen, *1914 Yılı Hareketleri*, 55–57.

9. See Edward J. Erickson, *Ordered to Die, A History of the Ottoman Army in the First World War* (Westport, CT: Greenwood Press, 2001), 25–34, for a detailed examination of the diplomatic and domestic aspects of the secret treaties.

10. Fevzi Çakmak, *Birinci Dünya Savaşı'nda Doğu Cephesi* (Ankara: Genelkurmay Basımevi, 2005), 10–15.

11. Akbay, *Askeri Hazırlıkları ve Harbe Girisi*, 167.

12. Ibid., 171.

13. Ibid., 173.

14. Ibid., 174.

15. Ibid., 175–76.

16. Ibid., 127.

17. Ibid.

18. Commandant M. Larcher, *La Guerre Turque Dans La Guerre Mondiale* (Paris: Chiron and Berger-Levrault, 1926), 66.

19. Ibid., 70.

20. Akbay, *Askeri Hazırlıkları ve Harbe Girisi*, 135–36.

21. David Woodward, *Armies of the World 1854–1914* (New York: G.P. Putnam's Sons, 1978), 89.

22. Larcher, *La Guerre Turque*, 65.

23. Ottoman Empire, therefore, did not have units such as the "First Reserve Corps" or the "16th Bavarian Reserve Infantry Division."

24. Akbay, *Askeri Hazırlıkları ve Harbe Girisi*, 121.

25. See Erickson, *Defeat in Detail*, 328–40, for a complete summary of units destroyed, captured, or inactivated during the Balkan Wars.

26. Ibid., 329.

27. See Erickson, *Ordered to Die*, 30–31; and Mustafa Aksakal, *The Ottoman Road to War in 1914: The Ottoman Empire and the First World War* (New York: Cambridge University Press, 2008), 150–60.

28. Akbay, *Askeri Hazırlıkları ve Harbe Girisi*, 157–62.

29. Sir G. Barclay to Sir Edward Grey, August 4, 1914, G. P. Gooch and Harold Temperley, eds., *British Documents on the Origins of the War 1898–1914, Vol. XI* (London, HMSO, 1926), 306.

30. Winston S. Churchill, *The World Crisis* (New York: Scribners, 1931), 280.

31. Akbay, *Askeri Hazırlıkları ve Harbe Girisi*, 162–76.

32. Ulrich Trumpener, *Germany and the Ottoman Empire* (Princeton: Princeton University Press, 1968), 54.

33. Ibid.

34. Bernd Langensiepen and Ahmet Guleryuz,. *The Ottoman Steam Navy* (Annapolis: Naval Institute Press, 1995), 44.

35. Ibid., 44–45.

36. Akbay, *Askeri Hazırlıkları ve Harbe Girisi*, 176 –78.

37. The lack of strategic space in Thrace still affects the modern-day Turkish general staff, which, in 2012, still stations four out of nine active army corps in the area of the Turkish straits and Istanbul.

7 IRREGULAR WAR IN CAUCASIA AND IN THE LEVANT

1. Report of the Committee on Asiatic Turkey, April 8, 1915, 21. FO 371/2486.
2. Sean McMeekin, *The Russian Origins of the First World War* (Cambridge, MA: The Belknap Press of Harvard University Press, 2011), 154.
3. Ibid. See also, e.g., facsimile of Araklyan's editorial in *Mshak*, September 20, 1914, which encouraged Ottoman Armenians to seek independence. Mehmet Perinçek, *Rus Devlet Arşivlerinden 100 Belgede Ermeni Meselesi* (Istanbul: Doğan Kitap, 2007), Document 20.
4. McMeekin, *The Russian Origins of the First World War*, 156. See also Mustafa Aksakal, *The Ottoman Road to War in 1914: The Ottoman Empire and the First World War* (New York: Cambridge University Press, 2008), 132. Aksakal cites correspondence between Sazonov and Goremykin.
5. Ibid., 158. McMeekin provides a facsimile of General Yudenich's memorandum of August 29, 1914 to Stavka. This is well in advance of the outbreak of hostilities between Russia and the Ottoman Empire.
6. Ibid. McMeekin provides a facsimile of General Yudenich's request of August 31, 1914, to Stavka for these quantities of arms.
7. Ibid., 161.
8. Ibid. McMeekin cites correspondence between Vorontsov-Dashkov and the Ministry of War located in the Russian archives as his source for this plan.
9. Report of A. A. Adamov, Russian Consul, Erzurum, November 1, 1914 (facsimile copy) in McMeekin, *The Russian Origins of the First World War*, 163–64.
10. This story is outside the framework of this book. See Michael A. Reynolds, *Shattering Empires, The Clash and Collapse of the Ottoman and Russian Empires 1908–1918* (Cambridge: Cambridge University Press, 2011), 117–19; and McMeekin, *The Russian Origins of the First World War*, 148–53.
11. G. Korganoff, *La Participation Des Arméniens à la Guerre Mondiale— sur le front du Caucase (1914–1918)* (Paris: Massis Editions, 1927), 10. The number of ARF *druzhiny* would grow later when Ishkhan Arghutian and Grigor Avsharian apparently organized another legion.
12. Antranig Chalabian, *General Andranik and the Armenian Revolutionary Movement* (USA: First Edition, 1988), 228.
13. Korganoff, *La Participation Des Arméniens à la Guerre Mondiale*, 10. Antranig was assisted by Dro, Amazaspe, and Kéri. Amazaspe is called Hamazapsp (Servandztian) by Chalabian.
14. Chalabian, *General Andranik and the Armenian Revolutionary Movement*, 229.
15. Ibid.
16. Telegraph Message Yudenich to Nikolayev, October 31, 1914, facsimile in Perinçek, *100 Belgede Ermeni Meselesi*, Document 23.

17. Chalabian, *General Andranik and the Armenian Revolutionary Movement*, 229.
18. Report to Headquarters, Third Army, August 25, 1914, ATASE archive 2818, record 59, file 2–4 cited in Reynolds, *Shattering Empires*, 116.
19. Report to Headquarters, Third Army, August 30–31, 1914, ATASE archive 2818, record 59, file 2–5 cited in Reynolds, *Shattering Empires*, 116.
20. Justin McCarthy, Esat Arslan, Cemalettin Taşkıran, and Ömer Turan, *The Armenian Rebellion at Van* (Salt Lake City: The University of Utah Press, 2006), 185. McCarthy cites reports in the Turkish military archives as the source of this information.
21. Muammer Demirel, *Birinci Dünya Harbinde Erzurum ve Çevresinde Ermeni Hareketleri (1914–1918)* (Ankara: Genelkurmay Basımevi, 1996), 17.
22. Enver to Headquarters, Third Army, September 25–26, 1914, ATASE archive 2818, record 59, file 2–19 cited in Reynolds, *Shattering Empires*, 116.
23. Report on Criminal Activity, Headquarters, Third Army to Ottoman general staff, October 8, 1914, ATASE archive 2818, record 59, file 2–85.
24. Report from 4th Reserve Cavalry Regiment to Headquarters, Third Army, October 20, 1914, ATASE archive 2818, record 59, file 2–80.
25. Report from Hudut Battalion to Headquarters, IX Corps, October 22, 1914, ATASE archive 2818, record 59, file 2–39.
26. Report from Headquarters, Third Army to Acting Commander-in-Chief (Enver), October 23, 1914, ATASE archive 2818, record 59, file 1–41/42.
27. The most comprehensive summary of the activities of the SO in the Caucasus during this period is found in Shaw's chapter on the *Teşkilat-ı Mahsusa* in Stanford J. Shaw, *The Ottoman Empire in World War I, Volume 1 Prelude to War* (Ankara: Türk Tarih Kurum Basımevi, 2006), 353–456.
28. Ibid., 363.
29. Shaw noted such friction existed between the Ministry of War and the Ministry of the Interior, so that when Enver sent Rıza to Trabzon Talat responded by sending Şakir to Erzurum. Ibid., 363.
30. Ibid., 374.
31. Ibid., 373–76. See also Kévorkian, *The Armenian Genocide*, 184. The contrast between Shaw and Kévorkian is significant with the Turkish position on the SO recruitment of undesirables characterized as being as forced by manpower shortages during mobilization while the Armenian position is the SO deliberately recruited dangerous and morally degenerate individuals.
32. See Sean McMeekin, *The Berlin-Baghdad Express: The Ottoman Empire and Germany's Bid for World Power* (Cambridge, MA: The

Belknap Press of Harvard University Press, 2010) for the most readable and comprehensive work on these remarkable Ottoman-German
expeditions.

33. Shaw, *Prelude to War*, 430.
34. Ibid., 431.
35. Ibid. and Kévorkian, *The Armenian Genocide*, 184–86. Again the
    contrast in views is significant. Shaw presents the SO as organized like
    the Armenian committees while Kévorkian presents the SO as a two-
    track secret organization.
36. Shaw, *Prelude to War*, 432.
37. See Arif Cemil Denker, *Birinci Dünya Savaşında Teşkilât-ı Mahsusa*
    (Istanbul: Arma Yayınları, undated), 81–96.
38. Shaw, *Prelude to War*, 451.
39. Fevzi Çakmak, *Birinci Dünya Savaşı'nda Doğu Cephesi* (Ankara:
    Genelkurmay Basımevi, 2005), 27.
40. Demirel, *Erzurum va Çevresinde Ermeni Hareketleri*, 42.
41. Çakmak, *Doğu Cephesi*, 27.
42. Kévorkian, *The Armenian Genocide*, 218.
43. Shaw, *Prelude to War*, 452. Shaw quotes Şakir's report and cites Arif
    Cemil as his source.
44. See, e.g., Kévorkian, *The Armenian Genocide*, 217–18; and Demirel,
    Erzurum va Çevresinde Ermeni Hareketleri, 39–44.
45. See, e.g., Kévorkian, *The Armenian Genocide*, 184; and Demirel,
    Erzurum va Çevresinde Ermeni Hareketleri, 43.
46. Kévorkian, *The Armenian Genocide*, 218.
47. David Gaunt, *Massacres, Resistance, Protectors; Muslim-Christian
    Relation in Eastern Anatolia during World War I* (Piscataway, NJ:
    Gorgias Press, 2006), 94–100.
48. Reynolds, *Shattering Empires*, 118.
49. Aziz Samih İlter, *Birinci Dünya Savaşı'nda Kafkas Cephesi Hatıraları*
    (Ankara: Genelkurmay Basımevi, 2007), 1–3. About 13,000 were
    Kurdish reserve tribal cavalrymen and the remainder were Ottoman
    regular army cavalrymen.
50. Belen, *1914 Yılı Hareketleri*, Kroki 3 (Map 3) following page 94.
51. The Ottomans organized three Mobile Jandarma divisions (*seyyar jan-
    darma tümen*) on August 6, 1914, in the Third Army area. These were
    the Erzurum and the Van Jandarma Divisions. The Erzurum Jandarma
    Division was inactivated on October 10, 1914 and its regiments returned
    to control of army corps. The Fourth Army activated the Aleppo Jandarma
    Division in August 1914 but it was deactivated shortly thereafter as well.
52. Hakkı Altınbilek and Naci Kır, *Birinci Dünya Harbi'nde Türk Harbi,
    Kafkas Cephesi 3ncü Ordu Harekâtı, Cilt II Birinci Kitap* (Ankara:
    Genelkurmay Basımevi, 1993), 122–323. In English, see W. E. D.
    Allen and Paul Muratoff, *Caucasian Battlefields: A History of the Wars
    on the Turco-Caucasian Border, 1828–1921* (Cambridge: Cambridge
    University Press, 1953), 240–50.

53. Belen, *1914 Yılı Hareketleri*, 96.
54. Altınbilek and Kır, *3ncü Ordu Harekâtı*, 600.
55. Ibid.
56. Ibid., 344.
57. Ibid., 293.
58. Ibid., Kroki 37 (Map 37).
59. İsmet Görgülü, *On Yıllık Harbin Kadrosu 1912–1922, Balkan-Birinci Dünya ve İstiklâl Harbi* (Ankara: Türk Tarih Kurum Basımevi, 1993), 109, 111.
60. Demirel, *Erzurum ve Çevresinde Ermeni Hareketleri*, 41–45; and Vahakn Dadrian, "The Role of the Special Organization in the Armenian Genocide during the First World War," Panikos Panayi (ed.), *Minorities in Wartime: National and Racial Groupings in Europe, North America and Australia in Two World Wars* (Oxford: Berg, 1993), 62.
61. Ottoman General Staff Orders, December 6, 1914, ATASE archive 2950, record H-6, file 1–267, reproduced in Altınbilek and Kır, *3ncü Ordu Harekâtı*, 339–40.
62. Altınbilek and Kır, *3ncü Ordu Harekâtı*, 349.
63. See Alaattin Uca, "Stange Müfrezesi'nin Harp Ceridesine Göre Kafkas Cephesi'nde Dr. Bahaeddin Şakir," *KMÜ Sosyal ve Ekonomik Araştırmalar Dergisi* vol. 13, no. 20 (2011); and Edward J. Erickson, "Armenian Massacres, New Records Undercut Old Blame," *The Middle East Quarterly* vol. XIII, no. 3 (Summer 2006) for information on Stange, Şakir, and their joint operations.
64. There were, apparently, two German officers in eastern Anatolia in the late fall of 1914 with the surname Stange. Various sources name them as Major Christian August Stange, a Prussian infantry officer, and Captain August Wilhelm Stange, a Prussian artillery officer. It is unclear from the author's research whether there actually were two officers, both named Stange in the empire at this time and, moreover, which of them actually led the detachment.
65. Altınbilek and Kır, *3ncü Ordu Harekâtı*, 602.
66. Ibid., 605.
67. Detachment Orders, December 29, 1914, ATASE archive 5257, record H-1, file 1–10, cited in Altınbilek and Kır, *3ncü Ordu Harekâtı*, 603.
68. Altınbilek and Kır, *3ncü Ordu Harekâtı*, 605.
69. Ibid., 608.
70. Ibid.
71. Ibid., 131; and Kroki 7 (Map 7).
72. Çakmak, *Doğu Cephesi*, Kroki 8 (Map 8).
73. Report from Headquarters at Saray, November 17, 1914, ATASE archive 2950, record H-6, file 1–196 cited in Altınbilek and Kır, *3ncü Ordu Harekâtı*, 292.
74. Altınbilek and Kır, *3ncü Ordu Harekâtı*, 334.
75. Çakmak, *Doğu Cephesi*, 43.

76. Chalabian, *General Andranik and the Armenian Revolutionary Movement*, 232.
77. Çakmak, *Doğu Cephesi*, 42–43.
78. Kévorkian, *The Armenian Genocide*, 225–26.
79. İlter, *Kafkas Cephesi Hatıraları*, 4–7.
80. Orders, Headquarters, Third Army, 1940 hours, November 22, 1914, ATASE archive 2821, record 31, file 1–16 reproduced in Altınbilek and Kır, *3ncü Ordu Harekâtı*, 304–305.
81. The author recognizes that this is simply speculation but this theory goes a long way toward explaining who might have perpetrated many of the massacres known to have been inflicted on the Armenians in the summer of 1915.
82. For summaries of this campaign, see Allen and Muratoff, *Caucasian Battlefields*, 249–85 and Erickson, *Ordered to Die*, 52–65.
83. Belen, *1914 Yılı Hareketleri*, 192. Western accounts of the Ottoman casualty figures for this campaign are frequently exaggerated with 90,000 dead being the most frequently used total. This number originates in Larcher's 1926 *La Guerre Turque Dans La Guerre Mondiale* and is undocumented. Larcher's figures are wildly inflated and unfortunately became the basis most of the subsequent literature on the campaign.
84. See, e.g., Peter Balakian, *The Burning Tigris,*, 176–79; and Taner Akçam, *A Shameful Act, The Armenian Genocide and the Question of Turkish Responsibility* (New York: Metropolitan Books, 2006), 125–27. These assertions appear to originate in the 1916 work of British wartime propagandist Arnold Toynbee.
85. Ibid.
86. See Allen and Muratoff, *Caucasian Battlefields*, XX.
87. Altınbilek and Kır, *3ncü Ordu Harekâtı*, Kroki 21 (Map 21).
88. Ibid., Kroki 22a (Map 22a).
89. G. Korganoff, *La Participation Des Arméniens à la Guerre Mondiale—sur le front du Caucase (1914–1918)* (Paris: Massis Editions, 1927), 15–17.
90. Mallet to Edward Grey, October 14, 1914, The National Archives (TNA), Kew, FO 438/3, 59458.
91. Cheetham to Edward Grey, November 12, 1914. TNA, FO 438/4, 70404. Boghos Nubar presented this idea to British military planners in Cairo.
92. Donald Bloxham, *The Great Game of Genocide; Imperialism, Nationalism, and the Destruction of the Ottoman Armenians* (Oxford: Oxford University Press, 2005), 80.
93. Ibid., Bloxham cites German and British archival records for this quote from Varandian.
94. Sailing Orders "Doris" from RH Peirse to CO, HMS Doris, December 13, 1914, TNA, CAB 137/1091.
95. Ibid., see paragraph 5.
96. Report from Larkin to Peirse, December 27, 1914, 1, TNA, CAB 37/124.

97. See also Vice Admiral Cecil Vivian Usborne, *Smoke on the Horizon: Mediterranean Fighting 1914–1918* (London: 1933), 20–40.

98. Report from Larkin to Peirse, December 27, 1914, 6.

99. Ibid., 8.

100. Ibid., 9.

101. Ibid., 5.

102. HMS Doris, Copy of Log, For January 1915, entry for January 7, 1915, TNA, ADM 153/40058 (hereafter HMS Doris, log entry for).

103. Report from Larkin to Peirse, January 17, 1915, 9, TNA, CAB 37/124.

104. Ibid., 9.

105. Ibid., 11.

106. Ibid., 16.

107. HMS Doris, log entry for January 20, 1915, TNA, ADM 153/40058.

108. HMS Doris, log entry for January 24, 1915, TNA, ADM 153/40058.

109. HMS Doris, log entry for January 30, 1915, TNA, ADM 153/40058. See Larkin's enclosure to Report of Proceedings February 8, 1915, for a list of prisoners by name, race, birthplace, and religion, TNA, CAB 37/124/13.

110. Ali Fuad Erden, *Birinci Dünya Harbinde Suriye Hatıraları* (Istanbul, 2003), 115. These are the memoirs of Ali Fuad, who was a Fourth Army staff officer in Damascus.

111. See Sailing Orders HMS Doris, December 13, 1914 and ciphered telegram from C.in C. East Indies, Port Said to *Admiralty*, January 8, 1915, TNA, ADM 137/1091, which reaffirmed the interdiction mission.

112. Report on Landing Facilities near Alexandretta, January 7, 1915, TNA, CAB 37/124/13.

113. Letter from Larkin to Peirse, February 6, 1915, TNA, CAB 37/124/13.

114. George H. Cassar, *Kitchener's War, British Strategy from 1914 to 1916* (Washington, DC: Brassey's Inc, 2004), see 120–24, for a particularly readable discussion of the War Council's deliberations and decisions regarding these events.

115. Memorandum Cheetham to Edward Grey, October 14, 1914, TNA, FO 438/4, 70404. Nubar continued to press the allies for an invasion of the Levantine coast (Cilicia) throughout the spring of 1915 and promised that they would be supported by a "unified rebellion of Armenians against Turkish authorities wherever possible." See Boghos Nubar to Sahag Catholicos of Cilicia, Heliopolis, Egypt, April 17, 1915, document 5 in V. Ghazarian (ed.), *Boghos Nubar's Papers and the Armenian Question, 1915–1918* (Waltham, 1996), 203. Nubar later led the Armenian delegation at Versailles in 1919.

116. Yigal Sheffy, *British Military Intelligence in the Palestine Campaign 1914–1918* (London: Frank Cass, 1998), 48–83. Sheffy noted that

the activities of January 1915 were among the most successful and that in 1915, 13 agents were successfully landed on the Levantine coast, but that at least 3 were intercepted by the Turks.

117. Memorandum by Lord Kitchener to Committee of Imperial Defence, "Alexandretta and Mesopotamia," March 16, 1915, CAB 37/124/12.

8   ENEMIES WITHIN

1. Professor John Hall (Emeritus), Department of Education at Saint Lawrence University in Canton, New York, lectured on the realities behind the human condition and its effect on decision-making. Professor Hall would point out that the truth and the facts were irrelevant to the discussion because perceptions of reality were often the determinants in human decision-making processes. Therefore understanding what people believed to be true rather than sorting out what was true may actually offer a better explanation of why historical events happened in the way that they did.

2. Hakkı Altınbilek and Naci Kır, *Birinci Dünya Harbi'nde Türk Harbi, Kafkas Cephesi 3ncü Ordu Harekâtı, Cilt II Birinci Kitap*, (Ankara: Genelkurmay Basımevi, 1993), 599–600.

3. Cipher from Third Army to Enver, January 29, 1915, ATASE, archive 2820, record 69, file 2–4.

4. Headquarters, V Corps Report, February 25, 1915, on the bombing incident in Ankara, ATASE, archive 2287, record 32, file 8. See also Muammer Demirel, *Birinci Dünya Harbinde Erzurum ve Çevresinde Ermeni Hareketleri (1914–1918)*, (Ankara: Genelkurmay Basımevi, 1996), 40–45. Demirel included the names of specific Armenian leaders and their locations, e.g., Bogos Boyaciyan from Toti and Ohannes Kokasyan from Velibaba.

5. Kemal Arı, *Birinci Dünya Savaşı Kronolojisi* (Ankara: Genelkurmay Basımevi, 1997), 105–10.

6. Guneş N. Eğe-Akter (trans.), *Babamın Emanetleri, Ragıp Nurettin E'ge'nin Birinci Cihan Harbi Günlükleri ve Harbin Sonrasi Hatiratı* (Istanbul: Isis Press, 2006), 56. See diary entry for February 23, 1915.

7. Justin McCarthy, Esat Arslan, Cemalettin Taşkıran, and Ömer Turan, *The Armenian Rebellion at Van* (Salt Lake City: The University of Utah Press, 2006), 187–90.

8. Ibid., 195.

9. Ibid.

10. Bloxham wrote in 2005 that "the distinction between acts of self-defense and acts of revolt remains blurred," and noted that it is difficult to separate acts of volunteerism from acts of desperation. See Donald Bloxham, *The Great Game of Genocide; Imperialism, Nationalism, and the Destruction of the Ottoman Armenians* (Oxford: Oxford University Press, 2005), 90. For more recent opposing viewpoints, see McCarthy

et al., *Armenian Rebellion*, 180–91; and Taner Akçam, *A Shameful Act, The Armenian Genocide and the Question of Turkish Responsibility* (New York: Metropolitan Books, 2006), 111–48.

11. First Division, Ottoman General Staff cable, directive 8682, February 25, 1915, ATASE, archive 2287, record 32, file 9.

12. Ibid. See paragraph 5.

13. Special ciphered correspondence no. 2086, Chief, Second Division, Ministry of the Interior, to Chief, Second Division, Ottoman General Staff, January 31, 1915, ATASE, archive 2029, file 2.

14. Russian ambassador to Foreign Ministry, Paris, February 23, 1915, Archives du ministère de Affaires étrangères (AMAE), Guerre 1914–1915, Turquie, tome 849, f. 214 reprinted in A. Beylerian, *Les Grandes Puissanes, l'Empire ottoman et les Arméniens dans les archives françaises 1914–1918* (Paris, 1983), 7.

15. Third Army to Supreme Command, February 26, 1915, ATASE, archive 2820, record 69, file 2–23 reproduced in reproduced in Hikmet Ozdemir and Yusuf Sarınay (eds.), *Turk-Ermeni Ihtilafi Belegeler* (Ankara: Egemenlik, undated), document 2.1.

16. Vasıf to governorates and armies, February 28, 1915, ATASE, archive 2820, record 69, file 2–23 reproduced in reproduced in Ozdemir and Yusuf Sarınay, *Turk-Ermeni Ihtilafi Belegeler*, document 2.2.

17. Third Army to Enver, March 15, 1915, ATASE, archive 412, record 647, file 51–2.

18. Altınbilek and Kır, *3ncü Ordu Harekâtı*, 587–88.

19. Report of Kemal, Kaimakam, March 15, 1915, ATASE, archive 2024, record 11. file 1–3 reproduced in ATASE, *Arşiv Belgeleriye Ermeni Faaliyetleri, 1914–1918, Cilt I* (Ankara: Genelkurmay Basımevi, 2005), 65–71.

20. Peter Balakian, *The Burning Tigris The Armenian Genocide and America's Response* (New York: Harper Collins, 2003), 197–209.

21. Intelligence office, 2nd Division to Intelligence office, Ministry of the Interior, March 25, 1915, ATASE, archive 311, record 1264, file 1 reproduced in ATASE, *Arşiv Belgeleriye Ermeni Faaliyetleri 1914–1918, Cilt I*, 77–78.

22. Fifth Army to Enver, March 6, 1915, ATASE, archive 2287, record 12, file 1–32.

23. Wagenheim to Bethmann-Hollweg, March 26, 1915, Politisches Archiv des Auswärtigen Amts (AP), AA/RI 4085 translated and reprinted at http://www.armenocide.de.

24. Roessler (Aleppo) to Bethmann-Hollweg, April 12, 1915, AP, AA/R14085, 1915-A-14801 translated and reprinted at http://www.armenocide.de.

25. Hilmar Kaiser, "Regional Resistance to Central Government Policies; Ahmed Djemal Pasha, the Governors of Aleppo, and the Armenian Deportees in the Spring and Summer of 1915," *Journal of Genocide Research* vol. 12, no. 3, 173–218.

26. Third Army Cipher 2763 to general staff, March 23, 1915, ATASE, archive 2024, record 12, file 1–11 reproduced in ATASE, *Arşiv Belgeleriye Ermeni Faaliyetleri 1914–1918, Cilt I*, 94–95.

27. Third Army report to Enver, April 14, 1915, ATASE, archive 2820, record 69, file 3 reproduced in ATASE, *Arşiv Belgeleriye Ermeni Faaliyetleri 1914–1918, Cilt I*, 79.

28. Şükrü, Erzurum to Headquarters, Ottoman Army, March 31, 1915, ATASE, archive 2061, record 21, file 1–18 reproduced in Inanç Atılgan and Garabet Moumdjian, *Archival Documents of the Viennese Armenian-Turkish Platform* (Klagenfurt: Wieser Verlag, 2010), 106–39.

29. Cemal to 2nd Directorate, April 5, 1915, ATASE, archive 2287, record 12, file 1–33.

30. Report by commander, SO volunteer battalion, April 6, 1915, ATASE, archive 2818, record 59, file 31.

31. Report from Tekirdağ to Enver, April 8, 1915, ATASE, archive 142, record 647, file 51.

32. Cipher 3079, Cemal to Enver, April 8, 1915, ATASE, archive 2287, record 12, file 1–34.

33. Cipher 3108, Cemal to Enver, April 9, 1915, ATASE, archive 2287, record 12, file 1–37.

34. Mahmud Kâmil to Enver, April 8, ATASE, archive 2820, record 69, file 3–33.

35. Cipher 3169, Cemal to Enver, April 14, 1915, ATASE, archive 2287, record 12, file 1–39.

36. Report from Third Army, April 19, 1915, ATASE, archive 142, record 647, file 37–20. See also Altınbilek and Kır, *3ncü Ordu Harekâtı*, 592.

37. McCarthy et al., *The Armenian Rebellion at Van*, 196. McCarthy cites Third Army reports from ATASE, archive 2818.

38. Roessler to Bethmann Hollweg, Aleppo, April 12, 1915, PA-AA/ R14085, Dok. A-14801 and Wangenheim to Bethmann Hollweg, Constnatinople, April 15, 1915, PA-AA/R14085, Dok. 026, translated and reprinted at http://www.armenocide.de.

39. Ibid., 197. Mc Carthy cites a Third Army report from ATASE, archive 2818.

40. Ibid., 200.

41. Ibid., 200–201. McCarthy cites Reports from Cevdat, April 20, 1915, ATASE, archive 2947, record 628, file 3–4.

42. Altınbilek and Kır, *3ncü Ordu Harekâtı*, 592.

43. Report from Cevdat Bey, April 21, 1915, ATASE, archive 2820, record 69, file 3–26 reproduced in Atılgan and Moumdjian, *Archival Documents of the Viennese Armenian-Turkish Platform*, 166–68.

44. Report from Cevdat Bey, April 22–23, 1915, ATASE, archive 2820, record 69, file 3–41 reproduced in Atılgan and Moumdjian, *Archival Documents of the Viennese Armenian-Turkish Platform*, 170–71.

45. Rafael De Nogales, *Four Years beneath the Crescent* (New York, 1926), 45.

46. Altınbilek and Kır, *3ncü Ordu Harekâtı*, 592.

47. Morgenthau to the Secretary of State, May 25, 1915, NARA, RG 353 (Internal Affairs, Turkey), roll 41, 2.

48. Announcement by ANDC to Sir J. Maxwell, CinC, Egypt, Cairo, July 24, 1915, document 119 in V. Ghazarian, *Boghos Nubar's Papers and the Armenian Question, 1915–1918*, 203.

49. Altınbilek and Kır, *3ncü Ordu Harekâtı*, 591.

50. W. E. D. Allen and Paul Muratoff, *Caucasian Battlefields: A History of the Wars on the Turco-Caucasian Border, 1828–1921*, (Cambridge: Cambridge University Press, 1953), 299.

51. G. Korganoff, *Le Participation Des Arméniens à la Guerre Mondiale—sur le front du Caucase (1914–1918)*, (Paris: Massis Editions, 1927), 21–23.

52. Anahide Ter-Minassian, "Van 1915," *Guerres mondiales et conflits contemporains*, 1989, Volume 153, issue 39, 46–50; and Antranig Chalabian, *General Andranik and the Armenian Revolutionary Movement* (USA: First Edition, 1988), 244.

53. Reynolds, Michael A. *Shattering Empires, The Clash and Collapse of the Ottoman and Russian Empires 1908–1918* (Cambridge: Cambridge University Press, 2011), 135. General Andranik's biographer, Chalabian, asserted that there were six regiments of Armenian volunteers, but that they were never employed en masse. See Chalabian, *General Andranik*, 229.

54. McCarthy et al., *The Armenian Rebellion at Van*, 215.

55. Allen and Muratoff, *Caucasian Battlefields*, 301.

56. DH ciphered cable, Başbakanlık Osmanlı Arşivi, Istanbul, Turkey (BOA), archive 53/345, cited in Demirel, *Erzurum ve Cevresinde Ermeni Hareketleri*, 48. Demirel noted the Erzurum to Aşkale and Erzurum to Bayburt lines were cut and that the road from Erzurum to Diyarbakir was cut in four locations. Later the train lines from Constantinople to Ankara were blown up as well.

57. Combat reports, April 15, 1915, ATASE, archive 2950, record H-13, file 1–29 cited in Altınbilek and Kır, *3ncü Ordu Harekâtı*, 618–19.

58. Ciphered message from Muammer Bey to Enver, April 22, 1915, ATASE, archive 142, record 647, file 54 and Ciphered message from Muammer Bey, April 22–23, 1915, ATASE, archive 2820, record 69, file 3–45.

59. Mahmud Kâmil to Enver, April 22, 1915, ATASE, archive 142, record 647, file 51–1.

60. Commander XI Corps to Third Army, 29 April 1915, ATASE, archive 2820, record 69, file 1–21.

61. Sıtkı Atamer, *41nci Piyade Tümen Tarıhçesi* (Ankara: ATASE unpublished staff study 1969), 3, ATASE, archive Folder 26–344.

62. Wagenheim to Bethmann-Holweg, April 15 and 25, 1915, AP, AA/RI 4085, translated and reprinted at http://www.armenocide.de.

63. Wagenheim to Bethmann-Holweg, May 8, 1915, AP, AA/RI 4085 translated and reprinted at http://www.armenocide.de.

64. Altınbilek and Kır, *3ncü Ordu Harekâtı*, 591–97.

65. Yahya Okçu and Hilmi Üstünsoy, *Birinci Dünya Harbi'nde Türk Harbi, Sina-Filistin Cephesi, Harbin Başlangıcından İkinci Gazze Muharebeleri Sonuna Kadar, IVncü Cilt 1 Kısım* (Ankara: Genelkurmay Basımevi, 1979), 698–704.

66. Şükrü Erkal, *Birinci Dünya Harbinde Türk Harbi, VIncı Cilt, Hicaz, Asir, Yemen Cepheleri ve Libya Harekatı 1914–1918* (Ankara: Genelkurmay Basımevi, 1978), 740–45.

67. See Edward J. Erickson, *Ordered to Die, A History of the Ottoman Army in the First World War*, (Westport, CT: Greenwood Press, 2001), for a comprehensive summary of the geography and weaknesses of the Ottoman railway system.

68. Atamer, *41nci Piyade Tümen Tarıhçesi*, 3, ATASE, archive Folder 26–344.

69. Okçu, *Sina-Filistin Cephesi*, 335–40. Additionally, the Fourth Army staff was also very concerned about the possibility of an Arab uprising in their rear centered on Aleppo and Damascus.

70. Instructions from the Minister of the Interior to the Govern ant of Adana, February 16, 1915, BOA DH, File 50/141 reproduced in ATASE, *Osmanli Belgelerinde Ermenile (1915–1920)* (Ankara: Osmanlı Arşivi Daıre, 1995), 20.

71. Report from Governor of Adana to Ministry of Internal Affairs, National Police Directorate, ATASE, archive 13, record 63, file 1–3.

72. Report from Ministry of Internal Affairs to Fourth Army, March 4, 1915, and Headquarters Fourth Army Cipher Number 2247, February 28, 1915. ATASE BDH, File 13, Folder 63, Index 2 (1–3).

73. The level of coordination between the Ottoman ministries in Constantinople was surprisingly effective and, in some cases throughout the war, put the Turks in possession of superior spatial and situational awareness compared to their enemies.

74. Message No. 8682, from First Division, General Staff to all armies, army areas, and general staff divisions, February 25, 1915 (coded for release February 27, 1915). ATASE BDH, File 2287, Folder 12, Index 9.

75. Orders from Ministry of the Interior, General Secretariat of Security to the Governor of Adana, March 2, 1915. BOA DH (Başbakanlık Osmanlı Arşivi—Dahiliye Nezareti Arşivi), File 50/141 reproduced in Ozdemir and Sarinay, *Turk-Ermeni Ihtilafi Belegeler*, document 3.

76. Ciphered telegram from Talat, Minister of the Interior to Fourth Army commander Cemal Pasha, April 11, 1915. BOA DH, File 52/93, reproduced in *Turk-Ermeni Ihtilafi Belegeler*.

77. Report N. 226 from Vice Consul Alexandretta (Hoffman) to Ambassador Wangenheim, Constantinople, March 7, 1915. AP-AA (Politisches Archiv des Auswartigen Amts) [German Foreign Ministry], Embassy Constantinople/Vol. 168 translated and reprinted at http://www.armenocide.de

78. Report No. 2234 from Consul Adana (Brüge) to Ambassador Wangenheim Constantinople, March 13, 1915. AP-AA, Embassy

Constantinople/Vol. 168, translated and reprinted at http://www .armenocide.de.

79. Ibid.

80. Ali Fuad Erden, *Birinci Dünya Harbinde Suriye Hatiraları* (Istanbul: Arma Yayınları, 2003), 52. At the time of the incident Ali Fuad was a staff officer in the Ottoman Fourth Army.

81. Ibid.

82. Letter from Chairman ANDCA to Grey, March 28, 1915, facsimile copy reproduced at http://armeniangenocidefacts.com.

83. Message from the Directorate of Security, Ministry of the Interior to the Fourth Army Command, May 23, 1915. BOA DH, File 53/94 reproduced in *Turk-Ermeni Ihtilafi Belegeler.*

84. Selahattin Karatamu, *Türk Silahlı Kuvvetleri Tarihi, IIIncü Cilt 6nci Kısım (1908–1920)* (Ankara: Genelkurmay Basımevi, 1971), 459–63.

85. Hermann Cron, *Imperial German Army, 1914–18: Organisation, Structure, Orders-of-Battle* (Solihull: Hellion and Company, 2002), 237.

86. Necmi Koral, Remzi Önal, Rauf Atakan, Nusret Baycan, and Selahattin Kızılırmak, *Türk Silahlı Kuvvetleri Tarihi, Osmanlı Devri, Birinci Dünya Harbi Idari Faaliyetler ve Lojistik, Xncu Cilt* (Ankara: Genelkurmay Basımevi, 1985), 115.

87. Tuncay Öğün, *Kafkas Cephesinin I. Dünya Savaşındaki Lojistik Desteği* (Ankara: Atatük Araştırma Merkezi, 1999), Section I, 29–108.

88. Koral et al., *Birinci Dünya Harbi Idari Faaliyetler ve Lojistik*, 102. Ottoman Army logistics doctrines as used in World War I were formulated in 1911 with the publication of *Menzil Hidematı Nizamnamesi.* By 1914 most of the field armies had published a secondary tier of instructions specific to their areas, e.g., *Ikinci Ordu Menzil Müfettişliği Hayvan Depoları Hakkinda Talimat* (Istanbul, 1914). Unrelated to this study, Ottoman logistics doctrines were refined during the war in 1917 as *Seferber Ordularda ve Menzillerde Geri Hidematı Rehberi.* I am indebted to Dr Mesut Uyar (Colonel, Infantry, Turkish Army) for this information.

89. Altınbilek and Kır, *3ncü Ordu Harekâtı*, 645.

90. I. Görgülü, *On Yıllık Harbin Kadrosu*, 104.

91. Altınbilek and Kır, *3ncü Ordu Harekâtı*, 645–49.

92. Akbay, *Askeri Hazırlıkları ve Harbe Girisi*, 186–87. The Ottoman 1st and 2nd Armies in Thrace stockpiled 34 and 38 days, respectively, while the 4th Army in Palestine stockpiled 24 days.

93. Koral, *Harbi Idari Faaliyetler*, 180–87.

94. 3rd Army report, ATASE, archive 139, record 636, file 10–2/4, cited in Altınbilek and Kır, *3ncü Ordu Harekâtı*, 657.

95. LoCI Reports, ATASE, archive 3055, record H-3, file 3–19 cited in Altınbilek and Kır, *3ncü Ordu Harekâtı*, 658.

96. Various reports, ATASE, archive 2130, record 833, file 16–20 cited in Altınbilek and Kır, *3ncü Ordu Harekâtı*, 662–63.

97. H. E. W., Strachan, *The First World War*, vol.1, *To Arms* (Oxford: Oxford University Press, 2001), 995–96.

98. Various reports, ATASE, archive 3027, record 3, file 1–17 cited in Altınbilek and Kır, *3ncü Ordu Harekâtı*, 665.
99. T. Sağlam, *Büyük Harpte 3ncü Ordu'da Sıhhı Hizmet* (Istanbul, 1941), 8–, cited in Altınbilek and Kır, *3ncü Ordu Harekâtı*, 662–63.
100. 4th Army orders, Damascus, November 12, 1914, reproduced in Yahya Okçu and Hilmi Üstünsoy, *Birinci Dünya Harbi'nde Türk Harbi, Sina-Filistin Cephesi, Harbin Başlangıcından İkinci Gazze Muharebeleri Sonuna Kadar, IVncü Cilt 1 Kısım* (Ankara: Genelkurmay Basımevi, 1979), 765–67.
101. Ibid., 675–76.
102. Altınbilek and Kır, *3ncü Ordu Harekâtı*, 671.
103. Ibid., 672. Major İrfan led 2,152 replacements forward on January 5, 1915.
104. Ibid., 674.
105. Strength report, ATASE, archive 140, record 640, file 6, cited in Altınbilek and Kır, *3ncü Ordu Harekâtı*, 676. A further 7,025 men remained in hospital.
106. Ibid.
107. Logistics reports, ATASE, archive 1261, record 539, file 1–9 cited in Koral, *Harbi İdari Faaliyetler,* 252.
108. Various reports, May 5, 1915, ATASE, Archive 1070, record 97, files 1–2/3/9 cited in Koral, *Harbi İdari Faaliyetler*, 269.
109. Computation of how much food and fodder a certain number of men and animals will consume follows a known formula. Ammunition usage, on the other hand, follows an unpredictable path of expenditure that is dependent on the tactical situation.
110. Koral, *Harbi İdari Faaliyetler*, 269.
111. Strength reports, ATASE, archive 1964, record 305, files 1–29/1–143 cited in Altınbilek and Kır, *3ncü Ordu Harekâtı*, 645.
112. See also Allen and Muratoff, *Caucasian Battlefields*, 287–89.
113. Ibid. See commentary on page 303 regarding the effectiveness of the Third army's reconstitution efforts.
114. Altınbilek and Kır, *3ncü Ordu Harekâtı*, 683.
115. Ibid.
116. 3rd Army Weapons/Munitions Report, May 3, 1915, ATASE, archive 2950, record 13, file 138 reproduced in Altınbilek and Kır, *3ncü Ordu Harekâtı*, Ek 3 (Document 3).
117. 3rd Army Logistics Situation, March 10, 1915, Altınbilek and Kır, *3ncü Ordu Harekâtı*, Kroki 113 (Map 113).
118. See Cengiz Mutlu, *Birinci Dünya Savaşında Amele Taburları* (Istanbul: IQ Kültür Sanat Yayıncılık, 2007), for recent work based on archival sources.
119. 3LoCI Situation Report, September 27, 1914, ATASE, archive 1129, record 27, file 1–2 reproduced in Altınbilek and Kır, *3ncü Ordu Harekâtı*, 647.

120. 3LoCI reports, TCGB, archive 3055, record H-28, file 1–11 cited in Altınbilek and Kır, *3ncü Ordu Harekâtı*, 696.

121. See, e.g., Balakian, *Burning Tigris*, 184–85; and E. J. Zürcher, *Ottoman Labour Battalions in World War I*, http://www.hist.net/kieser/aghet /Essays/EssayZurcher.html. Dr. Zürcher cites the work of Taner Akçam and Vahakn Dadrian. There is testimony that some Armenian soldiers were killed intentionally while assigned to the labor battalions; however, it is inaccurate to associate this characterization with the organization in general.

122. Reorganization Chart, August 30, 1916, ATASE, archive 3055, record H-10, file 4–127 reproduced in Altınbilek and Kır, *3ncü Ordu Harekâtı*, 721.

123. Altınbilek and Kır, *3ncü Ordu Harekâtı*, 721. See reorganization of Erzurum and Trabzon battalions.

124. TCGB, *Sina-Filistin Cephesi*, 684.

125. 4th Army Logistics Report, October 1915, ATASE, archive 1309, record 773, file 1/38 reproduced in Koral, *Harbi Idari Faaliyetler*, 665–66. In October 1915 the 4 LoCI had 17,970 officers and men assigned.

126. Priority message to 4th Army, April 22, 1915, ATASE, archive 18, record H-17, file 17–44.

127. Allen and Muratoff, *Caucasian Battlefields*, 233.

128. Demirel, *Erzurum ve Cevresinde Ermeni Hareketleri*, 19.

129. Ibid. See chart on page 19, which lists 21 known locations of Armenian arms caches containing 4,780 rifles.

130. Altınbilek and Kır, *3ncü Ordu Harekâtı*, 592–93.

131. Ibid., 676–77.

132. Kaiser, "Regional Resistance to Central Government Policies," 2.

133. Numerous warnings were sent from the Ministry of War to subordinate military commanders regarding the impending invasion. See, e.g., General Headquarter's Message, March 22, 1915, ATASE archive 4669, record H-13, file 1–2; and Otto Liman von Sanders, *Five Years in Turkey* (Nashville: The Battery Press, 2000, reprint of the 1928 edition), 56.

134. Wangenheim to Bethmann-Hollweg, Constantinople, April 30, 1915, PA-AA/R14085, Dok. 038, 1915-A-15363, translated and reprinted at http://www.armenocide.de.

135. Talat to Ottoman Army Commander-in-Chief, April 24, 1915, ATASE, archive 401, record 1580, file 1–3 reproduced in Atılgan and Moumdjian, *Archival Documents of the Viennese Armenian-Turkish Platform*, 170–71.

136. Ibid. German diplomatic reports also indicated the Interior Ministry's concerns regarding the linkages between prominent Armenians and the revolutionary committees. See Wangenheim to Bethmann Hollweg, Constantinople, April 30, 1915, PA-AA/R14085, Dok. 038, A-15363 translated and reprinted at http://www.armenocide.de.

137. Talat to Governors of provinces and cities, April 24, 1915, BOA, DH Şfr. No: 52/96–97–98 reproduced in Ozdemir and Sarınay, *Turk-Ermeni Ihtilafi Belegeler*, document 7.
138. Ministry of War directive, April 24, 1915, ATASE, archive 44, record 207, file 2–3.
139. Ibid.
140. Enver to Amy Commands, April 26, 1915, ATASE, archive 2287, record 12, file 12–1 98 reproduced in Ozdemir and Sarınay, *Turk-Ermeni Ihtilafi Belegeler*, document 9.

9   A NEW COURSE OF ACTION

1. Yahya Okçu and Hilmi Üstünsoy, *Birinci Dünya Harbi'nde Türk Harbi, Sina-Filistin Cephesi, Harbin Başlangıcından İkinci Gazze Muharebeleri Sonuna Kadar, IVncü Cilt 1 Kısım* (Ankara: Genelkurmay Basımevi, 1979), 31–332.
2. Operations Directorate, Ottoman General Staff, May 13, 1915, ATASE, archive 142, record 647, file 37–19.
3. Hakkı Altınbilek and Naci Kır, *Birinci Dünya Harbi'nde Türk Harbi, Kafkas Cephesi 3ncü Ordu Harekâtı, Cilt II Birinci Kitap*, (Ankara: Genelkurmay Basımevi, 1993), 676–77.
4. Ciphered telegram, Ministry of Finance to Governates, May 6, 1915, BOA, DH, Şfr, No. 52/249 reproduced in Hikmet Ozdemir and Yusuf Sarinay (eds.), *Turk-Ermeni Ihtilafi Belegeler* (Ankara: Egemenlik, undated), document 11.
5. Telegram 22, Reşid, Governor to Ministry of the Interior, April 27, 1915, ATASE archive 2820, record 69, file 3–52 reproduced in Inanç Atılgan and Garabet Moumdjian, *Archival Documents of the Viennese Armenian-Turkish Platform* (Klagenfurt: Wieser Verlag, 2010), 184–85.
6. Ciphered message from 3rd Army, May 19, 1915, ATASE, archive 401, record 1580, file 1–22.
7. Ibid.
8. Telegram 10, Ministry of the Interior to District officials of Vakfi Kebir, May 10, 1915, BOA Hr. Sys. Hu 110, 12–3, 12 reproduced in Atılgan and Moumdjian, *Archival Documents of the Viennese Armenian-Turkish Platform*, 210–11.
9. Ciphered message 25, Ministry of the Interior to 4th Army, May 23, 1915, BOA, DH, Şfr, No. 53/85 reproduced in Ozdemir and Sarinay, *Turk-Ermeni Ihtilafi Belegeler*, document 12.
10. See Edward J. Erickson, *Ordered to Die, A History of the Ottoman Army in the First World War* (Westport, CT: Greenwood Press, 2001), Table 4.2, 102, for the deployment of Ottoman army corps and divisions in April 1915.
11. Elements of this division began to arrive in the vicinity of Bitlis on June 7, 1915. See Kemal Ari, *Birinci Dünya Savaşı Kronolojisi* (Ankara: Genelkurmay Basımevi, 1997), 155.

12. İsmet Görgülü, *On Yıllık Harbin Kadrosu 1912–1922, Balkan-Birinci Dünya ve İstiklâl Harbi* (Ankara: Türk Tarih Kurum Basımevi, 1993), 141; and Fahri Belen, *Birinci Cihan Harbinde Türk Harbi, 1914 Yılı Hareketleri,* (Ankara: Genelkurmay Basımevi, 1964), "Activation of Divisions in the War," Chart following 250.

13. The documented absence of Ottoman military strength in the interior provinces of Anatolia in the spring of 1915 would seem to argue against the idea that attacks on the Armenian population were preplanned by the government.

14. Enver Pasha to Headquarters, 3rd Army, April 20, 1915, ATASE, archive 2820, record 100, file 2.

15. Message no. 5828, 3rd Army to Ministry of War, July 28, 1915, ATASE, archive 152, record 680, file 27–1. The 3rd Army reported the delivery of 2,000 rifles to the provincial governor of Diyarbakir for this purpose.

16. Kenneth O. Morgan, "The Boer War and the Media (1899–1902)," *Twentieth Century British History* vol. 13, no. 1 (2002), 12–16.

17. Max Boot, *Invisible Armies, An Epic History of Guerrilla Warfare from Ancient Times to the Present* (New York: Liveright Publishing Corporation, 2013), 378–88; and Daniel Marston and Carter Malakasian (eds.), *Counterinsurgency in Modern Warfare* (Oxford: Osprey Publishing, 2008), 113–30.

18. Boot, *Invisible Armies,* 364–77; and Marston and Malakasian, *Counterinsurgency in Modern Warfare,* 100–12.

19. Boot, *Invisible Armies,* 417; and Marston and Malakasian, *Counterinsurgency in Modern Warfare,* 136–39.

20. Pertev Demirhan, *Generalfeldmarschall Colmar von der Goltz, Das Lebensbild eines grossen Soldaten* (Göttingen: 1960), 74–77; and Feroze Yasamee, "Colmar Freiherr von der Goltz and the Boer War," Keith Wilson (ed.), *The International Impact of the Russo-Japanese War* (London: Palgrave, 2001), 193–210.

21. Yavuz Abadan, *Mustafa Kemal ve Çetelik* (Istanbul: Varlık Yayınevi 1996), 53–56; and Asım Gündüz, *Hatıralarım* (Istanbul: Kervan Yayınları, 1973), 29–32. Interestingly, Mustafa Kemal, himself a war academy graduate, wrote a training booklet after Gallipoli that included information about the Boer War. See Mustafa Kemal Atatürk, *Askeri Talim ve Terbiye Hakkında Görüşler* (Ankara: Genelkurmay Basımevi, 2011), 5 (translation of 1916 edition). I am indebted to Dr. Mesut Uyar for providing this information.

22. Kadri Alasya, *Türk Silahlı Kuvvetleri Tarihi, Balkan Harbi (1912–1913), Şark Ordudu II Cilt 1nci Kitap, Birinci Çatalca Muharebesi* (Ankara: Genelkurmay Basımevi, 1993), 62–63.

23. Report, Evacuation of Gallipoli, American Embassy, Constantinople to State Department, May 3, 1915, NARA, RG 353, Roll 41.

24. Bloxham, The Great Game of Genocide, 83–90.

25. Ministry of War directive, April 24, 1915, ATASE, archive 44, record 207, file 2–3.

26. Operations Division to Ministry of the Interior, May 2, 1915, ATASE, archive 44, record 207, file 2–1.

27. For varied commentary, see Yusuf Halaçoğlu, "Realities behind the Relocation," in Türkkaya Ataöv (ed.), *The Armenians in the Late Ottoman Period* (Ankara: Turkish Historical Society Printing House, 2001), 109–42; Donald Bloxham, *The Great Game of Genocide; Imperialism, Nationalism, and the Destruction of the Ottoman Armenians* (Oxford: Oxford University Press, 2005), 83–90; and Taner Akçam, *A Shameful Act, The Armenian Genocide and the Question of Turkish Responsibility* (New York: Metropolitan Books, 2006), 178.

28. Raymond H. Kévorkian, *The Armenian Genocide, A Complete History* (London: I.B. Tauris, 2011), 299–300. This number seems excessively high.

29. Ibid. See pages 279–621 for extensive commentary and documentation of the apprehension, imprisonment, and murder of the committee leadership in eastern Anatolia.

30. Ari, *Birinci Dünya Savaşı Kronolojisi*, 150. For German narratives of Ottoman appreciations, see, e.g., Wangenheim to Bethmann Hollweg, No. 449, Constantinople, July 16, 1915, Enclosure from Kuckhoff, PA-AA/R14086, Dok. 116, 1915-A-22101 translated and reprinted at http://www.armenocide.de.

31. H. S. Ayvazian to Nubar, July 8, 1915, reproduced in Ghazarian, *Boghos Nubar's Papers*, 145–48.

32. Wangenheim to Bethmann Hollweg, Constantinople, May 8, 1915, PA-AA/Ri4085, Dok. 044, 1915-A-15877, PA-AA/R14087, 1915-A-27584, translated and reprinted at http://www.armenocide.de.

33. Ciphered message, Talat to 4th Army, May 24, 1915, BOA, DH, Şfr, No. 53/94 reproduced in Ozdemir and Sarinay, *Turk-Ermeni Ihtilafi Belegeler*, document 15.

34. Ibid.

35. For the best, and most recent, scholarly analysis of this decision, see Hilmar Kaiser's superb article, "Regional Resistance to Central Government Policies: Ahmed Djemal Pasha, the Governors of Aleppo, and Armenian Deportees in the Spring and Summer of 1915."

36. Fuat Dündar, "Pouring a People into the Desert, the 'Definitive Solution' of the Unionists to the Armenians Problem," Ronald Grigor Suny, Fatma Müge Göçek, and Norman M. Naimark (eds.), *A Question of Genocide, Armenians and Turks at the End of the Ottoman Empire* (New York: Oxford University Press, 2011), 276–305.

37. Kaiser, 'Regional Resistance to Central Government Policies," 9–13.

38. Ibid., 11.

39. Talat to Prime Minister's Office, Confidential Memorandum 270, May 26, 1915, BOA, No. 326758, Siyasi, 53, reproduced in Ozdemir and Sarinay, *Turk-Ermeni Ihtilafi Belegeler*, document 17a.

40. Previously on May 2, Enver Pasha had recommended the forced reloca-
    tion of Armenians and resettlement of the vacated areas by Muslim refu-
    gees as a necessary solution to the problem of Armenian insurgency.
41. Ottoman Cabinet Decision No 33, May 30, 1915, BOA MVB 198/163
    reproduced in Atılgan and Moumdjian, *Archival Documents of the
    Viennese Armenian-Turkish Platform*, 226–27. The German ambassador
    noted that in order to "curb espionage and to prevent new Armenian
    mass uprisings" Enver used the state of war (or emergency) as the reason
    (or pretext) for closing Armenian schools, shutting down newspapers
    and relocating Armenians to Mesopotamia. See Wangenheim to Foreign
    Office, Constantinople, May 31, 1915, PA-AA/R14086, Dok. 072,
    1915-A-17493 translated and reprinted at http://www.armenocide.de.
42. Sublime Porte to Ministry of War, 842, May 31, 1915, ATASE,
    archive 401, record 1580, file 1–36 and Department of Critical Affairs
    Document No. 63 to ministries, May 31, 1915, BOA, 3267598,
    Siyasi, 53, reproduced in Ozdemir and Sarinay, *Turk-Ermeni Ihtilafı
    Belegeler*, document 17b.
43. Readers interested in this subject should refer to the document collec-
    tions produced by Ozdemir and Sarinay and Inanç and Moumdjian as
    well as the secondary analysis of Kévorkian, *The Armenian Genocide*
    and Kaiser, "Regional Resistance to Central Government Policies" for
    differing viewpoints.
44. Ciphered message from Talat to governates, July 4, 1915, ATASE,
    BOA, DH, ŞFR,No. 54/287, reproduced in Ozdemir and Sarinay,
    Turk-Ermeni Ihtilafı Belegeler, document 47.
45. Ciphered message No. 423 from Talat to governates, August 3, 1915,
    ATASE, BOA, DH, ŞFR,No. 54-A/252, reproduced in Ozdemir and
    Sarinay, *Turk-Ermeni Ihtilafı Belegeler*, document 63.
46. Ciphered message No. 5028 from Talat to governates, August 15,
    1915, ATASE, BOA, DH, ŞFR,No. 55/20, reproduced in Ozdemir
    and Sarinay, *Turk-Ermeni Ihtilafı Belegeler*, document 61.
47. Ciphered message No. 5029 from Talat to governates, August 15,
    1915, ATASE, BOA, DH, ŞFR,No. 55/19, reproduced in Ozdemir
    and Sarinay, *Turk-Ermeni Ihtilafı Belegeler* document 73.
48. Ciphered message No. 5030 from Talat to governates, August 15,
    1915, ATASE, BOA, DH, ŞFR,No. 55/18, reproduced in Ozdemir
    and Sarinay, *Turk-Ermeni Ihtilafı Belegeler*, document 75.
49. Ciphered message No. 5077 from Talat to governates, August 17,
    1915, ATASE, BOA, DH, ŞFR,No. 55/48, reproduced in Ozdemir
    and Sarinay, *Turk-Ermeni Ihtilafı Belegeler*, document 80.
50. Ciphered message No. 23 from Talat to Governate of Antalya Sanjak,
    August 17, 1915, ATASE, BOA, DH, ŞFR,No. 55/59, reproduced in
    Ozdemir and Sarinay, *Turk-Ermeni Ihtilafı Belegeler*, document 68.
51. Atamer, *41nci Piyade Tümen Tarıhçesi*, 3, ATASE, archive Folder 26–344.
52. Ibid.

53. Ibid., 4.
54. Okçu, *Sina-Filistin Cephesi, Harbin Başlangıcından İkinci Gazze Muharebeleri Sonuna Kadar*, 288. The four other tactical areas in Cemal's Fourth Army were the Birinci, Ikinci, Cebelilübnan Kıyıları, and the Akka-Hayfa-Yafa (First, Second, Lebanon Mountain and Haifa-Jaffa).
55. Fahri Belen, *Birinci Cihan Harbinde Türk Harbi, 1918 Yılı Hareketleri* (Ankara: Genelkurmay Basımevi, 1967), 248.
56. Atamer, *41nci Piyade Tümen Tarıhçesi*, 4.
57. Okçu, *Sina-Filistin Cephesi, Harbin Başlangıcından İkinci Gazze Muharebeleri Sonuna Kadar*, 282.
58. Ibid.
59. Necmi Koral, Remzi Önal, Rauf Atakan, Nusret Baycan, and Selahattin Kızılırmak, *Türk Silahlı Kuvvetleri Tarihi, Osmanlı Devri, Birinci Dünya Harbi Idari Faaliyetler ve Lojistik, Xncu Cilt* (Ankara: Genelkurmay Basımevi, 1985), 213–14.
60. . Okçu, *Sina-Filistin Cephesi, Harbin Başlangıcından İkinci Gazze Muharebeleri Sonuna Kadar*, 332. Thus to the Ottomans, the Armenian rebellion appeared to be an Entente orchestrated affair with the Russians supporting Armenian insurgents in northeast Anatolia and the French supporting Armenian insurgents in southeast Anatolia.
61. Ibid., Kroki (Overlay) 17.
62. Görgülü, *On Yıllık Harbin Kadrosu*, 141. Mehmet Emin's chief-of-staff was Major Mümtaz.
63. The city of Adana and 200 kilometers of coastline were transferred to the newly activated 44th Infantry Division.
64. Okçu, *Sina-Filistin Cephesi, Harbin Başlangıcından İkinci Gazze Muharebeleri Sonuna Kadar*, Kuruluş 5 (Organizational Chart 5).
65. Ibid., Kroki 18 (Map 18).
66. Ibid., 273.
67. Ibid.
68. See Kévorkian, *The Armenian Genocide*, 279–621, for extensive commentary and documentation of the massacres of villages and convoys.
69. Ibid., 303, 294–99. A fourth convoy left Erzurum on July 18. Kévorkian provides the most comprehensive record in the English language of the departure locations and the dates of the departing convoys.
70. Ibid., 393.
71. Ibid., 435–38.
72. Ministry of the Interior to Provinces, June 14, BOA, Dh, Şfr, 54/06 reproduced in Atılgan and Moumdjian, *Archival Documents of the Viennese Armenian-Turkish Platform*, 246–47.
73. Ibid., 455–56.
74. Kévorkian, *The Armenian Genocide*, 457.
75. Report from Van officials, June 15, 1915, ATASE archive 533, record 2082, file 2–20.
76. Kévorkian, *The Armenian Genocide*, 457.

77. Hratch Dasnabedian, *History of the Armenian Revolutionary Federation, Dasnaktutiun 1890/1924* (Milan: OEMME Edizioni, 1990), 114.

78. Army telegraph to corps commander, July 2, 1915, ATASE archive 2835, record 127, file 3–3 reproduced in Ozdemir and Sarinay, *Turk-Ermeni Ihtilafi Belegeler*, document 56.

79. Kévorkian, *The Armenian Genocide*, 458.

80. Ibid.

81. Ibid.

82. Altınbilek and Kır, *3ncü Ordu Harekâtı*, 702.

83. Ibid., 726.

84. Ibid., 730.

85. Incident Reports, 3rd Army, June 10, 1915, ATASE archive 18, record 19, file 19–26 and Staff Summaries, June 13, 1915, ATASE archive 18, record 19, file 19–34.

86. Ministry of War from Third Army, June 19, 1915, ATASE archive 401, record 1580, file 1–22 reproduced in ATASE, *Arşiv Belgeleriye Ermeni Faaliyetleri 1914–1918, Cilt I*, 189.

87. Ministry of the Interior to Ministry of War, June 23, 1915, ATASE archive 2287, record 12, file 15–2.

88. Report from Fuat Ziya to Commander, 3rd Army, July 18, 1915, ATASE, archive 3671, record 127, file 1–9.

89. Ciphered message, Ministry of the Interior to Governor, Sivas, July 20, 1915, BOA, DH, Şfr., No. 54-A/50 reproduced in Ozdemir and Sarinay, *Turk-Ermeni Ihtilafi Belegeler*, document 58.

90. Ari, *Birinci Dünya Savaşı Kronolojisi*, 161.

91. Aleppo to MajGen Veli, August 28, 1915, ATASE, archive 15, record 63, file 8, *Arşiv Belgeleriye Ermeni Faaliyetleri 1914–1918, Cilt I*, 232. This message confirms the overall shortages of rifles in the 3 and 4 LoCI previously identified in chapter 8.

92. Ibid.

93. Salahi Sonyel, *The Great War and the Tragedy of Anatolia* (Ankara: Türk Tarih Kurumu, 2001), 128–29.

94. Major General C. E. Callwell, War Office to Foreign Office, August 6, 1915, enclosing letters from Sykes to Callwell, July 14, 1915, NA, FO 371/2940/108253. Callwell was also a prolific military commentator and was well-known as the author of *Small Wars*.

95. Ibid., Sykes to Callwell, July 16, 1915.

96. Announcement by ANDC to Maxwell, CinC, Egypt, July 24, 1915, Ghazarian, *Boghos Nubar's Papers and the Armenian Question*, document 119, 203. See also Sonyel, *The Great War*, 129–30.

97. McMahon to Grey, July 17, 1915, NA, FO 371/2485/1067960.

98. McMahon to Foreign Office, September 24, 1915, NA, FO 371/2480/138051.

99. See also Major-General Sir C. E. Callwell, *Experiences of a Dug-Out 1914–1918* (London: Constable and Company, 1920), Chapters VIII,

IX, and XIV for commentary regarding the War Council and the Alexandretta invasion schemes.

100. Notes of the Naval Attaché, Constantinople, August 6, 1915, PA-AA/ BoKon/170, Dok. 131. A53a/1915/4647 translated and reprinted at http://www.armenocide.de.

101. Oppenheim to Bethmann-Hollweg, August 29, 1915, PA-AA/R14087, 1915-A-27584 translated and reprinted at http://www.armenocide.de.

102. Governor of Adana to Ministry of the Interior Police Directorate, July 29, 1915, ATASE archive 311, record 1264, file 9 reproduced in Atılgan and Moumdjian, *Archival Documents of the Viennese Armenian-Turkish Platform*, 370–71.

103. Cemal to Ottoman general staff, August 1–2, 1915, ATASE, archive 13, record 63, file 7 reproduced in Atılgan and Moumdjian, *Archival Documents of the Viennese Armenian-Turkish Platform*, 376–77.

104. Süleyman Faik, acting corps commander to Headquarters, 3rd Army, August 4, 1915, ATASE archive 2835, record 127, file 4–11 reproduced in Atılgan and Moumdjian, *Archival Documents of the Viennese Armenian-Turkish Platform*, 388–89.

105. Guneş N. Eğe-Akter, *Babamın Emanetleri, Ragıp Nurettin E'ge'nin Birinci Cihan Harbi Günlükleri ve Harbin Sonrasi Hatiratı* (Istanbul: Isis Press, 2006), 146.

106. Ciphered telegram from Muammer, governor of Sivas, August 2–3, 1915, ATASE archive 2835, record 127, file 4–26 reproduced in Atılgan and Moumdjian, *Archival Documents of the Viennese Armenian-Turkish Platform*, 378–79.

107. Atamer, *41nci Piyade Tümen Tarıhçesi*, 5.

108. Ibid.

109. Letter from American Consul, Aleppo to Morgenthau, June 14, 1915, NARA, RG 353 (Internal Affairs, Turkey), Roll 41.

110. Ali Fuad Erden, *Birinci Dünya Harbinde Suriye Hatıraları* (Istanbul: Arma Yayınları, 2003), 144–45.

111. Atamer, *41nci Piyade Tümen Tarıhçesi*, 5.

112. Erden, *Suriye Hatıraları*, 146 (see note 65).

113. The Musa Dag˘ mountain is in actuality a rugged extended area covering over 250 square kilometers.

114. Franz Werfel, *The Forty Days of Musa Dagh*, Geoffrey Dunlop (trans.) (New York: Viking Press 1934).

115. Ibid., 166.

116. Ibid., 225.

117. Ibid., 239.

118. Ibid., 240.

119. Ibid., 242–44.

120. Ibid.

121. Atamer, *41nci Piyade Tümen Tarıhçesi*, 6. This corroborates Werfel's information. See Werfel, *The Forty Days of Musa Dagh*, 324–30. Werfel

describes this battle as occurring on August 4, but Turkish sources place it on August 7.

122. Ibid.

123. Ibid.

124. Atamer, *41nci Piyade Tümen Tarıhçesi*, 6. The two Ottoman infantry battalions were authorized almost 2,000 men on paper. However, at this time the 1st and 2nd Battalions of the 131st Infantry Regiment were operating at less than half of their authorized strength or 44 percent of their required personnel. This reflected the low priority of units operating in this theater of operations

125. Ibid., 6.

126. The division was then assigned to the Ottoman XII Corps, which was commanded by Fahri Pasha.

127. Ibid.

128. Werfel, *The Forty Days of Musa Dagh*, 365–75.

129. Atamer, *41nci Piyade Tümen Tarıhçesi*, 8.

130. Ibid.

131. Ibid.

132. Ibid., 9. Evidently, this particular group of Armenians originated from the Gallipoli peninsula.

133. Ibid.

134. Merhum Kâmil Onalp, Hilmi Üstünsoy, Kâmuran Dengiz, and Şükrü Erkal, *Birinci Dünya Harbi'nde Türk Harbi, Sina-Filistin Cephesi, İkinci Gazze Muharebeleri Sonundan Mütarkesi'ne Kadar Yapılan Harekât, IVncü Cilt 2nci Kısım* (Ankara: Genelkurmay Basımevi, 1986), 698–704. See "Logistics and Support, Armenian Problems."

135. Atamer, *41nci Piyade Tümen Tarıhçesi*, 9.

136. Ibid.

137. Jandarma Headquarters to the Ministry of War, September 26, 1915, ATASE, archive 2287, record 13, file 3.

138. Atamer, *41nci Piyade Tümen Tarıhçesi*, 9.

139. Ibid.

140. Werfel, *The Forty Days of Musa Dagh*, 775–90.

141. Ciphered telegram from Cemal to Ottoman general staff, June 8, 1915, BOA, Dh, Şfr, archive 1–2, record 1030, file 11–13 reproduced in Atılgan and Moumdjian, *Archival Documents of the Viennese Armenian-Turkish Platform*, 234–35.

142. Ari, *Birinci Dünya Savaşı Kronolojisi*, 170.

143. Ibid., 170.

144. Ciphered message 5274 from Talat to Governor, Urfa, August 26, 1915, ATASE, BOA, DH, ŞFR,No. 55/230 reproduced in Ozdemir and Sarinay, *Turk-Ermeni Ihtilafı Belegeler*, document 86.

145. Headquarters, 4th Army to Foreign Ministry, September 16, 1915, BOA, Dh, Şfr, archive 1–2, record 1030, file 11–8 reproduced in Atılgan and Moumdjian, *Archival Documents of the Viennese Armenian-Turkish*

Platform, 290–91. The dates in the transcription of this document are contradictory.

146. District governor of Urfa to Ministry of the Interior1915, September 29, 1915, ATASE archive 2287, record 11, file 4–13 reproduced in Atılgan and Moumdjian, *Archival Documents of the Viennese Armenian-Turkish Platform*, 598–599.

147. Mete Şefik, *23ncü Piyade Tümen Tarıhçesi* (Ankara: Genelkurmay Basımevi, undated), 24, ATASE Record 26–412 (unpublished staff study).

148. Dasnabedian, *History of the Armenian Revolutionary Federation*, 115.

149. Hilmar Kaiser (ed.), *Eberhard Count Wolffskeel von Reichenberg, Zeitoun, Mousa Dagh, Ourfa: Letters on the Armenian Genocide, Second Edition* (London: Gomidas Institute, 2004), 21. Wolffskeel von Reichenberg's participation in these battles, while in command of and fighting alonside Ottoman soldiers against the Armenian revolutionary committees, appears to be unique and remains very controversial.

150. Ibid.,23.

151. Ibid., 24–25.

152. Şefik, *23ncü Piyade Tümen Tarıhçesi*, 25.

153. Kévorkian, *The Armenian Genocide*, 595. Kévorkian cites a letter from the American consul in Mersina to Ambassador Morgenthau dated July 26, 1915.

154. Ibid.

155. Şefik, *23ncü Piyade Tümen Tarıhçesi*, 25.

156. Kévorkian, *The Armenian Genocide*, 593–604.

157. Ciphered message, Governor of Izmit Sanjack to Ministry of the Interior, September 17, 1915, BOA, DH, Şfr., No. 68/67 reproduced in Arş.Ş. Mud.lüğü (T.C. Başbakanlık Devlet Archives staff), *Osmanli Belgelerinde Ermenile (1915–1920)* [English edition: *Armenians in Ottoman Documents (1915–1920)*] (Ankara: Osmanlı Arşivi Daıre, 1995), document 107.

158. Ciphered message, Governor of Eskişehir Sanjack to Ministry of the Interior, September 18, 1915, BOA, DH, Şfr., No. 68/72 reproduced in *Armenians in Ottoman Documents* (1915–20), document 111.

159. Ciphered message, Governor of Diyarbakır Sanjack to Ministry of the Interior, September 18, 1915, BOA, DH, Şfr., No. 68/71 reproduced in *Armenians in Ottoman Documents* (1915–20), document 112.

160. Ciphered message, Governor of Niğde Sanjack to Ministry of the Interior, September 30, 1915, BOA, DH, Şfr., No. 68/69 reproduced in *Armenians in Ottoman Documents* (1915–20), document 113.

161. See, e.g., the extensive reports contained in *Arşiv Belgeleriye Ermeni Faaliyetleri 1914–1918, Archival Documents of the Viennese Armenian-Turkish Platform, Armenians in Ottoman Documents* (1915–20), and *Turk-Ermeni Ihtilafi Belegeler.*

162. Ciphered message, Ministry of the Interior to Governor, Ankara, August 29, 1915, BOA, DH, Şfr., No. 55/290 reproduced in Ozdemir and Sarinay, *Turk-Ermeni Ihtilafi Belegeler*, document 89.

163. Ibid.
164. Taner Akçam, *The Young Turk's Crime against Humanity, the Armenian Genocide and Ethnic Cleansing in the Ottoman Empire* (Princeton: Princeton University Press, 2012), 202.
165. See, e.g., ciphered message, Ministry of the Governate of Aleppo, October 18, 1915, BOA, DH, Şfr., No. 199/35 reproduced in Ozdemir and Sarinay, *Turk-Ermeni Ihtilafi Belegeler*, document 124.
166. Ciphered message, Ministry of the Interior to Governor, Ankara, August 29, 1915, BOA, DH, Şfr., No. 55/290 reproduced in Ozdemir and Sarinay, *Turk-Ermeni Ihtilafi Belegeler*, document 89.
167. See ciphered messages, Ministry of the Interior to Governor, Kastamonu and Konya, October 23, 1915, BOA, DH, Şfr., No. 57/82 and 57/89 reproduced in Ozdemir and Sarinay, *Turk-Ermeni Ihtilafi Belegeler*, document 127 and 129.
168. Ciphered message, Ministry of the Interior to respective Governors, October 27, 1915, BOA, DH, Şfr., No. 57/135 reproduced in Ozdemir and Sarinay, *Turk-Ermeni Ihtilafi Belegeler*, document 133.
169. Ciphered message, Ministry of the Interior to all province and sanjack governors, March 15, 1916, BOA, DH, Şfr., No. 62/21 reproduced in Ozdemir and Sarinay, *Turk-Ermeni Ihtilafi Belegeler*, document 159.

10 AFTERMATH

1. Ciphered message 945, Ministry of the Interior to Governor, Ankara, May 27, 1916, BOA, DH, Şfr., No. 64/136 reproduced in Hikmet Ozdemir and Yusuf Sarinay (eds.), *Turk-Ermeni Ihtilafi Belegeler* (Ankara: Egemenlik, undated), document 172.
2. For two recent examples, see James L. Gelvin, *The Modern Middle East, A History* (Oxford: Oxford University Press, 2008), 172; and Margaret MacMillan, *Paris 1919, Six Months that Changed the World* (New York: Random House, 2003), 430.
3. Yusuf Halaçoğlu, "Realities behind the Relocation," Türkkaya Ataöv (ed.), *The Armenians in the Late Ottoman Period* (Ankara: Turkish Historical Society, 2001), 133; and Grigoris Balakian, *Armenian Golgotha, A Memoir of the Armenian Genocide, 1915–1918* (translated by Peter Balakian and Aris Sevag) (New York: Vintage Books, 2009), xvii.
4. Justin McCarthy, "The Population of the Ottoman Armenians," Ataöv (ed.), *Armenians in the Late Ottoman Period*, 77. McCarthy's data is based on a reconciliation of Ottoman census data and statistics from the Armenian Patriarchate.
5. Ahmed Emin Yalman, *Turkey in the World War* (New Haven: Yale University Press, 1930), 212.
6. Raymond H. Kévorkian, *The Armenian Genocide, A Complete History* (London: I.B. Tauris, 2011), 272–78.
7. Halaçoğlu, "Realities behind the Relocation," 134.

8. Murat Bardakçı, *Talât Paşa'nın Evrak-ı Metrûkesi* (Istanbul: Everest Yayınları, 2008).

9. Sabrina Tavernise, "Nearly a Million Genocide Victims, Covered in a Cloak of Amnesia," *The New York Times International,* March 9, 2009, A6.

10. Ara Sarafian, "Talaat Pasha's Black Book Documents His Campaign of Race Extermination, 1915–1917," *The Armenian Reporter,* March 14, 2009.

11. Ibid.

12. Ibid.

13. I am grateful for an analysis of the journal by Erman Sahin. Email to author from Erman Sahin, March 26, 2009.

14. Bardakçı, *Talât Paşa'nın Evrak-ı Metrûkesi,* passim.

15. Ara Sarafian, *Talaat Pasha's Report on the Armenian Genocide, 1917* (London: Gomidas Institute, 2011).

16. Ibid., 6. Sarafian's choice of a title, e.g., indicates that Talat produced a report about genocide rather than an exclusively tabular record of data concerning the number of Armenians remaining after the relocations. Moreover, Sarafian's eight-page introduction contains numerous assumptions and speculative characterizations of why Talat produced the journal.

17. Eric Lohr, *Nationalizing the Russian Empire, The Campaign against Enemy Aliens during World War I* (Cambridge, MA: Harvard University Press, 2003), 137.

18. Ibid., 139.

19. David Vital, *A People Apart, The Jews in Europe 1789–1939* (Oxford: Oxford University Press, 1999), 653.

20. Lohr, *Nationalizing the Russian Empire,* 140.

21. Ibid., 150.

22. Alexander V. Prusin, "The Russian Military and the Jews in Galicia," Eric Lohr and Marshall Poe (eds.), *The Military and Society in Russia 1450–1917* (Leiden: Brill, 2002), 537.

23. Lohr, *Nationalizing the Russian Empire,* 153.

24. See Yücel Güçlü, *The Holocaust and the Armenian Case in Comparative Perspective* (Lanham, MD: University Press of America, 2012), 65–102, for an interesting, and very well documented, exposition of "uneven treatment," which is defined by the author as exemptions, official acts of mercy, and Armenian power within the Ottoman elite.

Appendix A: The Relocation Antitheses

1. Henry Wadsworth Longfellow, *Evangeline, A Tale of Acadie* (Boston: Ticknor & Company, 1847), Stanza 6.

2. HQS, Department of the Army, *Counterinsurgency* (US Army Field Manual 3–24) (US GPO, December 15, 2006), 1–6.

Bibliography

Archival Sources

Foreign Office Papers (FO), The National Archives, Kew, UK.
National Archives of the United States, College Park, Maryland, USA.
Prime Minister's Office Ottoman Archives (BOA), Istanbul, Turkey.
Turkish General Staff Military History and Strategic Studies Directorate Archives (ATASE), Ankara, Turkey.
United States Congressional Record, 54th Congress, Sessions 1 and 2, USA.
War Office Papers (WO), The National Archives, Kew, UK.

Published Document Collections

Arş.Ş.Mud.lüğü (ATASE staff). *Arşiv Belgeleriye Ermeni Faaliyetleri 1914–1918, Cilt I* (Ankara: Genelkurmay Basımevi, 2005).
Arş.Ş.Mud.lüğü (ATASE staff). *Arşiv Belgeleriye Ermeni Faaliyetleri 1914–1918, Cilt III* (Ankara: Genelkurmay Basımevi, 2006).
Arş.Ş.Mud.lüğü (ATASE staff). *Arşiv Belgeleriye Ermeni Faaliyetleri 1914–1918, Cilt IV* (Ankara: Genelkurmay Basımevi, 2006).
Arş.Ş.Mud.lüğü (T.C. Başbakanlık Devlet Archives staff). *Osmanli Belgelerinde Ermenile* (1915–20) [English edition: *Armenians in Ottoman Documents (1915–1920)*] (Ankara: Osmanlı Arşivi Daıre, 1995).
Atılgan, Inanç, and Garabet Moumdjian. *Archival Documents of the Viennese Armenian-Turkish Platform* (Klagenfurt: Wieser Verlag, 2010).
Documents on Ottoman Armenians, Vol. II (Ankara: Prime Ministry Directorate of Press and Information, 1982).
Gooch, G. P., and Harold Temperley, eds. *British Documents on the Origins of the War 1898–1914, Vol. XI* (London: HMSO, 1926).
Ozdemir, Hikmet, and Yusuf Sarinay, eds., *Turk-Ermeni Ihtilafi Belegeler* (Ankara: Egemenlik, undated).
Perinçek, Mehmet. *Rus Devlet Arşivlerinden 100 Belgede Ermeni Meselesi* (Istanbul: Doğan Kitap, 2007).
Şimşir, Bilâl N., *British Documents on Ottoman Armenians, Volume III (1891–1895)* (Ankara: Turkish Historical Society, 1989).

Memoirs

Balakian, Grigoris. *Armenian Golgotha, A Memoir of the Armenian Genocide, 1915–1918* (translated by Peter Balakian and Aris Sevag) (New York: Vintage Books, 2009).

De Nogales, Rafael, *Four Years beneath the Crescent* (New York, 1926).

Djemal Pasha. *Memories of a Ottoman Statesman—1913–1919* (London: Hutchinson, undated).

Eğe-Akter, Guneş N., trans. *Babamın Emanetleri, Ragıp Nurettin E'ge'nin Birinci Cihan Harbi Günlükleri ve Harbin Sonrasi Hatiratı* (Istanbul: Isis Press, 2006).

Erden, Ali Fuad. *Birinci Dünya Harbinde Suriye Hatıraları* (Istanbul: Arma Yayınları, 2003).

İlter, Aziz Samih. *Birinci Dünya Savaşı'nda Kafkas Cephesi Hatıraları* (Ankara: Genelkurmay Basımevi, 2007).

Izzet Pascha, Ahmed. *Denkwürdigkeiten des Marschalls Izzet Pascha* (Leipzig, Germany: Verlag von K.F. Koehler, 1927).

Kut, Halil. *İttihat ve Terakki'den Cumhuriyete Bitmeyen Savaş: Kutülamare Kahramanı Halil Paşanın Anıları* (İstanbul: 7 Gün Yayınları, 1972).

Liman von Sanders, Otto. *Five Years in Turkey* (Nashville: The Battery Press, 2000, reprint of the 1928 edition).

Mehmet Talāt Pasha, *Talāt Paşa'nın Anıları* (ed. Alpay Kabacalı) (Istanbul: İletşim Yayinları, 1984).

Minasian, Rupen Der. *Rememberences of an Armenian Revolutionary, Vol. 7* (Tehran, 3rd edition, 1982).

Smith, Arthur D. Howden. *Fighting the Turk in the Balkans, An American's Adventures with the Macedonian Revolutionists* (New York: G.P. Putnam's Sons, 1908).

Torossian, Sarkis. *From Dardanelles to Palestine* (Boston: Meador Publishing Company, 1929).

Secondary Works

Abadan, Yavuz. *Mustafa Kemal ve Çeteçilik* (Istanbul: Varlık Yayınevi 1972).

Akbay, Cemal. *Birinci Dünya Harbinde Türk Harbi, 1nci Cilt, Osmanli Imparatorlugu'nun Siyası ve Askeri Hazırlıkları ve Harbe Girisi* (Ankara: Genelkurmay Basımevi, 1970).

Akçam, Taner. *A Shameful Act, The Armenian Genocide and the Question of Turkish Responsibility* (New York: Metropolitan Books, 2006).

———. *The Young Turk's Crime against Humanity, The Armenian Genocide and Ethnic Cleansing in the Ottoman Empire* (Princeton: Princeton University Press, 2012).

Aksakal, Mustafa. *The Ottoman Road to War in 1914: The Ottoman Empire and the First World War* (New York: Cambridge University Press, 2008).

Allen, W. E. D., and Paul Muratoff. *Caucasian Battlefields: A History of the Wars on the Turco-Caucasian Border, 1828–1921* (Cambridge: Cambridge University Press, 1953).

Altınbilek, Hakkı, and Naci Kır. *Birinci Dünya Harbi'nde Türk Harbi, Kafkas Cephesi 3ncü Ordu Harekâtı, Cilt II Birinci Kitap* (Ankara: Genelkurmay Basımevi, 1993).

Ari, Kemal. *Birinci Dünya Savaşı Kronolojisi* (Ankara: Genelkurmay Basımevi, 1997).

Ataöv, Türkkaya, ed. *The Armenians in the Late Ottoman Period* (Ankara: Turkish Historical Society Printing House, 2001).

Auron, Yair. *The Banality of Indifference: Zionism & the Armenian Genocide* (New Brunswick: Transaction Books, 2000), 218.

Ayışığı, Metin. *Mareşal Ahmet İzzet Paşa (Askerî ve Siyasî Hayatı)* (Ankara: Türk Tarih Kurumu Basımevi, 1997).

Balakian, Peter. *The Burning Tigris The Armenian Genocide and America's Response* (New York: Harper Collins, 2003).

Bardakçı, Murat. *Talât Paşa'nın Evrak-ı Metrûkesi* (Istanbul: Everest Yayınları, 2008).

Beehler, William H. *The History of the Italian-Turkish War, September 29, 1911 to October 18, 1912* (Annapolis, MD: The Advertiser-Republican, 1913).

Belen, Fahri. *Birinci Cihan Harbinde Türk Harbi, 1914 Yılı Hareketleri* (Ankara: Genelkurmay Basımevi, 1964).

Bloxham, Donald. *The Great Game of Genocide; Imperialism, Nationalism, and the Destruction of the Ottoman Armenians* (Oxford: Oxford University Press, 2005).

Boot, Max. *Invisible Armies, An Epic History of Guerrilla Warfare from Ancient Times to the Present* (New York: Liveright Publishing Corporation, 2013).

Çakın, Naci, and Nafiz Orhon. *Türk Silahlı Kuvvetleri Tarihi, IIIncü Cilt 5nci Kısım (1793–1908)* (Ankara: Genelkurmay Basımevi, 1978).

Çakmak, Fevzi. *Birinci Dünya Savaşı'nda Doğu Cephesi* (Ankara: Genelkurmay Basımevi, 2005).

Callwell, Colonel C. E. *Small Wars, Their Principles and Practice* (Lincoln, NE: University of Nebraska Press, 1996).

Cassar, George H. *Kitchener's War, British Strategy from 1914 to 1916* (Washington, DC: Brassey's Inc, 2004).

Cengiz, H. Erdogan, ed. *Enver Paşa'nın Anıları* (Istanbul: İletişim Yayınları, 1991).

Chadwick, French Ensor. *The Relations of the United States and Spain, Diplomacy* (New York: Russell & Russell, 1909).

Chalabian, Antranig. *General Andranik and the Armenian Revolutionary Movement* (United States: First Edition, 1988).

Childs, Timothy W. *Italo-Turkish Diplomacy and the War over Libya 1911–1912* (Leiden, NE: E.J. Brill, 1990).

Churchill, Winston S. *The World Crisis* (New York: Scribners, 1931).

Çiçek, Kemal. *Ermenilerin Zorunlu Göçü 1915–1917* (Ankara: Türk Tarih Kurumu, 2005).

Cron, Hermann. *Imperial German Army, 1914–18: Organisation, Structure, Orders-of-Battle* (Solihull: Helion and Company, 2002).

Dadrian, Vahakn N. *The History of the Armenian Genocide* (Providence: Berghahn Books, 3rd revised edition 1997).

———. *Warrant for Genocide, Key Elements of Turco-Armenian Conflict* (New Brunswick: Transaction Publishers, 1999).

Dasnabedian, Hratch. *History of the Armenian Revolutionary Federation, Dasnaktutiun 1890/1924* (Milan: OEMME Edizioni, 1990).

———. *History of the Organizational Structure of the Armenian Revolutionary Federation and Other Studies* (ed. Yervant Pampukian) (Beirut: Hamazkayin Press, 2009).

Demirel, Muammer. *Birinci Dünya Harbinde Erzurum ve Çevresinde Ermeni Hareketleri (1914–1918)* (Ankara: Genelkurmay Basımevi, 1996).

Demirhan, Pertev. *Generalfeldmarschall Colmar von der Goltz: Das Lebensbild eines grossen Soldaten* (Göttingen: 1960).

Denker, Arif Cemil, *Birinci Dünya Savaşında Teşkilât-î Mahsusa* (Istanbul: Arma Yayınları, undated).

Dennis, Peter, and Jeffrey Grey, eds. *1911, Preliminary Moves* (Canberra: Big Sky Publishing, 2011).

Erickson, Edward J. *Defeat in Detail, The Ottoman Army in the Balkans, 1912–1913* (Westport, CT: Praeger, 2003).

———. *Ordered to Die, A History of the Ottoman Army in the First World War* (Westport, CT: Greenwood Press, 2001).

———. *Ottoman Army Effectiveness in World War 1, A Comparative Study* (Abingdon, OX: Routledge, 2007).

Erkal, Şükrü. *Birinci Dünya Harbinde Türk Harbi, VInci Cilt, Hicaz, Asir, Yemen Cepheleri ve Libya Harekatı 1914–1918* (Ankara: Genelkurmay Basımevi, 1978).

Ertuna, Hamdi. *1911–1912 Osmanlı-İtalyan Harbi ve Kolağası Mustafa Kemal* (Ankara: Genelkurmay Basımevi, 1985).

———. *Türk Silahlı Kuvvetleri Tarihi, Osmanlı Devri, Osmanlı-İtalyan Harbi (1911–1912)* (Ankara: Genelkurmay Basımevi, 1981).

Farah, Caesar E. *The Sultan's Yemen, Nineteenth-Century Challenges to Ottoman Rule* (London: I.B.Tauris, 2002).

Ferguson, Niall. *The War of the World, Twentieth Century Conflict and the Descent of the West* (London: Penguin Books, 2006).

Foner, Philip S. *The Spanish-Cuban-American War and the Birth of American Imperialism 1895–1902*, Volume I: 1895–1898 (New York: Monthly Review Press, 1972).

Gaunt, David. *Massacres, Resistance, Protectors; Muslim-Christian Relation in Eastern Anatolia during World War I* (Piscataway, NJ: Gorgias Press, 2006).

Gawrych, George W. *The Crescent and the Eagle: Ottoman Rule, Islam and the Albanians, 1874–1913* (London: I.B. Tauris, 2006).

Gelvin, James L., *The Modern Middle East, A History* (Oxford: Oxford University Press, 2008).

Ghazarian, Vatche, trans. and ed. *Boghos Nubar's Papers and the Armenian Question 1915–1918* (Waltham: Mayreni Publishing, 1997).

Gooch, John. *The Plans of War, The General Staff and British Military Strategy c. 1900–1916* (New York: John Wiley, 1974).

Görgülü, İsmet. *On Yıllık Harbin Kadrosu 1912–1922, Balkan-Birinci Dünya ve İstiklál Harbi* (Ankara: Türk Tarih Kurum Basımevi, 1993).

Graff, Henry F., ed. *American Imperialism and the Philippine Insurrection (Testimony taken from Hearings on Affairs in the Philippine Islands before the Senate Committee on the Philippines-1902)* (Boston: Little, Brown and Company, 1969).

Güçlü, Yücel. *Armenians and the Allies in Cilicia 1914–1923* (Salt Lake City: University of Utah Press, 2012).

———. *The Holocaust and the Armenian Case in Comparative Perspective* (Lanham, MD: University Press of America, 2012).

Gündüz, Asım. *Hatıralarım* (Istanbul: Kervan Yayınları, 1973).

Gürün, Kamuran. *The Armenian File, The Myth of Innocence Exposed* (Nicosia: Rustem, 3rd edition 2001).

Hanioğlu, M. Sükrü. *Preparation for a Revolution, The Young Turks 1902–1908* (Oxford: Oxford University Press, 2001).

Hassassian, Manuel. *A.R.F. as a Revolutionary Party, 1890–1921* (Jerusalem: Hai Tad Publications, 1983).

Hovannisian, Richard. *The Armenian Genocide, Cultural and Ethical Legacies* (New Brunswick: Transaction Publishers, 2008).

HQS, Department of the Army. *Counterinsurgency* (US Army Field Manual 3–24) (US GPO, December 15, 2006).

Kaiser, Hilmar, ed. *Eberhard Count Wolffskeel von Reichenberg, Zeitoun, Mousa Dagh, Ourfa: Letters on the Armenian Genocide, Second Edition* (London: Gomidas Institute, 2004).

Kaligian, Dikran Mesrob. *Armenian Organization and Ideology under Ottoman Rule 1908–1914* (New Brunswick: Transaction Publishers, 2009).

Karatamu, Selahattin. *Türk Silahlı Kuvvetleri Tarihi, IIIncü Cilt 6nci Kısım (1908–1920)* (Ankara: Genelkurmay Basımevi, 1971).

Kasaba, Reşat, ed. *The Cambridge History of Turkey, Volume 4, Turkey in the Modern World* (Cambridge: Cambridge University Press, 2008).

Kévorkian, Raymond H. *The Armenian Genocide, A Complete History* (London: I.B. Tauris, 2011).

Klein, Janet. *The Margins of Empire, Kurdish Tribal Militias in the Ottoman Tribal Zone* (Stanford, CA: Stanford University Press, 2011).

Koral, Necmi, Remzi Önal, Rauf Atakan, Nusret Baycan, and Selahattin Kızılırmak. *Türk Silahlı Kuvvetleri Tarihi, Osmanlı Devri, Birinci Dünya Harbi Idari Faaliyetler ve Lojistik, Xncu Cilt* (Ankara: Genelkurmay Basımevi, 1985).

Korganoff, G. *La Participation Des Arméniens à la Guerre Mondiale—sur le front du Caucase (1914–1918)* (Paris: Massis Editions, 1927).

Kutay, Cemal. *Trablus-Garb'de Bir Avuç Kahraman* (Istanbul: Tarih Yayınları, 1963).

Lange-Akhund, Nadine. *The Macedonian Question, 1893–1908 From Western Sources* (New York: Columbia University Press, 1998).

Langensiepen, Bernd, and Ahmet Guleryuz. *The Ottoman Steam Navy* (Annapolis: Naval Institute Press, 1995).

Larcher, Commandant M. *La Guerre Turque Dans La Guerre Mondiale* (Paris: Chiron and Berger-Levrault, 1926).

Lewy, Guenter. *The Armenian Massacres in Ottoman Turkey, A Disputed Genocide* (Salt Lake City: The University of Utah Press, 2005).

Linn, Brian McAllister. *The U.S. Army and Counterinsurgency in the Philippine War, 1899–1902* (Chapel Hill, NC: The University of North Carolina Press, 1989).

Lohr, Eric. *Nationalizing the Russian Empire, The Campaign against Enemy Aliens during World War I* (Cambridge, MA: Harvard University Press, 2003).

MacMillan, Margaret. *Paris 1919, Six Months that changed the World* (New York: Random House, 2003).

Marston, Daniel, and Carter Malakasian, eds. *Counterinsurgency in Modern Warfare* (Oxford: Osprey Publishing, 2008).

McCarthy, Justin. *Death and Exile, The Ethnic Cleansing of Ottoman Muslims 1821–1922* (Princeton, NJ: The Darwin Press, Inc., 1995).

McCarthy, Justin, Esat Arslan, Cemalettin Taşkıran, and Ömer Turan. *The Armenian Rebellion at Van* (Salt Lake City: The University of Utah Press, 2006).

McMeekin, Sean. *The Berlin-Baghdad Express: The Ottoman Empire and Germany's Bid for World Power* (Cambridge, MA: The Belknap Press of Harvard University Press, 2010).

———. *The Russian Origins of the First World War* (Cambridge, MA: The Belknap Press of Harvard University Press, 2011).

Minakhorian, Vahan. *The Year 1915* (Venice: St. Ghazar Press, 1949).

Mutlu, Cengiz. *Birinci Dünya Savaşında Amele Taburları* (Istanbul: IQ Kültür Sanat Yayıncılık, 2007).

Nalbandian, Louise. *The Armenian Revolutionary Movement* (Berkeley: University of California Press, 1963).

Okçu, Yahya, and Hilmi Üstünsoy. *Birinci Dünya Harbi'nde Türk Harbi, Sina-Filistin Cephesi, Harbin Başlangıcından İkinci Gazze Muharebeleri Sonuna Kadar, IVncü Cilt 1 Kısım* (Ankara: Genelkurmay Basımevi, 1979).

Onalp, Merhum Kâmil, Hilmi Üstünsoy, Kâmuran Dengiz, and Şükrü Erkal. *Birinci Dünya Harbi'nde Türk Harbi, Sina-Filistin Cephesi, İkinci Gazze Muharebeleri Sonundan Mütarkesi'ne Kadar Yapılan Harekât, IVncü Cilt 2nci Kısım* (Ankara: Genelkurmay Basımevi, 1986).

Papazian, K. S. *Patriotism Perverted, A Discussion of the Deeds and the Misdeeds of the Armenian Revolutionary Federation, the so-called Dashnagtzoutune* (Boston: Baikar Press, 1934).

Pearson, Owen. *Albania and King Zog; Independence, Republic and Monarchy 1908–1939* (London: The Centre for Albanian Studies, 2004).

Perry, Duncan M. *The Politics of Terror, The Macedonian Liberation Movements 1893–1903* (Durham, NC: Duke University Press, 1988).

Ramsey, Robert D. III. *Savage Wars of Peace: Case Studies of Pacification in the Philippines, 1900–1902* (Fort Leavenworth, KS: CSI Press, 2007).

Reynolds, Michael A. *Shattering Empires, The Clash and Collapse of the Ottoman and Russian Empires 1908–1918* (Cambridge: Cambridge University Press, 2011).

Sarafian, Ara. *Talaat Pasha's Report on the Armenian Genocide, 1917* (London: Gomidas Institute, 2011).

Shaw, Stanford J. *The Ottoman Empire in World War I, Volume 1 Prelude to War* (Ankara: Türk Tarih Kurum Basımevi, 2006).

Shaw, Stanford J., and Ezel K. *History of the Ottoman Empire and Modern Turkey, Volume II* (Cambridge: Cambridge University Press, 1977).

Sheffy, Yigal. *British Military Intelligence in the Palestine Campaign 1914–1918* (London: Frank Cass, 1998).

Simon, Rachel. *Libya between Ottomanism and Nationalism, The Ottoman Involvement in Libya during the War with Italy (1911–1919)* (Berlin: Klaus Schwarz Verlag, 1987).

Sonyel, Salahi. *The Great War and the Tragedy of Anatolia (Turks and Armenians in the Maelstrom of Major Powers)* (Ankara: Türk Tarih Kurumu, 2001).

Sükan, Şadi. *Türk Silahlı Kuvvetleri Tarihi, Osmanlı Devri, Balkan Harbi (1912–1913), II Cilt 3ncü Kısım Edirne Kalesi Etrafındaki Muharebeler* (Ankara: Genelkurmay Basımevi, 1993).

Suny, Ronald Grigor, Fatma Müge Göçek, and Norman M. Naimark, eds. *A Question of Genocide, Armenians and Turks at the End of the Ottoman Empire* (New York: Oxford University Press, 2011).

Tierney Jr., John J. *Chasing Ghosts, Unconventional Warfare in American History* (Washington, DC: Potomac Books, Inc., 2006).

Tittoni, Renato. *The Italo-Turkish War (1911–1912)* (Kansas City, MO: Franklin Hudson Publishing Company, 1914).

Trask, David F. *The War with Spain in 1898* (New York: Macmillan Publishing Company., Inc, 1981).

Trumpener, Ulrich. *Germany and the Ottoman Empire* (Princeton: Princeton University Press, 1968).

Turfan, M. Naim. *Rise of the Young Turks; Politics, the Military and Ottoman Collapse* (London: I.B.Tauris, 2000).

Uyar, Mesut, and Edward J. Erickson. *A Military History of the Ottomans, From Osman to Atatürk* (Santa Barbara, CA: Praeger, 2009).

Vital, David. *A People Apart, The Jews in Europe 1789–1939* (Oxford: Oxford University Press, 1999).

Vratzian, Simon. *The Republic of Armenia* (Paris, 1928).

Wallach, Jehuda L., *Bir Askeri Yardımın Anatomisi* (Turkish edition of *Anatomie einer Miltaerhilfe*), trans. Fahri Çeliker (Ankara: Genelkurmay Basımevi, 1977).

Wilson, John. *CB, A Life of Sir Henry Campbell-Bannerman* (London: Constable and Company Limited, 1973).

Woodward, David. *Armies of the World 1854–1914* (New York: G.P. Putnam's Sons, 1978).

Yalman, Ahmed Emin. *Turkey in the World War* (New Haven: Yale University Press, 1930),

Yavuz, M. Hakan, and Peter Sluglett, eds. *War and Diplomacy, The Russo-Turkish War of 1877–1878 and the Treaty of Berlin* (Salt Lake City: University of Utah Press, 2011).

ARTICLES AND CHAPTERS

Adanır, Fikret. "Non-Muslims in the Ottoman Army and the Ottoman Defeat in the Balkan War of 1912–1913." In Ronald Grigor Suny, Fatma Müge Göçek, and Norman M. Naimark (eds.), *A Question of Genocide, Armenians and Turks at the End of the Ottoman Empire* (New York: Oxford University Press, 2011).

Dadrian, Vahakn. "The Role of the Special Organization in the Armenian Genocide during the First World War." In Panayi, Panikos (ed.), *Minorities in Wartime: National and Racial Groupings in Europe, North America and Australia in Two World Wars* (Oxford: Berg, 1993).

Davidson, Roderick. "The Armenian Crisis: 1912–1914." *American Historical Review* vol. 53, no. 3 (April 1948).

Dündar, Fuat. "Pouring a People into the Desert, the 'Definitive Solution' of the Unionists to the Armenians Problem." In Ronald Grigor Suny, Fatma Müge Göçek, and Norman M. Naimark (eds.), *A Question of Genocide, Armenians and Turks at the End of the Ottoman Empire* (New York: Oxford University Press, 2011).

Erickson, Edward J. "Armenian Massacres, New Records Undercut Old Blame." *The Middle East Quarterly* vol. XIII, no. 3 (Summer 2006).

Grant, Jonathan. "The Sword of the Sultan: Ottoman Arms Imports, 1854–1914." *The Journal of Military History* vol. 66, no. 1 (January 2002).

Halaçoğlu, Yusuf. "Realities behind the Relocation." In Türkkaya Ataöv (ed.), *The Armenians in The Late Ottoman Period* (Ankara: Turkish Historical Society Printing House, 2001).

Kaiser, Hilmar. "Regional Resistance to Central Government Policies: Ahmed Djemal Pasha, the Governors of Aleppo, and Armenian Deportees in the Spring and Summer of 1915." *Journal of Genocide Research* vol. 12, no. 3 (2010), 173–218.

Kodaman, Bayram. "The Hamidiye Light Cavalry Regiments, Abdülhamid II and the Eastern Anatolian Tribes." In Yavuz M. Hakan and Peter Sluglett (eds.), *War and Diplomacy, The Russo-Turkish War of 1877–1878 and the Treaty of Berlin* (Salt Lake City: University of Utah Press, 2011).

Libaridian, Gerard J. "What Was Revolutionary about Armenian Revolutionary Parties in the Ottoman Empire?" In Ronald Grigor Suny, Fatma Müge

Göçek, and Norman M. Naimark (eds.), *A Question of Genocide, Armenians and Turks at the End of the Ottoman Empire* (New York: Oxford University Press, 2011).

McCarthy, Justin. "The Population of the Ottoman Armenians." In Türkkaya Ataöv (ed.), *The Armenians in the Late Ottoman Period* (Ankara: Turkish Historical Society, 2001).

Morgan, Kenneth O. "The Boer War and the Media (1899–1902)." *Twentieth Century British History* vol. 13, no. 1 (2002).

Porch, Douglas. "Introduction to the Bison Books Edition," In Colonel C. E. Callwell, *Small Wars, Their Principles and Practice* (Lincoln, NE: University of Nebraska Press, 1996).

Prusin, Alexander V. "The Russian Military and the Jews in Galicia." In Eric Lohr and Marshall Poe (eds.), *The Military and Society in Russia 1450–1917* (Leiden: Brill, 2002).

Sanjian. Ara. "The ARF's First 120 Years, A Brief review of Available sources and Historiography." *Armenian Review* vol. 52, no. 3–4 (Fall–Winter 2011).

Sarafian, Ara. "Talaat Pasha's Black Book Documents His Campaign of Race Extermination, 1915–1917." *The Armenian Reporter*, March 14, 2009.

Tavernise, Sabrina. "Nearly a Million Genocide Victims, Covered in a Cloak of Amnesia." *The New York Times International*, March 9, 2009, A6.

Uca, Alaattin. "Stange Müfrezesi'nin Harp Ceridesine Göre Kafkas Cephesi'nde Dr. Bahaeddin Şakir." *KMÜ Sosyal ve Ekonomik Araştırmalar Dergisi* vol. 13, no. 20 (2011).

Uyar, Mesut, and A. Kadir Varoğlu. "In Search of Modernity and Rationality, The Evolution of Turkish Military Academy Curricula in a Historical Perspective." *Armed Forces & Society* vol 35, no. 1 (October 2009).

Yasamee, Feroz. "Colmar Freiherr von der Goltz and the Boer War." In Keith Wilson (ed.), *The International Impact of the Russo-Japanese War* (London: Palgrave, 2001).

DISSERTATIONS AND THESIS

Griffith, Merwin A. "The Reorganization of the Ottoman Army under Abdülhamid II, 1880–1897." Unpublished PhD dissertation, University of California, Los Angeles (1966).

Klein, Janet. "Power in the Periphery: The Hamidiye Light Cavalry and the Struggle over Ottoman Kurdistan, 1890–1914." PhD dissertation, Princeton University (2002).

Hatemi, Nilüfer. "Unfolding a Life; Marshal Fevzi Çakmak's Diaries." Unpublished PhD dissertation, Princeton University (November 2000).

Safi, Polat. "The Ottoman Special Organization—Teşkilat-ı Mahsusa: A Historical Assessment with Particular Reference to its Operations against British Occupied Egypt (1914–1916)." Unpublished MA thesis, Bilkent University (2006).

Stebbins, Jeffrey W. "Bell and Banner: Armenian Revolutionaries at the End of the Ottoman Empire." Unpublished MA thesis, US Naval Postgraduate School (December 2011).

Stoddard, Philip Hendrick. "The Ottoman Government and the Arabs, 1911 to 1918: A Preliminary Study of the Teşkilat-ı Mahsusa." Unpublished PhD dissertation, Princeton University (1963).

Uslu, Feride Çavdar. "Armenians of Adana (1914–1918)." Unpublished masters thesis, Afyonkarahisar Kocatepe University (May 2007).

Wilhite, Vincent S. "Guerrilla War, Counterinsurgency, and State Formation in Ottoman Yemen." Unpublished PhD dissertation, The Ohio State University (2003).

CONFERENCE PAPER

Tallon, James N. "The Young Turks and Ottoman Counter-Insurrectionary Operations." Unpublished conference paper, Society for Military History Annual Conference, Lisle, IL, June 9–12, 2011.

INDEX